THE CONTINENTAL MODEL

Selected French Critical Essays of the
Seventeenth Century, in English Translation

❧ THE CONTINENTAL MODEL ❧

Selected French Critical Essays of the Seventeenth Century, in English Translation

REVISED EDITION

EDITED BY

Scott Elledge and Donald Schier

Cornell Paperbacks

CORNELL UNIVERSITY PRESS

ITHACA AND LONDON

Published by arrangement with the University of Minnesota Press

Original edition, 1960, the University of Minnesota Press and Carleton College

Revised edition, 1970, Cornell University Press

First printing, Cornell Paperbacks, 1970

Permission to use the notes to Fontenelle's "Digression on the Ancients and the Moderns" from Robert Shackleton's Edition of *Entretiens sur la pluralité des mondes and digression sur les anciens et les modernes* (Oxford University Press, 1955) has been granted by Mr. Shackleton and Oxford University Press

International Standard Book Number 0-8014-9111-8

Library of Congress Catalog Card Number 79-130315

Printed in the United States of America by Vail-Ballou Press, Inc.

Preface to the Revised Edition

When we prepared the first edition of this book ten years ago, our aim was to introduce to students of English literary history some of the seventeenth-century French writers whose ideas had found their way into eighteenth-century English criticism. We thought translations would serve our readers better than the originals, because many serious students of English literature do not read French well. We decided to present the essays wherever possible in seventeenth- and eighteenth-century English translations, so as to preserve the English critical vocabulary and idiom in which many English writers and critics first read and discussed French "critic-learning." Since no contemporary translations existed for seven of the essays, Professor Schier translated these himself.

In the first edition we included only works which were not generally available and omitted Boileau's *Art of Poetry,* the best-known work of the greatest seventeenth-century French critic, because copies of it could be found in most academic libraries. In the revised edition, however, we have added Boileau—including the *Art of Poetry* in both the original and the Soame-Dryden verse translation, as well as two prose selections. The present book, therefore, is more useful and, of course, more comprehensive than the earlier edition. The special advantage of including both the original French and Soame and Dryden's English version of Boileau's *Art of Poetry* made us willing to delete Georges de Scudéry's Preface to *Alaric* and to make cuts in the selections from the works of Saint-Evremond, Bouhours, and Le Bossu.

No anthology can completely satisfy either its readers or the anthologist himself, who had to make compromises. And the efforts of anthologists to justify their choices seldom persuade the reader who would have preferred *x*, which was omitted, to *y*, which was included. In the notes we explain why we chose the essays we included. These pieces deal with matters that interested English critics of the century that followed: the epic and the romance; definition of the other genres; genius and the rules; the relative merits of the classics and contemporary works. Specifically French concerns, such as the *Querelle du Cid,* are only incidentally alluded to. But the debate between the "Ancients" and the "Moderns," which was easily exported, is illustrated. Most of our authors were on the side of the Ancients because that was the larger and more influential side, but the Moderns are represented by two of their most eloquent and effective spokesmen, Saint-Evremond and Fontenelle.

The writers we have chosen all were influential in England. Certain French writers, important in the history of French criticism, are omitted because their influence did not extend to England or was much less in England than in France. Malherbe's "Commentaire sur Desportes" was not published even in France during the seventeenth century. Vaugelas's *Remarques sur la langue française* (1647) went through at least twenty editions before the end of the century, and may have found some readers in England, but a book on usage is by its very nature untranslatable. Mesnardière's *Poétique* (1639) may have been, as W. P. Ker said, one of the "ancestors of Dryden's prose" (see the headnote to Chapelain's Preface to *Adone*); but later French students of Aristotle's *Poetics* (and of the elder Scaliger and Heinsius) were more original and more interesting. Balzac enjoyed some vogue in England, but it was his political writings that were most widely read; his ideas about literature reached England in the works of other French critics.

We have, of course, read all the contemporary translations in our collection against the original French texts and have made (within brackets) a few emendations in the interest of clarity and accuracy, but we have not attempted to present definitive texts of these often casually written translations. Pertinent background information for each author is given as a headnote to the notes for that selection. Notes are prefaced by a list of some of the major works on literary criticism in seventeenth-century France.

S. E.
D. S.

September 1970

vi

Contents

Contents

Introduction

Alfred North Whitehead, in writing of "The Century of Genius," makes the following judgment about the scientific and philosophical thought of the seventeenth century:

A brief, and sufficiently accurate, description of the intellectual life of the European races during the succeeding two centuries and a quarter up to our own times is that they have been living upon the accumulated capital of ideas provided for them by the genius of the seventeenth century. The men of this epoch inherited a ferment of ideas attendant upon the historical revolt of the sixteenth century, and they bequeathed formed systems of thought touching every aspect of human life. It is the one century which consistently, and throughout the whole range of human activities, provided intellectual genius adequate for the greatness of its occasions.[1]

This statement is particularly applicable to the literary theories of that period in France and, to a more limited extent, for the ideas concerning music and the representative arts. The greatness of the occasions was provided in the field of the theater by the genius of Corneille, Molière, Racine, and a few of their predecessors. In spite of some conflicts between the authors and the critics, there was a continuous, fruitful exchange between dramatic writing and formal criticism. Tensions and divergencies were lessened by the fact that there existed a common front against the pedants and the *précieux*.

Whitehead's image of "succeeding . . . centuries . . . living upon the accumulated capital of ideas provided for them by the genius of the seventeenth century" is equally appropriate for at least one century, the eighteenth, in the field of literary theory in France and England, and partly in Germany. Even Lessing, the opponent of French classicism, is deeply indebted to the body of ideas called *la doctrine classique,* and

ix

the speculative vigor of its representatives. Also in the nineteenth and twentieth centuries the genius of the seventeenth has continued to produce a determining influence on several great writers; those who have revolted against it have been forced to meet it on its own grounds.

Three major factors account for much of the impact of French classicism: first, the rational power and solid structure of a system of ideas that comprised and held together various elements and that allowed for modifications of key concepts and shifts of emphasis without losing its coherence; second, the continuity of this system, which was founded or was believed to have been founded on Aristotle's and Horace's poetics and on the great dramatic works of Classical Antiquity; and third, the existence of prestigious masterpieces whose authors made sincere efforts to conform to the best critical ideas of the doctrine. The fundamental error of the Moderns in their quarrel with the Ancients was that they misjudged the creative force inherent in artistic imitation (its theoretical formula is *imitatio, aemulatio,* and *inventio*), and divorced rules and norms from masterpieces which cannot be defined by a canon, not even a canon accepted by their authors as a guiding principle. The Moderns failed to see that the norms resulted from the interplay between the interpretation of creative achievements and the talent for formulating principles; they took them to be formal theories which could be applied by themselves.

The consolidation and codification of these theories taken abstractly characterize the neoclassicism of the eighteenth century and were still a feature of the interpretation of French classicism by historians of literature in the nineteenth. They are also reflected in the divided attitude of those eighteenth-century writers in France who criticized and undermined the rules and norms of the doctrine, while admiring Corneille's and Racine's tragedies. The situation in England was different from that in France with regard to the divided attitude, but in both countries the critics responsible for the development of eighteenth-century literary theories made constant use of and were heavily indebted to the ideas of the seventeenth century.

The editors of *The Continental Model* have selected a number of representative essays that influenced English criticism, among them essays that are not readily available elsewhere. The idea is an excellent one. No summary, however detailed, can make us understand the relationship between the seventeenth-century model and its interpretation by English critics, for their interpretation is based not on a unified doctrine but on individual works that represent varying developments and changing expressions of the fundamental positions. The index of authors and subject matter permits the reader (if he uses both kinds of entries) to find the passages in which the different authors deal with such issues as genres, rules, nature of plot, unity of action, place, and time, purpose of tragedy and comedy, propriety, credibility (verisimilitude and probability), pleasure and instruction as ends of art, the *je ne sais quoi,* taste, the Ancients and the Moderns, as well as the evaluation or interpretation of the great authors of Classical Antiquity. Quite apart from the significance of the texts for the student of literary theories in England, this collection is valuable for students of comparative literature, if only for the choice the editors have made of contemporary translations. Such translations invite cross-interpretation.

The perusal of the texts themselves, as opposed to the reading of the analyses made of them in histories of criticism or literature, reveals perspectives and themes which slip through the necessarily broad meshes of general histories or which can be noticed only because new methods of criticism have developed. Many readers will be surprised, upon reading the texts of *The Continental Model,* to see how closely the discussions of genres, allegory, metaphor, resemble those of recent structural critics. And finally, only the texts can disclose the individual characteristics of the authors and their thought, characteristics which throw an interesting light upon the theories.

Some reflections on authors and texts presented in this anthology may serve as an introduction to the texts themselves. It is impossible to understand the modifications which the classical doctrine underwent in the writings of Bouhours and Rapin if one does not follow closely the changing perspectives in the dialogues of Bouhours and study in Rapin the different evaluation of the emotions proper for a tragedy (he defends the presentation of tender feelings and considers the rousing of passions pleasant in itself) and of the effects which the emotions are to produce upon the audience. Bouhours is not only a theorist but a perceptive literary critic; his judgments on individual authors and their works will often be placed by the modern reader above the theoretical pronouncements. The criterion of *délicatesse* considered in itself and applied to authors rejected by Boileau and other conservative critics, the analysis of the interplay between truth and falsehood, of clarity, distinctness, and ambiguity, of the function of metaphor and hyperbole, illustrate a decisive change in literary taste. On the whole, Rapin is more restrictive and nationalistic than Bouhours, but his evaluation of probability in relation to truth and his interpretation of Aristotle as compared to that of Corneille attest to the variety of exegesis within the *doctrine classique*. The beginnings of a shift in the conception of the purpose of art (from the objective values of beauty, truth, moral instruction, to the subjective ends: the provoking of the activity of our faculties and the pleasure resulting from their free play) are to be found in some of the representatives of that doctrine.

Le Bossu, who is often associated with Rapin as neo-Aristotelian, lacks Rapin's literary talent and taste. His *Treatise of the Epick Poem,* which deals with principles applying also to tragedy (except for the choice of the hero and the subject matter) and which exerted a significant influence on the dramatic technique of structuring the play around a fable illustrating a moral point and on dramatic criticism in England, is rather formalistic and abstract. Le Bossu was held in high esteem by his contemporaries but was criticized by the Moderns for his allegorical interpretation of Homer. Voltaire ridiculed his method of first stating the neoclassical rules and then demonstrating that Homer and Virgil applied them; in England Sterne singled out Le Bossu in his satire on the rules and compasses of "connoisseurs" and critics.[2]

Corneille's discussion of the three unities—a discussion which can be fully understood only against the background of the struggle with the Academy in which Corneille became involved—is a striking example of the dialectics of freedom and constraint in the *doctrine classique*. Corneille not only pleads for flexibility and a liberal interpretation, but goes beyond the traditional quibbling over the correct interpretation of Aristotle and bases his argumentation on an examination of specific dramatic works, as well as on the artistic principles of the necessary concentration of the tragic plot and the illusion of reality.

Even Chapelain, called the founder of French classicism, and d'Aubignac, decried as its most dogmatic representative, are by no means as rigid as often claimed. Chapelain's flexibility is particularly striking. His preface to *Adone* is a surprising work: written in 1620, it is an early exposé of the *système classique* and establishes the rules for the epic almost two decades before the *Sentiments de l'Académie sur le Cid,* but it also shows Chapelain as a perceptive literary critic, and it has the characteristics of a paradox. Marino's *Adone* was, by virtue of its irregularities, digressions, and whimsicality, the least appropriate example of a classical epic. Chapelain was as aware of this as his readers. He solved the problem by skillfully combining his discussion of *Adone* with a presentation of the "true" rules of the epic. Every time Marino's work does not conform to the rules, its "novelty" is commended. Chapelain's essay, *On the Reading of the Old Romances,* is no less surprising; given the time when it was composed (1646), it is a bold defense of medieval romances for the light they throw on the French language, and on medieval culture and customs. Chapelain underlines their moral character and expresses his admiration for the medieval *merveilleux*. All in all, he shows a remarkable sense of history in this essay.

François Hédelin, abbé d'Aubignac, has often been criticized, but rarely was the ire against him as strikingly expressed as by Saintsbury:

In reading it [*La Pratique du théâtre*], the generous mind oscillates between a sense of intolerable boredom, and a certain ruth at the obviously honest purpose and industry that underlie the heaps of misapplied learning, and season the gabble of foolish authority-citing. . . . What he wants to do is to apply this theory to all the practical contingencies. And this he does through Unities and Episodes, through Acts and Scenes, through Narration, Discourse, Deliberation, everything, with sleuth-hound patience on his own part, and requiring Job's variety of that of his readers. . . . He cannot help his nativity of dulness, and at his very best he is a critic of dramaturgy, not of drama.[3]

In this book he is placed before Corneille, and he deserves it, for d'Aubignac admired Corneille greatly even after the quarrel. Racine, who created a form of tragedy of which d'Aubignac could not approve, still read the *Pratique* attentively and annotated his own copy, because, as Saintsbury discerned accurately, the abbé applies theory "to all the practical contingencies" and "at his very best he is a critic of dramaturgy." Starting from the sound (and at his time uncommon) premise that a play is meant to be performed and not merely to be read, he composed a practical manual for the authors of dramatic works, a manual which was still influential in the eighteenth century. This is not, however, his only contribution. He carried the important criterion of verisimilitude to its ultimate consequences; the real stage is transformed into the ideal stage. He insisted on the application of the rules in order to achieve the greatest concentration in the play; everything is reduced to its essence. The severest art form serves to create a complete illusion of reality in which the spectator participates to the fullest extent; he is transposed into the place and time of the play. One cannot help but admire the force of logic and the sense of art of a man for whom there was no excuse that prevailed against reason ("il n'y a point d'excuse contre la raison").[4]

Huet's justification of the novel and the rules he established had little influence on the later development of the genre, but they were often utilized for the defense of the dignity and usefulness of the novel. The remarkably erudite Bishop of Avranches was, like many of his illustrious contemporaries, a passionate reader of novels; this made him eloquent on the subject of the pedagogical virtues of the novel and man's natural desire for the romanesque. He also took a part in the writing of Madame de Lafayette's *Zayde* and—probably—her more famous *La Princesse de Clèves*. *The Original of Romances* was published as an introduction to *Zayde*. His tracing of the origins of the novel to oriental sources and the romances attests to a remarkable interest in history; it also served the purpose of stressing the novel's dignity by giving it a distinguished ancestry. His conception of the novel as a heroic poem in prose established the link with the epic, and his emphasis on the classical norm of epic probability even excluded the *merveilleux* from the novel. The application of this norm, however, dissociated the novel from history, and since the novel in its actual development tended toward history, the *De l'Origine des romans* can be said to present a retrospective poetics of the genre.

Saint-Evremond is sometimes called a "Modern" and is said to illustrate the transition from the seventeenth century, spellbound in literature and the arts by the perfection achieved in Classical Antiquity, to the eighteenth century, which believed in progress and evolution. In fact, Saint-Evremond remained in political and literary matters attached to the period of his youth and the "parti des mondains" (which was opposed to the fanciful and imaginary, to ornate style and the pedantry of the school, and which set the heart, its intuition, and the delicacy of feeling above rules and rigid rationalism), preferred Corneille as dramatist, and was skeptical about the novelties introduced by Racine. On the other hand, one may call him "modern," because he is critical toward Classical Antiquity and recognizes that every period has a character and spirit of its own. Above all, he is refreshingly cosmopolitan; his long exile in England probably contributed to his open-mindedness. Bouhours felt justified to write: "A German or Russian bel esprit is an oddity. . . . The bel esprit . . . is not at all compatible with the coarse temperament and the massive bodies of northern peoples. . . . This character is so suited to our nation that it cannot be found outside of France." [5] Rapin did not hesitate to belittle Dante, Petrarch, Boccaccio, Ariosto, Tasso, Lope de Vega, and Camoëns when he compared them to classical and French authors. When Saint-Evremond passes a negative judgment on some English tragedies, it is not from a sense of nationalism, but because the cruelty and savagery of the English stage offended his taste. He felt that the English dramatists spoke too much to the senses. With characteristic fairness, he adds that English criticism of French tragedies had some very good points, and he criticizes the French nation for referring everything to itself, for appreciating things only in so far as they are related to its standards. English comedy appealed very much to his taste, and Voltaire could add little to Saint-Evremond's judgments. His style and manner are quite different from those of the other authors in the anthology. Saint-Evremond does not write a treatise, he does not set forth rules or principles, he does not teach or prescribe. He speaks personally about his likes and dislikes; he reflects and meditates. His broad culture and his erudition are elegantly concealed. He has a philosophic mind and is a true man of letters; he writes, however, with the detachment of an aristocrat and *honnête homme*.

As for principles and theories, Boileau's *Art poétique* does not add anything essential to those of Chapelain and d'Aubignac, but the verse form in which he stated them in imitation of Horace [6] lent the charm of poetry to his theories and made them more forceful and pleasing. He adapted them not only to the taste of the literati, but also to their artistic criteria. More important still in the present context, he combined in the *Art poétique* the obiter dicta with literary criticism, a criticism which he had previously expressed in the form of brilliant satire. He still treated errors and abuses with irony, but now he also praised the great authors of his time for their achievement. In both cases he employed the instructive and lively form of applied criticism. Thus Boileau appears less as the legislator of the Parnassus than as the friend, adviser, monitor of creative poets, as the critical, stimulating consciousness in the complex genesis of great works. We may take the following passage as an expression of the role which he hoped to play:

Introduction

Faites choix d'un censeur solide et salutaire,
Que la raison conduise et le savoir éclaire,
Et dont le crayon sûr d'abord aille chercher
L'endroit que l'on sent foible et qu'on se veut cacher.
Lui seul éclaircira vos doutes ridicules,
De votre esprit tremblant lèvera les scrupules.[7]

One of the major reasons for his lasting influence is that he selected the writers who were indeed to win the acclaim and admiration of their contemporaries and of posterity.

Boileau's second major contribution to literary theory was his translation of the *Peri Hypsous* attributed to Longinus; the reverberation of this work in England, France, and Germany was immense. The frequently stated opinion that such a translation by the archpriest of neoclassicism is a paradox seems to us erroneous; it is based on a narrow conception of Boileau's other writings. In the present context we are primarily concerned with his *Préface* and one of his *Réflexions critiques:* following Longinus, Boileau frees the notion of the sublime from its connection with the rhetorical principle of the three levels of style and regards it as the expression of greatness of soul and mind; it does not consist in a stylistic technique, like high-flown prose or verse, but in great thoughts or lofty feelings. Though Boileau does not seem to have felt that this conception contradicted the rules of the *Art poétique* (as a matter of fact, the example of sublime expression which he quoted in the addition to his *Préface* is from one of Corneille's most regular tragedies), it drew attention to the faculties of the poet and admitted a subjective expression in art (apparent in Boileau's *Discours sur l'ode*), modified the concept of imitation of nature, and weakened the traditional alliance of Beauty and Truth; the sublime communicates itself directly, as it were, even in "very small words"; the heart speaks in simple language, which seizes the soul rather than dazzles the eye.

No less significant are the beginnings of historical thinking in literary theory which came out of the controversy with the Moderns. In the *Réflexions critiques* Boileau develops the idea of a "point of perfection and maturity" in the evolution of genres and poetic language and emphasizes more strongly than before that only posterity (the judgment of history) can and will decide the merit of works. Hume was to find later in the consensus of the ages the only objective criterion of taste. Confronted with the pseudo historicism of the Moderns, Boileau overcame the paralyzing antitheses of the tenacious quarrel and in a fine paradox unmasked the Moderns as unartistic rationalists.

Fontenelle is considered to be a "Modern" because he rejected the model character of Classical Antiquity, ridiculed the praise bestowed upon Antiquity, criticized its shortcomings, and found many contemporary works of art superior to those of Greece and Rome. Though these points are important, Fontenelle is modern in a more radical way.

There are in his *Discours sur l'églogue* several observations on writers of pastorals in various centuries and on the different forms of the genre, but the perspective in which they are seen is philosophical, psychological, and strictly contemporary rather than literary and historical. According to Fontenelle, the pastoral answers our desire for happiness, for freedom from care and ambition, and our longing for leisure and idleness (*paresse*). The latter two, however, must not be static; they need the animation of tender, simple, delicate, and faithful love. There should exist an emotional balance and an intellectual as well as artistic one. The true (the tranquillity and simplicity of country life) and the false (the concealment of the real condition of shepherds) will have to be combined; the elements of gallantry and *finesse d'esprit* must not contradict the simplicity of a shepherd. One might say that for Fontenelle the merit of the pastoral consists in the ideas which it suggests and in the happy surprise which a reconciliation of contrasts evokes in a reader's mind. Theocritus' coarseness, Virgil's high-flown philosophical notions and political visions, are as much to be avoided as clownishness, exercises in *mots d'esprit,* conceits, and exaggerated or old and threadbare figures.

Though the attacks against his critical remarks on the pastorals of Classical Antiquity are mentioned only at the end of the *Digression,* Fontenelle had them in mind when he decided to deal with the principle of the quarrel between the Ancients and Moderns. The reader who turns to the *Digression* after having waded through the literary and philological argumentation of the *Querelle* gives at first a sigh of relief when he sees the debate reduced to fundamental issues. Only later does he realize the radical nature of Fontenelle's thought which cuts the links, established in seventeenth-century literary theory, between Classical Antiquity, nature, and reason. In the *Digression* even more than in the writing on the pastoral, not only the main argument but the very way of presenting and discussing the issue is modern. Fontenelle opposes the cult of Classical Antiquity and criticizes the belief in its authority and moral superiority; he also rejects antiquated modes of thinking that are incompatible with modern philosophic reasoning and with science. To the notion of a point of perfection reached in an exemplary past he opposes the progressing perfectibility of reason and the steady increase of knowledge. Taking reason as the exercise of the mind and nature as the sum total of physical laws, he denies their metaphysical, mythical, or anthropological foundation. If he recognizes "perfection" in certain authors of the past, the term is no longer a historical norm, but designates high achievement. He even discards the cyclical conception of history, an idea which he entertains for a while as image and allegory. History becomes a varying relationship in time: those who are called now the Moderns will one day be the Ancients. May they not become the object of excessive admiration!

The *Digression* and the first edition of La Bruyère's *Les Caractères* appeared in the same year, and they seem to illustrate two aspects of the final stage of the seventeenth century: the turning toward a new era and the consciousness of the end of a great epoch. "We are come too late . . . to say anything which has not been said already"; these first words of the opening chapter of *Les Caractères* have a melancholic, disillusioned ring! "We can do nothing now but glean after the ancients and the most ingenious of the moderns." La Bruyère is painfully aware of the plight of the latecomer, but as he wrote his *Caractères,* he must have realized that he also occupied a unique vantage point. He had reached a high degree of consciousness, denied to those who first said all that now has been said.

The first chapter of *Les Caractères,* entitled "Des Ouvrages de l'esprit," is La Bruyère's *ars poetica;* he remains faithful on the whole to the norms and values of Boileau's *Art poétique,* but he is more broadminded, as his remarks on preclassical writers show. The battle had been won, after all. He is an "Ancient," but in retrospect; he feels and makes the reader feel that the great period has passed. He is conscious not only of its criteria and its style, but also of more general issues: what it means to be an author, to compose a work, to appear on the stage, to be a reader or a spectator, to formulate a judgment. Hence his touchiness as a writer, his defensiveness, his acute awareness of the public, and, above all, his preoccupation with the problem of expression. After all has been said, the art of expression is the saving grace. La Bruyère is deliberately a stylist. He is the last to be able to state peremptorily: there is in art a point of perfection; he who is sensitive to it has good taste. There *is* good and bad taste. The point of perfection had been reached, and La Bruyère still acknowledged the norms. In the eighteenth century, taste becomes a problem of criticism and a philosophic issue.

Owing to the high degree of consciousness and to the keen awareness of the importance of expression and the criterion of expression, the chapter on "Des Ouvrages de l'esprit," like the entire work to which it is a prelude, is a unique introduction to the values, norms, ideas, and style of the French seventeenth century. It could be written only by someone who is still part of an era yet already removed from it.

HERBERT DIECKMANN

September 1970

THE CONTINENTAL MODEL

Selected French Critical Essays of the
Seventeenth Century, in English Translation

"But critic-learning flourished most in France." POPE

Jean Chapelain LETTER OR DISCOURSE BY MONSIEUR CHAPELAIN TO MONSIEUR FAVEREAU, KING'S COUNSELLOR ON THE BOARD OF EXCISE, CONVEYING HIS OPINION OF THE POEM "ADONE" BY THE CHEVALIER MARINO

I already knew, both from you and the Chevalier Marino, that you had determined to assemble the learned and detailed observations you have made on his poem *Adone*, and I was overjoyed to think that since this fine work was about to appear, so rare a mind had taken the trouble to reveal subtly its riches and excellence, when I received in your letter the confirmation of what I had believed until then; but your letter is phrased in such a way that you seem to await my answer to learn whether I think such a critical appreciation is likely to redound to your honor, and whether in my opinion the poem is worth the time you would have to give to it. To this I shall reply that I am greatly astonished at two things: the first, that you could now conceive any doubts, however small, about a work which you know to be by that great man, which he communicated to you himself, and whose beauties, as he read it to us, you have often repeatedly admired in my presence; it is as though you had changed and now, alone among critics, refused to recognize that the works of Marino are flawless, and that they bear in his name their inviolable passport. The other thing which astonishes me even more is this: granted that the scorn which the chevalier has several times expressed to us of this poem might have given you serious grounds for doubt; and granted that the modesty you profess so precisely prevents you from depending upon yourself and makes you mistrust that solid judgment upon which others of the most judicious rely so willingly; in short, granted there was real reason to fear and doubt; the astonishing thing is, I say, that among so many skillful people who esteem you and who are at your disposal, you were willing to cast your eyes upon such weakness

3

as mine in the hope and desire of drawing from it some good result. That is indeed a thing of which I do not believe you will be able to clear your conscience. I am a man without a name, without authority, without importance in the world, and if it were not that I fear to contradict a too favorable judgment you once made of me, I should say a man without the learning and the training necessary to speak worthily of so elevated a subject. From this you see what may be expected of me. However, in order not to excuse myself from a thing you order me to do, and from which you leave me no liberty to seek exemption, being unable because of the distance between us to tell you by word of mouth how it appears to me, I shall set my opinion down for you on this paper, protesting beforehand, however, that I disavow my own sentiments from this moment if you judge that they diverge, however slightly, from the goal of truth; nor do I do this without promising myself that you will read the discourse benignly as is your custom, paying attention not to me, who shall write it, but only to the weight and genuineness of the things which are to be said in it.

I say then, in order to answer your question, that I consider the *Adone*, in the form in which we saw it, a good poem, built up and developed in all its novelty according to the general rules of the epic, and the best of its genre which can ever be published.

Now in the reasonable proof of this opinion of mine it might be thought necessary for me to say what *poetry* is, how many kinds of it there are, what the nature is of each, especially of that which the Greeks call *epopoeia* and for which we have not yet found a name, in order to see how, while remaining within these principles — granted that this poem is not typical of the epic — it has been permitted to the poet to introduce a genre different from the traditional one and which may nevertheless be included in the epic as to kind — a point we must demonstrate in order to establish the success of the poem. But since I am speaking to you who are aware of all that, in order not to prolong this essay unnecessarily I shall omit all definitions and divisions as presupposed and sufficiently dealt with by others, and shall concentrate with regard to the first heading, which concerns the basic value of the poem, upon examining three points to be encountered therein which are subject to doubt and to objection, and on the validity of which depends the proof of my position: the *novelty* of the literary genre; the *choice* of the subject; and its *credibility*.

As to *novelty*, I can, in the first place, imagine two kinds: the one blameworthy and unnatural, the other praiseworthy and natural. That novelty which is unnatural has two subdivisions, of which the first might be called perfect in its imperfection; this occurs when to a body of one nature is conjoined a body of another nature, as was the case with the satyrs in antiquity and in our time with the half-men, half-dogs. Here novelty consists in the excess of monstrosity. The second kind might be called imperfect and occurs when to a body of one nature there is attached another body of the same nature without their being unified and fused, with the result that these two segments do not appear to be and do not produce two distinct beings each independent of the other; we see examples of this in those human monsters having two heads, in hermaphrodites, and in Siamese twins; here the novelty is merely monstrous without excess. Natural novelty is also of two sorts, the first perfect in its perfection, occurring when a non-monstrous thing which has never existed before first comes to light, as when, in a place where water had never appeared, one sees suddenly a clear stream burst forth. The other, less perfect, occurs when, in a thing already known, one discovers some perfection thitherto unrecognized, as if in that same known spring one happened after a while to note some particular virtue which had not been perceived before. Now to reduce these four kinds of novelty to the terms of a fable, that is to say, of the subject of a poem, I include in the first group of the unnatural, daydreams, and the stories nurses tell to children, or, if you prefer, some of the stories of Straparola,[1] the Italian author, in which, without being constrained to do so by the needs of allegory, he makes irrational animals talk and act as men talk and act. In the second I put romances of all kinds if they do not have either unity of action or unity derived from the principal characters. In the first group of natural novelties I include the original discovery of the arts and sciences, as for example, poetry produced by Apollo in his time or by another; that kind of novelty is the most excellent in that it opens the way for those who come afterwards to discover the special virtues of an art. To the second group I assign the invention of genres, as of the heroic by Homer or Orpheus, or of the lyric by Sappho; this kind of invention, although it is really less excellent, has nevertheless much merit in the eyes of those who make the first discovery, and the same is true proportionately of the understrappers. Grant me that word and also those I shall be forced to use in dealing with this subject, because as far as I know our language does not have any words suitable to express these ideas, and I am not bold enough to launch new words for general use. Now, coming back to the subject, I say that the *Adone* is neither of the first nor the second kind of

5

unnatural novelty since, as you know, the fable has unity of action and unity of character and since, for example, there is in it no mixture of sacred history with profane poetry. It does not belong, either, among the first group of natural novelties, because being a poem and an epic poem, as we shall show later, poetry and the epic are presupposed before it. If it has novelty, then, it must be of the second kind, that is to say, of the praise-worthy sort, and that is what I maintain; here are my reasons.

The *significant action*, according to Aristotle, is either represented or narrated. When it is represented tragedy results; when it is narrated epic results. I define a significant action as a notable event, whether of good or of ill fortune, occurring to persons illustrious in themselves or who are made so by the quality of the event. Now of these kinds of actions some can occur in war, as in tragedy the death of Capaneus [2] or the events in the *Antigone*; and in the epic, the death of Hector or that of Turnus; others occur in peace as, in tragedy, *Atreus* [3] or *Medea*. It is true that for the epic there is, as far as I know, no example of this latter kind; but that there may be one is clearly seen in that tragedy and epic do not differ in subject, and that only the way in which the subject is treated, by representation or by narration, sets up a distinction between them. Now it is certainly true that between representation and narration there is difference only in the incidents, for the purpose of both is none other than to set the chosen sub-ject before the eyes, whether by means of scenic display or by words alone (both being instruments of imitation); this being true, nothing can be ac-ceptable in the one which is not acceptable in the other. But there is no doubt that tragic representation accommodates itself to events which have occurred in time of peace, and thus one may soundly conclude that epic narration cannot refuse the same peacetime actions. Otherwise, if the sig-nificant action, which occurred in peacetime and was suitable to serve as a subject for the tragic poet, could not so serve for the epic poet, it would follow that they do not both use the same subject, which is against the hy-pothesis. I do not deny certainly that just as among tragedies those are more frequently seen and are better which are deeply involved in the tu-mult of war, so among epics those which have war for their subject are the first in dignity, since they have the advantage of events and of the relief given by a stormy background and by violent struggles attendant upon the most important affairs; I mean only that just as the first tragedies do not exclude the others simply because they happen to be favored with a richer subject, so the epic, being of the same eminence and having the same obli-

6

gations, since a significant action is the subject common to both, cannot reject a second type of itself on the mere statement of the pre-eminence of the first.

Having thus resolved the first problem, and having supposed, as is in fact the case, that the poem *Adone* takes its rise from a deed done in time of peace, accompanied by peaceful circumstances, and which has no complications other than those which peace admits of, nor embellishments other than those which peace allows, it is clear that being new, the poem is of the second class of novelties, the poet having discovered by means of it something new in a kind of writing which was already well known; that is to say he found to be included in the epic besides the heroic, which is a war poem of a kind already familiar, this other which is a poem of peace not previously known, the less so because poets, hitherto enticed by the grandeur of martial subjects as being most susceptible of various encounters and unexpected events having the most remarkable consequences, and ambitious to acquire for themselves a name in the description of something which, like war, is the greatest among human actions, have thrown themselves so avidly and so unanimously upon this kind of poem that they seem to have overlooked the possibility of writing one in the contrary manner. But however overlooked or neglected — I am inclined to think rather the latter — this second has been, insofar as it constitutes another division of the epic, if our friend has considered its basic theory, as I believe, and if he has wanted to put it into practice and to give it vogue, I say not only that his poem is good because it is new and of a praiseworthy kind of novelty, but beyond this that poetry will be infinitely obliged to him as to one who felicitously extends its frontiers and who rightly amplifies and augments its scope and domain.

Since we have proved the reality of this new kind of writing by the example of tragedy, which, merely because it includes deeds of both war and peace, is nevertheless not divided and does not produce two kinds of itself, treating both equally and without difference in style or omission of events, it seems that the epic also, making use of the same deeds, ought to treat them in the same way without any difference in characters or composition; and thus instead of two kinds there would be only one. This, however, was not our conclusion, and I shall say first that although in appearance tragedies of both subjects seem to have only one single mode of composition, they are not so undifferentiated, especially as regards style, that anyone who wished to examine them carefully could not yet find some diversity among them; and secondly I shall say that even if this were not true, the question of treatment is not the same in tragedy and in the epic: for in the first the poet is not concerned with whether the action takes place in war or in peace but only with whether it has particular complications, which results in this, that the subject being one in this respect it can be treated in only one way, whereas in the heroic epic the question of war is important, and so important that without it the heroic would no longer be heroic because the complication, which inseparably constitutes its nature, occurs in it probably only with respect to war, as being the source of its complication and entanglement; and similarly in this new genre the question of peace ought also to enter, in order inseparably to form its essence, which will result in this, that the epic, being divided into two kinds by this means, will require two kinds of treatment. But in a word, when I alleged the tragedy as proof, I ought to have been satisfied that it supported me on the subject of peace as well as that of war; for as far as treating the latter is concerned, the technique is always different depending upon the different considerations which one brings to it, and things are considered either in all their nakedness or with regard to necessary circumstances as we see by the difference between the historian's style and the poet's, even when they are dealing with the same occurrences and the same events. Now since war and peace have notably different tempos and almost opposite circumstances, and since it is necessary to treat things which are different and opposed by differing means, if the difference as such can constitute a separate genre, there is no doubt that since this sort of poem has, in the state of peace which informs it throughout, the difference which can make it a distinct genre, it must then constitute a genre distinct from the heroic and consequently must require different treatment.

And this genre, in view of the opposition between peace and war, will be such, if you please, with respect to the heroic, as comedy, in view of the contrast between an action which is insignificant and one which is significant, is with respect to tragedy, and the same opposition will be found proportionately between the one and the other as exists between comedy and tragedy, provided that the universal rules governing their general constitution and what the poets call consistency are equally observed in them, which will be seen hereafter to be precisely the case with the poem of which we are speaking. And moreover, if we found the conception of this new genre on the basis of a significant action which has occurred in time of peace, I shall say it is necessary that the subject of the poem to which one is willing to grant this designation be significant without an admixture of war; significant, if possible, through its principal characters, and above all significant through the event; that the particular complications be as great as the chosen subject permits while yet not removing it from the relationship which it ought properly to have with the repose of peace and the ordinary events of peacetime; that the composition should thus incline more to simplicity than to complexity as should also the episodes therein principally considered, because of the nature of peace which does not furnish narrative substance, that is to say diversity of action; that all efforts ought to be devoted to descriptions and detail and this more concerning things associated with peace than war, as palaces, gardens, architecture, games, and other similar things, what is not in this category being treated only when necessary and as it were in passing; that love should have the principal place and that everything should issue from it and revolve about it, other subjects being considered only as accessory and ancillary to this one; finally, that comic situations may occur in it, but modest ones, or modestly told: all these conditions are indeed proper to peace, you understand, and yet they do not include the exact contrary of things which are important in war. You know also that the *Adone* everywhere conforms perfectly to this conception, and as the climax of perfection remember that it is a mixed genre yet not debased, as befits its nature which is as it were in suspension between tragedy and comedy, the epic and the romance; it is in some ways grave and lofty, both as regards the characters and the catastrophe, and it is also simple and low both in the actions which precede the conclusion and in the detailed descriptions. I am not speaking here of the style which accompanies it, since it has the same antitheses to the heroic style as its subject has to the heroic subject, but I am certain its novelty will be all the more estimable since the brilliance of antiquity will be found everywhere in it and the graces of the moderns will give it color.

And indeed so many rich and strong conceptions fill the body of the poem that, even if the composition of the poem were irregular, vicious, and haphazard, without any basis in reason (the contrary of which opinion has in part been demonstrated and in part will be demonstrated), nevertheless one would have to admit that the intention of giving the world a poetic genre like this one, where all things may find their place, was never anything but very beautiful and very useful; for how many beautiful inspirations may we believe have been lost or are lost every day for lack of a place where they may be used worthily; and how many profitable things

9

may we think have gone astray and been buried in the ruins of antiquity which, had poets undertaken their expression, regularly or irregularly, would still be alive in the memory of mankind for the public benefit, since everyone knows by experience that there is nothing which is preserved for so long a time, impregnable and invincible to all the shocks of time, as poetic monuments? Oh, how I should extol our friend for having been the inventor and the first advocate of this novelty if I had for his defense only what I have said! But we shall see that the ancients in the two greatest languages practiced what he did before him. I am speaking neither of the *Odyssey* nor of the *Ethiopian History* [4] — both of these compositions have more complications than peace admits of, and it is easy to judge that they were never modeled on the prototype of this poem — but there has come down to us from Musaeus or perhaps from Nonnus [5] a poem very similar to this one, concerning the loves of Hero and Leander; and Claudian elaborated a long poem founded on the rape of Persephone,[6] of which we have a fragment, in the same style and with similar actions although much less unified than those which are here, so that not only on the basis of reason but on that of the most valid authority this novelty will be no more in itself than a renewal and as it were a legitimate correction of a defect which existed in the division of the epic; and thus for being too well founded it will merit less praise. If hereupon it should be claimed that the poems mentioned come to an end in a few lines whereas *Adone* is extremely long, I should reply first that the allegation is not true for Claudian's poem, and that secondly, even if our poet had given himself an unexampled free hand he would have been justified in doing so since the subject-matter of peace allows this, as appears from what has been said above, and since it is only the episodes which he has developed at length, and these episodes, as you know, accommodate themselves to greater or lesser development, there being nothing which controls this in detail except necessity or the poet's preference; this is shown clearly by the episode of Ariadna in the epithalamium of Catullus,[7] which is less necessary and less probable than any one of those which are in the *Adone*, but which all the same has a greater place in this little poem than the principal subject, which concerns the loves of Peleus and Thetis. It can thus be seen that no difficulty arises from this mooted length. Add to this that everything in the poem being excellent, and it being moreover impossible ever to have too many things which are excellent, only the poet loses by that length, and he does not understand, as he has told me a hundred times, why it is taken as binding upon other poems since he wants to be as free in the other major works which he has promised as if he had never thought of this one; in this he shows only too clearly the difference between his mind and that of the ordinary man, for he is unable to do things negligently or pettily, not even those which are petty and negligible.

The question of novelty being thus dealt with, the problem of *choice of subject*, which we have placed second of the three things to be considered, does not consequently need much argument. Choice is said to be good when it is commensurate with the plan one has, and bad in the contrary case; consider the man who, wanting to build a palace, chose a suitable site, the proper materials, and the tools with which to arrange them according to the desired effect: such a man would be said to have chosen well because he kept in view his goal, which is his building, to which goal all those things are related and necessary; but a man who, in order to make a suit or a picture, provided himself with the same equipment and had the same plans would make himself ridiculous and would be said to have chosen ill because he did not consider his goal for which all that equipment is useless. If that is granted, I say the choice of fable for *Adone* is very good and very judicious, and that for this new idea of a poem of peace, which Marino probably stumbled upon, no other subject of greater plausibility or suitability could have been chosen or found, the more so since, as we have said, the action is significant in both ways, occurs in time of peace, is simple rather than complicated, turns entirely on love, and is seasoned with the sweet circumstances of peace and the moderate salt of mirth. But if he had used that fable in an ordinary heroic poem, how reprehensible that would have been! However, that can never have been his intention, and I am convinced that if you forced him to declare what his purpose was, he would tell you that he does not present the poem as heroic or tragic or comic, the term epic alone being suitable to it, although the poem has some admixture of all the other three. And if it is permissible to make a conjecture about these things, one of the principal reasons which probably led him to this choice was to show the existence between two extremes, that of great goodness as seen in the heroic poem, and that of great imperfection as seen in the cluttered romance, of an area to which the poet who could not aspire so high and who would disdain to stoop so low might restrict himself, in order to work with commendation and without fear of losing the title of poet.

After the choice of subject comes the question of *credibility* or the belief which one may have in the subject — a point important above all others since it is said that where belief is lacking attention or feeling also fail; but where feeling does not exist there cannot be any emotion nor consequently any *katharsis*, nor any improvement in the morals of mankind, which is the purpose of poetry. Belief is then absolutely necessary in poetry. But what belief can we have in a fable which is admitted to be a fable? This kind: belief in the meaning which we draw from it; that is to say, the tendency of the imagination to accept that a thing is rather than is not, is acquired in two ways: the one imperfect and incapable of persuading, as being the mere report either of an historian or of another (and I call this incapable of persuading because the sincerity of men is unknown and because most often it is called into question over the slightest difficulty which arises); the other perfect and persuasive because of the probability of the thing reported, whether by the historian or by another; this latter is the natural, efficacious means of acquiring belief to which the first is reduced even when it professes the truth, if it be right that of two stories which are contraries or differently told we always put faith in that which has the greater degree of probability; this happens when the first way is highhanded and subject to rejection, for then the second gains its end gently even while vigorously seizing the imagination of the listener, and by the consistency of the things contained in the report makes him favorable to it. But of these two, since the one is proper to the historian, so one must recognize that the other is proper to the poet, the more so since history treats things as they are and poetry as they ought to be, so that the first cannot accept a false thing however probable it may appear, and the second cannot refuse it provided it has verisimilitude; and the reason for this is the fact that the one considers a detail with the intent only to report it; and that is why in histories cases and events are all different and unregulated as is suitable for what is at the mercy of fortune, for fortune makes the wicked prosper as much as the good, and ruins without distinction of persons the one as well as the other, whereas poetry, one of the sublime sciences which in its classification is not far removed from philosophy, takes first consideration of the universal, treating its subject in detail only with the intention of deducing from it something specific for the instruction of everyone and the common benefit; and that is why in poems the consequences of a good or bad action are always similar, according to the genre; the good man is recognized as such and the wicked man is punished, since their actions result from virtue or vice whose nature it is to reward or to destroy those who follow them; to such an extent is this true that when reading history I learn only what happened to Caesar or Pompey, without any certain profit and without moral instruction, whereas in reading poetry, behind the episodes of Ulysses or Polyphemus I see what one may reasonably suppose will generally happen to any who commit the same acts; just as by that abstraction from the specific which poetry requires of me I no longer consider, in the poems of the ancients, Aeneas as pious and Achilles angry (and the same can be said of all the other actions and passions of mankind) but rather piety with its consequences and anger with its effects so as fully to learn the nature of them. In order to achieve this result the same ancients, urged on by zeal and these considerations, and judging that the truth of events, since they depend on chance, deflected their very laudable intentions through fortuitous and uncertain happenings, with one accord banished the truth from their Parnassus, some composing by caprice without mixing in anything that was truthful while others contented themselves with changing the truth and altering it insofar as it was opposed to their idea; but not one of them made a practice of recalling it except when it accommodated itself to them, that is to say, to justice and reason, and unless it had verisimilitude, which in this instance, rather than truthfulness, serves as the instrument by which the poet puts man on the road to virtue; to which end examples of evil are as useful as those of good, provided they be considered as intended for instruction and be requited as they deserve. For all this either the Achilles of Homer or the Aeneas of Virgil will serve as proof, for if we believe certain writers, neither of these was ever so enraged or so virtuous as he has been pictured to us; nevertheless, since Homer and Virgil intended to suggest by their names the psychological dimensions of the deeds attributed to them, they made them so and were in no way concerned if the details of truth suffered, provided mankind in general profited by the verisimilitude. Now since this verisimilitude is a representation of things as they ought to occur, according as human judgment, born and trained to the idea of good, foresees and determines them; and since the truth is reduced to this and not this to the truth, there is no doubt that because verisimilitude is an attribute of poetry (that is to say, since the poet treats only what ought to be and since what ought to be is always compatible with verisimilitude, for these two things are reciprocal) and since this verisimilitude stimulates the imagination and makes the reader judge that everything came about easily as described, as he does not judge truth to have done except insofar as it has

13

verisimilitude, there is no doubt, I say, that poetry should be believed since it has in its favor that which in itself produces belief, whereas history proceeds more highhandedly and has in its favor only the naked truth which cannot be believed without other aid and comfort. Thus it will suffice for the approval of a poem that it have verisimilitude because of the quick impression which verisimilitude makes upon the imagination, the latter being captivated and controlled by it as the poet intends.

Having thus discussed the subject in general, we may apply what we have said to our friend's poem in this way: it is clear that if one wishes to deny the truth of the plot, and the succession of events seems likely to make us admit its fabulous quality — although this is not certain in view of the fact that there is mention in writing of the tears shed for Adonis, and since according to the ancient rhapsodes and mythologists there is no fable, especially of those concerning the deities, which was not founded upon some real event — the poem will not cease for that reason to follow the laws of art and will not lose credibility, because truth is not of the essence of poetry, and even if truth should be found there, since it is considered not truth but only fable, for the reason that we have discussed, and since verisimilitude alone is sought for, as long as the poem has that quality as you know it does, so long will it have credibility for men; and the more it loses through historical inaccuracies the more it will gain through a sufficiency of probability.

In order to show further the right and necessary falseness of poems I could have instanced the allegory with which they ought to be associated, but since allegory is irrelevant to the discourse on verisimilitude, it being a self-conscious operation of the intellect as it moves from one outward appearance to another and not of the imaginative faculties, I have reserved a discussion of it for this place. *Allegory*, then, according to the general opinion of learned men, is a part of the conception of the poem, and is the second fruit which one can gather from it. Now as it happens that allegory is most often incompatible with the real sequence of events, poets obliged to include it will always prefer rather to falsify the truth, which occurs in their works only incidentally, than to neglect the allegory which must be there by the nature of things; of this we have a notable proof in the fables Aesop gave to his country. Have they any verisimilitude, let alone truth, insofar as concerns the speeches, words, subtleties, foresight, and other things which he attributes to his animals? And yet they have come down to us with the general applause of mankind, who, on reading the fable, go straight to its meaning (that is to say, to the other reality which is meant), by usefully applying what Aesop has said about an impossibility to what is possible, without troubling to examine its degree of possibility; this indicates more than clearly that in the other fables, I mean in ordered poems closer to us than Aesop's, and overlooking the test of truth as an unimportant thing, we need consider only whether the desired profit is in fact found in them.

At this point, if I am not mistaken, the qualities which could keep this poem from being a poem, that is to say good in its poetic genre, have been sufficiently clarified and it has been sufficiently shown that they do not deprive this work of the nature of a poem. There remain now to be considered those which would make it a poem, and it will be proved, if possible, that *Adone* has all the principal qualities of epic poems hitherto accepted; and as for those which it has not, I shall show that it could not have them without impropriety; and consequently that it is good in the highest degree. This is the second premise of the proposition which we must now try to establish with complete proof.

In any narrative poem I consider two things: the *subject* and the *manner* in which it is treated. The first consists in the structure of the fable, which, according to my personal division, properly includes *plot* and *structure* and to a lesser degree *consistency* and *passions*. The second is the *style*, which serves to express all these things and includes *conceits* and *phrasing*. But each of these has its own rules and conditions which as the poem approaches them more closely make it more a poem, that is, bring it closer to perfection. Let us see how *Adone* accommodates itself to them.

First I divide the *plot* of any poem into two aspects, the first *diversity*, the second the *marvelous*. This diversity is acquired in two ways, from the *nature* of the subject and from its *episodes*. That diversity which arises from its nature is like an emanation of things flowing spontaneously from the natural abundance of the subject; thus in the heroic poem the events which constitute the complication, and without which the poem would not be heroic, are said to engender diversity arising from the nature of the subject; and in this new kind of poem about peace, ordinary, uncomplicated events would produce it also if tranquillity could admit of a diversity of incidents and not the contrary. The diversity which results from the episodes is like an assemblage of things which are suitable to the subject but not essential to its nature: for example, (1) in the heroic poem everything which enters into the fable without contributing to the principal event

15

and which nevertheless is suitable to it, which will probably be very little because its complicated nature gives it enough subject-matter in itself without its being forced to seek more elsewhere; and (2) in this new conception all that enters uselessly or unnecessarily into the poem but still without impropriety, which may be a great deal in view of its natural poverty — all these things, I say, are considered to produce the diversity engendered by episodes. The first diversity makes the fable necessary, the second enriches it with ornament. The *marvelous* has the same sources; the nature of the subject produces the marvelous when by a concatenation of causes not forced nor extrinsic to the action one sees events produced which are either unexpected or out of the ordinary; the marvelous takes place in the *episodes* when the fable is sustained by ideas and richness of language only, so that the reader neglects the subject to dwell on the embellishments. But before including these things in our remarks we must assume that the analysis of any poem consists, first of all, in the recognition of its subject so it may be related to the theory of the poetic genre, and then in determining whether the poem observes the rules laid down for the genre.

To come down to cases then, because it has a new subject and because it constitutes a new genre opposed, as we have said, to the heroic, to which belong the first kinds of diversity (those which arise from the nature of the subject), and because of the nature of its new idea, which is to have more episodes than subject-matter, the *Adone* does not accommodate itself to these first kinds of diversity and dwells rather on the latter kinds which result from the episodes in which it is so rich. Now it dwells on these not because there are no diversity and nothing of the marvelous of these first kinds in the body of the fable insofar as it admitted of them, but mostly because the poem must, for the perfection of its type, treat of what the heroic poem has not been able to treat of; and since the one is sustained only by its events which occur in war and troubles, so the other maintains itself only by means of simple, vain events furnished by an action occurring in the tranquillity of peace; despite this, however, the poet has neglected nothing in the *Adone* of what might increase both the diversity and the marvelous in the nature of the subject itself; his interweaving of the plot elements, in the form in which we saw it, if you remember, testifies sufficiently to that; and to prove that he would have done wrong to have gone about it in any other way, I shall argue as follows. If, in order to produce more diversity and more of the marvelous of the first kinds in the *Adone*

16

than there are, Marino had introduced other subjects than those which are there, as he would have had to do to achieve that result, these subjects would have had to be either of the same type or of a different one; if of the same he must have inserted important actions by the gods other than those which belong to the fable, for of unimportant actions there can be no more, I mean of those which merely enhance the subject; but if he had included other important actions, even though they enhanced the subject, the action would have been dislocated and consequently could be criticized according to our second subdivision under *novelty* as being against nature; that is to say that other important actions would have stifled the principal one and the *Adone* would no longer be the handsome Adonis but a many-headed Hydra. If the actions inserted had been of a different kind, i.e., human actions, they must either have served the general plan of the work or not. Those which would so have served could have been either important or unimportant; if important they would have dislocated the unity of the action neither more or less than important actions of the same kind, and moreover would have added to that dislocation a difference in kind, which is no small difference. As for unimportant actions, they are to be found in the poem as are those of the same kind, as many, indeed, as the subject allowed, and handled both in the ancient style, which is the manner I hold in highest esteem for this kind of effect, and in the modern, which I should not approve of in this poem if it appeared in more than one canto (divine certainly in itself and called by the author *Gli Errori*) because of the absurdity which the mixture of genres and the confusion of periods seems to me to bring about; but if he had made the actions of a different kind, not subordinate to the plan, they would all have been important actions with the result that the same difficulties noted above would have been encountered, and hence the composition could have shown only the opposition between the divine and the human, which would have been monstrous and not suitably knit together and so would have fallen into the first classification of unnatural novelties and would have had no unity of action, nor consistency of genre, nor suitable connective cladding. So much for diversity. As for the marvelous, now, it could not be made greater in the poem except by adding new occasions for it; but this could not be, both because of what has been said about diversity and because the poet cannot attribute to a received fable (as he can to history) another event than that known to be part of it; and the reason, I think, is that the relation between history and what is accepted as true is the same as that between poetry and what is accepted as probable; now just as the historian, having once received and recognized the truth as such, cannot alter it in any way at all, that is to say, can neither add to nor take away from it, so the poet, receiving a fable from another writer and recognizing it as probable, that is to say as having previously been reduced to verisimilitude, that immutable object of poetry, confines himself to the fable without being able to innovate in any way whether by suppressing part of it or by adding to it of his own invention; hence just as we say that truth must play the role of verisimilitude in history as far as the historian is concerned so that he can change nothing in it however useful he thinks that might be, so one may say that a fable having verisimilitude must take the place of truth for poetry as far as the poet is concerned, and so for the same reason he must not alter it, however advantageous it might be for him to do so. But to return to the subject, since the poet could add nothing to the subject-matter, so he could not disclose other marvels in the poem than those which are there since the fable is in itself more than fully treated and all possible artifice had been employed in it. Granted even that he was free to make that addition, aside from the fact that the fable would then have been overladen (which would have been against his original conception) he would also have run the risk of creating a diversity of action as has previously been said in the discussion of diversity. Now the unity of action, among the general rules which every epic poem must observe, is in especial the principal one without which the poem is not a poem but a romance. If then to preserve that unity the poet has kept himself within the limits of the chosen fable, although this procedure is in itself sterile as far as the first ways of producing diversity and marvels are concerned, he has done only what he had to do, and the seeking of diversity and the marvelous according to the other ways is suited to the conception of his new poem.

If you should now ask me which of these two manners seems to me the nobler, that which arises from the nature of the subject or that which arises from the episodes only, or, to clarify the matter by an example, whether it is the heroic which has an inherent complication or this new genre which has unalterable tranquillity, I shall admit in all simplicity that it is the first according to my lights, and I consider the other only second to this, even though several reasons might make me think otherwise. For if among these reasons you consider the fable you will remember that the ancients recognized three kinds: the first the Romans called *motoria* since it contained in itself the agitation and entanglement which subsequently appeared in the treatment of the subject, these being artfully arranged to bring about a happy or unhappy ending as required by the subject; the second was called *stataria* since it was less agitated and more tranquil than the other, consisted of ordinary events, and ended without great ceremony so that the spectator came to believe in it; the third was called *mixed* since it partook of the one and the other. Now to say which of these three was the most esteemed among the ancients would be difficult, and it would appear obvious that the calm one enjoyed no less consideration than the others since they often made use of it, and since poetry with its special procedures does more for it than for the two others. Here is why. The purpose of poetry being utility, although this is achieved by means of pleasure, it appears likely that whatever has utility as its object, i.e., whatever tends toward utility, is more estimable for that very reason than whatever has as its object pleasure alone, i.e., whatever halts at pleasure; and thus fables which are in good moral standing since they have utility as their goal are more important to poetry than those whose morality is dubious since they have as their object pleasure alone. That the calmer kind of fables have utility as their object I see no reason to doubt; for if the utility of poetry consists in the purgation of vicious passions, it is clear that this effect is obtained rather from those poems which are not complicated and entangled than from those which are. That this is true everyone will admit: what is to produce a purging must do so by constant application and without slackening, by continuous effort and without interruption; and the fact is that the simplicity of calm fables gives them this quality in the highest degree since they never leave their subject and are bound to give a detailed description only of the passion which is their subject, a state of things which is far from being characteristic of those fables which have complexity inherent in their nature, for that complexity scatters the descriptions about piecemeal and through the jumble of many different events blunts the effect and weakens the vigor which any one of them in its simplicity might have. Therefore the ancients, taking this into consideration, were as careful as possible even in their great poems not to overload them with subjects, recognizing that although in their diversity and capacity to produce the marvelous they might cause pleasure, they also obscured the goal of utility at which all good writers aim their inventions; that is in part why romances are so scorned among the learned, for without any idea of perfection to which they may conform they pile adventure upon adventure, and include fights, love-affairs, disasters, and other things, of which one well treated would make a laudable effect, whereas together they destroy each other, and so romances remain at best the amusement of fools and the horror of the sophisticated who cannot bear even to look at them, knowing that in their confusion they are remote from the purpose of poetry: for to purge it is first necessary to move, and since one cannot move another without first making an impression on him — an impression which is produced by ways both suitable and continuous — and since moreover these tales, by the quality as well as by the quantity of their subject-matter, are utterly incapable of making an impression, one cannot reasonably hope for that purgation through them. As opposed to these and even to heroic poems, since in the conception of the new poem diversity does not consist in events whose number or entanglement may distract from or destroy the impression, but in descriptions which help to create it and consequently to produce the desired utility, it is obvious that we may say the goal of poetry is fully achieved by the new poem and that for this reason the new genre would take first place. All this is part of what he might say on the subject who wished to praise everything in the poem and to show everything in it to be at the highest degree of excellence. But since that is by no means my intention here, and since I am not willingly carried away by appearances when I have some knowledge of the truth, the conclusion I come to in the matter is this: it is certain that the real purpose of poetry is utility which consists in the purgation we have described above but which is obtained from pleasure alone as a gate is taken by storm, so that without pleasure there is no poetry and on the other hand the more pleasure to be found in it the more poetical it is and the better it achieves its purpose which is utility. Now the pleasure of any reading may be divided into three kinds: when it comes from those events which are separate and plain, without arrangement; when it comes from descriptions alone, that is to say, when events are subordinated to descriptions; and when events and descriptions both produce pleasure by a judicious and moderate combination so that the one does not hinder the other and the events nevertheless appear to have the advantage. The first is an abuse in poetry and is not proper to it as much as to history; it occurs without the authority of any good ancient poet. Hence when we consider the nudity of ancient poems of bad form, and the confusion and multiplicity of their principal actions, we may liken them to modern romances whose wild structure the stupid public adores because it has a natural liking for imperfection. The new conception of a poem of peace is related to the second kind of pleasure in reading, and here poetry is found in its absolute purity free from anything foreign to it except such as may serve as a foil. The last kind raises poetry above itself and causes it to be embodied, without in any way altering its nature, in a subject which it wishes to treat for the subject's sake and not its own; to this kind is attributed the conception of the heroic poem. Now that we have excluded the first kind of pleasure from any poetical composition, no one can deny that of the remaining two the first, which arises from descriptions alone, is as far below the other, which includes events clothed in description, as description alone is inferior to the thing described; or one might say that since the description merely makes use of the event as a foil, it is inferior to the event (attribute to necessity the tiresome repetition of this term, but I consistently mean by it the subject) which uses description as a mere accompaniment; thus when description makes use of the event, since the event is not the most important element in the amalgam, it is not found in the description in all its perfection, whereas when the event makes use of description, the event itself is entirely there since it is most important, and the description, although not equally important, is nevertheless as perfect as if it were; this is because description is the essence of poetry and ought never to be lacking in it. And thus on the one hand, if the first kind of these remaining two types of pleasure, which assimilates to itself this new conception, is more purely poetic, that is to say, if it more than the other confers on the writer the name of poet, because the virtue of any artisan, among whom we include the poet, is not judged by the richness of his material but by the rarity of his skill in treating it, on the other hand the second type of pleasure, which is induced by the traditional epic poem, will be more richly poetic, being aided and carried to perfection by the predominance of the event which is perfect in itself; I mean which is considered to be perfect in its form and which is treated primarily because of the goodness inherent in it. These are the reasons which have led me to say, while recognizing the form of the *Adone* as partaking of this new conception, that it yields the first place to the form of the heroic poem and that it must be content with the second place which its nature gives it.

To *plot* may be reduced the parts of the poem generally called *quantitative*, that is to say the complication of the fable and its unraveling (if I may imitate the Italians in the formation of these terms which do not in any way express what is meant by the interweaving of the parts of the fable

21

and its development). Now although these parts are not to be found in the *Adone* insofar as concerns the kind of principal action so much esteemed among the writers of heroic poems, i.e., the marvelous, with or without recognitions, yet they are there just the same; but if they are there in something less than perfection the defectiveness of the subject is the cause of it. Now it was proved above that the choice of this subject was made necessary by the novelty of the above-mentioned conception, and because in that conception the subject-matter, or event, was least considered. Of the subdivisions included under the composition of the fable, the second of those properly so-called is the structure, of which, if it is to be good, two things are usually required: the first, that the poet should not begin his narration *ab ovo*,[8] seeking the first cause of the action and having the story proceed in the same order as it occurred in time, as Statius and Silius Italicus wrongly did, not to mention that Lucan could have done otherwise; the other that the peripeteia, I mean the conversion or the change of fortune,[9] must occur in it, whether the change be from good to bad or from bad to good. If it is argued that the author of *Adone* has transgressed this first law, I say he could not have observed it, or at least that he ought not to have done so. But it seems obvious to me in the first place that he could not have followed it, for if he had given another arrangement to the work than the one it has, if, for instance, he had begun the story at the arrival of Adonis in the forest of Cyprus or in the palace of love or even further back, it is clear he would irremediably have lost the chance to inform the reader of Venus' passion, a thing which cannot be passed over since it is absolutely of the essence of the fable, he would, I say, have lost the chance, for since Amor alone knew of this passion it would have been inconsistent with the proper behavior of a son toward his mother to present him as boasting to anyone of his vengeance; it would also have been unreasonable, for his boasting would have given him cause to fear the anger of Venus and to anticipate some new punishment from her; and as far as Apollo and Neptune are concerned, both of whom knew something of this vengeance because they had helped in it, they could not tell it to others either except at the cost of a serious departure from the subject of the fable, and even then there would have been a great loss both in the general outline of the affair and in the details which enter into it so usefully; all these things Amor alone knew. In the second place it appears that the author ought not to have followed the rule even if he had been able because that reversal of chronology which is sought in poems is in itself more a recourse and an expedient than a beauty, a necessity, even an embarrassment rather than something marvelous; I mean that the judicious ancients made use of it not expressly to produce that highly recommended suspense, which is nevertheless very different from the marvelous as will be clear to anyone who examines the question, but only to recall and as it were to reincorporate in the body of their compositions what could have happened before the previous year, in which their action is described as having occurred; and they proceeded in this way for several reasons: the first, in order to restrict the course of the action to one year, a period whose limits were accepted by all those who wished successfully to treat a significant action in narrative poetry as the limit of one natural day was accepted by all who wrote for the stage; the second, so as not, through continuous narration, to overload their poems with more main actions, even if they were related to a single one, than the subject could profitably admit of; and the third, so as not to corrupt their works by several different actions each independent of the other, which would have made their writings defective in unity. For if the action of their poems had not lasted longer than a year or had not contained more subject-matter than their perfection required, or had not included independent actions, it is obvious that authors would not have forsaken the natural order which is not forced for another where there is constraint and where the imagination is overworked; the example of Claudian is decisive on this point as is that of others like Musaeus and Nonnus who follow the easy order. But in the *Adone* the fable does not stretch beyond a year, nor is the crowd of events very great, nor is what precedes the love of Venus very separate from the main action, and so it was not necessary, in order to avoid these evils, to have recourse to that ὕστερον πρότερον; [10] the poet would then have been mistaken if he had subjected himself to this law and forsaken the natural way which, as long as it is convenient, is always the best. Now the change of fortune in the poem is of the most pathetic kind even though it is lacking in the marvelous for the reasons we have set forth above, and is of the kind most efficacious in purging the passions, especially the tragic passion; but alas! with what circumstances is it accompanied! Considering all these things, I have been a hundred times astonished at what our chevalier has said and repeated to me, that he was not satisfied with the poem, and that if it were to be done over again he would give it a different form; but then I thought that in his case the greatness of his intelligence furnished him ideas which could not be arrived at by reasonable discourse, each idea being unknown to all until he discovered it; and besides, since I could not come to any other conclusion, I thought that what he said was only to test me and to set me thinking, especially since until now I have not been able to conceive of anything which is opposed to this interpretation.

After the proper subdivisions of composition we come now to those aspects of a poem which are less closely related to the composition, of which the first has been designated *consistency*. It could be defined as a natural inclination, confirmed by practice, whether for good or for evil, which is likely to be found in poetic characters endowed with four conditions (as the ancients said, but with only two as I hold): *goodness, propriety, resemblance,* and *equality*; now the first two are reciprocal since what is good is proper and what is proper is good, so that happenings attributed to an evil nature, even though they are evil in themselves, must be called good since they are proper to the person. For example, if cruel men like Diomedes or Mezentius [11] were introduced into a poem, the consistency of their cruelty would be considered good because it would fit them; thus Armida's [12] artifice and magic are good, not morally speaking but from the poetic point of view. Otherwise, in making a poem, the poet would be forced to shape it entirely of virtuous people, which is against usage and against reason. The latter two, on the other hand, which are resemblance and equality, are also the same thing, or almost so, since the one requires that the character presented be made similar to what has been learned about his inclinations through tradition or by the testimony of authors; and the other demands, if the character has not hitherto been known for one habit rather than another, or if he is entirely invented, that he be made to continue throughout the poem in the same posture as was attributed to him at first; one might just as well say that a character presented must be such throughout the poem as he was when either borrowed from another or created by the author at the beginning. But that these conditions of consistency have been precisely observed in the *Adone* is obvious, and first, as far as the good and the proper are concerned, should anyone obstinately try to erect the good into a category different from the proper, I answer that among good things love is considered to be very good and even the severest critic could class it no lower than among the neutral things, which is all one to the poet; aside from the fact that only the outcome of things determines their goodness or badness, if the outcome of the loves of Adonis by their disastrous end, as in tragedies, is to purge away the filth that is found in that passion, it is good, and renders the whole action good with respect to this end; but if one dwells on the proper instead, what is more proper to youth and beauty than the chase and the amorous passions? Secondly, regarding the similar and the equal, no matter how they are considered, what is there in this poem either received from tradition or entirely invented by the poet, which is not consistent to the end? Instead of making a more precise demonstration of this I shall trust to your memory so as not to bore you with details.

The *passions*, following our classification, constitute the second subdivision of these secondary aspects of composition and seem to be of the same type as consistency, being derived from it, for passion is nothing but a perturbation supervening in the animal faculty through a strong operation and, if I dare put it that way, an extraordinary tension of the natural inclination. As for that, the ordinary rules for the expression of the passions are known to you, and I shall say only that all those relating particularly to love are so efficaciously and skillfully handled in the *Adone* that the poet has left far behind him the most famous writers in this genre; and I dare say that those who follow his example most closely in the future still will never come very near to him. You have examples of this very clearly set forth in the beginning of his book and there is no need to examine them more closely here.

The subject having now been justified, the question of style arises, and of this we have made two divisions, the *conceits* and the *phrasing*. Concerning the *conceits*, all of whose differences and effects you are familiar with, I shall say boldly that this noble mind has so excelled in this work that I do not believe, either in the case of the passions or in that of the descriptions, that similar felicities have ever occurred to a human mind. It is really in this aspect of his work that he has achieved diversity and the marvelous, things which other poets seek in the mere invention of episodes; and in this respect where another might have been cloying and disgusting, he has succeeded in being so charming and agreeable that the length of the poem will seem inadequate to anyone who has some little judgment of what good reading is. As for the phrasing, now, if I am allowed without reproof to judge the beauty of a tongue which is not natural to me, the diction is so beautiful in itself, so Tuscan, so carefully chosen, so pregnant, that never has there been a poet in whatever language who had this gift in a higher degree than he; and of conceits and phrasing he has compounded a style which, whether in sweetness or in seriousness, as well as in really poetic inspiration, has no equal unless in certain ancient authors, and which will never be surpassed except by Marino himself.

But because this style is free and diffuse and because some even of the ancients have made judgments against it in their writers, calling it garrulousness, it will be good to see whether Marino's style, which follows that of the ancient writers, is subject to the same objection and whether it deserves blame or praise. It is an accepted maxim that any style must be suitable to the subject, the more so, as they say, because words are the natural expression of the idea, and the idea is nothing but the pure image of the thing itself. Now there are three kinds of subjects to which all others may be reduced: one is called grave or elevated, another humble or low, and the third a mixture of both; this last is called intermediate because it is small with respect to the great or the extraordinary, and great with respect to the ordinary and the petty. The first kind of subject includes all heroic deeds, the cyclical rise and fall of nations, the ruination or establishment of illustrious families, brave enterprises, and similar things; the second includes trickery, examples of gullibility, light loves, the quarrels and reconciliations which occur in civil and peaceful life among people of low estate and which do not produce public disturbance because of the low rank of the people involved; the third includes plots made up of mixtures of those events which are attributed to particular persons, even those who are great and illustrious, but which produce no other consequence than complaints and tears instead of wars and the subversion of the state. But as a thing is said to be average when it appears to partake of the two opposed extremes, so a subject is more properly called intermediate when it includes the serious and low; the seriousness may be found in the people and the lowness in the passions or ordinary events, or else the seriousness may be in the event and the extraordinary passions, and the lowness in ordinary people and circumstances. In ancient times the masters of eloquence sought in these three kinds of subjects the different forms or characteristics of style needed to treat them properly according to their differences; and to the first they assigned, if it was simply tragic, the style they merely called serious; if it was heroic also, that called both grave and magnificent, i.e., figured — you can easily see why; for the second they prescribed a common, trivial, discursive, smooth-flowing style, correct and understandable but knavish and jesting; to the third they assigned a style which was also intermediate, having some admixture of each of the others but sweetened and tempered — something of the serious

26

and the magnificent in those places where the subject resembled the heroic or the tragic whether in dealing with people or events; and something of the popular or the common in those, whether concerning events or people, where it resembled the ordinary and the comic. Once these points are agreed upon, if one considers the nature of the subject of *Adone*, there is no doubt that it will be seen to belong to the genre of the intermediate subject, nor that in consequence the subject had to be treated in the intermediate style. Now the theory of this style requires that things be expressed clearly but not basely, this latter quality being an inconvenience ordinarily associated with its characteristic frankness (which we would interpret as clarity if we should some day begin to want to understand thoroughly what true learning consists of), the more so since to bring things before the eyes one must descend to details and to the statement of relationships and subordinations which, however, it seems impossible to explain without baseness; Homer himself in so doing fell into this pit. But the greater the difficulty in finding this intermediate style which is expressive but not distasteful to the reader, the greater also the praise due to the mind which found it and to the judgment which had the skill to make use of it precisely in a subject which not only permits this but requires it for its own perfection; you may judge particularly whether the fable of *Adone* does this by what we have said about it above. If then our friend used this style on this occasion he must have done so more by judicious choice than by compulsion, and he merits special praise for this as being the first of the moderns who has ventured upon detailed description, in which the essence of poetry consists (I mean by this its energy and imitation) and that, moreover, without having played his subject false and without having stooped to what is base; consider, I beg of you, what subject he chose in order to achieve this success, and how elevated it is in its simplicity. No one denies that of all things the vastest and most susceptible of different facets is human passion, the unique image of raw nature, nor that among all the passions love and jealousy hold first place; now consider whether these are found in the *Adone* and in what way. In truth one could scarcely find a plot or any development of a fable involving the marvelous which is worthy of being compared with that simple way of narrating which Marino has reestablished in his poem, wherein both as regards passions and descriptions that magnificent clarity, that is to say — if I may — that floridity or elegance of style, has been maintained with such complete possession of the ideas, so great care for the language and such precise regard for the scansion of the verse and the conformity which ought to exist between the verse and the subject, that no one could ask for more: I find this all the more worthy of admiration since these are the thorniest things in poetry and the last to be mastered. If Scaliger, that great critic of the preceding century, were still alive, I do not doubt that in approving this work he would point out what we have shown here nor that the same thing for which he blamed Lucan, whose subject did not allow him to expatiate, would cause him to praise Marino, whose subject required that he treat it as he did. What leads me to this conjecture is the fact that Scaliger did not criticize copiousness in Claudian, whose intemperance is not slight, nor in Ovid, who expatiated to excess, whatever Quintilian may have said, for Scaliger no doubt realized that the one was fleshing out a simple fable which needed these external aids to give it relief, and that the other was giving life and speech to passions which are inexhaustible springs whose end is never seen. But since I said that the style of the *Adone* is perfect in its genre, I am sure you understand that it has all the qualities and general conditions of a good style, i.e., that the narration is very smooth, that the comparisons are naturally clear, being drawn from things well-known, finally, that as to the transitions nothing is left to be desired; and that thus since the principal virtue of this conception lies in the excellence of the style, and since this latter is the most excellent of all to the despair of carping critics, you see that the poem *Adone*, because of its style, will never have an equal in its genre. That is why, without dwelling at greater length on this final point, and without mentioning either the allegory included in the fable, as being sufficiently elucidated by the poet in the discourses with which he makes a practice of prefacing each canto, or the courageous competition into which he has entered with the ancients on the most important of their subjects, including the phrasing and even the conceits, as well as the detailed inventions hitherto unattempted by any other than himself, I shall, so as not to follow indiscreetly on your traces, conclude this wearisome catalogue by affirming to you as I did at the beginning that I consider *Adone*, in the form in which I remember having seen it, a good poem built up in all its novelty according to the general rules of the epic, and as the best in its genre which will ever be published.

Such then is the opinion you wanted from me concerning our friend's work; to support it more firmly I could have extended to greater length the things I have said in few words, for I should still have much to say if I were speaking to a person less understanding or less predisposed in favor of Marino, that is to say, in favor of the truth. Now should the affection which you have for him lead you to think I have meanly praised him here, remember you did not set me that task, and consider that in taking up my pen in order to satisfy you I have not intended to crown him with laurel but to show you succinctly that I knew why he deserved the crown. It seemed to me, since I was required only to give my opinion about his poem, that I was satisfying my obligation by telling you in plain words what I thought of it and the reasons why I held that opinion; and because of my nature you ought to have expected that I would not force my feelings in return for the friendship which Marino is kind enough to have for me; indeed, if there had been in the poem the slightest thing which I judged severely you would find it noted here in all freedom because, as I say, I do not love my friends more than my frankness and because I do not know what it is to squeeze out praise for them at the expense of the truth, consideration for the truth being so dear to me that what might disturb me about this essay would not at all be to have praised wrongly — that causes me no worry — but not having you before me so that if what I have said is perhaps subject to objection, I might hear your arguments and defend myself by replying to them at once, or else if the objections were unanswerable, so that I might relinquish my error immediately, ask for mercy, and profit from my shame by learning what I did not know. Had you wanted to compel me to panegyrize and praise Marino to the skies as he deserves, either I should have asked you for a longer time in which to prepare or I should have asked you to do it yourself, using that admirable pen which both in prose and verse and in one language or the other recognizes no rival which aims higher than it does. But allow me to tell you what I think: since I have no reason to suppose you wanted that from me, neither can I believe you waited until you had my opinion to make up your mind on this subject; I know too well both your ability and my own lack of knowledge to have any faith in such an idea as that, which without edifying you in the slightest would have entirely destroyed that modesty which alone my friends have until now esteemed in me; and I cannot come to any other conclusion than that you wished to test whether your authority was powerful enough to lead me into vanity and to induce me to think myself capable of making a judgment on the matter, preferring to inflict on yourself an annoying reply rather than not to plumb my weakness to the depths; and if this were true I should have nothing to oppose to that subtle scheme but my affection and the vow of cheerful compliance with

29

which I have bound myself to you, and which, since your first request made me shut my eyes to any other consideration, has led me to reply to you as I have done on the subject of the *Adone*, and obliges me further to tell you that you ought to carry out the fine plan you have of working on the poem; and to show you more clearly that I believe you should do so and that there is in it honor to be won for you, I boldly warn you that if you do not do it I shall try my best to accomplish the task; you will have, then, to address yourself to it, first in your own interest and secondly to deliver Marino from the well-grounded fear he would have, should I undertake it, of coming ill-arrayed from my hands. Farewell.

Jean Chapelain ON THE READING OF THE OLD ROMANCES,

DIALOGUE FOR MONSEIGNEUR JEAN-FRANCOIS-PAUL DE

GONDY, ARCHBISHOP OF CORINTH AND COADJUTOR IN THE

ARCHBISHOPRIC OF PARIS, LATER CARDINAL DE RETZ

You complain, my Lord, of not having been present at the conversation which Monsieur Ménage, Monsieur Sarasin, and I [13] had a few days ago on the reading of our old romances, and you show some regret that things were said there in your absence which one would not have expected so miserable a subject to call forth. What can I answer, except that there was never a more legitimate complaint? For indeed that diversion was owing to you for many reasons and among them because it began or at least it was conceived in your presence, during the journey we made last autumn with you. But, my Lord, permit us in our turn to complain that we missed you sorely on that occasion; I especially, who was, I do not know how, led to talk the most, particularly desired that you might have been there to hold me to moderation, to set me right, and to enlighten my darkness. There are so few things you do not know, your learning is so broad, your judgment so clear, you express yourself so lucidly, so force-fully, so eloquently, that if you had been present one might indeed have said that nothing was overlooked in the thorough discussion of the question. If it was through some mistake that you were not present, it must have been fortune's mistake and one for which we are all ready to make amends. We may still help you to enjoy that conversation, for all traces of it are not effaced; and I will wager that my bad memory will recall them easily and also will portray them faithfully for your satisfaction. However, because you are not always at leisure and because this recital could not be delayed without running the risk of being less exact and of losing many of its essential parts, it is best to commit it to paper so that you may pass your time with it free of constraint and it may await your leisure without spoiling. I shall report the exact words as they were uttered by each of us without any embellishment except that which they derive from the subject and which is sometimes found in spontaneous discourse where nothing is premeditated.

If I were speaking to another than you, my Lord, I should have to describe the temper and the qualities of the men who took part in the discussion, and inform you of the goodness, the learning and the wit for which Monsieur Ménage is remarkable and of the fine and varied knowledge which Monsieur Sarasin has acquired and which is added to the quickness of his mind and strengthened by his experience in the affairs of the world. I should have to give you a little sketch of my own inclinations and undertakings, and in showing you my faults I should reveal to you also my boldness in having embarked upon a work so little proportioned to my talents. But since the first has been a friend of yours for so long, since the second holds so high a place in your esteem, and since, for my part I am, to my shame, so well known to you, I shall not take the time to paint our collective portrait, for in any case it could only make us all blush, each in a different manner. I shall only say, my Lord, without other preliminary, that when these two gentlemen came to visit me a few days ago they caught me over a book which you have no doubt heard of but which probably you have never been tempted to read. Monsieur Ménage, who is completely devoted to the ancient Greeks and Romans and whose knowledge of them scarcely allows him to admit that there is good to be found in anything the moderns may do, discovering me with this book [14] which even the moderns mention only with scorn, said to me with his usual gaiety and making sport of me, "What! so this is the Virgil you have taken as a model, and Lancelot is the hero in whose image you are forming the Count de Dunois? I confess I should not have expected that of a man to whom antiquity is not unknown and whom we have heard speak reasonably of its philosophers, its poets and its orators."

I was forestalled in my answer by Monsieur Sarasin who had formerly taken pleasure in that kind of reading and with whom I had discussed it more than once.

"*Lancelot*," said he, "is not his Virgil but his Ennius, in whom, as in manure, he thought he might find a ruby or a diamond with which to deck his Maid. I have read that book and did not find it too disagreeable. Among the things in it which pleased me is this: that I saw in it the source of all the romances which for four or five centuries were the most refined diversion of the courts of Europe and prevented barbarism from mastering the world completely."

"You praise it," said I, "far beyond what it deserves. It is a barbarous thing which barbarians liked, but it is not so throughout. It is better however to let Monsieur Ménage keep whatever opinion of it he likes than to force him to listen to a defense of it. I shall merely defend myself, for I should not want him to leave here convinced that I have lost all taste for good literature because he found me seriously engaged upon a book which he thinks very bad and which in his estimation is no less Gothic in the events than in the characters. He will be very much surprised and will feel very much indebted to me when he learns that it was only out of respect for him that I became attached to it. The fact is that when Monsieur Arnauld came back this winter from Dunkirk laden with so fine a conquest [15] and when that event had reawakened the desire I have always had of casting my eyes on this book so as to observe a little in it the language and the style of our ancestors, I decided to read it principally in the hope of finding there important matter for the *Treatise on the Origins of Our Language* which our scornful friend has started and which is already far along, but he shall know nothing more of it. We have dug up this treasure for him but we shall keep it hidden from him; we shall give it to Monsieur Conrart [16] who wants it for a work of the same plan or even a vaster one, and God knows how well he will make use of it with the solid sense he has and the good taste he shows in these matters."

"If I believed that," replied Monsieur Ménage, "I should be mortified at the hastiness of my judgment and angry at myself for having scorned so useful a book."

"In my opinion you should take him up on that," said Monsieur Sarasin to me, "and while he is in that good humor you can overwhelm him with those riches whose existence he doubts."

"I beg you to do so," went on Monsieur Ménage; "indeed, I defy you, if begging is not enough, so that whether out of kindness or out of spite you will do me a favor I hardly dare hope for."

"You could do that favor for yourself," I replied, "and it cannot be a great one if it is not even worth the seeking. You have only to read and note. However bad you may consider this book to be, it must be for you a classic work; its antiquity gives it that status, and the difference between the language of the book and your own proves its antiquity only too well.

You will have the pleasure of finding in it words so old that they are all worn out; indeed, they are dead in the language, for they are not intelligible or are so only through what goes before or what comes after. You will see others so strange that, since you will not be able to understand them by guesswork or by any other way, you will have to fall back on Monsieur de Salmonet, who will enlighten you through the perfect knowledge he has of his language, provided the words do not have an English root or do not come from Scotland. You will sometimes be in doubt owing to the resemblance to be found there between French sayings and phrases and those in Spanish and Italian which are either their originals or copies of them. You will see a good many which are no longer in use but whose source is not hard to find. On the other hand you will encounter some which have come down to us from remote times not only in their purity but even in their elegance, so that they are among our most agreeable expressions and are heard only among the best speakers. You will find there noun and verb formations, sequences of pronouns, omissions of the articles, constructions, and inversions which seem ridiculous to most of those who read them, but which will serve as torches to light your way more easily to an understanding of the dependence of French on Latin. In a word, you will observe there, through a comparison of the old style and the new, what changes the language has undergone, how it shed bit by bit its original rusticity, and by what roads it passed to arrive at the sweetness, the majesty, and the abundance which we now find in it. And do not think you will have to cover much ground in order to obtain examples of all these things. Each page — why do I say each page? — each sentence, each line will furnish you with such a quantity that if you are embarrassed it will be by their number."

Monsieur Ménage, confused by my remarks and not certain of how to judge them, said that all those statements were fine and that half of them would justify him in having a good opinion of the book if they were as solidly established as they were boldly advanced.

I replied, as I had already said, that proof would be easy and that we should not have to go far; but in order to teach him not to take people at their word I would not give him proof: rather he should find it himself.

"What!" said he, "will you be so cruel, so rigorous? To refuse to convince me and to want me to convince myself! If it is as easy as you say, you cannot decently refuse me, and so I am suspicious of your argument. Well, well, since I must, I shall investigate, and we shall see at leisure if there are grounds for believing in all you say. However, as a single favor, I shall ask you for just one example of that elegance which is both old and new, which has traversed so many ages without being corrupted, and which is not less beautiful now because it was beautiful five hundred years ago. If you can show me that miracle I shall have no more trouble in believing the rest and shall not want a fuller illustration."

"I prefer," said I, "that you should seek the illustration yourself, and if I give you the example you ask for, it is on the condition that you will do so. Could anyone say nowadays in a nobler way that he loves someone extremely than by saying 'He is the man I love best in all the world?' Yet this was said more than four hundred years ago, as can be shown by more than twenty places in this book."

"But if that turn of phrase," he answered, "is as usual as you say it is, it seems to me modern enough so that I should deduce from it the contrary conclusion, and instead of believing it is old because it is in the book, I should say for that very reason that the book is not old."

"There is wit," I replied, "in twisting the argument in that way, but there is no solidity. For since this book is filled with terms either unknown or no longer used, and elegant turns of phrase are only scattered through it, the presumption in favor of its antiquity is much stronger than that of its modernity. But we are not reduced to mere presumption. We have conclusive proofs and unimpeachable witnesses. Three hundred years ago Boccaccio mentioned Lancelot, Tristan, and Gallehaut of the Distant Isles as heroes celebrated by writers of the past. About three hundred and fifty years ago Petrarch spoke of them and of their adventures as dreams and reveries. More than thirty years before him Dante says that Lancelot was the cause of a tragic event which, as he calculated, could not have been very recent. Thus you can see as clear as daylight that this romance was written more than four centuries ago, and I know no older French books except perhaps the chronicles of Joinville and Villehardouin.[17]

"As for its antiquity," said Monsieur Sarasin, "that is indisputable; a cursory reading is convincing on that point; but I should not believe it is more than four centuries old, and I do not see how you will prove convincingly that it is as much as five."

"Nor do I claim to be able to do so," I replied. "But do you have a good reason to show that it is not so old?"

"My position," he said, "is the negative — a choice I am free to make. The burden of proof is on you."

35

I was about to reply when Monsieur Ménage said: "You are arguing about nothing and it is of no importance to the question which of you says yes or no. As far as antiquity is concerned I do not consider there is much difference between four centuries and five centuries; and if you proved to me that the book is older than four you could easily make me believe it is close to five."

"So," said Monsieur Sarasin, "after the proof we have given you we have at least won this point from you, that the book is good for something and that the French language may receive from its authority a remarkable enrichment. But," he went on, addressing me, "do you limit its merit to the utility which the language may draw from it?"

"Would that not be enough," I replied, "even if there were no other? I have already told you that when first I began to read it that was the only advantage I sought in it. I admit nevertheless that, because its words forced me to look at things, I have found in it reason to show Monsieur Ménage, if he makes me angry enough, that other than linguistic profit may be drawn from it."

"That's what comes," cried Monsieur Ménage, "of granting something to people like you. Instead of being happy with the favor you have received, you authorize yourselves by our generosity to make new claims. I should really like to know what other profit can be got from that miserable carcass, which is horrible and repulsive even to the crude and the ignorant. Do you expect to show me in that barbarian a Homer or a Livy? What you propose is scarcely anything less."

"Now, now," I said, "we have not taken leave of our senses and we are not making any such odious comparisons. We know the dignity of those great men and the vulgarity of the writer, whoever he was, that composed the romance. But the main difference we see between Homer and him is in the style and in the mere expression of feelings. We see the first always noble and always sublime in this respect, and the second always rustic and prosy; as to the events they are scarcely truer in the one than in the other; and fables for fables, when I examine them closely I don't know which are the more ingeniously invented or even in which of the two verisimilitude is better observed."

"That is no new opinion of yours," interrupted Monsieur Ménage. "What you are saying reminds me of what you once said on this subject: that just as the poems of Homer were the fables of the Greeks and Romans, so our old romances are the fables of the French and the English."

"I still consider the point well taken," I replied, "and if you are reminding me of it in order to reproach me you are no longer the same man who praised my remark as a reflection which, on the basis of what you said, I might even consider excellent."

"I am not holding it against you," said he, "but I am bringing it up in order to show you on what principle your reasoning is based."

"Well," I replied, "Aristotle, who made a mystery of that poet [Homer] and who took him to be the prototype of his art, attributed to him the glory of following the rules — a glory it is very unlikely he ever aspired to. There is but good and bad luck in this world. If Aristotle were to come back and take it into his head to find the subject-matter of a poetics in *Lancelot* I am sure he would succeed just as well as with the *Iliad* and the *Odyssey*, and that his intelligence or his authority would easily overcome the inconveniences which he might encounter. I can assure you of this at least, that the magic which is everywhere in the *Lancelot* would not be more difficult for him to accommodate to the rules than the divinities which Homer used so eccentrically, whatever the allegorical significance given them by his hollow commentators."

"But," said Monsieur Sarasin, "if you consider magic to be as plausible in poetic machinery as Homer's divinities, why did you rather make use in your *Maid* of angels and demons which are related to those divinities instead of magical operations which not only are established in the old romances but which Tasso himself introduced into his poem with so much success? What reason had you in so free a choice to prefer the old style to the new?"

"The argument is *ad hominem*," said Monsieur Ménage, "and presses him hard; I should very much like to hear the answer."

"You may be sure," I replied, "that the answer is ready, but because it would need a long discussion and would take us far from the subject we are dealing with now, we shall put it aside for another occasion. However since, as you know, that is one of the principal difficulties of modern poetry, I considered its nature and basis when I made the plan of my work, and if I decided not to use magic, the reason was not that I thought it bad but merely unnatural to my subject owing to the circumstances of its time, place, and character and its illumination by the excessively bright light of history; besides that, I should require much more discretion in the use of magic in our romances than in the use of Homer's divinities. Moreover, to speak frankly, since my heroic poem came after so many others, if I wished to distinguish myself from the ordinary I had to do it with the quintessence of art and exquisite verismilitude, moving the action by machinery which might appear necessary but which was not, and show that one can write a poem in the Christian style without going along the beaten track of magic, for that would have deprived me of the glory of originality. But to return to the point from which we started, I beg you to consider what a reasonable reader must think of that division and opposition of celestial powers, of the wounding of Mars and Venus by a mortal man, of Vulcan who sets fire to the Scamander, of Neptune and Apollo who work as laborers in the building of the walls of Troy; decide whether the most subtle allegory can satisfy a reason offended by such absurdities, and whether *Lancelot* contains any extravagances to which a speculative mind might not give interpretations as favorable as those given by the commentators of Homer to his. Nevertheless I respect the antiquity of Homer and I freely admit that in the detail of his works there are seeds of astronomy, geography, the art of oratory and even of philosophy which bear witness to the excellence of his doctrine and which put him above comparison."

"Still you gave him a pretty good drubbing," said Monsieur Sarasin, "and that is the least you can say in his favor without declaring yourself his enemy in everything."

"I said enough good of him," I answered, "so that no one can reasonably accuse me of being opposed to him. What if I had treated him as Scaliger [18] did, and if instead of putting him above comparison I should have preferred not to choose between Virgil and him?"

"But," said Monsieur Ménage, "do you not want us to compare *Lancelot* and Livy?"

"The choice," I replied, "that anyone would claim to make between *Lancelot* and Livy would be as mad as that between Virgil and Livy, between the false and true. *Lancelot* is not Livy because the actions which are narrated in it are remote from any truth. If, however, the romance is not comparable to Livy in historical truth, since it is composed only of fabulous events, I daresay it is comparable to him in the description of mores and customs of which both provide perfect images, the one of the times of which he wrote, the other of those in which it was written."

"You are embarking," said Monsieur Ménage, "on a strange affair — that of presenting as truthful a writer who, by your own admission, is completely imaginative."

Monsieur Sarasin interrupted him to say: "He probably didn't do it without thinking. Before condemning him we must hear him out and see how he will escape the paradox. The point is subtle enough in all conscience and deserves a fuller explanation."

"I am convinced," I replied, "of the truth of the statement I made on the subject, and you will be also when I have finished explaining it, or I am very much mistaken. Yet I make it only as a reasonable guess, and I shall be satisfied if you merely consider it probable. For the first basis of my opinion I accept as a fact that the period in which *Lancelot* was written was a time of deep ignorance, when all the scholarly disciplines were dead, and when not only abstruse and difficult sciences were unknown, but when even history, chronology, and cosmography were as confused as it is possible to imagine. All human subtlety was turned either to scholastic theology or to the thorns of jurisprudence, without anybody's having the slightest suspicion that literature existed in the world, for the Greeks and Romans were known only by name. As a second basis I assume that any writer who invents a fable of which human actions are the subject can only present his creatures and make them act in a way conformable to the mores and beliefs of his time, since it is generally admitted that our ideas scarcely go beyond what we see and hear. Since the author's goal is to please the public, he will seek to attain his goal by events which are easily believed; he will use descriptions only of what ordinarily happens or is usually done because pleasure arises only from nature or from habit, and unless one has a depraved taste it is difficult to find pleasure in chimerical imaginings; there must be a relationship between the object and its persuasive power; if the mind is to accept what is presented to it the thing presented must be either natural or well known, for the unknown and the impossible, far from satisfying the mind, will but prove disgusting. On these bases I think I can say that *Lancelot*, which was composed in the darkness of our modern antiquity, and without the benefit of erudition other than experience with the world, is a faithful narration, if not of what happened among the kings and knights of that time, at least of what everybody was convinced might happen, perhaps because of the traces of similar things which had often occurred in the preceding centuries. I think I can assure you even more emphatically that it is a faithful representation and, so to speak, a certain and exact history of the mores which prevailed in the courts of that time. Just as doctors diagnose the peccant humor of their patients from their dreams, so one can judge the mores and the actions of bygone times from the daydreams in these writings. One of the reasons which does most to confirm me in this opinion is the seriousness with which all Europe took this work and the avidity with which all nations sought diversion in it. Novelty, I admit, attracts the curiosity of men, who are rarely excited by what they already know. But we must distinguish among novelties and say that the novelty of events attracts the curious, but not novelty of mores, which astonishes and wounds more than it pleases. Another reason which persuades me to this belief is the great conformity which we find among the customs, and sometimes even among the actions, which we see represented in this fabulous book and those we find in Gothic, Danish, English, and even French stories of that time or of times closer to our own. Read Olaüs Magnus, Saxo Grammaticus, the original of Polydore Virgil and of Buchanan, our *Lives* of Saint Louis, Bertrand du Guesclin, Marshal de Bouciquaut, and the Chevalier Bayard, our Froissarts and our Monstrelets;[19] you will note, if not in all at least in some, shadows and traces of the things which are developed to excess in this romance and similar writings. I need Monsieur Duchesne at this point, for he would fortify my sentiments by his observations, since nothing of these matters has escaped the vast knowledge he has acquired about our antiquity through the unearthing of so many manuscripts and documents. In his stead I might have asked the help of my neighbor, the Baron d'Auteuil, who is scarcely second to Monsieur Duchesne,[20] had I foreseen that you would involve me in this argument. Since they are not here I shall refer you to what Monsieur de la Colombière has just published in his *Théâtre de Chevalerie*, and which might in itself sufficiently guarantee the truth of what I have been saying."[21]

"That aspect of things," said Monsieur Sarasin, "leaves me with no difficulties whatever, and your conception and its proof have satisfied me much more than I had hoped. And to show you that I am not saying this from mere politeness I shall reinforce your proof with a similar one which has just occurred to me." Then turning to Ménage, he said: "Do you not agree that the old tapestries, old paintings, old statues which have come down to us from our ancestors are the true originals of the clothing, the hair-dressings, and the shoes of their times and that, as those relics show us the styles of the times, one may say, as Monsieur Chapelain has done, that the old romances paint for us to the very life the mores and the customs of those same times?"

"It seems likely," said Monsieur Ménage, "and although at first I found the proposition very strange, to show you my open-mindedness I confess it seems to me not unreasonable and that I should consider it true in a pinch."

"Then," said I, "you agree that this book is both fictional and historical, at least that it is often fictional in the events but historical for the rest."

"But you too must agree," replied Monsieur Ménage, "that there is to be found in it no event which deserves the attention of a man of taste, that it is devoid of all art, of all surprise, of all that stimulates the curiosity, and that very often there is found in it a kind of simple-mindedness which comes very close to silliness and foolishness."

"I willingly admit that," said I, "and even more than you require. I have argued nothing else the whole day. The author is a barbarian who wrote in barbarous times for an audience of barbarians; he never imagined a work might be planned so that it would have a reasonable arrangement, a proper proportion among its parts, a subtle plot, or a natural conclusion. He goes as far as is humanly possible; he is always in the same posture and always sings the same note; he is rough, rugged, antipodal to the graces. When in difficulties his only recourse is to magic, which is always at his command and which he has turned into an art as ordinary as the tailor's or the cobbler's. Finally it can be said that he is entirely lacking in wit and that no one can read a single page of his without a yawn and a headache. I am sure you do not think I have such bad taste as to read this book for anything but its language when I take from serious business the time needed to leaf through it. It seems to me I am giving you full measure by saying as many bad things about this book as you could wish. In exchange I ask in my turn that you take my word for this: that it contains all the good things I have mentioned and more besides, if possible."

"What other good things can you say of it," replied Monsieur Ménage, "after having assured us that it is the historian of the mores of its time and that there is to be found in it a supplement to the annals which have come down to us, but which inform us only of the births and deaths of princes with the events which marked their reigns, whereas this book, as you describe it, makes us familiar with those princes and shows us the depths of their souls?"

"Say rather," went on Monsieur Sarasin, seeing that he was stopping there, "that it reveals to us their character and that of their courtiers, that it teaches us how they talked together, that it shows us how deeply they were imbued with the maxims of true honor, how religiously they held to their word, how they managed their love-affairs, how far they were able to carry on a decent friendship, what gratitude they showed for favors, how high an idea they had formed of valor, and finally what feelings they had about Heaven and what respect for holy things."

"If Monsieur Sarasin," said I to Monsieur Ménage, "had added the customs they invariably followed, he would have left me nothing to say on this subject; for excepting that, you and he have mentioned everything; yet this is enough, as anyone will see who thinks about it, so that if you admit it all to be true, you are compelled to say that this bad book is nevertheless a good one, and that there is profit to be had from it which it would be hard to get elsewhere."

I fell silent after these words, and Monsieur Ménage did not intend to pursue the discourse any further, for he showed himself by his silence to be satisfied with it; but then Monsieur Sarasin replied: "If he will not take your word for it I shall vouch for it with mine, and if need be by my oath as an eye-witness; for I have seen in the book all that you saw there, and if I had not read it I could not have made the same reflections about it you have made and which do not admit of contradiction. Therefore I shall say that anything you might add to what you have said, by way of a fuller explanation of this subject, would be superfluous from my point of view; but from that of Monsieur Ménage it might well be different since he has not seen what I have seen and in the end he is not obliged to believe us without proof."

I replied: "If he could not find out for himself, if we forbade him to read the book, if we required him to take us on trust, you would be right to talk that way and to demand proofs of me for him."

"And besides, have we not sufficiently discussed a subject as base as this one? Have we not wallowed long enough in the depths of barbarism and," went on Monsieur Sarasin, turning to Monsieur Ménage, "as your Mamurra would say, in the cloaca of caliginous centuries and in the bilge of apedestic nations?" [22]

"The choice is mine," said Monsieur Ménage to me, "whether I shall take your refusal for a defeat and hence doubt everything you have claimed up to now."

"There is an eye-witness," I answered, "who gives you his word for it, and even if you doubted mine you would be forced to respect his and not to change your opinion so fast."

"He may doubt my sincerity," said Monsieur Sarasin then, "and yours too, but he cannot allow you to stop when you are so well on the road; the important thing is to confirm the new convert in his faith."

"But," said I, "since you think it necessary, do it yourself, for you can do it incomparably better than I and have the necessary graces as I do not."

"I am not to be caught by such flattery," he replied, "and Monsieur Ménage would not follow the new scent even if I were vain enough to imagine he had nothing to lose by doing so."

"Nevertheless," I said, "you must bear your part of the burden; do not imagine that in this you are a mere onlooker."

"In order to satisfy you," said he, "I prefer to promise him an ample discussion whenever he wants it of one of the points which I have only listed, on the condition that you now give him a sample of each, so that before finishing with you he may be assured that we are honorable men and that we affirm only what can be proved. I do not expect you to treat these subjects profoundly. You would need more time and more breath. A summary and a few light touches will be enough to satisfy him until something better is possible."

"I see there is no way to evade this," I replied, "and moreover you are in my house where you are the masters: it would be uncivil of me not to obey. I shall then point out to Monsieur Ménage that one learns from this romance better than from any history of that period how Christian Europe was; I mean how deeply the nations were really attached to the divine cult. Here are a few evidences of that. Make those knights as eager as you want in their perilous quests, whether to preserve their honor or to aid some oppressed person; yet not a day passes that the author does not have them attend mass, and nothing is clearer in the whole book than the care he takes to have them regular in their duty, even to the point of putting these words occasionally into their mouths: 'I have not missed mass one day of my life if it was in my power to attend.' If he involves them in a doubtful enterprise he has them turn toward a monastery and, in order to take it to witness their promises, has them utter aloud before it the terms of their pledge; or else he has them presented with relics on which they swear that they will do what they have undertaken; this is what they call *swearing by the saints*. I shall not mention his famous Holy Grail with its unexpected appearances and difficult adventures, nor the conditions of virginity, purity, and innocence which he requires of the knight destined to end them."

"We can easily believe that," said Monsieur Ménage, "after what we have learned of the zeal of those old days from the narration of the Bishop of Tyre [23] and of Joinville, and from the other histories of the Crusades which have caused so much debate in the east and south."

"You believe it," I replied, "on the word of those writers who are no doubt better than the author of *Lancelot*; but you believe it only because they report generalities whereas in the latter you see the individual actions and the very words of the characters as they were done and uttered by the real men of the period. And if we had not decided to glide lightly over each of these subjects I could show you by an infinite number of examples that you are not at liberty to doubt the powerful impression religion had made on their minds nor the sincerity and the reverence with which they submitted to its mysteries."

"You do not say with what knowledge," pointed out Monsieur Ménage.

"I have already mentioned," said I, "their deep ignorance of everything. But why should their understanding and their knowledge matter when only their piety and their faith are concerned?"

"Indeed," said he, "they must have been very ignorant to have been able to combine the goodness and virtue attributed to them with the insults which, it is said, the author has them utter to passers-by and because of which one or the other usually is left dead at the meeting-place. One must live in the deepest darkness to think it possible to adjust the license of utter wantonness to the humblest devotion, and to suppose unscrupulous slaughters and remorseless debaucheries were in no way contrary to the holy laws these knights professed to follow so exactly. There is reason to think the princes of those times were very brutish and that they knew but little of civil government. Ours are much more civilized, when you examine the question, to have suppressed those odd knights and to have replaced them by captains of the watch through whom they have put an end to those disorders which otherwise would have destroyed society."

"Those old princes and their old subjects," I said, "had a plentiful supply of the ignorance they needed for the adjustment you speak of. They held that all of religion consisted in believing firmly in Jesus Christ, and beyond this they made few general reflections about good and evil where natural inclinations were concerned. The priests themselves barely knew how to read, and instructed the people only through the sermon, as was laid down in their ceremonials. If occasionally one of them chanced to take up the study of literature or to raise his mind to the contemplation of heavenly movements, he was at once taken to be a magician or a heretic. Other men, especially the knights, knew nothing but how to fight well, and the women knew nothing beyond how to love well those who fought well. These were the only principles by which they regulated their actions and feelings."

"Are those not animals you are describing," said Monsieur Ménage, "are they not *silvestres homines*, etc.?"[24]

"I am describing them to you as they were," I answered, "and although if you look at them from the point of view you have taken nothing could be more brutish and more savage, yet if one is willing to take another point of view and to seek the root of things, it would not be impossible to find in them something resembling reason, or at least to show that they were not wholly brutes."

"I beg of you to demonstrate that," said Monsieur Sarasin, "for as to this point I admit I am on the side of Monsieur Ménage and I do not see how they can be excused."

"It is well known," I said, "that among northern peoples might has always made right and that the only virtue they recognize is valor. They feel that courage is the instrument by which one attains ease and security in life, and that without it both the preservation and the increase of property are unthinkable. Imbued with that opinion and deprived of any other kind of understanding, they founded, as we see, their whole policy on power alone, and when they formed states these were always military states. Without having heard of Achilles, each of them behaved like him who *Jura negat sibi nata, nil non arrogat armis.*[25] I am aware that little is known of the manner of their ancient government as it existed in the confines of their native lands such as Gothia and Scandia, Sarmatia and Scythia;[26] but it can easily be judged from the swarms of peoples who formerly came out of them and who, under the names of Cimbrians, Teutons, Huns, Goths, Alans, Danes, and Norsemen, overran and subjugated every part of Europe. All their law was only what is called custom, and they gave themselves up to brigandage and violence as a right of conquest, much as Alexander did. Even when in the course of time they grasped the idea that justice was a concept necessary for the maintenance of society and to give a firm basis for their usurpations, when they found it appropriate to make use of it they refused to trust its administration to the laws. The wisest among them held that crimes could rightly be punished if they were only suspected, and that provided they acted in good faith the same men could be both judges and executioners. On this idea were founded the false and the true quests among their adventures for the protection of the weak and the punishment of the wicked, for which they received a mandate when they were raised to the order of chivalry."

"With the result," said Monsieur Ménage, "that the knights were really officers of the law whom the princes sent after robbers and whom they set on the tracks of salt-smugglers and counterfeiters."

"With the result," I said, "that they resembled an army of men like Hercules sent by their Eurystheuses [27] to purge the world of monsters and tyrants. In truth I do not see much difference between Hercules errant and Lancelot errant; and a man wanting to do justice to everybody would decide that Lancelot and his fellows were nothing but Hercules while Hercules and his fellows were much like Lancelots. But, to come back to our argument, from the custom of exercising justice individually there has come down to us the custom of being unwilling to satisfy an offense against honor through a magistrate or a prince, even though God and reason have set them up no less for this than for robberies and murders; and to insist on reparation by our own hands as if the honor of a gentleman could be vindicated only by the sword, not the sword of justice but that of the individual who considers himself offended. And that abuse, gentlemen, is a relic of the former brutality of the French which the light of the Gospel and the authority of the laws have not yet been able to root out from the souls of their descendants. From the same source come those other customs, which are not less barbarous, and which are preserved still in Scotland and in the Isles, as well as those which the inaccessible forests of Ireland have preserved intact and uncorrected for so many centuries whether they concern the tyranny of the lords or the servitude of the vassals, the freedom and purity of marriage, or the security of the weak against the unbridled violence of their powerful neighbors. All this means that the French and the English, being the successors of these brutal tribes, before experience and teaching had uprooted their uncivilized habits, apparently observed the same ways of behaving and put all their trust in valor, using it either to preserve or to increase the extent of their domination. Justice counted for almost nothing among them, and it was a great thing when princes dispensed it once in their lives while making a progress through their provinces as is still done today among the northerners. Ecclesiastics were shut up in hermitages and monasteries; valor reigned alone by its own right, and to it alone pleasures and honors were reserved. The knights were the favored class and the sole arm of the monarch, who for the reasons I have mentioned fed that courage by all the means which those crude times and the sensual bent of youthful minds could suggest to his imagination. For this was invented that Round Table, which was nothing but an Order similar to that of the Garter, to the honors of which were admitted none but those who by acts of superlative valor had deserved to be made companions of the king. So it came about that those who had obtained that highest of favors preferred to die a hundred times rather than to fail their lord once, or to lose the name of brave men by refusing dangers or even by not seeking them out. And because valor was sovereign in the hearts of young men, and because the hearts of persons of that age can be touched only by love of glory and love of women, so as to strengthen the former by the latter, the policy of those olden days was to erect into a kind of law the idea that a lady's heart was the prize of courage, thereby sharpening the fidelity which vassals owed to their lord by the hope, not only of glory, but also of the pleasure which the possession of beauty gives. For this reason princes had established in their courts promiscuous and public love-making as a praiseworthy thing — a situation which has been imitated among modern courts in that of Isabella of Castile and Catherine de Medici; with this single difference that in the earlier ones it was unimportant whether a villainy occurred, for each lady was free to satisfy her lover without being disgraced. This was openly done with the connivance, or rather, at the suggestion of the kings, who were hindered in their own designs by the modesty and virtue of the ladies, since these served only to rebuff knights who were not civilized enough to participate in a long affair and who had no conception of Platonic love. The same princes, for the same ends, had suggested to the ladies that of all the virtues valor alone was to be prized in a knight, and if they wanted something besides it should be faithfulness in love."

"And for them," said Monsieur Sarasin, "the obligation on this last point was reciprocal and the amusing thing is this: the learned lawgivers required that mistresses be faithful to their lovers when they could easily deceive them without being discovered, whereas wives were allowed to be unfaithful to their husbands, provided the scandal was public."

"If we take these things for granted . . ." I went on.

"That is exactly right, 'take for granted,'" interrupted Monsieur Ménage, "for I see no proofs of all this and I should put you in a difficult position if I were to deny the truth of what you say."

"I do not have," said I, "any individual author by whom I can prove this to you, but I do have the author of the *Lancelot* itself, the author of *Tristan*, and the whole swarm of writers of old romances such as *Merlin*, *Arthur*, *Perceforest*, who all agree on the same points and who all wrote in an age when minds were not very inventive or were incapable of reacting against the mores and customs of the times. And the agreement of so many writers about such circumstances as these may pass for partial proof which is enough in this kind of a situation where I promised you only reasonable guesses defensible only before people as pliable as yourself. But since what leads you to be more suspicious of my supposition is what I am telling you about the promiscuity of the ladies of that time — a promiscuity based on the idea that it brought no dishonor — I think I can make their behavior seem more than probable to you by citing a custom maintained in Scotland long after Christianity had been accepted by which the kings had first pleasure after the marriage of their principal ladies, and the great lords a similar tribute from those of their vassals, a custom once observed in Normandy as we see by the dues which certain lords still collect on this precedent at the marriage of their subjects. Now anyone who considers this situation carefully will see that it is of the same nature as that which I accept on the testimony of the romances, except that it is even more reprehensible since it was not excused by love and was but mere brutality. If we take these things for granted, then it does not require great subtlety to conclude that even though the expedient chosen by the princes was violent and indecent, nevertheless it served their ends; and that if they were inexcusable insofar as concerns fairness and modesty they could be justified on grounds of logic and necessity since their limited diligence led them to no other way of maintaining and extending their power."

"If the point is not entirely proved," said Monsieur Sarasin, "it is at least colorable, and I am inclined to believe it."

"If Monsieur Ménage," I replied, "had the same inclination, I should be satisfied and should ask no more."

"I shall not tell you my opinion," responded Monsieur Ménage, "because I am still in doubt, and my decision is not yet made."

"In my opinion," said Monsieur Sarasin, "we should not wait for your decision, and it would be better," he said, turning to me, "for you to continue to show him the other good qualities of this book according to your observations and reflections."

"Let us settle them in a few words," I said, "since we are pledged to discuss them, and let us be careful not to be as lengthy on the remaining points as we have been on this one. First, the style of conversation between these knights and their ladies, which is, as I suppose, that of the time when the book was written, was simple and unadorned, without anything genteel or charming in it, but sensible, clear, and laconic, saying only what was necessary but everything that was essential, *morata* rather than *urbana*, [28] somewhat like the Roman speech of Numa's day; [29] in a word, not very gallant but very solid. From this you will conclude that it is not a clever book or one from which we learn how to behave in good company. On the other hand you see in it the quality of the mind of this past century; you can see how far its barbarism had come on the road to reason; finally you can see what progress the French nation has made in four or five hundred years, not only in language but in the arts of discourse, which is not a disagreeable subject for consideration nor an entirely useless piece of knowledge. Besides this, one may note in these rustic adventures how deep-rooted in the hearts of these knights errant were the love of fairness and the hatred of injustice as these were conceived by them; hence the violent deeds they did in their fights against those whom they met in their quests most often grew out of other violent deeds done to ladies, orphans, and generally to the weak and the deserving.

"From this one may rise to a consideration very different from the last if we are but willing to note how far the centuries which approach our own, as they have come closer to the light of reason, have fallen away from virtue, and if we but consider into what disorders and corruptions souls have fallen from having, as I may say, eaten of the fruit by which they distinguish good from evil. But if there is anything in this kind of reading which pleases me, it is the high point of honor of which each knight makes a precise profession, and the never-ending fear they have lest they do or say something by which their reputation may be in any way smirched or lest they have something with which to reproach themselves even though they alone know of it. If I am touched by anything in the book it is that jealous care for their pledged word, the principle of always doing exactly what they have promised — an ethic worthy of the admiration of more civilized ages, which, because it was constantly practiced, leaves far behind the empty ostentation of the theory that one can teach by precepts. For, although these knights often give a promise very lightly and carry it out at an unsuitable time, what we must complain about is the awkwardness of the writer who plots badly and applies that virtue badly; but what we must esteem is the fixed and resolute intention of the men of those times never to fail in their word, whatever harm may come to them from standing by it.

"What shall I say to you of their undying gratitude for favors done them, their eagerness and the labors they undertook to find an opportunity for repayment, and their conviction that they were always indebted even after they had doubly repaid? I include here their obvious displeasure when they considered they had not shown deep enough appreciation for services received, and the penitences which they imposed upon themselves. These are virtues common to the principal characters of the book and which appear so uniform in it that one cannot doubt they were ordinary in those old days, provided one recalls my supposition that if he wanted to please his contemporaries, the writer could not give his heroes mores other than those of the time. I leave you to judge whether such noble impulses and praiseworthy habits could sow bad seed in the minds of readers; whether the knights who had them were not decent barbarians and admirable boors, and whether there are not grounds for surprise that our sophistication may be enlightened as to its duty by their ignorance; whether blind men like these can serve as guides to those who see as well as we do; and finally whether they did not have great virtues in terms of pure nature while we are covered with vices in the midst of the teachings of art.

"As for valor it is at its apogee among them; I do not say this because of the greatness of their acts, which are almost always exaggerated and impossible, but because of their great contempt for life when their honor was ever so slightly engaged, because of their brave way of fighting, and because of their honest admission of their disadvantage when the worst had happened. I am willing to say that in this our century is their equal and that among the nobility of our times there are but few cowards capable of foul play or the denial of a favor received. I maintain only that those ruffians of the past, who cheated in nothing else, were, in single combat, as shrewd as any of us; and as for frankness, civility, courtesy, modesty in talking of themselves, as well as for vigor and bravado, if they did not surpass us, at least they were not inferior to us, and could boast of having carried that aspect of military virtue to the refinement it has today; that is to say they could boast of having taught it to us, though it be almost the only good lesson we have been willing to take from them. If we wish to talk now of their perfect friendship, based as it was on esteem and virtue, who were ever nobler or more ardent friends than Lancelot and Gallehaut, or

to put it better, Gallehaut and Lancelot, as soon as the former had been
told of Lancelot's extraordinary merit?

"See the effects of this friendship. Because of it alone he gave back to
King Arthur his life and the kingdom which he had almost entirely taken
away, and, as a climax of deference, asked pardon of the King for his own
victory and offered him in homage his own estates. He allowed Guinevere
to have a larger share of Lancelot than himself. For love of Lancelot he
took her in when Arthur drove her from Logres. Finally he died of sorrow
at the news of Lancelot's death. Achilles did not love Patroclus so much
nor Theseus Pirithoüs, and there is nothing approximating this in the
Toxaris [30] although it was written to celebrate perfect friendship, and
after so many years learned men have imagined nothing more perfect. Our
own times furnish no comparable examples; what am I saying, furnish no
examples? Men of our day do not even conceive such examples, or if they
conceived them would laugh at them as empty vaporings and would call
mad a man warmed by so fine a passion."

"But even if we granted you all that," said Monsieur Ménage, "and even
if we accept all these points as sound, how will you deal with the question
of the gallantry of your old knights, since it could not have been very admirable; even you have admitted that they were entirely lacking in wit?"

"I have not promised," I answered, "to justify this romance in all respects, and from the way I have spoken of it you must have seen that I was
far from approving everything in it. Speaking frankly, the question of
Lancelot's gallantry is one which I should not like to undertake to defend,
especially since I am convinced that while love may exist without wit, for
that passion has its seat more in the heart than in the head, it is very unlikely that there can be gallantry in which wit has no part and which hence
is totally devoid of grace. Even so, if I condemned all the gallantry of
Lancelot I should be afraid of the trap into which the author of *Don
Quixote* fell when he made game of the knights errant and their strange
adventures merely because he failed to consider, as we have done, the
times in which they were active and the accepted mores of the period. For
if it were allowable to turn to ridicule whatever is not the usage of our
century or the place in which we live there is nothing so serious and so true
in antiquity or foreign literature in which a clever wit might not find substance for his own amusement and that of others. For myself, I hold that
we must be just and that we must look at things with all their attendant
circumstances in order to make a sound judgment. Our way of pleasing

the ladies and of persuading them of our love is completely contrary to that of ancient times. Shall I for that reason esteem only ours to be good? I am not presumptuous enough to believe that there is nothing good except what I do. I shall not call Lancelot's gallantry bad; I shall merely say it is different from ours, and if it achieved the same effect as ours why should I grudge the admission that it is just as good? I shall not say it, however, because I prefer gallantry to be gallant and I admit that Lancelot's is crude. But to satisfy everybody I think one must say that gallantry is an equivocal term which sometimes designates the art of pleasing the ladies so as to be loved by them, and sometimes the love of them, devoid of method and art. By the first definition we can agree that Lancelot is the least gallant of men, that he has no idea of how to get into his mistress's good graces by studied words and by the art of following her about; that he does not seek to win her by the handsome ordering of his person, and that he does not depend on the elegance of his attire, on melodious serenades, or on striking ballet-like attitudes. By the second definition there was never so perfect a gallant as Lancelot. He does not pretend to be in love, he really is; he loves as much in absence as in presence; the mere sight of Guinevere puts him beside himself, makes him speechless, and incapable of any other thought. He is frenzied at the thought of having displeased her, and this thought sends him out to race through the fields; he invokes her in his greatest perils; he is faithful to her when he has the greatest opportunities to betray her; he belongs to her more than to Galahad, although Galahad bore for him the most ardent friendship that was ever seen.

"You must judge which of these two kinds of gallantry is the more obliging to the ladies and whether the latter is as ridiculous as it appears to the bloods of the present time. For myself I shall not decide so delicate a question in which stylish prejudice does not allow natural freedom of choice. I shall say only that one cannot condemn, except at the risk of being over-bold, the second kind of gallantry, where the lady is sincerely adored and where, instead of words, she is given deeds; in which the eyes and the ears find less satisfaction but where the mind and the heart find it whole and entire. Indeed, I should have great difficulty in replying to anyone who, in its defense, would show me how noble is that gallantry which proves passion by seeking dangers, as also by blood and victories, and how great an advantage it has over that which finds its proofs only in coquetries and assiduities or, at most, in dinners, concerts, and jousting.

"I should have great difficulty in persuading him that a fine dance-step is more valuable than a good sword-thrust, that handsome furniture or elegant races are more important than jousts with whetted blades or than bitter fights to the death or gifts of vanquished prisoners. If he were to add that the state of society at that time gave value only to such actions as these, and hence that ladies could admire no others and thought themselves loved and well served only by them; or finally that tourneys, combats, and quests were the style of those times as courts, the comedy, and balls are in ours; if I did not grant that he was right to prefer that kind of gallantry to ours, nevertheless I should be forced to concede that it can in no way be considered ridiculous."

"If he were to speak to me," said Monsieur Sarasin, "as you pretend he might do, I should reply as you say you should, and only the most unjust man in the world would not hear both sides of the argument and would decide on the testimony of only one litigant."

"It seems to me," said Monsieur Ménage, "that I am of your opinion, and that this point has been as well examined as the others."

"After that," I replied, "I have nothing more to say in order to prove to you that however bad this book may be, there is yet something good in it, and it is not entirely disgraceful for me to have been found with it by a scholar like yourself."

"You have only the customs left to discuss," he said, "and then you will have discharged your duty toward us."

"I have grown hoarse with talking," I answered, "and for the customs I am tempted to refer you to the authority on customs in the kingdom of Logres, [31] I mean the book *Lancelot* itself where you will find them thick-sown; or perhaps you will prefer to await the publication of the *Treatise* which Monsieur Le Fèvre, the great antiquary, is devoting to them,[32] for he supports almost all his observations by passages he takes from *Lancelot*, of which he makes his chief stock as far as customs are concerned. In general I shall say only that they have the character of the mores of that remote time, and whether they be true or false it is obvious that most of them were instituted to give security to the ladies and to feed the valor in the souls of the knights; but the first objective serves the second. I shall cut this discussion short and leave the matter obscure so that you will be curious enough to seek enlightenment."

At this statement I arose as did they, though they were complaining I had skimped on this last part, especially Monsieur Ménage, whose appetite had been whetted by this legal matter and who would have been much interested in seeing then and there what Gothic jurisprudence was like and what affinity it might have with Roman law. He threatened to complain to you, my Lord, and said to me as I walked with them to the door, "Yes, I shall look over the Lancelot code, and I shall even study it with Monsieur Seingeber; it would be amusing if he were to abandon the Code of Justinian for this new one."

"Anything can happen," said I, "if it be only to change your field of study and to avoid ever finishing what you have begun."

Monsieur Sarasin was much amused at this reproach, and both went away laughing, thus showing much satisfaction at the conversation we had had, although it was excessively long for so scanty and meager a subject.

Jean-François Sarasin DISCOURSE ON TRAGEDY OR RE-
MARKS ON "TYRANNIC LOVE" BY MONSIEUR DE SCUDERY

The *Amour tyrannique* by Monsieur de Scudéry is so perfect and so finished a poem that if Time had not grudged to the age of Louis the Just the birth of Aristotle, or if Monsieur de Scudéry had written during the Alexandrian Empire, I really think the philosopher would have modeled a part of his *Poetics* on that excellent tragedy and that he would have drawn from it examples as beautiful as those from the *Oedipus*, which he particularly admired.

Since this divine man, having noted all the faults of the Greek poets and reduced to rule what he found excellent in their works, has taught us what opinion we ought to have of the poems of others and the rules we ought to follow for our own, there has not perhaps been a single dramatic writer who has profited so well from his remarks nor so faithfully followed his precepts as Monsieur de Scudéry.

If this were to be a critical discourse instead of an essay dedicated to the merit of my friend and to the defense of his play, I should have to include here a complete examination of the tragic writers, to raise many objections and to produce many quotations and examples; but since I write only to enhance his reputation I shall content myself with pointing out the beauties of his work without paying any attention to the vices of others and without establishing his reputation on the ruin of theirs; and I shall have accomplished my purpose if I confirm the learned in the good opinion they have of this play and leave all my readers persuaded of its excellence.

Should I be obliged later on in my discourse to compare with this work certain passages from the ancients, my purpose will be to reinforce my defense by this means; and if I should happen to challenge them I shall do so without tediousness or affectation and even then only where it appears to me necessary. Indeed, I have no intention of burdening this essay with useless erudition nor of planning out exactly its composition.

55

Panegyrists need the graces of eloquence and the strength of rhetoric but those who write commentaries do not, and since I am simply making a few remarks about *L'Amour tyrannique* rather than a eulogy of it, I shall put elocution by for another occasion. I shall be satisfied to treat this subject with the order and simplicity which are proper to the argumentative style.

However, since this style is ordinarily thorny and since very plain order is dry and barren I shall temper that harshness and barrenness in certain places so as to provide some source of pleasure for the mind.

Before making a judgment of this tragedy (for that is how we shall describe it and not as a tragicomedy, for reasons which we shall put forward in their proper place), we must see what are the purpose and usefulness which these compositions are assumed to have and what has been taught about them by the philosopher we are following. For since all works approach perfection in proportion as they come nearer to fulfilling their purpose, we shall be easily able to examine later whether the same is true of Monsieur de Scudéry's and whether it has the degree of perfection we hope to find in it.

Since the tragic muse is principally concerned with stirring the passions of the audience through the appalling adventures she represents before them, Aristotle thought the purpose of tragedy was to calm those passions and to restore to the spectators' souls that tranquillity and serenity which she had taken away from them. He thought pity and terror were the passions stirred by tragedy and hence that tragedy ought to repress them and reduce them to a reasonable level of intensity after having excited and stirred them; and he calls that way of calming our souls the expiation or, if you prefer, the purgation of the passions and tensions.

This was his opinion of those passions:

He did not include them among the vices nor did he allow them to be numbered among the virtues, and so without defending them and without banishing them from human life he hoped that wise men might become accustomed to them and come to a reasonable decision concerning how far and when they ought to accept and receive them.

This excellent familiarity with them was to result, in his opinion, from the presentation of tragedies, for just as we acquire perfection in an art through practice so we achieve temperance in the passions when we are used to seeing those things which excite them in our imagination.

Good surgeons calmly dress the most dangerous wounds, while the inexperienced tremble at the task. Habit produces in physicians an insensitivity toward their patients, and veteran regiments who come to grips daily with the enemy attack him without the fear and the indiscipline which are common in raw recruits.

The same thing is true of a man who sees suffering every day: he is touched by it but only to the point proper to a wise man, and the fact that he sees habitually spectacles which produce terror and pity in him results in his being moderate and serene.

Since these things are presented in the theater and since the stage re-echoes with the cries of Hecuba, Electra, and Antigone; since we see there Oedipus, Atreus, and Aegisthus and since the stage may properly be called the tiltyard of the passions, it is also to the performance of these tragic poems in which these personages appear that one must go in order to mould the passions and to lead them to that perfect philosophical reasonableness to which they never attain without contributing much to the acquisition of virtue and the mastery of learning.

Such was the opinion of Aristotle concerning the purpose of tragedy, which for that reason he called *the government of the passions*. It is clear from this that he was not of the opinion of those who consider the final purpose of these sublime compositions to be the pleasure of the people. We particularly want to make that statement here so as to enlighten those others and so as to judge whether Monsieur de Scudéry's work may excite those violent emotions which prepare the mind for virtue and discipline and whether it has that degree of perfection which we hope to find in excellent tragedies.

For this reason we must examine it according to the rules of the philosopher and judge from the way its separate parts conform to the rules how well the whole conforms to the idea of tragedy. Thus we shall follow the methodical clarity which is always characteristic of the Sage's teachings, and even jealousy will have no grounds for alleging that we are flattering Monsieur de Scudéry, for we shall be examining his composition according to the severe precepts of the greatest critic in the world.

That remarkable man has defined tragedy as follows: "Tragedy is the imitation of a serious action, complete and proper in its magnitude, which through action and not only by speech excites pity and terror, but afterwards leaves a moderate reasonableness in the mind of the spectators."

From the above definition we have eliminated rhythm and music, which are not now in use.

The philosopher, I say, having thus defined tragedy, divides it into six essential parts, of which the final two are related to the others and depend upon them.

The first four are Plot, Character, Thought, and Diction; the last two are Spectacle and Song.

Since of these latter two the first is the concern only of the scenic designer and the second, which made all the charm of the ancient stage, is no longer in use on our own, we need speak only, if we have the leisure, of the remaining four, which concern the poet, in order to see whether our author has a thorough knowledge of them and whether he has made proper use of them in his *L'Amour tyrannique.*

Just as the Plot, which Aristotle takes to be the subject of tragedy, and which includes both the action and the arrangement of the action, which he calls *the structure of the incidents,* is the first in the order of his division so it is first in the order of excellence. The philosopher adduces beautiful arguments in its favor; he calls it *the soul of a tragedy* and claims that without it tragedy cannot be perfect.

Indeed, since the purpose is always the most important thing, the reason for all actions and that upon which everything else depends; since the purpose of tragedy is the representation of human good or ill fortune; and since men are neither fortunate nor unfortunate except insofar as they act; it follows that the plot is the most important part of the tragedy because it includes the action, and the action includes that happy outcome or that catastrophe whose representation is the purpose of tragedy.

And certainly, since without a plot a poet making use of Character, Thought, and Diction, as well as other things, would no more make a real play than a painter would make a good picture by mixing confusedly black lacquer, ultramarine blue, and other colors without representing anything; and since on the contrary with one single action a poet could well make a fine tragedy just as a painter can draw a beautiful figure with red chalk or charcoal, I see no reason to doubt that the plot is the principal part of a thing which cannot exist without it, or that it ought to be considered before the other parts of a composition since they depend upon it so completely.

Moreover, since the last thing men learn in the arts, and that only after much practice and diligence, is what is excellent and perfect in them, the ancient poets who did not yet know how to treat the plot by rule, although they made divine use of the other aspects of tragedy, are adequate witnesses that the plot, which they came to understand only at the end of their period, is beyond all doubt the perfection and crown of a fine tragedy.

If I had to give examples in support of this last argument, our own drama would provide enough of them for me, and I should not be forced to hunt them up among the fragments of Greek drama. Among us tragedy is relatively new and so, although we see it in its full perfection, we also saw its infancy; for this reason the same poets who now give us well-composed works produced very unsatisfactory ones in the past.

Not so very long ago the plot was what they paid least attention to; they worked only on the versification and treated indifferently all sorts of subjects. Provided that in their plays they had mixed up love and jealousy, duels, disguises, prisons, and shipwrecks on a stage divided into several areas, they considered they had written an excellent dramatic poem:

> Post hoc
> securi cadat an recto stet fabula talo.[1]

In this regard we are under great obligation to Monsieur Mairet, [2] who was the first to take care in plotting the action, who cleared the way for correct works with his *Silvanire* and who restored the dignity of tragedy with his *Sophonisbe*; one may well say of him that he was born for the glory of our century and for that of our nation's poetry. A little later Monsieur de Scudéry's *La Mort de César* [1636] was successfully presented. This play is certainly incomparable in its kind and no doubt always will be, for the vigor of its ideas and the magnificence of its verse make it worthy of the majesty of ancient Rome, and it follows the rules in its every aspect. Since then some of our authors have learned from a more precise study of dramatic art how important the plot is and how absolutely necessary to the perfection of tragedy; they have since then produced several fine pieces and happily made amends for their first transgressions.

I have dilated somewhat upon the importance of the plot before examining that in my friend's work so as to show how necessary the plot is and how much glory he deserves for having handled it so well.

I claim to have noticed this technical excellence in his work and a part of this essay will be devoted to demonstrating it.

A thing cannot be called beautiful unless it has the order and magnitude which are suitable and proportionate to its nature. The closer a thing comes to this optimum magnitude the more it approaches perfection, and conversely it is defective in proportion as it exceeds or falls short of that optimum size. Tall men are handsome but dwarfs and giants are deformed.

The same thing is true of the plot of a tragedy; for it, too, there is an optimum magnitude; and just as bodies are not beautiful without being of a certain size, so a tragedy cannot be beautiful if it is not of a certain length, and if it does not attain that optimum length which is proper to it and which through its very nature it cannot exceed without becoming defective.

Although Aristotle leaves the exact length to the poet's judgment he nevertheless restrains him with certain rules. He thinks the action may grow and be continued until it is absolutely necessary, because of the nature of the thing represented, to bring about the climax, which is its last development, for it is then that good fortune turns to bad or disaster becomes felicity.

One needs no other example than that of *L'Amour tyrannique* to clarify that doctrine and to show how completely the play conforms to it.

Tiridate, having driven Tigrane and Polyxène to Amasia, takes the town by assault. This victory does not satisfy him; he must have the husband and wife who are the objects of his hatred and his love as well as the causes of the war. At that moment misfortune causes the unhappy lovers to fall into his hands. He will have no happiness unless he possesses Polyxène and puts her husband to death; he therefore decides upon these violent actions and the lovers choose to die. Tigrane begs poison of his wife; she sends it to him. Tiridate intercepts it and owing to an ambiguous letter thinks his own life is at stake. This changes his love to hatred and he debates whether to put both Tigrane and Polyxène to death. He decides to do so. He gives the order. This, it seems to me, is the last development which the action had necessarily to reach and beyond which it could not go without changing course. This is also the point at which the poet brings it to an end and the moment when Polyxène's brother, who seizes the tyrant unawares, changes the misfortune of the lovers into supreme joy and the happiness of Tiridate into unhoped-for disaster, from which, however, he escapes through the recognition of his faults and the goodness of those he had unjustly offended.

I shall not mention here Orosmane or Ormène even though these two characters do much to complete the greatness of the tragedy and play important roles in its denouement and structure; that is a pleasure which I leave to my readers and one which will serve to enlighten them as to the ingeniousness of the poet's plotting.

Indeed, when I consider the smoothness with which the action is led to its climax I must confess that I am entranced; Aristotle did not prescribe anything better, and Monsieur de Scudéry has followed his precepts exactly.

The second rule laid down by the philosopher for the greatness of a tragedy is the one called by our dramatic writers *the unity of time*, for the action occurs in time and, depending upon the time needed for its completion, it may be described as great, small, or excessive. This rule, according to Aristotle, was invented to relieve the memory of the spectators, and since actions embracing several years or several days would be too complicated for the memory to retain them without effort, and since actions completed in a few hours would not occupy it enough, the philosopher has considered it proper to limit the length of the action to the time of one full day and has established the principle that those events which might occur between two suns are the only ones suitable to tragedy.

And certainly, leaving aside the effort and attention needed to follow the representation of actions occurring over several years and which would have burdened the memory of the audience and wearied their patience, the composition of tragedies without the unity of time would not have been an art at all. The episodes which Aristotle urges on the playwright so strongly and which must be treated so delicately would have been banished from it; it would not have been necessary to choose a plot and to plan them carefully; a single tragedy could have been made from the history of a whole century; the masterpieces of the greatest poets would have been exposed to the depredations of the lowliest versifiers.

This defect, for all it is so gross and contrary to common sense, was not avoided by all the Roman poets. Certain of their works are deformed by this irregularity; the time-span of Plautus's *Amphitryon* covers nine full months, involving as it does the love of Jupiter for Alcmena, her pregnancy, and the birth of Hercules as well as his conception. All this is the result of Plautus's eagerness to present the universe with this giant-killer, and his reluctance to end the play before the demi-god is born.

The tragic author who has described the death of Hercules on the stage and whose plays are included among those of Seneca, although in Heinsius's [3] opinion they are not by him — that tragic author fell into the same fault; his stage is divided into several places and his actions last several days. In the beginning he presents Hercules to us in Euboea; later he has him offer sacrifices on the Cenaean Promontory, and it is there that he takes the shirt stained with the blood of Nessus; it is there that the poison begins to take effect; it is in that place that he amazes himself by crying out:

61

Hic caelum horrido
clamore complet.[4]

It seems to me it would have been proper for the poet to finish his torments in that same place and that he might easily have lighted his funeral pyre from the flames of his sacrifice. The poet should have remembered that it takes four days to go from the Cenaean Promontory to Mount Oeta, where he has Hercules die; he should have considered that it was not proper to burn Hercules slowly nor credible that a poison of which he had said

Quidquid illa tabe contractum est labat [5]

should act with such delay and take its effect only in this long space of time.

Our modern writers, who for the most part have broken the rule we are speaking of, have not been prepared to do it so lightheartedly as the ancients.

They have sometimes included a succession of several years in the same tragedy; nor have they been satisfied to sin only for the learned, for their faults have been made public, and the audience has been amazed to see the same actors grow old in the course of the play so that those who had been lovers in the first act appeared decrepit in the fifth.

No doubt the desire to include a number of effective episodes in their plays and the fear that a period of twenty-four hours would not afford enough of them led these writers into this mistake; the charm of the spectacle brought them to revolt against the severity of the tragic precepts, and the large number of events which a long time-span so easily provided induced in them a scorn for those plots which they considered less attractive because they were more close-knit and Aristotelian.

They will pardon me if I point out that they have not considered carefully what events may happen in one day and that they have boisterously condemned a rule which they did not clearly understand; this would not have happened if they had sought instruction, with reflection, in good poets; they would have found there well-filled days and many events occurring in a few hours; they might even, in the events of one day, have had enough material left over for a second tragedy, or they might have had to be satisfied with the occurrences of a few hours only, or even been forced to cut out superfluous events from that very period of time in which they were afraid of not finding enough action for a single play.

They must agree with me that the day which was the last of the siege of

62

Troy as well as of Priam's empire was one of those busy days filled with a succession of events. Would anyone want more events than are there, and could one not very rightly and properly take those included between this line of the second book of the *Aeneid*

> Ergo omnis longo soluit se Teucria luctu [6]

and this one

> Hic finis Priami favorum etc.? [7]

It seems to me there is a good deal of subject-matter there, enough to fill a day; and I do not see that our dramatic writers can complain of the shortness of a time in which they find a group of such considerable events and so many important actions.

On the contrary that multitude of events compressed into one day is so important and so beautiful that this very compression is one of the reasons why Aristotle did not hesitate to prefer tragedy to the epic and to find in favor of Sophocles against Homer. Here is what he says in the final chapter of his *Poetics*:

ἔτι τῷ ἐν ἐλάττονι μήκει τὸ τέλος τῆς μιμήσεως εἶναι: τὸ γὰρ ἀθροώτερον ἥδιον ἢ πολλῷ κεκραμένον τῷ χρόνῳ.[8]

Our author, who recognized the importance of that maxim, has observed it religiously; among the many things which take place on the stage he was careful to include skillfully arranged episodes and external embellishments; he has made good use of all the time he was able to devote to the subject, but he was able to stay on this side of the furthest time limit instead of going beyond it; if they examine his play carefully and make allowance for the time needed to carry out the actions it involves, all just critics will conclude that he could have had several hours left over and that he was not in too much of a hurry.

Indeed, if we agree that not much time is needed to take an almost unwalled town, concerning which Tiridate says

> The rams have breached the wall that girds the town;
> The first assault which I am now to lead
> Will end the war and win the kingly crown

and if we consider that the tyrant was hated by his own soldiers, as Pharnabase tells him

> It seems your men their arms but sadly bear,
> In spilling foeman's blood they shed a tear

and nobly deceived by Phraarte, the Prince of Phrygia was able to reach a point only three leagues from his camp without Tiridate's being informed of this move, the prince having indeed come

> with wagons light,
> Through shadows' favor marching in the night,
> By forests' darkness hidden from all sight.

It is obvious that since these two actions, which must be the two longest in the play, need no more than a few hours for their accomplishment, the rest of the action might easily take place in much less time than that between two suns; thus it is easy to justify what is true in itself and to judge a play justly, provided one be free of boredom and preoccupation.

A writer who neglects the rule which our poet has so happily observed will ordinarily neglect also the one calling for unity of action. This rule is not less important nor less difficult, and it is not easy to arrange things so that in a long period of time only those things occur which are not detached from each other and which can all be related to the same subject.

The term "unity of action" has not been well understood and so has brought about many mistakes; even today it causes writers to make strange errors. Many have understood it to mean the actions of a single hero such as Theseus, Hercules, or Achilles as opposed to the actions of different men which are all related and connected with the same goal; hence on this bad foundation they have constructed works whose parts had no connection or relationship and they made poems about an accumulation of different actions because they had all happened to the same man. Good tragic writers have carefully avoided this mistake and even in the epic Homer and Virgil have escaped it; and although the time-span of their works is much greater than in the tragedy and although there was room for an infinite number of actions, they nevertheless admitted only those which were related to the same purpose and which were necessary for the ornamentation of the poems. Thus Virgil, whose purpose is only to bring Aeneas to the shores of the Tiber, took care not to describe to us all that had ever happened to him; and Homer has not told us everything he knew about Ulysses' adventures, nor did he treat the Trojan war like that poet whom Horace makes game of in the *Ars poetica*:

Nec gemino bellum Troianum orditur ab ovo.[9]

I cannot resist mentioning here an error of Joachim du Bellay's [10] which I regret; he considered it strange that the writers of his time did not work on the adventures of Amadis or Lancelot or Tristram of Lyonesse, for he took those books to be legitimate subjects for an epic poem and imagined that the *Orlando Furioso* of Ariosto followed the rules of the genre.

And in my opinion Ronsard, carried away by that mistaken opinion, would have made his Francus a knight errant if he had gone ahead with his poem and had departed from the *Aeneid*; at least he had already begun to involve him with giants and to have him enter the lists to defend ladies' honor. Thus we see that those great men did not yet have a knowledge of the rules of poetry although they were well read in the poets.

It is then not what happens to a single person that makes unity of action but rather the actions of several men if these actions can all be related to the same subject.

One may use *L'Amour tyrannique* as an illustration of this doctrine, for we see in it how all events are related to the violent love of Tiridate and depend upon it. Polyxène, on the point of falling into the tyrant's hands, begs her husband to kill her and makes him swear to go on living after her so as to avenge her; she obtains both these desires after much difficulty, and Tigrane, thinking he has killed her, enters the camp of Tiridate in disguise intending to stab him. He turns to his sister for help and she, instead of helping him in this bloody design, tries to dissuade him from it by pointing out that Polyxène is not dead but a prisoner. This piece of information produces the effect that is to be expected on a passionate heart, and he is led to scorn all other considerations; as he is about to throw himself into the crowd of Tiridate's guards to assassinate him, Tigrane is recognized and arrested.

If you connect these various ornaments to their goal or purpose, which we have described in dealing with the magnitude of the plot, you will find they observe all the rules necessary to that unity of action we are speaking of.

In the first place, all these actions, which can be reduced to one, are so closely related and connected that one cannot be admitted without the succeeding one which depends upon it either through logical necessity or through verisimilitude.

Moreover, not one of them produces its effect if it is separated from the others, whereas all together they conform to the large action of which they are component parts.

Finally, they are so obviously real parts of this whole that not one of them can be cut out without destroying the plot, or at least without changing the nature of the play.

Since all these things are necessary to the unity of action, and since they can all be found in our poem, we must conclude it is perfect in this regard, and that in this regard as in others we should be unjust in withholding the laurel from our author.

No doubt he deserves much praise for this unity but also no less for the unity of place; never has a stage been better arranged or less cluttered than his; and despite the large number of adventures which take place on it the only scene needed is a bastion in the town of Amasia and Tiridate's tents which are so close to it that Ormène says

> And now the favor of Mars upon him falls;
> Already his tents are pitched beneath the walls.

Hardy, [11] who really gave dignity to tragedy (which had been played on platforms built in the streets and at crossroads), among the many defects which the ignorance of his period makes excusable, was especially prone to this one: he could never keep the scene in one place. He changed countries and crossed the seas without scruple and one was often amazed to see that a character who had just spoken in Naples had moved to Cracow while other actors recited a few lines or the orchestra played a tune.

But although almost all his plays have this defect, in no one of them is it more obvious than in the one entitled *Bigamie*; there has never been such an endless peregrination as that play contains. The author made as bold use of Pegasus in it as does Ariosto of the hippogriff; and Count Gleichen in the French play travels as far as Astolfo in the Italian poem.

This defect of Hardy's did not die with him, any more than did the reputation of his works; the writers who followed him kept that changing scene for a long time; their lyres, like those of Orpheus and Amphion, had the privilege of building cities and of removing cliffs and forests; and their stage was like those geographical maps which on their small scale represent the whole extent of the earth.

Nowadays, although the license is no longer permitted and there are no more supporters of that heresy, a few traces of it still remain, and our poets are not diligent enough to protect themselves completely from it: their scene may indeed be in a single city but not in a single place; the audience cannot tell whether the actors are talking in a house or in the street; the stage is like a common room, private for no one and where anyone may do whatever he wants.

Since not a single beauty is missing from *L'Amour tyrannique*, we must also expect not to find a single defect in it; therefore the poet, as we have already said, does not make the walls fall as they did at the trumpets of Jericho, and all events occur in one place.

It is not enough for a tragedy to follow the rules for length, for the time required for the events, and for unity of place and action; if it is to be perfect it must also arouse pity and terror and it must produce these emotions in the souls of the audience.

What is more, these passions and emotions must be caused not only by the lines recited or the things described but also by the arrangement of the action and the nature of the plot, which therefore is of the essence of tragedy and is its principal ingredient, as we have proved above.

And yet, although all good tragedies must necessarily produce these emotions, nevertheless the kind of tragedy we call *mixed*, which the Romans named better than we do *implexam* and the Greeks excellently, as is their custom, πεπλεγμένην, [12] causes these emotions much more intensively than does simple tragedy which contains nothing unexpected, nothing surprising.

My friend's tragedy is of the first kind, and without flattery one can say that it is an excellent one of the kind.

Indeed the reversal of the situation and the recognition, which are two of the aspects of the plot, have so important and so beautiful a place in *L'Amour tyrannique* that perhaps *Oedipus*, which is the only Latin tragedy of that kind which has been preserved, does not accommodate them in a more beautiful or more finished way.

And the reversal, in fact, which may be defined as "an unexpected change in the action and an event contrary to what was expected or awaited," could not be found without much searching, I assure you, which would be more Aristotelian than the one in our play.

Is it not true that when Tiridate appears in that terrible tribunal where he is to condemn Tigrane, Polyxène, his wife, and his father-in-law, when we see come before him those innocent victims loaded with chains and apparently abandoned of all save virtue and constancy, and when the rage of the tyrant and his injustice have pronounced the cruel verdict "Put them to death," is it not true, I say, that everyone pities those crowned victims and believes that heaven has not strength enough to draw them back from a death which is so close and which seems so assured? And yet, in accordance with the nature of the play and the structure of the plot their help arrives. Troilus changes the nature of things. Tiridate falls from that throne to which violence and betrayal had raised him, and by an unexpected reversal and a course of events entirely contrary to the one awaited, Orosmane finds himself in a position to condemn the tyrant.

The arrival of Polyxène's noble brother shows the poet's skill and by the means he used to rescue the princes one may admire his judgment. Several points in the structure of the play allow the audience to foresee this help; they are prepared for it by the brave deception of Phraarte and by the blindness of the tyrant who puts into his hands the command of the army (in which the learned may note a divine bit of technique), and finally they are fully informed of it through the conference between Phraarte and the Phrygian whom Troilus is supposed to have sent to him.

Seneca in his *Agamemnon* made a serious mistake in the very thing from which Monsieur de Scudéry draws one of his principal beauties: Strophius, whom he introduces to save Orestes and Pylades, appears on the stage like a god from the machine. Nobody expected him. In the whole play there is no preparation for this entrance, and it is so far from everybody's thoughts that he is compelled himself to tell his name to the audience;

> Phocide relicta, Strophius Elea inclytus
> palma revertor.[13]

His reason for coming is only to kiss Agamemnon's hand and to rejoice with him over the fall of Troy:

> Causa veniendi fuit
> gratiari amico etc.[14]

But is it not charming of the poet to have him come with the fastest horses in Greece to carry off Orestes and protect him the more surely from his mother's cruelty:

> Vos Graecia nunc teste, veloces equi,
> infida cursu fugite praecipiti loca.[15]

The best one can say of him is that although he took good care for his children's safety, he was not equally careful to save his reputation.

We learn from this that in ancient times writers made serious mistakes and that our critics ought not to praise antiquity so highly at the expense of our century and the works of our day.

The help of Troilus and the fall of Tiridate produce the *anagnorisis*, which is what the philosopher calls that recognition of people, events, places or other things which produces some effect or which causes some important change in the play.[16] It depends upon the reversal, and cannot exist without it, but the converse is not true since the reversal is found alone in many tragedies.

In this play the *anagnorisis* is very natural and easy, for Tiridate, seeing his ingratitude compensated by the good actions of Ormène and hearing her speak these lines:

> If his reign ends so also must my day;
> If he be punished I must also pay.
> His fate and mine forever interlinked . . .

begins to understand these:

> But to free us all from suffering
> We have no dearth of poison . . .

and to realize his crime and the innocence of those he had condemned. From this result his repentance, his reconciliation and finally the remarkable changes in this marvelous play.

Now I, who always judge as much as possible without prejudice, and who ordinarily am more severe than indulgent toward the works of my friends and who try to resemble that good and wise man of whom Horace says

> Fiet Aristarchus, nec dicet, cur ego amicum
> Offendam in nugis? [17]

I admit that I have never thought of the structure of this fable, even without the aid of the poetry and the spectacle, without shedding in secret those tears which no one has been able to keep from shedding at its presentation and which have sprinkled the galleries and the main floor alike.

Certainly, if I have some understanding of poetics and if my friends have not deceived me on that score, I am prepared to state boldly that it is not possible to find an action better suited to tragedy than that of *L'Amour tyrannique* and that Monsieur de Scudéry created a masterpiece when he found that marvelous subject.

I must also point out, without, however, dwelling on the point, how well Monsieur de Scudéry observes that rule by which the reversal and the recognition must lead toward and concern the same end, for we see that just as the unexpected change in the fortunes of Orosmane, Ormène, Polyxène, and Tigrane has for its purpose a happy ending to the play, Tiridate's recognition of his own faults leads to this same conclusion and makes it possible for him to participate in the general felicity.

It must also be said that of all the kinds of recognition (which may be reduced to six: those brought about through natural or accidental marks, by the intervention of the poet, by the memory, by logical deduction, by deceit or finally, without exterior signs, those that are inherent in the fable and in the structure of the plot) this one, on the word of Aristotle himself, is the first and best

πασῶν δὲ βελτίστη ἀναγνώρισις ἡ ἐξ αὐτῶν τῶν πραγμάτων [18]

It is the one our poet has used and through which Tiridate, with an astonishment and a wonder which must really have surprised even him, recognizes by the very writing-tablets which had persuaded him of his kinsmen's crime the fact of their innocence and his own injustice.

These two beautiful details, which are of such great importance, almost escaped me among the infinite number to be found in this excellent piece of work, in part because of the eagerness I bring to this essay which I am writing in a turmoil of enthusiasm; for *L'Amour tyrannique* is a garden which would be completely denuded if we were to pluck only the most beautiful flowers, and besides, the nature of this preface, which is that of a familiar essay rather than of a studied treatise, has forced me to eliminate from consideration many extrinsic ornaments in the poem whose effectiveness depend upon a knowledge of recondite literary doctrines; thus I am far from taking into account the lesser beauties of the play and through haste from making the thorough examination of this fertile poem which a man of greater leisure would devote to so advantageous a subject.

The scene of suffering, which the Greeks call πάθος and the Romans *perturbatio*, follows so logically from the reversal and the recognition and depends upon them so completely, that the philosopher makes it the third division of the mixed plot.

This element is not completely banished from what we have called the simple fable nor can there be any tragedy which fails to produce pity and terror either through the artifice of language and what is recited on the stage or through fate and the way things occur. But the really tragic quality is inherent in the dramatic idea and does not depend upon the spoken word or the stage action, for it is the nature of the plot to imitate events which by their occurrence evoke pity and terror.

Moreover, since what can be educed from the interrelation of events is probably preferable to what can be introduced into the plot from the outside (as we said when we were discussing the different kinds of recognition according to Aristotle's classification), it follows that reversals which the plot contains within itself and which are to be found in the very subject are to be more highly esteemed than those inserted into the plot, especially since the former are more logical and more excellent.

The same thing is true of the arguments with which rhetorical technique reinforces eloquence and which Aristotle for that reason esteems much less than those which do not depend on forensic skill; and just as bad orators fell back on laws, witnesses, and pactions because they did not know the real rules of eloquence and could not make proper use of rhetorical effects, so poets of the past and even some of our own day depend upon the actor's skill to evoke pity and terror, the more so because they have none of their own.

These faults are committed by the writer who bloodies the stage, who shows effects produced by magic and unbelievable metamorphoses, and who presents impossibilities to the public view.

> Nec pueros coram populo Medea trucidet,
> nec humana palam coquat exta nefarius Atreus,
> nec in avem Progne vertatur, Cadmus in anguem.[19]

Because of this mistake, Nero, who was born for the eternal shame of poetry, chose plots full of murders which were dangerous and sometimes fatal to the actors, for he took pleasure in seeing real blood shed on the stage and satisfied his lust for cruelty by the presentation of these appalling spectacles. This is what Suetonius [20] reports of that unhappy actor who, while playing before Nero the role of Icarus, fell near the Emperor's chair as he was attempting his first flight and spattered with his blood that bloodthirsty monster.

We may say then that the plot must be so well constructed that even without stage settings or the aid of actors or horrifying spectacles it cannot be listened to or read without producing its effect and without evoking pity and terror.

This is Aristotle's opinion and what sovereign reason requires, and it is what the learned find worthy of applause in our play. For in truth, who does not experience these two passions which are so violent and so appropriate to tragedy? And who can consider without emotion the strange fall of Tiridate? At the moment when he falls from that felicity which injustice and fate had given him he recognizes in himself the enemy and persecutor of his father-in-law, the ruination of all his kingdom, an unfaithful husband, an infamous lover, an incestuous rival, and almost a parricide and executioner of his own kinsmen.

Indeed, without adding to all these disasters the torments of Orosmane, Ormène, Polyxène, and Tigrane, without mentioning the disgraceful chains loaded upon these illustrious persons, a man can but tremble with horror and grow soft with pity at the mere recital of these adventures, and has no need for the effects of the stage setting, the vigorous interpretation of actors, or the power of poetry.

If I am permitted in this essay to unveil the secrets of art and to divulge the most jealously guarded mysteries of poetry, this must be because I am speaking in my friend's favor and addressing myself only to the small group of true connoisseurs.

Let us say then both for them and for him that since the change upon which the emotions and the suffering of a play depend can lead only to felicity or to disaster, and since the characters must all be virtuous or vicious or at a point equidistant from these two extremes, the poet must make use of one of these kinds of people to excite pity and horror and thus to achieve the goal which tragedy proposes for itself.

Now as to witnessing the passage of a good man from felicity to ill fortune: it seems to me that this change will probably not touch the soul in the way we want because, since pity and terror are induced in men by the things they see happening to others and which they fear may happen to themselves, it is unlikely that if a calamity befalls a good man the soul will be moved by these passions or that the spectators will fear misfortune caused by their probity since this latter ordinarily has as·its recompense good fortune in life, and this is Aristotle's argument in the various books of his *Rhetoric*.

However, the ill fortune of a bad man is no more useful and certainly produces no more emotion than that of a good man, for it appears to be the effect of divine justice, and the good fortune of the evil man, which always seems unjust, excludes pity. No one commiserates with a wicked man on his downfall because he is believed to deserve that punishment and because no one fears the same for himself since each man takes a flattering view of his own probity and since, to tell the truth, the great majority of men are passably good.

There remains to be considered only that third type of man who is neither deeply criminal nor deeply virtuous and who alone will actually produce the emotions to which dramatic writers aspire and who is defined by the philosopher in the third book of the *Ethics*. He who sins through imprudence does not deserve to be called a good man because he has not

72

lived up to his duty; but he cannot either be called wicked, for his sin is without premeditation, as they say in the schools.

Thus behave those who have yielded up their judgment to one of the passions and who are no longer their own master, who let themselves be carried away by the torrent; just as diseased eyes are poor judges of colors these minds, clouded and deprived of light, act only from the force of the passion, consider right whatever passion dictates, and no doubt are to be pitied because they imagine they are acting heroically when in fact they are committing appalling crimes.

Monsieur de Scudéry's Tyrant is a perfect example of this kind of character, and the confession he makes in Act III, scene 3, reveals this fact to us while showing that love is the cause of all these tragic events.

To begin with, he discovers that he loves Polyxène, his sister-in-law:

> In truth 'tis Polyxena I adore:
> I will not hide this fateful passion more.

Then his passion leads him to believe that it is right to love her:

> She is too lovely not to be desired;
> I have eyes; by her my soul is fired;
> Her glance is like an arrow in my heart;
> Could living man not feel her beauty's smart?

And then he concludes that he would be mad not to feel this passion:

> In truth 'twould be surprising lov'd I not.

Hence we must not be surprised that he is prepared to use any means to win Polyxène, and he continues as follows:

> What though she flee me to the furthest pole
> I'll seek for her where swiftest torrents roll;
> I'll follow her through desert and through wood,
> Across the sea, etc.

He lifts the mask still further and exposes his complete blindness when he is contradicted by the wise Pharnabase who had been his tutor and who tries to recall to virtue that mind possessed by passion. This is what he says after the fall of Amasia:

> If when the battle's done I find my Queen,
> Let her by throngs of witnesses be seen:
> I'll lead this lovely captive weak and tame
> Triumphant through the streets in public shame.
> I hold my love is just when it gives joy.

When we consider the sentence of death he pronounces against this beautiful woman and examine the sentiments caused by so violent and so disprized a love, we must conclude that throughout the play Tiridate has been dominated by a violent passion, that he has done wrong without premeditation as we have said before, and that his intelligence, killed or stifled by his passion, had no share in his crimes.

I am not surprised this play had so many admirers and that everybody left the theater after its presentation with his soul deeply moved and his eyes wet with tears, for the tyrant who is its protagonist, to whom all the events are related, has all the qualities necessary to cause in others the emotions of fear and pity. He is neither too virtuous nor too wicked, for although he does commit evil acts, he is driven to them by a greater force; his misfortune does not come upon him because of his evil-doing, the more so because he thinks it is right both to love Polyxène and to condemn her to death; and finally, in order greatly to increase the pity and horror of the play and to push these emotions to their uttermost limits, at the moment when he sees two kings and two queens in chains at his feet he is himself overthrown, stripped of the purple, constrained to bear the same chains he had imposed upon others and to pass from the extreme of good fortune to a lamentable calamity.

But since the ambitions of many people must come together to bring about all these complications, and one cannot be enough for this purpose, it follows also that these people must be enemies, or neutral toward each other, or joined by friendship or blood so that they may be driven to act.

But since the desire to avenge ourselves and to injure our enemies is certainly innate in us all and the accomplishment of such acts seems to our minds sweeter than honey, as Homer says, and since the reasons for which men hate each other seem rightfully odious to everybody, how shall the means of the vengeance which we choose to wreak upon our enemies touch the spectators who are likely to consider all such means justified? The spectators must be touched by the fear of misfortunes whose causes they detest and they must be made to look with pity upon the misfortunes which they themselves wish to their enemies.

The same remark may be made concerning those disasters which occur among neutral characters who neither love nor hate, who excite no emotions, who act without passion, and whose misfortunes leave no sadness in the soul except that which we are obliged to feel for suffering humanity.

Hence it is only the Tiridates, the Ormènes, the Tigranes, the Polyxènes, the Orosmanes who can terrify and soften our hearts; in other words, it is only the Husbands, Wives, Fathers-in-law, and Brothers- and Sisters-in-law who can touch us deeply; only the misfortunes of people joined by blood and friendship give us terror and pity.

They do this certainly in Monsieur Scudéry's play. The misfortunes he shows on the stage have touched the greatest hearts in the world as well as the lowest, and not one of these spectators came away without having profited from that calming of the passions which is one of the ends of tragedy.

Finally, of all the means by which Aristotle teaches that pity and horror may be excited, the one he prefers, which is that after having committed a crime one be led to acknowledge it,[21] is not omitted from this excellent tragedy.

From the moment that Tiridate condemns his relatives to death he is a criminal, even though his passion really commits the crime, and, as we have said, partially excuses it. He says this himself after having acknowledged his sin; it is remorse which tortures him so agonizingly and makes him wish for death because he holds himself unworthy to live; and this desire for death shows clearly that there is nothing feigned or superficial in his repentance. Here is how he comes to that acknowledgment:

> Now that the blindfold's gone, I see my error:
> At last my crime is clear; I shake with terror.

This is how he begs Ormène to avenge herself:

> Love me no more; in honor you're constrained
> To grant my heart the death which it awaits.
> Take vengeance, punish me, etc.

It is in these terms that he addresses the princes he had persecuted:

> O princes, outraged by my insolence
> Give all your aid to his just indignation;
> Spare not my blood, avenge your degradation.
> I am your foe who must be greatly feared.

And finally this is how he begs for death:

> My death will save you; that's all my desire.

With these lines the complication of the plot, or what the Romans called *connection*, comes to an end; at this point the denouement or resolution of the plot begins.

These two divisions, which contain all the tragic action, are totally opposed, and must be treated in completely different ways: the first includes not only those things which are properly a part of the plot but also those which can be distinguished from it, such as the episodes, the descriptions and whatever is added to increase either the length or the beauty of the work, and in general whatever the poet brings in for the ornamentation of his poem, whereas the second excludes all extraneous beauties, concerns itself only with the subject, and admits of nothing superfluous.

Despite the great number of ornaments which Monsieur de Scudéry's genius and learning have scattered so prodigally throughout his tragedy the episodes must claim a share of our praise as they have contributed to his reputation; he has worked them out carefully; he has not allowed himself the least poetic license; he has varied them for visual effect; now he charms his audience with wonderful descriptions expertly planned like the one in the fourth act where he describes a city taken and given up to fire and pillage; again he touches the soul of the spectators with the sight of nations enslaved; at still other times he makes use of Pharnabase to teach virtue with greater success and with greater pleasure for the listener than are commonly achieved in the schools or in academic chairs.

These episodes derive both from the subject and from the plot; they are useful; and their primary technical advantage is that they serve to advance the action which nevertheless does not move too fast and comes to its end only after having attained the magnitude required by the structure of the plot. Indeed, the sad state of Amasia's citizens does not touch Tiridate; the lessons of its governor do not restrain him from vice; and Ormène does not allow herself to be so far carried away by the description of her country's ruin that she determines upon and consents to the death of its tyrant; these are the moments when the poet has very skillfully worked out the episodes and the purpose for which they are included.

There is nothing like this in the denouement, which is much more severe since its nature does not allow all these ornaments. It contains only action and only matters related to the plot, nothing that can be or ought to be cut out, and nothing extrinsic or not absolutely necessary.

It remains for us only to consider the conclusion of the plot, which is a happy one. This quiet issue from so many troubled and unhappy events, this peaceful conclusion found in the greater number of our tragic plays and appearing to resemble the tone of comedy, has led our poets to describe these plays as tragicomedies. Some poets are convinced that if the ending is not bloody the play cannot be called a tragedy. Therefore they have brought together two contrary things and have made a monster by combining two natures each good in itself, and they have forgotten the precepts of their master:

> sed non ut placidis coeant immitia, non ut
> serpentes avibus geminentur, tigribus agni.[22]

Aristotle, who includes the happy ending in his enumeration of the purposes of tragedy,[23] gives us no reason to share the opinion of those poets. The examples of Alcestis, the two Iphigenias, of Io and Helen support and confirm the example of the present play; and although most tragedies spill blood on the stage and end with someone's death, we need not conclude from this that the ending of all such plays must necessarily be in disaster. Yet above all we must be careful not to mix into them anything comic.

And indeed how convincing would it be for the actors to have the buskin on one foot and the sock on the other, or for them to wear both the chimer and a simple parti-colored dress? How shall a king's orders, the murders, the despairs, the violent deaths, the banishments, the parricides, the incests, the burnings, the battles, the weeping and wailing and funeral pomps, which are things to be found in tragedy, be made compatible with the games, the feasts, the weddings, the avarice of old men, the tricks and drunkenness of the slaves and parasites, which are things to be found in comedy? And who could reasonably imagine that the author would want at one and the same time to excite in the spectators pity and horror, delight and pleasure, tears and laughter, or that he would seek to calm their souls by stirring them deeply, these being the different purposes which the two kinds of plays seek to achieve?

It is for these sound and convincing reasons that we have called *L'Amour tyrannique* a tragedy throughout this essay. But it could also be so described because it is so perfect and so finished that one can truthfully say it lacks nothing which the philosopher prescribes or which the severest critics seek in such works.

Let no one allege here in opposition the *Amphitryon* of Plautus which we have already censured; that author sins against the rules of comedy in almost every one of his plays. Menaechmus is so deeply in love that he seems maddened, and that is a tragic passion; in another comedy Alesimacchus comes on the stage to kill himself, a thing inexcusable in comedy; in short, the authority of a man of whom Horace says

> Quam non adstricto percurrat pulpita socco [24]

ought not lead another to break the rules which the wisest of philosophers has established.

As far as the Greeks are concerned, the same thing must be said of Euripides' *Cyclops*, which Julius Caesar Scaliger excludes from the canon of true tragedies because it contains too many comic elements; and indeed who could allow in a serious play what the Cyclops says of Bacchus when, in a casual meeting, he asks how it is possible for a god to live in a bottle?

Monsieur de Scudéry knew very well that his play was a tragedy and yet he gave it the title of tragicomedy so as to show that he was willing to conform to accepted custom and that he preferred to accommodate himself to convention instead of following sovereign reason too scrupulously.

Up to this point we have discussed the plot, which the philosopher considers the most important part of tragedy and, unless I am mistaken, we have shown that he was right to call it the soul of tragedy; we have shown that in this respect Monsieur de Scudéry's work is above all praise, and we would have continued to point out in it the consistency of the characters, of the emotions and of the diction (in which discussion we should no doubt have included matter to satisfy the connoisseurs and instruct the ignorant) if a journey which we are about to make beyond the mountains had not prevented us from ending this essay as we had planned.

But aside from the fact that this would have delayed the publication, which is imminent, and would have increased public impatience for a long time, and aside from the fact that our very good friend Monsieur de la Mesnardière has wonderfully treated these three subjects in the great work on poetic theory which he is about to publish,[25] anyone can see how religiously our author has followed the philosopher's precepts.

Aside from all this, I say, we have considered that the plot was the aspect of a play which is least frequently discussed and yet is the most important, and hence that it was right for us to dwell on it and to demonstrate the incomparable beauty in that of *L'Amour tyrannique* which Monsieur de Scudéry has so marvelously invented; and as for character, emotion, and diction one would have to be completely lacking in common sense not to recognize in this play the consistency of the first, the nobility of the second, and the majestic purity of the third.

It is true that if we had followed the beaten track of prefaces to books of our day we should also have avoided speaking of the plot, for following the example of other writers we should only have scattered three or four handfuls of flowers in the path of the work, filled two or three pages with words like *good* and *beautiful*, given praise without explaining the reason for it, wearied the reader by useless flattery, and awarded a crown to the author on our own private authority.

But we should no doubt have had the same experience as others have commonly had: nobody would have believed us and instead everyone would have made fun of our eulogies and refused to judge the reputation of our friend on the basis of conventional praise.

It has then seemed best to adduce at every point the authority of reason and erudition and not to praise Monsieur de Scudéry except after having consulted Aristotle, to award no crowns except at the philosopher's hands, and to establish his glory only on a foundation which would have nothing to fear from either the envious or from calumniators.

And yet we freely admit that even with all these advantages our essay would not have sheltered the play from the incursions of those two enemies of beautiful things, and perhaps we ought to have defended further the truths we have just demonstrated and thus to show the envious that we are

Et cantare pares respondere parati [26]

had that great genius of our century, the shame of past centuries and the marvel of those which are to come, the divine CARDINAL DE RICHELIEU, not spared us this labor.

Having been charmed by the play and convinced that only unjust and impertinent things could be written against so perfect a work, this great man forbade its author to reply if ever human malice should attack him to the prejudice of truth.

Therefore we consider that the tragedy is above attack by the envious both because of its own merit and because of the protection (which it would be more than sacrilegious to violate) granted to it by ARMAND, THE TUTELARY DEITY OF LETTERS.

The voice of that ORACLE pronounced these very words: "L'AMOUR TYRANNIQUE" IS A WORK WHICH HAS NO NEED OF BEING SHELTERED FROM ATTACK, FOR IT PROVIDES ITS OWN DEFENSE.

François Hédelin, abbé d'Aubignac THE WHOLE ART OF THE STAGE

Book I, Chapter 3

WHAT IS TO BE UNDERSTOOD BY THE ART OF THE STAGE

It may seem very rash, or at least superfluous, to treat of poetry after that so many authors both ancient and modern have given us books upon that subject full of learning, and more particularly have taken pains to make observations upon dramatic poetry as being the most agreeable and yet the hardest to succeed in. But if we may believe with Seneca that all truths have not been yet spoken, we may assure it in the subject which I undertake, for all I have seen yet that concerns the stage contains only the general maxims of dramatic poetry, which is properly the theory of the art, but as for the practice and application of those instructions, I never met with anything of that kind hitherto, all the discourses that are upon that subject being only paraphrases and commentaries upon Aristotle with great obscurity and little novelty.

I do not pretend here to trouble myself about satisfying the criticisms of grammarians or the scruples of logicians, who, it may be, will not freely admit of this distinction in an art whose rules seem all to tend to practice. I am sure all the rational and polite learning will not oppose me in it, since it is natural in all arts to distinguish the knowledge of the maxims and the use of them, besides that in the execution of all general rules there are

NOTE: The complete title of d'Aubignac's book gives a good indication of its contents: *The Whole Art of the Stage, Containing not only the rules of the dramatic art, but many curious observations about it, which may be of great use to the authors, actors and spectators of plays, together with much critical learning about the stage and plays of the ancients.* The translation of 1684 says that the book was "Written in French by the command of Cardinal Richelieu, by Monsieur Hédelin, Abbot of Aubignac, and now made English."

observations to be made of which there is no mention when one teaches only the theory, and which nevertheless are of great importance. Thus architecture teacheth the beauty and symmetry of buildings, their noble proportions, and all the rest of their magnificent appearance, but does not descend to express a thousand necessary contrivances of which the master of the house is to take care when he puts his hand to the work. If the art of playing upon the lute were reduced into rules, it could teach only general things, as the number of the strings and touches, the manner of making the accords, the measures, passages, quavers, etc., but still one would be forced to have recourse to the master himself to learn in the execution of all this the nicest way of touching the strings, the changing of the measures, the most graceful way how to give a good motion to one's playing, and many more particulars which could not well be committed to writing and so must either be neglected or learned of the masters themselves.

The same thing has happened to the stage. There have been ample treatises of dramatic poems, the original of them, their progress, definition, species, the unity of action, measure of time, the beauty of their contrivance, the thoughts, manners, language which is fittest for them, and many other such matters, but only in general, and that I call the theory of the stage; but for the observations to be made upon those general rules, as how to prepare the incidents to unite times and places, the continuity of the theatral action, the connection of the scenes, the intervals of the acts, and a thousand other particulars of which there is nothing left in antiquity, of which all the moderns have said so little that it is next to nothing — all this, I say, is that which I call the art or practice of the stage. As for the ancients, if they have writ nothing about it as to the practical part, it is because that perhaps in their time it was so common that they could not believe anybody capable of not knowing it, and indeed if one look into their works and make but the least reflection upon the art they use, one may perceive it almost everywhere.

But for the moderns, they for the most part have been entirely ignorant of it because they have neglected the reading of the poems of those great masters, or if they have read them, it was without taking notice of the nicest beauties with which they are adorned. Therefore it must be set down for a maxim out of context, that it is impossible to understand dramatic poetry without the help of the ancients and a thorough meditation upon their works.

Book II, Chapter 6

OF THE UNITY OF PLACE

After the poet has ordered his subject according to the rules we have given, or, it may be better, which his own industry and study may furnish him with, he must reflect that the best part of it must be represented by actors, which must be upon a stage fixed and determined, for to make his actors appear in different places would render his play ridiculous by the want of probability, which is to be the foundation of it.

This rule of unity of place begins now to be looked upon as certain, but yet the ignorant and some others of weak judgment do still imagine that it cannot but be repugnant to the beauty of the incidents of a play, because that they, happening often in great distance of place, cannot but lose by this constraint, and therefore whatsoever reason you oppose against their imaginations, they fancy a false impossibility in the execution and reject stubbornly all that's said to convince them. On the other side, those that are but half read in antiquity do well perceive the strength of what it alleged for this rule, but yet they make objections so unbecoming a literate thinking man that they have often moved pity in me, though I had more mind to laugh at them. It is the property of little geniuses not to be able to comprehend many things at the same time so as to reduce them to a point, their judgment not being able to assemble so many images as they must have present all at once, and therefore they make so many difficulties that it is easy to see they would be glad that there were reasons wanting to convince them.

As for the truly learned, they are thoroughly convinced of the necessity of this rule, because they see clearly that probability can no ways be preserved without it. But I may boldly say that hitherto no one of them has explained this rule and made it intelligible, either because we do not take the pains of making all the necessary reflections upon the works of the ancients to discover the art which is most commonly hid in them, and which always ought to be so, [under] an apparent necessity of the subject or the interest of the actors; or else because nobody strives to go beyond the first great masters, and what they have neglected is given over most commonly by their followers.

Aristotle has said nothing of it, and I believe he omitted it because that this rule was in his time too well known, the Choruses which ordinarily remained upon the stage from one end of the play to the other marking the unity of the scene too visibly to need a rule for it. And indeed, would it not have been ridiculous that in the play called the *Seven before Thebes* the young women who make the Chorus should have found themselves sometimes before the palace of the king and sometimes in the camp of the enemies without ever stirring from the same place? And the three famous tragedians of the Greeks whose works we have are so punctual in the observation of this rule and do so often make their actors say where they are and whence they come that Aristotle must have supposed too much ignorance in his age and in those who should read these poets if he had gone about to explain so settled a rule. But since the ignorance and barbarity of some past ages have brought such disorder upon the stage to make people in the play appear in different parts of the world on the same stage, it will not be amiss to give here at length the reason of this rule so well practised by the ancients, and that in honor of some of our modern poets who have very handsomely imitated them.

To understand it, then, we must have recourse to our ordinary principle, which is, that the stage is but a representation of things; and yet we are not to imagine that there is anything of what we really see, but we must think the things themselves are there of which the images are before us. So Floridor[1] is much less Floridor than the Horatius of whom he acts the part, for his dress is Roman, he speaks, acts, thinks as that Roman did at that time; but as that Roman could not but be in some place acting and speaking, the place where Floridor appears does represent that where Horatius was, or else the representation would be imperfect in that circumstance.

This truth well understood makes us to know that the place cannot change in the rest of the play since it cannot change in the representation, for one and the same image remaining in the same state cannot represent two different things. Now it is highly improbable that the same space and the same floor, which receive no change at all, should represent two different places, as, for example, France and Denmark, or, within Paris itself, the Tuileries and the Exchange. At least to do it with some sort of color, one should have of that sort of theatres which turn quite round and entire that so the place might change as well as the persons acting, and to do this, the subject of the play ought to furnish some reason for this change, and as that cannot well happen but by the power of God Almighty, who changes as He pleases the face of nature, I doubt it would be hard to make a reasonable play without a dozen miracles at least.

Let it then be allowed for a certain truth that the place where the first actor who opens the play is supposed to be ought to be the same place to the end of the play, and that, it not being in the ordinary course of nature that the place can receive any change, there can be none likewise in the representation, and, by consequence, that all your other actors cannot rationally appear in any other place.

But we must remember that this place which cannot be supposed to change is the area or floor of the stage, upon which the actors walk, and which the ancients called by the name of *proscenium*; for as that represents that spot of ground upon which the persons represented did actually walk and discourse, which could not turn about or change on a sudden or without a miracle, so, when you have once chosen the place where you intend your action to be begun, you must suppose it immovable in all the rest of the play, as it was in effect and really.

It is not the same with the sides and end of the theatre, for as they do but represent those things which did actually environ the persons acting and which might receive some change, they may likewise receive some in the representation, and it is in that that consists the changing of scenes and other ornaments of decoration which always ravish the people and please the best judges when they are well done. So we have seen upon our stage a temple adorned with a noble front of architecture, which, coming to be set open, showed the inside of it where in perspective were descried pillars and an altar and all the other ornaments of a church extremely well done, so that the place did not change and yet had a fine decoration.

We are not, nevertheless, to imagine that the poet's *capriccio* is to rule these decorations, for he must find some color and appearance for it in his subject.

So, for example, he might feign a palace upon the seaside, forsaken and left to be inhabited by poor fishermen. A prince landing or being cast away there might adorn it with all the rich furniture fit for it, after this by some accident it might be set on fire, and then behind it the sea might appear, upon which one might represent a sea fight; so that in all the five changes of the stage the unity of place would still be ingeniously preserved. Not but that the very floor or *proscenium* may change too, provided it be superficially, as if some river should overflow it, as the Tiber did in the time of Augustus, or if flames came out of the earth and covered the face of it. In all these cases the unity of place would not be broke. But, as I have said already, the subject of the play must furnish probable reasons for these changes, which I repeat the oftener because I am still afraid that it will not make impression enough in the reader.

It is not enough neither to say that the floor or stage should represent a place immovable. It must, besides, be a place supposed open in the reality as it appears in the representation, for since the actors are supposed to go and come from one end of it to the other, there cannot be any solid body between to hinder either their sight or motion. Therefore the ancients did use to choose for the place of their scene in tragedies some public place, as that before the gate of a palace, and in their comedies, some part of a town where different streets met and where the houses of the principal actors were supposed to be, because these places were most fitly represented by the empty stage adorned with the figures of those houses. Not that they always followed this, for in the *Suppliants* and in the *Ion* of Euripides, the scene is before a temple, and in the *Ajax* of Sophocles, the scene is before his tent pitched in the corner of a forest. In the *Rudens* of Plautus, it is before the temple and some scattered houses from whence one sees the sea. And indeed all this depends upon the poet's invention, who according to his subject chooses the place the most convenient for all that he has a mind to represent and adorns it with some agreeable appearance.

One may judge from all this how ridiculous was the wall in the *Thisbe* of [the] poet Théophile, it being placed upon the stage and Pyramus and she whispering through it; and when they went out, the wall sunk that the other actors might see one another. For besides that the two places on each side of the wall represented the two chambers of Pyramus and Thisbe, and that it was contrary to all appearance of reason that in the same place the king should come and talk with his confidents, and, much less, that a lion should come and fright Thisbe there, I would fain know by what supposed means in the action itself this wall could become visible and invisible, and by what enchantment it was sometimes in being and then ceased quite to be again. The fault is not less in those who suppose things done upon the stage which have not been seen by the spectators, it not being probable they could have been done without being seen, or else things must be supposed to have been invisible in the reality of the action, upon which, I think, one of our modern poets fell into a great error of this kind, having placed a bastion upon the stage and having afterwards caused the town to be taken by that bastion, which was never seen to be either attacked or defended.[2]

As for the extent which the poet may allow to the scene he chooses, when it is not in a house, but open, I believe it may be as far as a man can see another walk and yet not know perfectly that it is he. For to take a larger space would be ridiculous, it being improbable that two people, being each of them at one end of the stage without any object between, should look at one another and yet not see one another; whereas this distance, which we allow often, contributes to the working of the play by the mistakes and doubts which a man may make by seeing another at a distance. To which the theatres of the ancients do very well agree; for, being as they were, threescore yards in front among the Romans and little less among the Grecians, it was pretty near the proportion we allow them.

I desire the reader, besides, to consider that if the poet did represent by his stage all the places and rooms of a palace or all the streets of a town, he should make the spectators see not only all that happened in his story but all that was done besides in that palace or in the town. For there is no reason to hinder the spectators from seeing all that, nor why they should see one thing sooner than another, particularly considering that since they can see at the same time into the garden of the palace and into the king's cabinet, according to the subject of the play, they must likewise hear and see all that is done there besides the theatral action, except there were an enchantment to show only that which the poet had a mind to and hide all that was not of his subject. Besides, the stage would never be empty of any of the actors, except they went out of the palace or town, for since the place represents the palace with its garden, court, and other apartments, one cannot forbear seeing anyone who should go from any of those apartments into the court or garden, and, by consequence, as long as any of the actors were in the extent represented by the stage, they cannot avoid being seen. To which it cannot be answered that to mark the different apartments there may be curtains to shut and draw, for these curtains are fit for nothing but to toss their inventors in them like dogs in a blanket.

I have spoken so clearly of this in my *Terence Justified* that I have nothing more to say against this gross piece of ignorance.

If it be said besides that the poet has the liberty of showing and hiding what he pleases, I grant it, provided there be a probability that one thing be seen and another not. But there would need a singular invention to contrive that ever and anon the same persons acting and speaking in a palace should be seen and not be seen, for that would be making of the walls to sink and rise, go backwards and forwards every moment. This may be enough to show the error of those who upon the same scene represent

Spain and France, making their stage not only almost as big as the earth, but likewise causing the same floor to represent at the same time things so far distant from one another and that without any apparent cause of so prodigious a change.

We may likewise observe how they are mistaken that suppose in one side of the stage one part of the town, as, for example, the Louvre, and on the other side, another part, as the Place Royale, thinking by this fine invention to preserve the unity of place. Indeed, if two parts or quarters of a town thus supposed were not far from one another, and the space between were really empty of houses, such a thing were not improper, but if between the two places there are many houses and solid bodies, I would then ask how it comes to pass that those houses do not fill up the empty place of the stage, and how, if they do, an actor can see another place at the other end of the stage beyond all these houses, and, in a word, how this stage, which is but an image, represents a thing of which it has no resemblance.

Let it then be settled for a constant maxim that the *proscenium* or floor of the stage can represent nothing but some open place of an ordinary extent where those that are represented by the actors might naturally be in the truth of the action. And when we see it written, "The Scene is at Aulis, Eleusis, or Argos," it is not that the place where the actors appear is all that town or province, but only that all the intrigues of the play, as well what passes out of the sight of the spectators as what they see, are treated in that town of which the stage takes up but the least part.

Thus in the prologue of the last comedy of Plautus, the poet, explaining the place of the scene, says that he begs of the Romans a little space in the middle of their noble buildings to transport thither the town of Athens without the help of architects.[3] Upon which Samuel Petit [4] observes that we ought not to imagine that Plautus pretends to place all the city of Athens in that of Rome, but only a small part of it where the things represented in the play did come to pass, to wit, the quarter of the Plotaeans, and of all that quarter only the place where Phronesion lived. And he confirms this by the mending of two Greek words, of which he pretends one Latin one was made by a mistake, and by a verse which he mends by some manuscripts which he had seen, making the Prologue then speak thus: "I abridge here the town of Athens upon this stage during this play, and in this house lives Phronesion."

These are the only authorities of any either ancient or modern authors that I have found concerning the place of the scene. Castelvetro indeed says that tragedy requires but a small space, but since he has not explained himself better, we are not bound to guess in his favor.

These things, then, once settled for the doctrine or theory, I have thought of what follows for the practical part. The poet does not desire to represent to his spectators all the particulars of his story, [but only the principal and most beautiful circumstances. On the one hand he cannot do so since he would have to include too many incidents and transactions; thus he is obliged to suppose some of them to be beyond the view of the spectators. On the other hand he should not do so, since there are a hundred horrible, indecent, low, and almost useless things which he must hide, informing the spectators of them either by a mere narration which corrects them, or by an easy act of the imagination.] He must then first of all consider exactly what persons he most wants and cannot well be without, then let him choose a place where they may probably meet; for as there are places which certain persons cannot leave without extraordinary motives, so there are others where they cannot be without great reason. A nun cannot leave the place of her retreat but upon some pressing motive, and a woman of honor cannot accompany Messalina to the place of her infamous debauches.

Besides, he must observe whether or not in his subject there be not some circumstances or notable incident which it will be necessary to preserve for the beauty of his play and which cannot happen but in a certain place, for then he must accommodate to that the rest of his parts. So he that would show Celadon half dead upon the shore and found there by Galatea must, of necessity, place his scene upon the bank of a river and accommodate to it the rest of the theatral action. Plautus followed this method in his *Rudens*, where he desired to show the relics of a shipwreck and therefore was forced to place his scene on the seaside, where all the rest of his adventures are very dexterously brought to pass.

The poet, having chosen the place, must examine next what things are fittest to be showed with delight to the spectators and be sure to represent them. As for the others not so fit to be seen, they must be told some way that they may be supposed done, and that in places so near the stage that the actor who tells them may be supposed to have been there and back again from the time he has been absent from the stage, or else he must be supposed gone before the play began, for then he may come as far off as you will. All which Terence hath observed in his third comedy, where the two slaves, Syrus and Dromo, had been sent a great while before for Clitophon's mistress, and, by consequence, all that Syrus tells of their negotiation is very credible — what time soever there needed for the dressing of the lady and the doing of all the rest.

And if the things or places to be spoke of in the play have been done too far from the scene or are in themselves too remote, one must bring them nearer in the representation, which may be done two ways: either by supposing that they happened in other places nearer when it is all one to the story (as Donatus [5] observes that in plays country houses are always supposed to be in the suburbs), or else by supposing the places nearer than they really are when it is impossible to change them; but in this last, one must observe not to bring known places so near that the spectator cannot follow the poet in his belief. As, for example, if a man should bring the Alps or Pyrenaean mountains in the place of Mount Valerian that so he might bring an incident to play which else he could not, the scene being at Paris, truly the rigor of the rule would be followed as to the unity of the scene and its decencies, but beauty of the art, which is to please and persuade, would be lost. It is therefore that I cannot approve of this force upon nature as to the distance of places which we see done in the *Suppliants* and the *Andromache* of Euripides, in the *Captives* of Plautus and some other pieces of antiquity. I speak not here of our modern poets, for all the world knows there never was anything so monstrous in this point as the plays we have seen in Italy, Spain, and France, and indeed, except the *Horatius* of Corneille, I doubt whether we have one play where the unity of the scene is rigorously observed — at least I am sure I have not seen any.

It is necessary to give one advertisement more to the poet in this place, which is that none of his actors ought to come upon the scene without some apparent reason, since else it is not probable they should be there, and he must avoid to follow the example of a poet who made a princess come a-purpose out of her tent upon the stage which was before it to say some passionate complaints of a secret misfortune of hers, for it was much more probable that she should make them in her tent.[6] Therefore he ought to have feigned either that the company of some people in the tent was importunate and troublesome to her and that to avoid them she came out, or else he ought to have given her some sudden impatience to look out, and then, as naturally upon reflections of our misfortunes we are carried to expressions of them, he might have put in her mouth what words he had thought necessary for his subject. Thus when the passion of some person upon the scene is to be showed by some narration which the spectator has had already and which cannot be repeated without disgust, one must suppose the thing to have been told that person in some place near the scene and make him come in near towards the end of it with words in his mouth expressing the knowledge of the thing and causing the passion he is to show afterwards upon the stage. The examples of this are frequent among the ancients, and the imitation of them cannot but succeed well.

Book II, Chapter 7

THE EXTENT OF THE THEATRAL ACTION, OR OF THE TIME FIT TO BE ALLOWED A DRAMATIC POEM

There is no question more debated than this which I am now treating. The poets make it their discourse, and the players scarce talk of anything else, as well as those who frequent the theatres; nay, the ladies in their *ruelles* undertake to decide it, and all this while the thing is so little understood that I have a great deal of reason to endeavor to explain it carefully. To talk with some knowledge, then, of this matter one must consider that a dramatic poem has two sorts of time, each of which has a different and proper lasting.

The first is the true time of the representation; for though this sort of poem be but an image, and so ought to be considered as having a representative being, nevertheless one ought to consider that there is a reality in the very representation. For really the actors are seen and heard, the verses are really pronounced, and one suffers really either pleasure or pain in assisting at these representations, and there is a real time spent in amusing the audience, that is from the opening of the stage to the end of the play. This time is called the lasting of the representation.

Of this time the measure can be no other but so much time as will reasonably spend the patience of the audience, for this sort of poem being made for pleasure, it ought not to weary and fatigate the mind; and it must not likewise be so short as that the spectators go away with an opinion of not having been well nor enough diverted. In all this, experience is the faithfullest guide and tells us most commonly that a play cannot last above three hours without wearying of us, nor less without coming short of pleasing us. I have seen a very learned gentleman who was present at the representation of the *Pastor Fido* in Italy who told me that never was anything so tedious, it having lasted too long, and that this play, which ravishes the reader because he can lay it by when he will, had most horridly disgusted the spectators.

There is another observation to be made here, which is that the time which we allow the representation may be spent many other ways.

The ancients had in their tragedies many different mixtures, as *mimes*, *pantomimes*, and other buffoons. These diversions pleased the people, and yet I do not believe they made the representations longer than those of our time, for besides that these interludes were short, their tragedies themselves were not of above a thousand verses and those verses much shorter than our heroic ones. Therefore the poet must take great care that if his play be of the ordinary length, his interludes be not too long, for let them be never so pleasing, they will disquiet the spectator in the impatience which he will naturally have to know the event and success of the story.

The other time of the dramatic poem is that of the action represented so far as it is considered as a true action and containing all that space which is necessary to the performing of those things which are to be exposed to the knowledge of the spectators from the first to the last act of the play.

Now this time is the chief time, not only because it is natural to the poem, but because also it all depends on the poet's invention and is made known by the mouth of his actors according as his ingenuity can suggest him the means of doing it, and this is the time so much talked of in our days. The three Greek tragics, Aeschylus, Euripides, and Sophocles, allow but a few hours to the lasting of the theatral action in their poems, but their example was not followed by the poets who succeed them; for Aristotle blames those of his time for giving too long an extent to the lasting of their plays, which makes him set down the rule, or rather renew it from the model of the ancients, saying that tragedy ought to be comprehended in the revolution of one sun. I do not know whether this rule was observed by those that came after him as by the authors of those tragedies which carry the name of Seneca, which are regular enough in this circumstance. But for all those that I have seen which were made at the reestablishment of learning in Spain and France, they are not only irregular in this point but in all the other most sensible rules, insomuch that one would admire that men of learning should be the authors of them. When I first had the honor to be near Cardinal Richelieu, I found the stage in great esteem but loaded with all these errors and particularly with that of exceeding the time fit to be allowed in tragedy. I spoke of it in those plays which were acted at court, but I was generally opposed and, most commonly, turned into ridicule both by the poets, the actors, and the spectators. And when I, to defend myself, began to allege the ancients, I was paid with this answer, that what they had done was well for their time, but nowadays they would be laughed at if they were here, as if the general reason of mankind could grow old with time. And accordingly we see that at last it has prevailed over prejudice and ignorance to make all the world confess that the time of a tragedy ought to be short and limited. But because even in this there are different interpretations given to Aristotle, and that some poets do believe to circumscribe too narrowly the lasting of the theatral action would be to spoil most of the incidents, I will here give the true explanation of the rule and ways of practising it with success. Aristotle has said that one of the principal differences which is between an epic poem and a tragedy is that the first is not limited in any time and that the second is comprehended in the revolution of one sun. Now though Aristotle does express himself in few words, yet I cannot understand how there was ground for so much dispute. For since he says the revolution of one sun, it cannot be meant the annual revolution, for that is the time generally allowed to an epic poem, and there is none of the most indulgent that have offered to extend the rule to that excess in tragedy. It remains then to say he means the diurnal revolution but as the day is considered two ways — the one with regard to the *primum mobile*, which is called the natural day and is of twenty-four hours, and the other by the sun's presence upon the horizon between his rising and setting, which is called the artificial day. It is necessary to observe that Aristotle means only the artificial day, in the extent of which he makes the theatral action to be comprehended. Castelvetro and Piccolomini upon Aristotle's poetic are of this opinion against Segni, who extends the rule to the natural day of twenty-four hours.[7]

The reason of this is certain and founded upon the nature of dramatic poems, for this sort of poem ought to carry a sensible image of the actions of human life. Now we do not see that regularly men are busy before day nor much after night, and accordingly in all well governed places there are magistrates to watch those who employ the night, naturally designed for rest, in the actions of the day.

Besides, we have said, and it cannot be called in question, that the theatral action ought to be one, and not comprehend any other actions which are not necessary to the intrigue of the stage. Now how can that be observed in a play of twenty-four hours? Would it not be a necessity that the persons acting should sleep and eat and busy themselves in many things which would not be of the subject of the play, and though the poet should say nothing of it, yet the spectators must needs conceive it so.

But, besides, the action of the stage is to be continued and not interrupted or broken. Now that could not be in a play of twenty-four hours; nature could not without some rest endure so long an action, since all that men can commonly do is to be in action for the daytime.

Moreover we cannot omit a reason of the ancients which originally is essential to tragedy, which is that the choruses which they used did not regularly use to stir off the stage for the whole play or at least from the time they first came on, and I do not know with what appearance of probability the spectators could have been persuaded that people who were never out of their sight should have stayed twenty-four hours in that place, nor how, in the truth of the action, they could imagine that those whom they represented had passed all that time without satisfying some necessities of nature.

After all, we can never better understand Aristotle than by those three excellent tragic poets whom he always proposes for examples who have regularly observed not to give above twelve hours to their plays. And I do not think that there are any of their works which do comprehend the whole space between the rising and setting of the sun.

It being most certain that their stage generally opens after sunrise and is shut up before sunset, as one may observe in the comedies of Plautus and Terence, it is therefore that Rossi,[8] an Italian, allows but eight or ten hours. And Scaliger, more rigorously but more reasonably, would have the whole action performed in six hours. It were even to be wished that the action of the poem did not take up more time than that of the representation; but that being hard and almost impossible, in certain occasions the poet has the liberty to suppose a longer time by some hours, in which the music that marks the intervals of the acts, and the relations of the actors upon the stage while others are busy off of it ([together] with the natural desire of the spectators to see the event), do all contribute very much and help to deceive the audience so as to make them think there has passed time enough for the performance of the things represented.

What we have said hitherto of Aristotle's rule might suffer some difficulty in those plays which represent actions that happened in the night, if we did not own that he has forseen the objection when he says that "tragedy endeavors to comprehend its action in the revolution of one sun, or in changing that time a little," for by that means he lets us know that the poet is not always bound to place his action between sunrising and sunsetting, but may take a like time out of twenty-four hours and place his action in the night, as in the *Rhesus* of Euripides and some other plays of the ancients of which we have nothing but fragments in Athenaeus. Nay, he may take some of his time in the day and the rest in the night, as Euripides has done in his *Electra* and Plautus in his *Amphitryon*. They that upon this of Aristotle have said that he gave leave to exceed the revolution of a sun and go some hours beyond did not well understand him, having taken the word "changing" for "exceeding."

But without standing upon this scrupulous niceness, I must tell the poet that he need not fear to spoil his play by straitening his incidents in so small a compass of time; for quite contrary, it is that which shall make his play agreeable and wonderful, it is that which will afford him the means of introducing extraordinary surprises and passions which he may carry as far as he will. Let him consider well *Horatius, Cinna, Polyeucte*, and *Nicomedes*, the latter works of Monsieur Corneille, and I believe he cannot but agree to it.

Now, to contribute for my share to the necessary means of practising this rule, I here deliver my thoughts.

First, let the poet be very careful in choosing the day in which he will comprehend all the intrigues of his play, and that choice ought generally to be made from the most noble incident of the whole story, that is, from that incident which is to make the catastrophe and to which all others do tend, like lines to their center; and if he be free to take what day he will, his best will be to pitch upon that which will most easily bear the assemblage and concurrence of all the incidents of the stage. So Corneille, being to represent the death of Pompey, took the last day of his life because he could not do otherwise, but when he was to make his *Cinna*, he chose what day he pleased for to facilitate the bringing in of the conspiration of Cinna with the deliberation of Augustus whether he should forsake the Empire or no. The choice being thus made, the next sleight is to open your stage as near as it is possible to the catastrophe, that you may employ less time in the negotiation part and have more liberty in extending the passions and discourses which may please; but to execute this luckily the incidents must be prepared by ingenious contrivances, and that must appear upon occasion in the whole conduct of the action.

This we may observe in the *Ion* of Euripides, the *Amphitryon* of Plautus, and the *Andria* of Terence. Corneille practises it likewise well in *Horatius* and *Cinna*. The stage in *Horatius* is opened but a moment before the combat of the three Horatiuses against the three Curiatiuses who are told of their being chosen to fight against each other as soon as they come upon the stage. And Cinna had already made his conspiracy before the opening of the stage, which opens just before the sacrifice which was to be the pretext of the execution of it.

Things being thus disposed, the poet must next study to bring together the incidents all in one day so artfully that there appear no force nor constraint in the effecting of it. And to succeed in this he must rectify the time of those things that happened before the opening of the stage, and suppose some of them to come to pass that day, though they really happened before, but he must join them with so much art as they may seem to be naturally connected and not put together by the poet's invention.

Thus Sophocles makes that Creon, who was sent to Delphos to consult the Oracle, comes back just at the same time that the news comes to Thebes of the death of Polybius, king of Corinth, though these two things did not happen on the same day. So Plautus makes Amphitryon return victorious that very night that Alcmena is brought to bed of Hercules. But that which one must particularly have a care of is not to conjoin the time of the incidents with so much precipitation that probability be destroyed by it, as in the *Suppliants* of Euripides, the *Captives* of Plautus, and some other pieces of the ancients which I cannot approve of, though for some other considerations they are not unexcusable. They are indeed according to the rule of time, but without any of the graces of the art. In a word, we must still remember that Aristotle, in giving his rule of the confining tragedy to the revolution of one sun, means that the poet ought so to press his imagination as to order all the events of his theatre in that time, but so as not to offend probability, which is always the principal rule and without which all the others become no rules at all.

Book IV, Chapter 5
OF DIDACTIC DISCOURSES OR INSTRUCTIONS

This is new subject in our dramatic art, I not having found anything in those authors who have composed great volumes about it, and I am the first that have made observations upon it such as I may boldly say ought not to be despised by our poets.

I understand then by didactic discourses those maxims and general propositions which contain known truths and are only applied in the play according as the subject will allow, tending more to instruct the audience in the rules of morality than to explain any part of the intrigue afoot. An example may illustrate the thing better. Suppose then the poet had a mind to treat this proposition: "The gods are just, and were they not so, they would cease to be gods." Or this: "A general instinct cannot be suspected of error." Or this: "A subject that rebels against his prince is criminal." I say that a poet often endeavors to set out some of these maxims by a great number of verses upon which he demurs a great while, leaving all that time his subject and the intrigue of the stage and keeping himself still upon general notions.

Now as to these didactic discourses, I distinguish them into two sorts; some I call physical and the others moral ones.

I call those physical or natural which make a deduction or description of the nature, qualities, or effects of anything, without distinction whether it be in the rank of natural or supernatural things or of the number of artificial compounds.

Under the notion of moral discourses I comprehend all those instructions which contain any maxim of religion, or politics, or economics, or that anyways regard human life.

To come after this to my observations, we must lay it down as a maxim that all these didactic discourses are of their own nature unfit for the stage because they are cold and without motion, being general things which only tend to instruct the mind but not to move the heart, so that the action of the stage, which ought to warm our affections, becomes by them dull and indifferent. Young people who come to read Euripides and Sophocles admire the first much more than the latter, and yet Sophocles almost always carried the prize from Euripides upon the stage and that by the judgment of all the Athenians. This mistake of the young reader proceeds from this, that they being themselves not thoroughly instructed in those maxims and finding a great many of them in Euripides, as well about religion as politics and moral ones, they are charmed to see such truths so nobly expressed, and the things themselves, being new to them, please them beyond measure. It is for this that Quintilian, in his precepts of rhetoric, advises young people to the lecture of Euripides before Sophocles. In all which they do not observe that Sophocles makes the groundwork of his plays of those very truths as well as Euripides, but he does it with so much art that he utters them in a pathetic manner as well as in a didactic one; whereby the people of Athens departed almost always pleased and charmed by the high passions which Sophocles fills his stages with, but were more used to Euripides's maxims which he so often beats over to them and by that means did not consider them as anything rare and extraordinary. And from thence it proceeds that in our modern plays those very places in which the poets have labored by noble verses and high words to express some great maxim have least succeeded, because that falling into the didactic way they forsake the business of the stage and let the action cool. From thence it comes likewise that all actors that appear with the pedantic character of teaching, such as are the governor of a young prince, a doctor, a governess, or the like, are still ill received by the audience; the very presence of them displeases and imprints the character of ridicule upon the most serious piece. I am confident that if the Linco in *Pastor fido* appeared upon our stage, he would be hissed off of it, notwithstanding all the good counsel he gives Sylvio; and that which makes me believe it the sooner is that one of our best modern plays lost half its due applause by there being a governor to a young prince who was giving him advice in the midst of most violent passions with which he was tormented, that being neither the time, nor the stage the place, for such instructions.

We do not see neither that either astrologers, conjurers, high priests, or any of that character do much take, for the very reason that they can hardly speak without pretending to teach or else talk in generals of the power of the gods, the wonderful effects of nature, and such things which cannot fail of being tedious when they are prolixly expressed. Scaliger will not allow them in the very epic poems; much less can they be received in the dramatic but ought to be quite banished the stage.

We must observe, besides, that physical instructions about nature and its effects are yet less welcome than moral ones, because that it is hard an actor should speak so long as to explain the nature of a thing without disgusting the audience, which soon grows weary of being ill taught the thing the poet would have him learn; which together with the little concern the no passion of the stage raises in him makes the whole very disagreeable. We have a notable example of this in *Mariamne*,[9] where a long discourse is made of the nature of dreams. The thing is very fine, and the nature of them well explained, but it interrupts an agitation of the stage begun by Herod's trouble at his waking. The audience would fain know the cause of his disturbance and the particulars of his dream, but instead of that, there is a long discourse of the nature of dreams in general, to which the spectator gives but little attention as being thereby disappointed of his chief expectation.

To all this it may be objected that the stage is a place of public instruction, and that the dramatic poet is to instruct as well as please, and therefore that didactic discourses may be proper enough or at least ought not to be condemned.

I confess that the stage is a place of instruction, but we must well understand how that is meant. The poet ought to bring his whole action before the spectator, which ought to be so represented with all its circumstances that the audience be fully instructed; for as dramatic poetry does but imitate human actions, it does it only to instruct us by them, and that it does directly and properly. But for moral maxims which may incite us either to the love of virtue or stir us up to hate vice, it does it indirectly and by the *entremise* of the actions themselves; of which sentiment Scaliger is so much as I dare quote him for my warrantee in this opinion. Now this may be done two ways: the first, when the action of the stage is so judiciously managed that it shows the force of virtue triumphing in the midst of persecutions, after which it is often happily rewarded, but if it is totally overwhelmed by them it remains glorious even in its death. By this all the deformities of vice are discovered; it is often punished, but when even it triumphs and overcomes, it is in abomination with the audience who thereupon are apt to conclude with themselves that it is better to embrace virtue through the hazard of persecution than to follow vice even with hopes of impunity.

It is thus principally that the stage ought to be instructive to the public — by the knowledge of things represented; and I have always observed that it is not agreeable to the audience that a man who swerves from the way of virtue should be set right and repent by the strength of precepts and sentences. We rather desire it should be by some adventure that presses him and forces him to take up reasonable and virtuous sentiments. We should hardly endure that Herod should recall his sentence against Mariamne upon a remonstrance of one of the seven wise men of Greece; but we are pleased to see that after the death of the queen, his love becomes his tormentor, and, having opened his eyes, drives him into so sincere a repentance that he is ready to sacrifice his life to the regret he has for his crime.

As for the other way of teaching morality, it depends much on the ingeniousness of the poet when he strengthens his theatral action with divers pithy and bold truths, which being imperceptibly worked into his play are, as it were, the nerves and strength of it. For, in a word, that which I condemn in common didactics is their style and manner of expression, not the things themselves, since those great truths which are, as it were, the foundation of the conduct of human actions, I am so far from banishing them off the stage that quite contrary I think them very necessary and ornamental — which to attain I give these following observations.

First, these general maxims must be so fastened to the subject and linked by many circumstances with the persons acting that the actor may seem to think more of that concern of his he is about than of saying fine things; that is, to speak in terms of rhetoric, he must reduce the thesis to the hypothesis and of universal propositions make particular applications, for by this means the poet avoids the suspicion of aiming to instruct pedantically, since his actors do not leave their business which they are about. For example, I would not have an actor spend many words to prove that "Virtue is always persecuted," but he may say to the party concerned, "Do you think to have better measure than virtue has always had, and can you expect to be privileged from persecution more than Socrates or Cato?" And so continue a little, speaking still to the party present and upon the subject in hand, by which means these discourses seem a little to keep off from being too general precepts and so, disgust the less.

Secondly, in all these occasions the poet must use figurative speech, either by interrogation, irony, or others that his fancy shall suggest; for these figures, by not circumstancing minutely the general propositions, make them more florid, and so, by ornaments, free them from the didactic character. As, for example, if there be a design of advising a young woman to obey her parents, instead of preaching downright obedience to her, I think an irony would do better. As thus: "That's a fine way indeed for a virtuous young lady to attain the reputation of a good daughter, to be carried away by her own passions and neglect not only the censure of the best sort of people but break through all the fences of duty and honor."

My third observation is that when any of these great maxims are to be proposed bluntly and in plain words, it be done in as few as may be; by that means they do not cool the stage but add something to the variety of it. But there must be care taken that this do not happen in the midst of a violent passion, for besides that in those cases men do not naturally speak sentences, the actor cannot then appear with that moderation which those reflections require. Seneca is very guilty of this fault in all his tragedies, where most commonly in the heat of passion all his fine commonplaces are bestowed upon the audience.

We have, nevertheless, some examples of didactic propositions made in direct terms and at length, not without some success, in Corneille, which to attain as well as he requires the same ingenuity and art. The expressions must be strong and seem to have been said only for that particular subject to which they are applied, and that requires a particular genius and much study to accomplish.

I have observed, besides, that common truths, though in a didactic style, yet do very well upon the stage in the mouth of a rogue or a cheat when his character is known; for the spectator is delighted to see him cunningly use all the maxims and discourses of a good man to intents and purposes quite contrary, so that by that means it is all figurative and moves the attention of the audience.

One may likewise successfully enough burlesque all these common truths, but that can be performed nowhere but in comedy, where, by that means, they forsake their natural state and are disguised under a new appearance which causes both variety and ornament. But tragedy in its own nature is too grave to admit of anything so low and buffoon as this would be; neither do I remember to have met with anything of that kind in any serious tragedy — I say serious tragedy because that in satirical tragedy there was admitted a mixture of heroic actions and low buffooneries, and therefore this disguising of serious precepts might have room among the rest in them.

Pierre Corneille OF THE THREE UNITIES OF ACTION, TIME, AND PLACE

The two preceding discourses and the critical examination of the plays which my first two volumes contain have furnished me so many opportunities to explain my thoughts on these matters that there would be little left for me to say if I absolutely forbade myself to repeat.

I hold then, as I have already said, that in comedy, unity of action consists in the unity of plot or the obstacle to the plans of the principal actors, and in tragedy in the unity of peril, whether the hero falls victim to it or escapes. It is not that I claim that several perils cannot be allowed in the latter or several plots or obstacles in the former, provided that one passes necessarily from one to the other; for then escape from the first peril does not make the action complete since the escape leads to another danger; and the resolution of one plot does not put the actors at rest since they are confounded afresh in another. My memory does not furnish me any ancient examples of this multiplicity of perils linked each to each without the destruction of the unity of action; but I have noted independent double action as a defect in *Horace* and in *Théodore*, for it is not necessary that the first kill his sister upon gaining his victory nor that the other give herself up to martyrdom after having escaped prostitution; and if the death of Polyxène and that of Astyanax in Seneca's *Trojan Women* do not produce the same irregularity I am very much mistaken.

In the second place, the term unity of action does not mean that tragedy should show only one action on the stage. The one which the poet chooses for his subject must have a beginning, a middle, and an end; and not only are these three parts separate actions which find their conclusion in the principal one, but, moreover, each of them may contain several others with the same subordination. There must be only one complete action, which leaves the mind of the spectator serene; but that action can become complete only through several others which are less perfect and which, by serving as preparation, keep the spectator in a pleasant suspense. This is what must be contrived at the end of each act in order to give continuity to the action. It is not necessary that we know exactly what the actors are doing in the intervals which separate the acts, nor even that they contribute to the action when they do not appear on the stage; but it is necessary that each act leave us in the expectation of something which is to take place in the following one.

If you asked me what Cléopâtre is doing in *Rodogune* between the time when she leaves her two sons in the second act until she rejoins Antiochus in the fourth, I should be unable to tell you, and I do not feel obliged to account for her; but the end of this second act prepares us to see an amicable effort by the two brothers to rule and to hide Rodogune from the venomous hatred of their mother. The effect of this is seen in the third act, whose ending prepares us again to see another effort by Antiochus to win back these two enemies one after the other and for what Séleucus does in the fourth, which compels that unnatural mother [Cleopatra] to resolve upon what she tries to accomplish in the fifth, whose outcome we await with suspense.

In *Le Menteur* the actors presumably make use of the whole interval between the third and fourth acts to sleep; their rest, however, does not impede the continuity of the action between those two acts because the third does not contain a complete event. Dorante ends it with his plan to seek ways to win back the trust of Lucrèce, and at the very beginning of the next he appears so as to be able to talk to one of her servants and to her, should she show herself.

When I say that it is not necessary to account for what the actors do when they are not on stage, I do not mean that it is not sometimes very useful to give such an accounting, but only that one is not forced to do it, and that one ought to take the trouble to do so only when what happens behind the scenes is necessary for the understanding of what is to take place before the spectators. Thus I say nothing of what Cléopâtre did between the second and the fourth acts, because during all that time she can have done nothing important as regards the principal action which I am preparing for; but I point out in the very first lines of the fifth act that she has used the interval between these latter two for the killing of Séleucus, because that death is part of the action. This is what leads me to state that the poet is not required to show all the particular actions which bring about the principal one; he must choose to show those which are the most ad-

102

vantageous, whether by the beauty of the spectacle or by the brilliance or violence of the passions they produce, or by some other attraction which is connected with them, and to hide the others behind the scenes while informing the spectator of them by a narration or by some other artistic device; above all, he must remember that they must all be so closely connected that the last are produced by the preceding and that all have their source in the protasis which ought to conclude the first act. This rule, which I have established in my first *Discourse*, although it is new and contrary to the usage of the ancients, is founded on two passages of Aristotle. Here is the first of them: "There is a great difference," he says, "between events which succeed each other and those which occur because of others." [1] The Moors come into the *Cid* after the death of the Count and not because of the death of the Count; and the fisherman comes into *Don Sanche* after Charles is suspected of being the Prince of Aragon and not because he is suspected of it; thus both are to be criticized. The second passage is even more specific and says precisely "that everything that happens in tragedy must arise necessarily or probably from what has gone before." [2]

The linking of the scenes which unites all the individual actions of each act and of which I have spoken in criticizing *La Suivante* is a great beauty in a poem and one which serves to shape continuity of action through continuity of presentation; but, in the end, it is only a beauty and not a rule. The ancients did not always abide by it although most of their acts have but two or three scenes. This made things much simpler for them than for us, who often put as many as nine or ten scenes into each act. I shall cite only two examples of the scorn with which they treated this principle: one is from Sophocles, in *Ajax*, whose monologue before he kills himself has no connection with the preceding scene; the other is from the third act of Terence's *The Eunuch*, where Antipho's soliloquy has no connection with Chremes and Pythias who leave the stage when he enters. The scholars of our century, who have taken the ancients for models in the tragedies they have left us, have even more neglected that linking than did the ancients, and one need only glance at the plays of Buchanan, Grotius, and Heinsius, of which I spoke in the discussion of *Polyeucte*, to agree on that point. We have so far accustomed our audiences to this careful linking of scenes that they cannot now witness a detached scene without considering it a defect; the eye and even the ear are outraged by it even before the mind has been able to reflect upon it. The fourth act of *Cinna* falls below the others through this flaw; and what formerly was not a rule has become one now through the assiduousness of our practice.

I have spoken of three sorts of linkings in the discussion of *La Suivante*: I have shown myself averse to those of sound, indulgent to those of sight, favorable to those of presence and speech; but in these latter I have confused two things which ought to be separated. Links of presence and speech both have, no doubt, all the excellence imaginable; but there are links of speech without presence and of presence without speech which do not reach the same level of excellence. An actor who speaks to another from a hiding-place without showing himself forms a link of speech without presence which is always effective; but that rarely happens. A man who remains on stage merely to hear what will be said by those whom he sees making their entrance forms a link of presence without speech; this is often clumsy and falls into mere pretense, being contrived more to accede to this new convention which is becoming a precept than for any need dictated by the plot of the play. Thus, in the third act of *Pompée*, Achorée, after having informed Charmion of the reception Caesar gave to the king when he presented to him the head of that hero, remains on the stage where he sees the two of them come together merely to hear what they will say and report it to Cléopâtre. Ammon does the same thing in the fourth act of *Andromède* for the benefit of Phinée, who retires when he sees the king and all his court arriving. Characters who become mute connect rather badly scenes in which they play little part and in which they count for nothing. It is another matter when they hide in order to find out some important secret from those who are speaking and who think they are not overheard, for then the interest which they have in what is being said, added to a reasonable curiosity to find out what they cannot learn in any other way, gives them an important part in the action despite their silence; but in these two examples Ammon and Achorée lend so cold a presence to the scenes they overhear that, to be perfectly frank, whatever feigned reason I give them to serve as pretext for their action, they remain there only to connect the scenes with those that precede, so easily can both plays dispense with what they do.

Although the action of the dramatic poem must have its unity, one must consider both its parts: the complication and the resolution. "The complication is composed," according to Aristotle, "in part of what has happened off stage before the beginning of the action which is there described, and in part from what happens on stage; the rest belongs to the resolution.

The change of fortune forms the separation of these two parts. Everything which precedes it is in the first part, and this change, with what follows it, concerns the other." [3] The complication depends entirely upon the choice and industrious imagination of the poet and no rule can be given for it, except that in it he ought to order all things according to probability or necessity, a point which I have discussed in the second *Discourse*; to this I add one piece of advice, which is that he involve himself as little as possible with things which have happened before the action he is presenting. Such narrations are annoying, usually because they are not expected, and they disturb the mind of the spectator, who is obliged to burden his memory with what has happened ten or twelve years before in order to understand what he is about to see; but narrations which describe things which happen and take place behind the scenes once the action has started always produce a better effect because they are awaited with some curiosity and are a part of the action which is being shown. One of the reasons why so many illustrious critics favor *Cinna* above anything else I have done is that it contains no narration of the past, the one Cinna makes in describing his plot to Emilie being rather an ornament which tickles the mind of the spectators than a necessary marshaling of the details they must know and impress upon their memories for the understanding of what is to come. Emilie informs them adequately in the first two scenes that he is conspiring against Augustus in her favor, and if Cinna merely told her that the plotters are ready for the following day he would advance the action just as much as by the hundred lines he uses to tell both what he said to them and the way in which they received his words. There are plots which begin at the very birth of the hero like that of *Héraclius*, but these great efforts of the imagination demand an extraordinary attention of the spectator and often keep him from taking a real pleasure in the first performances, so much do they weary him.

In the resolution I find two things to avoid: the mere change of intention and the machine. Not much skill is required to finish a poem when he who has served as the obstacle to the plans of the principal actors for four acts desists in the fifth without being constrained to do so by any remarkable event; I have spoken of this in the first *Discourse* and I shall add nothing to that here. The machine requires no more skill when it is used only to bring down a god who straightens everything out when the actors are unable to do so. It is thus that Apollo functions in the *Orestes*: this prince and his friend Pylades, accused by Tyndarus and Menelaus of the death of Clytemnestra and condemned after prosecution by them, seize Helen and Hermione; they kill, or think they kill the first, and threaten to do so the same with the other if the sentence pronounced against them is not revoked. To smooth out these difficulties Euripides seeks nothing subtler than to bring Apollo down from heaven, and he, by absolute authority, orders that Orestes marry Hermione and Pylades Electra; and lest the death of Helen prove an obstacle to this, it being improbable that Hermione would marry Orestes since he had just killed her mother, Apollo informs them that she is not dead, that he has protected her from their blows and carried her off to heaven at the moment when they thought they were killing her. This use of the machine is entirely irrelevant, being founded in no way on the rest of the play, and makes a faulty resolution. But I find a little too harsh the opinion of Aristotle, who puts on the same level the chariot Medea uses to flee from Corinth after the vengeance she has taken on Creon. It seems to me there is a sufficient basis for this in the fact that she has been made a magician and that actions of hers as far surpassing natural forces as that one have been mentioned in the play. After what she did for Jason at Colchis and after she had made his father Aeson young again following his return, and after she had attached invisible fire to the gift she gave to Creusa, the flying chariot is not improbable and the poem has no need of other preparation for that extraordinary effect. Seneca gives it preparation by this line which Medea speaks to her nurse:

Tuum quoque ipsa corpus hinc mecum aveham; [4]

and I by this one which she speaks to Aegeus

I shall follow you tomorrow by a new road.

Thus the condemnation of Euripides, who took no precautions, may be just and yet not fall on Seneca or on me; and I have no need to contradict Aristotle in order to justify myself on this point.

From the action I turn to the acts, each of which ought to contain a portion of it, but not so equal a portion that more is not reserved for the last than for the others and less given to the first than to the others. Indeed, in the first act one may do no more than depict the moral nature of the characters and mark off how far they have got in the story which is to be presented. Aristotle does not prescribe the number of the acts; Horace limits it to five; [5] and although he prohibits having fewer, the Spaniards are obstinate enough to stop at three and the Italians often do the same thing. The Greeks used to separate the acts by the chanting of the chorus, and since I think it reasonable to believe that in some of their poems they made it chant more than four times, I should not want to say they never exceeded five. This way of distinguishing the acts was less handy than ours, for either they paid attention to what the chorus was chanting or they did not; if they did, the mind of the spectators was too tense and had no time in which to rest; if they did not, attention was too much dissipated by the length of the chant, and when a new act began, an effort of memory was needed to recall to the imagination what had been witnessed and at what point the action had been interrupted. Our orchestra presents neither of these two inconveniences; the mind of the spectator relaxes while the music is playing and even reflects on what he has seen, to praise it or to find fault with it depending on whether he has been pleased or displeased; and the short time the orchestra is allowed to play leaves his impressions so fresh that when the actors return he does not need to make an effort to recall and resume his attention.

The number of scenes in each act has never been prescribed by rule, but since the whole act must have a certain number of lines which make its length proportionate to that of the others, one may include in it more or fewer scenes depending on whether they are long or short to fill up the time which the whole act is to consume. One ought, if possible, to account for the entrance and exit of each actor; I consider this rule indispensable, especially for the exit, and think there is nothing so clumsy as an actor who leaves the stage merely because he has no more lines to speak.

I should not be so rigorous for the entrances. The audience expects the actor, and although the setting represents the room or the study of whoever is speaking, yet he cannot make his appearance there unless he comes out from behind the tapestry, and it is not always easy to give a reason for what he has just done in town before returning home, since sometimes it is even probable that he has not gone out at all. I have never seen anybody take offense at seeing Emilie begin *Cinna* without saying why she has come to her room; she is presumed to be there before the play begins, and it is only stage necessity which makes her appear from behind the scenes to come there. Thus I should willingly dispense from the rigors of the rule the first scene of each act but not the others, because once an actor is on the stage anyone who enters must have a reason to speak to him or, at least, must profit from the opportunity to do so when it offers. Above all, when an actor enters twice in one act, in comedy or in tragedy, he must either lead one to expect that he will soon return when he leaves the first

107

time, like Horace in the second act and Julie in the third act of *Horace*, or explain on returning why he has come back so soon.

Aristotle wishes the well-made tragedy to be beautiful and capable of pleasing without the aid of actors and quite aside from performance.[6] So that the reader may more easily experience that pleasure, his mind, like that of the spectator, must not be hindered, because the effort he is obliged to make to conceive and to imagine the play for himself lessens the satisfaction which he will get from it. Therefore, I should be of the opinion that the poet ought to take great care to indicate in the margin the less important actions which do not merit being included in the lines, and which might even mar the dignity of the verse if the author lowered himself to express them. The actor easily fills this need on the stage, but in a book one would often be reduced to guessing and sometimes one might even guess wrong, unless one were informed in this way of these little things. I admit that this is not the practice of the ancients; but you must also allow me that because they did not do it they have left us many obscurities in their poems which only masters of dramatic art can explain; even so, I am not sure they succeed as often as they think they do. If we forced ourselves to follow the method of the ancients completely, we should make no distinction between acts and scenes because the Greeks did not. This failure on their part is often the reason that I do not know how many acts there are in their plays, nor whether at the end of an act the player withdraws so as to allow the chorus to chant, or whether he remains on stage without any action while the chorus is chanting, because neither they nor their interpreters have deigned to give us a word of indication in the margin.

We have another special reason for not neglecting that helpful little device as they did: this is that printing puts our plays in the hands of actors who tour the provinces and whom we can thus inform of what they ought to do, for they would do some very odd things if we did not help them by these notes. They would find themselves in great difficulty at the fifth act of plays that end happily, where we bring together all the actors on the stage (a thing which the ancients did not do); they would often say to one what is meant for another, especially when the same actor must speak to three or four people one after the other. When there is a whispered command to make, like Cléopâtre's to Laonice which sends her to seek poison,[7] an aside would be necessary to express this in verse if we were to do without the marginal indications, and that seems to me much more intolerable than the notes, which give us the real and only way, following the opinion of Aristotle, of making the tragedy as beautiful in the reading as in performance, by making it easy for the reader to imagine what the stage presents to the view of the spectators.

The rule of the unity of time is founded on this statement of Aristotle "that the tragedy ought to enclose the duration of its action in one journey of the sun or try not to go much beyond it." [8] These words gave rise to a famous dispute as to whether they ought to be understood as meaning a natural day of twenty-four hours or an artificial day of twelve; each of the two opinions has important partisans, and, for myself, I find that there are subjects so difficult to limit to such a short time that not only should I grant the twenty-four full hours but I should make use of the license which the philosopher gives to exceed them a little and should push the total without scruple as far as thirty. There is a legal maxim which says that we should broaden the mercies and narrow the rigors of the law, *odia restringenda, favores ampliandi*; and I find that an author is hampered enough by this constraint which forced some of the ancients to the very edge of the impossible. Euripides, in *The Suppliants*, makes Theseus leave Athens with an army, fight a battle beneath the walls of Thebes, which was ten or twelve leagues away, and return victorious in the following act; and between his departure and the arrival of the messenger who comes to tell the story of his victory, the chorus has only thirty-six lines to speak.[9] That makes good use of such a short time. Aeschylus makes Agamemnon come back from Troy with even greater speed. He had agreed with Clytemnestra, his wife, that as soon as the city was taken he would inform her by signal fires built on the intervening mountains, of which the second would be lighted as soon as the first was seen, the third at the sight of the second, and so on; by this means she was to learn the great news the same night. However, scarcely had she learned it from the signal fires when Agamemnon arrives, whose ship, although battered by a storm, if memory serves, must have traveled as fast as the eye could see the lights.[10] *The Cid* and *Pompée*, where the action is a little precipitate, are far from taking so much license; and if they force ordinary probability in some way, at least they do not go as far as such impossibilities.

Many argue against this rule, which they call tyrannical, and they would be right if it were founded only on the authority of Aristotle; but what should make it acceptable is the fact that common sense supports it. The dramatic poem is an imitation, or rather a portrait of human actions, and it is beyond doubt that portraits gain in excellence in proportion as they resemble the original more closely. A performance lasts two hours and would resemble reality perfectly if the action it presented required no more for its actual occurrence. Let us then not settle on twelve or twenty-four hours, but let us compress the action of the poem into the shortest possible period, so that the performance may more closely resemble reality and thus be more nearly perfect. Let us give, if that is possible, to the one no more than the two hours which the other fills. I do not think that *Rodogune* requires much more, and perhaps two hours would be enough for *Cinna*. It we cannot confine the action within the two hours, let us take four, six, or ten, but let us not go much beyond twenty-four for fear of falling into lawlessness and of so far reducing the scale of the portrait that it no longer has its proportionate dimensions and is nothing but imperfection.

Most of all, I should like to leave the matter of duration to the imagination of the spectators and never make definite the time the action requires unless the subject needs this precision, but especially not when probability is a little forced, as in the *Cid*, because precision serves only to make the crowded action obvious to the spectator. Even when no violence is done to a poem by the necessity of obeying this rule, why must one state at the beginning that the sun is rising, that it is noon at the third act, and that the sun is setting at the end of the last act? This is only an obtrusive affectation; it is enough to establish the possibility of the thing in the time one gives to it and that one be able to determine the time easily if one wishes to pay attention to it, but without being compelled to concern oneself with the matter. Even in those actions which take no longer than the performance it would be clumsy to point out that a half hour has elapsed between the beginning of one act and the beginning of the next.

I repeat what I have said elsewhere,[11] that when we take a longer time, as, for instance, ten hours, I should prefer that the eight extra be used up in the time between the acts and that each act should have as its share only as much time as performance requires especially when all scenes are closely linked together. I think, however, that the fifth act, by special privilege, has the right to accelerate time so that the part of the action which it presents may use up more time than is necessary for performance. The reason for this is that the spectator is by then impatient to see the end, and when the outcome depends on actors who are off stage, all the dialogue given to those who are on stage awaiting news of the others drags and action seems to halt. There is no doubt that from the point where Phocas exits in the fifth act of *Héraclius* until Amyntas enters to relate the manner of his death, more time is needed for what happens off stage than for the speaking of the lines in which Héraclius, Martian, and Pulchérie complain of their misfortune. Prusias and Flaminius, in the fifth act of *Nicomède*, do not have the time they would need to meet at sea, take counsel with each other, and return to the defense of the queen; and the Cid has not enough time to fight a duel with Don Sanche during the conversations of the Infanta with Léonor and of Chimène with Elvire. I was aware of this and yet have had no scruples about this acceleration of which, perhaps, one might find several examples among the ancients, but the laziness of which I have spoken will force me to rest content with this one, which is from the *Andria* of Terence. Simo slips his son Pamphilus into the house of Glycerium in order to get the old man, Crito, to come out and to clear up with him the question of the birth of his mistress, who happens to be the daughter of Chremes. Pamphilus enters the house, speaks to Crito, asks him for the favor and returns with him; and during this exit, this request, and this re-entry, Simo and Chremes, who remain on stage, speak only one line each, which could not possibly give Pamphilus more than time enough to ask where Crito is, certainly not enough to talk with him and to explain to him the reasons for which he should reveal what he knows about the birth of the unknown girl.

When the conclusion of the action depends on actors who have not left the stage and about whom no one is awaiting news, as in *Cinna* and *Rodogune*, the fifth act has no need of this privilege because then all the action takes place in plain sight, as does not happen when part of it occurs off stage after the beginning of the act. The other acts do not merit the same freedom. If there is not time enough to bring back an actor who has made his exit, or to indicate what he has done since that exit, the accounting can be postponed to the following act; and the music, which separates the two acts, may use up as much time as is necessary; but in the fifth act no postponement is possible: attention is exhausted and the end must come quickly.

I cannot forget that although we must reduce the whole tragic action to one day, we can nevertheless make known by a narration or in some other more artful way what the hero of the tragedy has been doing for several years, because there are plays in which the crux of the plot lies in an obscurity of birth which must be brought to light, as in *Oedipus*. I shall not say again that the less one burdens oneself with past actions, the more

111

favorable the spectator will be, because of the lesser degree of trouble he is given when everything takes place in the present and no demands are made on his memory except for what he has seen; but I cannot forget that the choice of a day both illustrious and long-awaited is a great ornament to a poem. The opportunity for this does not always present itself, and in all that I have written until now you will find only four of that kind: the day in *Horace* when two nations are to decide the question of supremacy of empire by a battle; and the ones in *Rodogune, Andromède,* and *Don Sanche.* In *Rodogune* it is a day chosen by two sovereigns for the signature of a treaty of peace between the hostile crowns, for a complete reconciliation of the two rival governments through a marriage, and for the elucidation of a more than twenty-year-old secret concerning the right of succession of one of the twin princes on which the fate of the kingdom depends, as does the outcome of both their loves. The days in *Andromède* and *Don Sanche* are not of lesser importance, but, as I have just said, such opportunities do not often present themselves, and in the rest of my works I have been able to choose days remarkable only for what chance makes happen on them and not by the use to which public arrangements destined them long ago.

As for the unity of place, I find no rule concerning it in either Aristotle or Horace. This is what leads many people to believe that this rule was established only as a consequence of the unity of one day, and leads them to imagine that one can stretch the unity of place to cover the points to which a man may go and return in twenty-four hours. This opinion is a little too free, and if one made an actor travel post-haste, the two sides of the theater might represent Paris and Rouen. I could wish, so that the spectator is not at all disturbed, that what is performed before him in two hours might actually be able to take place in two hours, and that what he is shown in a stage setting which does not change might be limited to a room or a hall depending on a choice made beforehand; but often that is so awkward, if not impossible, that one must necessarily find some way to enlarge the place as also the time of the action. I have shown exact unity of place in *Horace, Polyeucte,* and *Pompée,* but for that it was necessary to present either only one woman, as in *Polyeucte*; or to arrange that the two who are presented are such close friends and have such closely related interests that they can be always together, as in *Horace*; or that they may react as in *Pompée* where the stress of natural curiosity drives Cléopâtre from her apartments in the second act and Cornélie in the fifth; and both enter the great hall of the king's palace in anticipation of the news they are expecting. The same thing is not true of *Rodogune*: Cléopâtre and she have interests which are too divergent to permit them to express their most secret thoughts in the same place. I might say of that play what I have said of *Cinna*, where, in general, everything happens in Rome and, in particular, half of the action takes place in the quarters of Auguste and half of it in Emilie's apartments. Following that arrangement, the first act of this tragedy would be laid in Rodogune's antechamber, the second, in Cléopâtre's apartments, the third, in Rodogune's; but if the fourth act can begin in Rodogune's apartments it cannot finish there, and what Cléopâtre says to her two sons one after the other would be badly out of place there. The fifth act needs a throne room where a great crowd can be gathered. The same problem is found in *Héraclius*. The first act could very well take place in Phocas's quarters, the second, in Léontine's apartments; but if the third begins in Pulchérie's rooms, it cannot end there, and it is outside the bounds of probability that Phocas should discuss the death of her brother in Pulchérie's apartments.

The ancients, who made their kings speak in a public square, easily kept a rigorous unity of place in their tragedies. Sophocles, however, did not observe it in his *Ajax*, when the hero leaves the stage to find a lonely place in which to kill himself and does so in full view of the people; this easily leads to the conclusion that the place where he kills himself is not the one he has been seen to leave, since he left it only to choose another.

We do not take the same liberty of drawing kings and princesses from their apartments, and since often the difference and the opposition on the part of those who are lodged in the same palace do not allow them to take others into their confidence or to disclose their secrets in the same room, we must seek some other compromise about unity of place if we want to keep it intact in our poems; otherwise we should have to decide against many plays which we see succeeding brilliantly.

I hold, then, that we ought to seek exact unity as much as possible, but as this unity does not suit every kind of subject, I should be very willing to concede that a whole city has unity of place. Not that I should want the stage to represent the whole city, that would be somewhat too large, but only two or three particular places enclosed within its walls. Thus the scene of *Cinna* does not leave Rome, passing from the apartments of Auguste to the house of Emilie. *Le Menteur* takes place in the Tuileries and in the Place Royale at Paris, and *La Suite* shows us the prison and

Mélisse's house at Lyons. *The Cid* increases even more the number of particular places without leaving Seville; and since the close linking of scenes is not observed in that play, the stage in the first act is supposed to represent Chimène's house, the Infante's apartments in the king's palace, and the public square; the second adds to these the king's chamber. No doubt there is some excess in this freedom. In order to rectify in some way this multiplication of places when it is inevitable, I should wish two things done: first, that the scene should never change in a given act but only between the acts, as is done in the first three acts of *Cinna*; the other, that these two places should not need different stage settings and that neither of the two should ever be named, but only the general place which includes them both, as Paris, Rome, Lyons, Constantinople, and so forth. This would help to deceive the spectator, who, seeing nothing that would indicate the difference in the places, would not notice the change, unless it was maliciously and critically pointed out, a thing which few are capable of doing, most spectators being warmly intent upon the action which they see on the stage. The pleasure they take in it is the reason why they do not seek out its imperfections lest they lose their taste for it; and they admit such an imperfection only when forced, when it is too obvious, as in *Le Menteur* and *La Suite*, where the different settings force them to recognize the multiplicity of places in spite of themselves.

But since people of opposing interests cannot with verisimilitude unfold their secrets in the same place, and since they are sometimes introduced into the same act through the linking of scenes which the unity of place necessarily produces, one must find some means to make it compatible with the contradiction which rigorous probability finds in it, and consider how to preserve the fourth act of *Rodogune* and the third of *Héraclius*, in both of which I have already pointed out the contradiction which lies in having enemies speak in the same place. Jurists allow legal fictions, and I should like, following their example, to introduce theatrical fictions by which one could establish a theatrical place which would not be Cléopâtre's chamber nor Rodogune's, in the play of that name, nor that of Phocas, of Léontine or of Pulchérie in *Héraclius*, but a room contiguous to all these other apartments, to which I should attribute these two privileges: first, that each of those who speaks in it is presumed to enjoy the same secrecy there as if he were in his own room; and second, that whereas in the usual arrangement it is sometimes proper for those who are on stage to go off, in order to speak privately with others in their rooms, these latter might meet the former on stage without shocking convention, so as to preserve both the unity of place and the linking of scenes. Thus Rodogune, in the first act, encounters Laonice, whom she must send for so as to speak with her; and, in the fourth act, Cléopâtre encounters Antiochus on the very spot where he has just moved Rodogune to pity, even though in utter verisimilitude the prince ought to seek out his mother in her own room since she hates the princess too much to come to speak to him in Rodogune's, which, following the first scene, would be the locus of the whole act, if one did not introduce that compromise which I have mentioned into the rigorous unity of place.

Many of my plays will be at fault in the unity of place if this compromise is not accepted, for I shall abide by it always in the future when I am not able to satisfy the ultimate rigor of the rule. I have been able to reduce only three plays, *Horace, Polyeucte*, and *Pompée,* to the requirements of the rule. If I am too indulgent with myself as far as the others are concerned, I shall be even more so for those which may succeed on the stage through some appearance of regularity. It is easy for critics to be severe; but if they were to give ten or a dozen plays to the public, they might perhaps slacken the rules more than I do, as soon as they have recognized through experience what constraint their precision brings about and how many beautiful things it banishes from our stage. However that may be, these are my opinions, or if you prefer, my heresies concerning the principal points of the dramatic art, and I do not know how better to make the ancient rules agree with modern pleasures. I do not doubt that one might easily find better ways of doing that, and I shall be ready to accept them when they have been put into practice as successfully as, by common consent, mine have been.

Charles de Saint-Evremond SELECTIONS FROM

"THE WORKS OF M. DE SAINT-EVREMOND"

1668

A DISSERTATION ON RACINE'S TRAGEDY CALLED "THE GRAND ALEXANDER"

Since I have read *The Grand Alexander*, the old age of Corneille does not so much alarm me, and I am not so apprehensive that the writing of tragedies will end with him.[1] However, I could wish that before his death he would adopt the author of this piece, and like a tender father give a right cast to the judgment of one who alone deserves to be his successor. I wish that he would give him a good taste of antiquity, which he enjoys to so much advantage; that he would make him enter into the genius of those dead nations, and know judiciously the character of heroes that are now no more. This is, in my opinion, the only thing which is wanting in so great a genius. Some of his thoughts are strong and bold; his expressions equal the force of his thoughts. But then you must give me leave to say he is not acquainted with Alexander or Porus. By his performance one would think that he had a mind to give the world a greater idea of Porus than of Alexander, in which it was not possible for him to succeed; for the history of Alexander, as true as it is, has much of the air of a romance in it, and for an author to make a greater hero than him is to affect to deal in fiction, and rob his work not only of the credit of truth but the agreeableness of probability. Let us not therefore imagine anything greater than this conqueror of the world, otherwise our imaginations will range too far and soar too high. If we would give other heroes an advantage over him, let us take from them the vices which he had and give them the virtues which he had not. Let us not make Scipio greater, although there never was amongst the Romans a soul so aspiring as his; he should be made more just, more disposed to do good, more moderate, more temperate, and more virtuous.

Let not those that are most partial to Caesar against Alexander allege in his favor either passion of glory, greatness of soul, or firmness of resolution. These qualities are so conspicuously shining in the Grecian that to have had them in a higher degree would have been to have had them to excess; but let them make the Roman more wise in his undertakings, more dexterous in his affairs, one that better understood his own interests and was more master of himself in his passions.

A very nice judge of the merits of men is contented to compare to Alexander the man whom he thought worthy of the highest character. He durst not attribute to him greater qualities, but took away from him the bad: *Magno illi Alexandro, sed sobrio nec iracundo simillimus.*[2]

Perhaps these considerations influenced our author in some measure; perhaps, to make Porus the greater man without diving into fables, he thought it convenient to lessen his Alexander. If that was his design, it is impossible for him to have executed it better, for he has made him so moderate a prince that a hundred others may be preferred to him as well as Porus. Not but that Hephestion gives us a fine idea of him, that Taxila and Porus himself speak advantageously enough of his greatness; but when he appears himself he has not force enough to sustain it, unless out of modesty he has a mind to appear an ordinary man amongst the Indians in a just repentance for having been ambitious to pass for a god amongst the Persians. To speak seriously, I can here discern nothing of Alexander but his bare name; his genius, his humor, his qualities appear to me nowhere. I expect to find in an impetuous hero such extraordinary motions as should excite my passion, but I find a prince of so little spirit that he makes no manner of impression upon me. I imagined to find in Porus a greatness of soul which would be somewhat more surprising to us; an Indian hero should have a different character from one of ours. Another heaven, if I may so speak, another sun and another earth produce other animals and other fruits. The men seem to be of another make, by the difference of their faces, and still more, if I dare say so, by a distinction of reason. Both their morals and a wisdom peculiar to their climate seem there to overrule and guide another sort of men in another world. Porus, however, whom Quintus Curtius [3] describes an utter stranger to the Greeks and Persians, is here purely French. Instead of transporting us to the Indies, he is carried into France, where he is so well acquainted with our humor that he seems to have been born or at least to have passed the greatest part of his life among us.

They that undertake to represent some hero of ancient times should enter into the genius of the nation to which he belonged, of the time in which he lived, and particularly into his own. A writer ought to describe a king of Asia otherwise than a Roman consul: one should speak like an absolute monarch, who disposes of his subjects as his slaves; the other, like a magistrate, who only puts the laws in execution, and makes their authority respected by a free people. An old Roman should be described furious for the public good, and moved by a fierce sense of liberty, different from a flatterer of Tiberius's time, who knew nothing but interest, and abandoned himself to the slavery of the age. We should not make the same description of persons of the same condition and the same time when history gives us different characters of them. It would be ridiculous to make the same description of Cato and Caesar, Catiline and Cicero, Brutus and Mark Antony, under pretence that they lived at the same time in the same republic. The spectator, who sees these ancients represented upon our theatres, follows the same rules to judge exactly of them as the poet doth to describe them well, and the better to succeed in this he removes his mind from all that he sees in fashion; he endeavors to disengage himself from the humor of his own time, he renounces the inclination of his own nature if it is opposite to that of the persons represented: for the dead cannot know our manners, but reason, which is of all times, may make us entertain theirs.

One of the greatest faults of our nation is to make all center in it, even to that degree as to call those very persons strangers in their own country who have not exactly either our air or manners. Upon this score we are justly reproached for not knowing how to esteem things but by the relation they have to us, of which Corneille made a sad but undeserved experiment in his *Sophonisbe*. Mairet, who described his [Sophonisbe as] unfaithful to old Syphax, in love with the young and victorious Massinisse, pleased the whole world, in a manner, by hitting upon the inclination of the ladies and the true humor of the courtiers. But Corneille, who makes the Greeks speak better than the Greeks, the Romans than the Romans, the Carthaginians than the citizens of Carthage speak themselves — Corneille, who is almost the only person that has a true taste of antiquity, has had the misfortune not to please our age for representing [the genius of these nations, and preserving] the true character of Hasdrubal's daughter. Thus to the disgrace of our judgments, he that has surpassed all our authors, and has, in this respect, perhaps, even surpassed himself by allowing to those great names all that was their due, could not oblige us to do him the same piece of justice, being enslaved by custom to set a value on those things the present mode recommends, and little disposed by reason to esteem those qualities and sentiments which are not agreeable to our own.

Let us then conclude, after so long a reflection, that Alexander and Porus ought to have preserved their characters entire; that it was our business to view them upon the banks of Hydaspes such as they were, not theirs to come to the banks of the Seine to study our nature and speak our thoughts. The speech of Porus should have had something more unusual and extraordinary in it. If Quintus Curtius has made himself admired for his oration of the Scythians, where he gives them thoughts and expressions natural to their nation, this author might have rendered himself as much admired by representing to us the rarity of a genius of another world.

The different conditions of these two kings, in which both of them behaved themselves so gallantly, their virtue differently exercised in the variety of their fortune, bespeak the attention of historians, and oblige them to describe them to us. The poet, who is at liberty to add to the truth of things, or at least to set them off with all the ornaments of his art, instead of using colors and figures to embellish them has taken away much of their beauty; and whether the scruple of saying too much of them did not suffer him to say enough, or whether it is owing to the barrenness of his invention, he falls vastly short of the truth. He might have entered into their most private thoughts, and have drawn from the bottom of those great souls, as Corneille has done, their most secret motions; whereas he scarce goes so far as their bare outside, little curious to remark well what appeared, and little prying to discover what lay concealed.

I could have wished that our author had laid the stress of his skill in giving us a just representation of those great men, and that in a scene worthy of the magnificence of the subject he had carried the greatness of their souls as high as it was possible. If the conversation of Sertorius and Pompey had such an influence upon our minds, what should not we expect from that of Porus and Alexander upon a subject so uncommon? I could likewise have wished that the author had given us a greater idea of this war. And, indeed, the passage of the Hydaspes is so strange that it is hardly to be conceived: a prodigious army on the other side the river, with terrible chariots and elephants, at that time formidable; the lightning, thunder, and tempests, which occasion a general confusion, and above all,

119

when so large a river must be passed over in skins; in short, a hundred dreadful things which astonished the Macedonians, and which made Alexander say that at last he had found a danger worthy of himself; all this, I say, ought to have raised the imagination of the poet, both in the description of the preparations and the recital of the battle.

However, he scarce mentions the camps of these two kings, whom he robs of their true character to enslave them to imaginary princesses. All that is either great or valuable amongst men, the defense of a country, the preservation of a kingdom, does not excite Porus to the battle; he is encouraged to it by the beautiful eyes of Axiana alone, and the design of his valor is only to recommend himself by it to her. Thus knights-errant are described when they undertake an adventure, and the finest genius, in my opinion, that Spain has produced never makes Don Quixote enter the lists before he has recommended himself to Dulcinea.

A maker of romances may model his heroes according to his fancy. Neither is it of great importance to confine oneself religiously to the true character of an obscure prince, to whose reputation we are perfect strangers. But those great persons of antiquity, so famous in their age, and better known amongst us than the living themselves, the Alexanders, the Scipios, and the Caesars, ought never to lose their characters in our hands. For the most injudicious spectator perceives that he is offended when an author ascribes faults to them which they had not, or when he takes from them virtues which had made upon his mind an agreeable impression. Their virtues, once established, interest our self-love near as much as our own real merit, and it is impossible to make the least alteration in them without making us feel this change with violence. Above all things, we ought not to injure the reputation of their genius in the war to render them more illustrious in their amours; we may give them mistresses of our own inventing, we may mix passion with their glory, but let us take care of making an Antony of an Alexander, and not ruin a hero confirmed for so many ages merely to favor a lover of our own creating.

To banish love out of our tragedies as unworthy of heroes is to take away that secret charm which unites our souls to theirs by a certain tie that continues between them. But then to bring them down to us by this common sentiment, don't let us make them descend beneath themselves, nor destroy what they possess above men. Provided this discretion be observed, I dare affirm that there are no subjects where so universal a passion as love is may not be introduced naturally and without violence. Besides, since women are as necessary in the representation as men, we should give them frequent occasions to speak of that which is most agreeable to their nature, and [of] which they talk better than anything else. Take away from some of the fair sex the expression of amorous thoughts and from others those private familiarities into which the mutual confidence they have in each other leads them, and you reduce them for the most part to very tedious conversations. Most of their motions as well as their discourses should be the effects of their passion; their joy, their sorrow, their fears, and their desires ought to have a little tincture of love in order to be taking.

If you introduce a mother rejoicing for the happiness of her dear son, or afflicting herself for the misfortune of her poor daughter, her satisfaction or her grief will make but a weak impression upon the spectators. To affect us with the tears and complaints of this sex, show us a mistress that bewails the death of a lover, and not a wife that laments the loss of a husband. The grief of mistresses, which is tender and endearing, has a far greater influence upon us than the affliction of an inveigling, self-interested widow, who, as sincere as she happens to be sometimes, always gives us a melancholy idea of funerals and their dismal ceremonies. Of all the widows that ever appeared upon the theatre, I can endure none but Cornelia, [4] because instead of making me think of fatherless children and a wife without a spouse, her affections, truly Roman, recall to my mind the idea of ancient Rome and of the great Pompey.

This is all that may reasonably be allowed to love upon our theatres: let our writers be contented with this, so far even as the severest rules of the drama will allow of it, and let not its greatest favorers believe that the chief design of tragedy is to excite a tenderness in our hearts. In subjects truly heroic, a true greatness of soul ought to be maintained above all things. That which would be pleasing and tender in the mistress of an ordinary man is often weak and scandalous in the mistress of a hero. She may entertain herself, when alone, with those inward conflicts she feels in herself; she may sigh in secret for her uneasiness, and trust a beloved and virtuous confidante with her fears and griefs. But supported by her glory and fortified by her reason, she ought always to remain mistress of her passions, and to animate her lover to great actions by her resolution instead of disheartening him by her weakness.

It is, indeed, an indecent sight to see the courage of a hero softened by tears and sighs; but then, if he haughtily contemns the grief of a beautiful person that loves him, he rather discovers the hardness of his soul than the resolution of his heart.

To avoid this inconvenience, Corneille has no less regard to the character of his illustrious ladies than to that of his heroes. Emilie encourages Cinna to execute their design, [5] and answers all the scruples that oppose the assassinating of Augustus. Cleopatra has a passion for Caesar, and leaves nothing undone to preserve Pompey.[6] She had been unworthy of Caesar if she had not declared against the base treachery of her brother, and Caesar undeserving of her if he had been capable of approving so infamous an action. Dircé, [7] in *Oedipus*, vies greatness of courage with Theseus, turning upon herself the fatal explanation of the oracle which he would apply to himself out of love to her.

But above all we ought to consider Sophonisbe, [8] whose character might be envied by the Romans themselves. We ought to behold her sacrifice the young Massinisse to old Syphax for the good of her country; we ought to see her hearken as little to the scruples of duty in quitting Syphax as she had done to the sentiments of love in losing Massinisse. We ought to see her subject the strongest inclinations, all that binds, all that unites us, the most powerful ties, the most tender passions, to her love for Carthage and her hatred for Rome. In a word, we ought to see her, when being utterly abandoned, not wanting to herself, and when those hearts which she had gained to save her country failed her expectations, to owe to herself the last support, to preserve her glory and her liberty.

Corneille makes his heroes speak with so exact a decorum that he had never given us the conversation of Caesar with Cleopatra [, as beautiful as it is (and it is beautiful to the point of making this lover's discourse attractive even to disinterested persons) if Caesar had realized what tasks were facing him in Alexandria]. He had certainly let it alone but that the Battle of Pharsalia was fully won, Pompey dead, and all his party dissipated. As Caesar then believed himself to be the master of all, an author might justly enough make him offer a glory of which he was in full possession and a power in all probability well settled. But when he discovered Ptolemy's conspiracy, when he beheld his affairs in an ill condition and his own life in danger, he is no more a lover that entertains his mistress with his passion, but a Roman general that acquaints the queen with the danger that threatens them, and leaves her in haste to provide for their common security.

It was therefore very ridiculous to busy Porus wholly with his love just before a great battle which was to decide his destiny, nor is it less preposterous to make Alexander quit the field when the enemy begin to rally. One should have introduced him impatient to find out Porus, and not make him leave the fight with precipitation only to pay a visit to Cleophile —he that was never troubled with any such amorous disorders, and who never thought a victory complete till he had either destroyed or pardoned. That which is harder upon him still is that he is made to lose much on one side without gaining anything on the other. He is as indifferent a hero in love as in war, and thus the history is disfigured without any ornament to the romance. We find him a warrior whose glory cannot inflame our courage and a lover whose passion cannot affect our tenderness.

This is what I had to say of Alexander and Porus. If I have not regularly tied myself to an exact criticism, it is because instead of entering into particular criticism I rather chose to enlarge myself upon the decorum that ought to be observed in the discourses of heroes and the difference of their characters; upon the good and ill usage of the tenderness of love in tragedies, which is rejected too severely by those that ascribe everything to the motions of pity and fear, and is too nicely pursued by those that have no relish but for these sorts of sentiments.

1672

OF ANCIENT AND MODERN TRAGEDY

There were never so many rules to write a good tragedy by, and yet so few good ones are now made that the players are obliged to revive and act all the old ones. I remember that the Abbé d'Aubignac wrote one according to the laws he had imperiously prescribed for the stage. This piece had no success, notwithstanding which he boasted in all companies that he was the only French writer who had exactly followed the precepts of Aristotle; whereupon the Prince of Condé said wittily: "I am obliged to Monsieur d'Aubignac for having so exactly followed Aristotle's rules, but I will never forgive the rules of Aristotle for having put Monsieur d'Aubignac upon writing so bad a tragedy."

It must be acknowledged that Aristotle's *Art of Poetry* is an excellent work; but, however, there is nothing so perfect in it as to be the standing rules of all nations and all ages. Descartes and Gassendi have found out truths that were unknown to Aristotle. Corneille has discovered beauties for the stage of which Aristotle was ignorant; and as our philosophers have observed errors in his *Physics*, our poets have spied out faults in his *Poetics*, at least with respect to us, considering what great change all things have undergone since his time. The gods and goddesses amongst the ancients brought everything that was great and extraordinary upon the theatre, either by their hatred or their friendship, by their revenge or their protection; and among so many supernatural things, nothing appeared fabulous to the people, who believed there passed a familiar correspondence between gods and men. Their gods, generally speaking, acted by human passions; their men undertook nothing without the counsel of the gods, and executed nothing without their assistance. Thus in this mixture of the divinity and humanity there was nothing which was not credible.

But all these wonders are downright romance to us at this time of day. The gods are wanting to us, and we are wanting to the gods; and if, in imitation of the ancients, an author would introduce angels and saints upon our stage, the devouter sort of people would be offended at it and look on him as a profane person, and the libertines would certainly think him weak. Our preachers would by no means suffer a confusion of the pulpit and theatre, or that the people should go and learn those matters from the mouth of comedians which themselves deliver in their churches with authority to the whole people.

Besides this, it would give too great an advantage to the libertines, who might ridicule in a comedy those very things which they receive at church with a seeming submission, either out of respect to the place where they are delivered or to the character of the person that utters them.

But let us put the case that our doctors should freely leave all holy matters to the liberty of the stage; let us likewise take it for granted that men of the least devotion would hear them with as great an inclination to be edified as persons of the profoundest resignation; yet certain it is that the soundest doctrines, the most Christian actions, and the most useful truths would produce a kind of tragedy that would please us the least of anything in the world.

The spirit of our religion is directly opposite to that of tragedy. The humility and patience of our saints carry too direct an opposition to those heroical virtues that are so necessary for the theatre. What zeal, what force is there which Heaven does not bestow upon Néarque and Polyeucte? And what is there wanting on the part of these new Christians to answer fully the end of these happy gifts? The passion and charms of a young, lovely bride make not the least impression upon the mind of Polyeucte. The politic considerations of Félix, as they less affect us, so they make a less impression. Insensible both of prayers and menaces, Polyeucte has a greater desire to die for God than other men have to live for themselves. Nevertheless this very subject, which would make one of the finest sermons in the world, would have made a wretched tragedy if the conversation of Pauline and Sévère, heightened with other sentiments and other passions, had not preserved that reputation to the author which the Christian virtues of our martyrs had made him lose.

The theatre loses all its agreeableness when it pretends to represent sacred things, and sacred things lost a great deal of the religious opinion that is due to them by being represented upon the theatre.

To say the truth, the histories of the Old Testament are infinitely better suited to our stage. Moses, Samson, and Joshua would meet with much better success than Polyeucte and Nearchus, for the wonders they would work there would be a fitter subject for the theatre. But I am apt to believe that the priests would not fail to exclaim against the profanation of these sacred histories, with which they fill their ordinary conversations, their books, and their sermons; and to speak soberly upon the point, the miraculous passage through the Red Sea, the sun stopped in his career by the prayer of Joshua, and whole armies defeated by Samson with the jawbone of an ass — all these miracles, I say, would not be credited in a play because we believe them in the Bible; but we should be rather apt to question them in the Bible because we should believe nothing of them in the play.

If what I have delivered is founded on good and solid reasons, we ought to content ourselves with things purely natural, but at the same time, such as are extraordinary; and in our heroes to choose the principal actions which we may believe possible as human, and which may cause admiration in us as being rare and of an elevated character. In a word, we should have nothing but what is great, yet still let it be human. In the human, we must carefully avoid mediocrity, and fable in that which is great.

I am by no means willing to compare the *Pharsalia* to the *Aeneid*; I know the just difference of their value; but as for what purely regards elevation, Pompey, Caesar, Cato, Curio, and Labienus have done more for Lucan than Jupiter, Mercury, Juno, Venus, and all the train of the other gods and goddesses have done for Virgil.

The ideas which Lucan gives us of these great men are truly greater, and affect us more sensibly, than those which Virgil gives us of his deities.

The latter has clothed his gods with human infirmities to adapt them to the capacity of men; the other has raised his heroes so as to bring them into competition with the gods themselves. *Victrix causa deis placuit, sed victa Catoni.*[9] In Virgil, the gods are not so valuable as the heroes; in Lucan, the heroes equal the gods.

To give you my opinion freely, I believe that the tragedy of the ancients might have suffered a happy loss in the banishment of their gods, their oracles, and their soothsayers.

For it proceeded from these gods, these oracles, and these diviners, that the stage was swayed by a spirit of superstition and terror, capable of infecting mankind with a thousand errors, and overwhelming them with more numerous mischiefs. And if we consider the usual impressions which tragedy made at Athens in the minds of the spectators, we may safely affirm that Plato was more in the right, who prohibited the use of them, than Aristotle, who recommended them; for as their tragedies wholly consisted in excessive motions of fear and pity, was not this the direct way to make the theatre a school of terror and of pity, where people only learnt to be affrighted at all dangers, and to abandon themselves to despair and every misfortune?

It will be a hard matter to persuade me that a soul accustomed to be terrified for what regards another has strength enough to support misfortunes that concern itself. This perhaps was the reason why the Athenians became so susceptible of the impressions of fear, and that this spirit of terror which the theatre inspired into them with so much art became at last but too natural to their armies.

At Sparta and Rome, where only examples of valor and constancy were publicly shown, the people were no less brave and resolute in battle than they were unshaken and constant in the calamities of the Republic. Ever since this art of fearing and lamenting was set up at Athens, all those disorderly passions which they had, as it were, imbibed at their public representations, got footing in their camps and attended them in their wars.

Thus a spirit of superstition occasioned the defeat of their armies, as a spirit of lamentation made them sit down contented with bewailing their great misfortunes when they ought to have found out proper remedies for them. For how was it possible for them not to learn despair in this pitiful school of commiseration? The persons they usually represented upon it were examples of the greatest misery and subjects but of ordinary virtues.

So great was their desire to lament that they represented fewer virtues than misfortunes, lest a soul raised to the admiration of heroes should be less inclined to pity the distressed; and in order to imprint these sentiments of affliction the deeper in their spectators, they had always upon their theatre a chorus of virgins or of old men, who furnished them upon every event either with their terrors or their tears.

Aristotle was sensible enough what prejudice this might do the Athenians, but he thought he sufficiently prevented it by establishing a certain *purgation*, which no one hitherto has understood, and which in my opinion he himself never fully comprehended. For can anything be so ridiculous as to form a science which will infallibly discompose our minds, only to set up another, which does not certainly pretend to cure us? Or to raise a perturbation in our souls for no other end than to endeavor afterwards to calm it by obliging it to reflect upon the dejected condition it has been in?

Among a thousand persons that are present at the theatre, perhaps there may be six philosophers who are capable of recovering their former tranquility by the assistance of these prudent and useful meditations; but the multitude will scarce make any such judicious reflections, and we may be almost assured that what we see constantly represented on the theatre will not fail, at long run, to produce in us a habit of these unhappy motions. Our theatrical representations are not subject to the same inconveniencies as those of the ancients were, since our fear never goes so far as to raise this superstitious terror, which produced such ill effects upon valor. Our fear, generally speaking, is nothing else but an agreeable uneasiness, which consists in the suspension of our minds; it is a dear concern which our soul has for those subjects that draw its affection to them.

We may almost say the same of pity as it is used on our stage. We divest it of all its weakness, and leave it all that we call charitable and human. I love to see the misfortune of some great unhappy person lamented; I am content with all my heart that he should attract our compassion; nay, sometimes, command our tears; but then I would have these tender and generous tears paid to his misfortunes and virtues together, and that this melancholy sentiment of pity be accompanied with vigorous admiration, which shall stir up in our souls a sort of an amorous desire to imitate him.

We were obliged to mingle somewhat of love in the new tragedy, the better to remove those black ideas which the ancient tragedy caused in us by superstition and terror. And in truth there is no passion that more excites us to everything that is noble and generous than a virtuous love. A man who may cowardly suffer himself to be insulted by a contemptible enemy will yet defend what he loves, though to the apparent hazard of his life, against the attacks of the most valiant. The weakest and most fearful creatures — those creatures that are naturally inclined to fear and to run away — will fiercely encounter what they dread most to preserve the object of their love. Love has a certain heat which supplies the defect of courage in those that want it most. But to confess the truth, our authors have made as ill an use of this noble passion as the ancients did of their fear and pity; for if we except eight or ten plays where its impulses have been managed to great advantage, we have no tragedies in which both lovers and love are not equally injured.

We have an affected tenderness where we ought to place the noblest sentiments. We bestow a softness on what ought to be most moving; and sometimes when we mean plainly to express the graces of nature, we fall into a vicious and mean simplicity.

We imagine we make kings and emperors perfect lovers, but in truth we make ridiculous princes of them; and by the complaints and sighs which we bestow upon them where they ought neither to complain nor sigh, we represent them weak, both as lovers and as princes. Our great heroes upon the theatre do often make love like shepherds; and thus the innocence of a sort of rural passion supplies with them the place of glory and valor.

If an actress has the art to weep and bemoan herself after a moving, lively manner, we give her our tears at certain places which demand gravity; and because she pleases best when she seems to be affected, she shall put on grief all along, indifferently.

Sometimes we must have a plain, unartificial, sometimes a tender and sometimes a melancholy whining love, without regarding where that simplicity, tenderness, or grief is requisite; and the reason of it is plain: for as we must needs [have] love everywhere, we look for diversity in the manners, and seldom or never place it in the passions.

I am in good hopes we shall one day find out the true use of this passion, which is now become too common. That which ought to sweeten cruel or calamitous accidents, that which ought to affect our very souls, to animate our courage and raise our spirits, will not certainly be always made the subject of a little affected tenderness or of a weak simplicity. Whenever this happens, we need not envy the ancients; and without paying too great a respect to antiquity, or being too much prejudiced against the present age, we shall not set up the tragedies of Sophocles and Euripides as the only models for the dramatic compositions of our times.

However, I do not say that these tragedies wanted anything that was necessary to recommend them to the palate of the Athenians; but should a man translate the *Oedipus*, the best performance of all antiquity, into French, with the same spirit and force as we see it in the original, I dare be bold to affirm that nothing in the world would appear to us more cruel, more opposite to the true sentiments which mankind ought to have.

Our age has at least this advantage over theirs, that we are allowed the liberty to hate vice and love virtue. As the gods occasioned the greatest crimes on the theatre of the ancients, these crimes captivated the respect of the spectators, and the people durst not find fault with those things which were really abominable. When they saw Agamemnon sacrifice his own daughter, and a daughter too that was so tenderly beloved by him, to appease the indignation of the gods, they only considered this barbarous sacrifice as a pious obedience, and the highest proof of a religious submission.

Now, in that superstitious age, if a man still preserved the common sentiments of humanity, he could not avoid murmuring at the cruelty of the gods like an impious person, and if he would show his devotion to the gods, he must needs be cruel and barbarous to his own fellow-creatures; he must, like Agamemnon, offer the greatest violence both to nature and to his own affection. *Tantum religio potuit suadere malorum,* says Lucretius,[10] upon the account of this barbarous sacrifice.

Nowadays we see men represented upon the theatre without the interposition of the gods; and this conduct is infinitely more useful both to the public and to private persons, for in our tragedies we neither introduce any villain who is not detested, nor any hero who does not cause himself to be admired. With us, few crimes escape unpunished and few virtues go off unrewarded. In short, by the good examples we publicly represent on the theatre, by the agreeable sentiments of love and admiration which are discreetly interwoven with a rectified fear and pity, we are in a capacity of arriving to that perfection which Horace desires: *Omne tulit punctum, qui miscuit utile dulci,*[11] which can never be effected by the rules of the ancient tragedy.

I shall conclude with a new and daring thought of my own, and that is this: we ought, in tragedy, before all things whatever, to look after a greatness of soul well expressed, which excites in us a tender admiration. By this sort of admiration our minds are sensibly ravished, our courages elevated, and our souls deeply affected.

1685

OF THE POEMS OF THE ANCIENTS

No man pays a greater veneration to the works of the ancients than myself. I admire the design, the economy, the elevation of spirit, the extent of knowledge which are so visible in their compositions; but the difference of religion, government, customs, and manners have introduced so great a change in the world that we must go, as it were, upon a new system to suit with the inclination and genius of the present age.

And certainly my opinion must be accounted reasonable by all those who will examine it. For if we give quite opposite characters when we speak of the God of the Israelites and of the God of the Christians, though it be the same deity; if we speak otherwise of the Lord of Hosts, of that terrible God who commanded to destroy the enemy to the very last man, than we do of that God patient, meek, merciful, who enjoins to love them; if the creation of the world is described with one genius and the redemption of men with another; if we want one kind of eloquence to set forth the greatness of the Father, who hath made all things, and another kind to express the love of the Son, who was pleased to suffer all: why should there not be a new art, a new genius to pass from the false gods to the true one; from Jupiter, Cybele, Mercury, Mars, Apollo, to Jesus Christ, the Virgin Mary, our angels, and our saints?

Take away the gods from the ancients, and you take from them all their poems. The constitution of the fable is in disorder, and the design of it turned upside down. Without the prayer of Thetis to Jupiter, and the dream which Jupiter sends to Agamemnon, there will be no *Iliad*; without Minerva, no *Odyssey*; without the protection of Jupiter and the assistance of Venus, no *Aeneid*. The gods assembled in heaven, and there debated what was to be done upon earth; they formed resolutions, and were no less necessary to execute than to take them. These immortal leaders of parties among men contrived all, gave life to all, inspired force and courage, engaged themselves in fight; and if we except Ajax, who asked nothing of them but light, there was no considerable warrior that had not his

130

god upon his chariot as well as his squire, the god to conduct his spear, the squire to direct his horses. Men were pure machines whom secret springs put in motion, and those springs were nothing else but the inspiration of their gods and goddesses.

The divinity we serve is more favorable to the liberty of men. We are in his hands, like the rest of the universe, by way of dependence, but in our own to deliberate and to act. I confess we ought always to beg his protection. Lucretius himself asks it, and in that very book where he attacks providence with all the force of his wit he falls a-praying, and implores that power which governs us to be so gracious as to avert all misfortunes from him.

Quod procul a nobis flectat natura gubernans.[12]

However, we should not introduce this formidable majesty upon every trifling occasion, whose very name ought never to be used in vain. If the false divinities are mixed in fictions, it is no great matter; those are downright fables and vain effects of the poet's imagination. As for Christians, they should give nothing but truth to Him who is truth itself, and they should adapt all their discourses to His wisdom and to His goodness.

This great change is followed by that of manners, which by reason of their being civilized and softened at present cannot suffer that wild and unbecoming freedom that was assumed in former times. It is this change that makes us nauseate the vile and brutal scolding between Achilles and Agamemnon. Upon this score Agamemnon appears odious to us, when we see him take away that Trojan's life whom Menelaus, upon whose account the war was made, had generously pardoned. Agamemnon, the king of kings, who ought to have shown an example of virtue to all the princes and the people, the base Agamemnon kills this miserable wretch with his own hand. It is on the same account that Achilles fills us with horror when he butchers young Lycaon, who entreated him so tenderly for his life. It is then we hate him even to his virtues, when he ties the body of Hector to his chariot and drags him inhumanely to the camp of the Greeks. I loved him as a valiant man, and as the friend of Patroclus; the cruelty of this action makes me abhor his valor and his friendship. It is quite otherwise with Hector: his good qualities return into our minds; we pity and lament him the more for his sufferings; his idea on the sudden becomes very dear and raises all our thoughts in his favor.

Let it not be said in the behalf of Achilles that Hector had killed his dear Patroclus. The resentment of this death doth not excuse him to us. An affliction that could permit him to suspend his revenge, and to tarry till his arms were made before he went to the combat — an affliction so patient ought not to have carried him to this unusual barbarity after the fight was over. But let us acquit friendship of an imputation so odious; the sweetest, the tenderest of all virtues does not use to produce effects so contrary to its nature. Achilles had really this cruelty in the bottom of his nature. It is not to the friend of Patroclus, but to the inhumane and inexorable Achilles, that it belongs.

This all the world will easily agree to. However, the vices of the hero are no faults in the poet. Homer's design was to paint nature such as he saw it, and not to improve it in his heroes. He has described them with more passions than virtues; now passion has its foundation in nature, and virtue is a thing acquired by the improvement of our reason.

Politics had not yet united men by the bonds of a rational society, nor polished them enough for others; morality had not yet accomplished them for themselves. Good qualities were not sufficiently distinguished from the bad. Ulysses was prudent and fearful, provident against dangers, industrious to get out of them, valiant sometimes, when there was less danger to be so than otherwise. Achilles was valiant and fierce, and, what Horace would not set down in his character for him, condescending sometimes to puerile follies. As his nature was uncertain and irregular, hence it came to pass that his behavior was sometimes fierce and sometimes childish. One while he drags the body of Hector in a barbarous manner, now he whines to the goddess his mother, like a child, to drive away the flies from that of Patroclus, his dear friend.

Their customs differ no less from ours than their morals. Two heroes ready for the combat would not amuse themselves nowadays in setting forth their genealogy; but it is easy to observe in the *Iliad*, nay in the *Odyssey* and the *Aeneid* too, that such a method was then practised. Men harangued before they fought, just as they make speeches in England before they are hanged.

As for comparisons, discretion will teach us to use them more sparingly than the ancients. Good sense will render them just, invention new. The sun, the moon, the elements, will lend us no more of worn-out magnificence. Wolves, shepherds, and flocks will not afford us a simplicity too much known and threadbare.

I am of opinion there is an infinite number of comparisons that are more like one another than the things they are compared to. A goshawk that strikes a pigeon, a sparrow hawk that dares the little birds, a falcon that makes a stoop, are liker one another in the swiftness of their flight than the men to whom they are compared for their impetuosity. Take away the distinction of the names of goshawk, sparrow hawk, and falcon, you will find the very same thing. The violence of a whirlwind that roots up trees more resembles that of a storm which raises disorders of another kind than the objects to which it is compared. A lion whom hunger drives from his den, a lion pursued by hunters, a lioness furious and jealous of her whelps, a lion against whom a whole village assembles, and who for all that retires with pride and indignation — all this is a lion differently represented, but still a lion, which doth not afford us ideas different enough.

Sometimes comparisons take us from objects that employ us most by showing us another object that makes an unseasonable diversion. I am ready to consider two armies that are drawn out to engage, and I employ all my thoughts to observe the behavior, order, and disposition of the troops. On a sudden, I am transported to the shores of a sea, which is swelled by the fury of the winds, and I am in more danger to behold shipwrecked vessels than broken battalions. These vast thoughts which the sea affords me efface the former. Another represents to me a mountain or a forest all on fire. Whither doth not the idea of such a burning carry one? If I were not a perfect master of my own thoughts, I might insensibly be led to the last universal conflagration. From this terrible burning I am hurried to an image of lightning, and these diversions so much take me off from the first image that employed me that I lose entirely that of the battle.

We think to embellish objects by comparing them to eternal, immense, infinite beings; but in truth we lessen instead of advancing them. To say that a woman is as handsome as Madame Mazarin is to praise her more than if you compared her to the sun: for the sublime and wonderful create esteem; the impossible and the fabulous destroy that very commendation which they pretend to bestow. Truth was not the inclination of the first ages; a useful lie and a lucky falsehood gave reputation to imposters and pleasure to the credulous. It was the secret of the great and the wise to govern the simple, ignorant herd. The vulgar, who paid a profound respect to mysterious errors, would have despised naked truth, and it was thought a piece of prudence to cheat them. All their discourses were fitted to [this] advantageous design, in which there was nothing to be seen but fictions, allegories, and similitudes— nothing appeared as it was in itself. Specious and rhetorical outsides hid the truth of things, and comparisons too frequently used hindered the reader from minding the true objects by amusing him with resemblances.

The genius of our age is quite opposite to this spirit of fables and false mysteries. We love plain truth; good sense has gained ground upon the illusions of fancy, and nothing satisfies us nowadays but solid reason. To this alteration of humor we may add that of knowledge; we have other notions of nature than the ancients had. The heavens, that eternal mansion of so many divinities, are nothing else with us but an immense and fluid space. The same sun shines still upon us, but we assign it another course, and instead of hastening to set in the sea it goes to enlighten another world. The earth, which was immovable in the opinion of the ancients, now turns round in ours, and is not to be equalled for the swiftness of its motion. In short, everything is changed, gods, nature, politics, manners, humors, and customs. Now is it to be supposed that so many alterations should not produce a mighty change in our writings?

If Homer were now alive, he would undoubtedly write admirable poems; but then he would fit them to the present age. Our poets make bad ones, because they model them by those of the ancients, and order them according to rules which are changed with things which time has altered.

I know there are certain eternal rules, grounded upon good sense, built upon firm and solid reason, that will always last. Yet there are but few that bear this character. Those that relate to the manners, affairs and customs of the ancient Greeks make but a weak impression upon us at present. We may say of them as Horace has said of words: they have their certain period and duration. Some die with old age.

Verborum interit aetas.[18]

Others perish with their nation, as well as their maxims of government, which subsist not after the empire is dissolved. So it is plain, there are but very few that have a right to prevail at all times, and it would be ridiculous to regulate matters wholly new by laws that are extinct. Poetry would do ill to exact from us what religion and justice do not obtain.

To this servile and too much affected imitation is owing the ill success of all our poems. Our poets have not genius enough to please without employing the gods, nor address to make a good use of what materials our religion could afford them. Tied to the humor of antiquity but confined to the doctrines of this age, they give the air of Mercury to our angels, and that of the fabulous wonders of paganism to our miracles. This mixture of ancient and modern has made them succeed very ill. And we may say that they neither know how to draw any advantage from their fictions nor make a right use of our truths.

To conclude, the poems of Homer will always be a masterpiece, but they are not a model always to be followed. They will form our judgment and our judgment will regulate the present disposition of things.

1685

OF THE WONDERFUL THAT IS FOUND IN THE POEMS OF THE ANCIENTS

If we consider the wonderful in the poems of antiquity, divested of the fine thoughts, the strong passions, and the noble expressions with which the works of the poets are adorned; if we consider it, I say, destitute of all ornament and come to examine it purely by itself, I am persuaded that to a man of good sense it will appear no less ridiculous than that of knight-errantry. Nay, the latter is in this regard the discreeter of the two because it supposes all pernicious, dishonest, and base things done by the ministry of devils and magicians, whereas the poets have left the most infamous exploits to the management of their gods and goddesses. Yet this hinders not but that poems have been always admired and books of chivalry ridiculed. The first are admired for the wit and knowledge we find in them, and the other despised for the absurdities they are filled with. The wonderful in the poems supports its fabulous extravagance by the beauty of the discourse and by an infinite number of useful discoveries that accompany it. That of chivalry discredits even the foolish invention of its fable by the ridiculousness of the style in which it is written.

Be it how it will, the wonderful in the poems has begotten that of knight-errantry, and certain it is that the devils and conjurers cause much less harm in this way of writing than the gods and their ministers did in the former. The goddess of arts, of knowledge, and wisdom inspires the brav-

135

est of all the Greeks with an ungovernable fury, and suffers him not to recover his senses she had taken from him, but only to make him capable of perceiving his folly and by this means to kill himself out of mere shame and despair. The greatest and most prudent of the goddesses favors scandalous passions, and lends her assistance to carry on a criminal amour. The same goddess employs all sorts of artifices to destroy a handful of innocent people who by no means deserved her indignation. She thought it not enough to exhaust her own power and that of the other gods, whom she solicited to ruin Aeneas, but even corrupts the god of sleep to cast Palinurus into a slumber and so to order matters that he might drop into the sea; this piece of treachery succeeded, and the poor pilot perished in the waves.

There is not one of the gods in these poems that does not bring the greatest misfortunes upon men or hurry them on to the blackest actions. Nothing is so villainous here below which is not executed by their order or authorized by their example, and this it was that principally contributed to give birth to the sect of the Epicureans, and afterwards to support it. Epicurus, Lucretius and Petronius would rather make their gods idle and enjoy their immortal nature in an uninterrupted tranquillity than see them active and cruelly employed in ruining ours. Nay, Epicurus by doing so pretended he showed his great respect to the gods, and from hence proceeded that saying which my Lord Bacon so much admires: *Non deos vulgi negare profanum, sed vulgi opiniones diis applicare profanum.*[14]

Now I do not mean by this that we are obliged to discard the gods out of our works, and much less from those of poetry, where they seem to enter more naturally than anywhere else:

Ab Jove principium Musae.[15]

I am for introducing them as much as any man; but then I would have them bring their wisdom, justice, and clemency along with them, and not appear, as we generally make them, like a pack of impostors and assassins. I would have them come with a conduct to regulate, and not with a disorder to confound everything.

Perhaps it may be replied that these extravagancies ought only to pass for fables and fictions, which belong to the jurisdiction of poetry. But I would fain know what art and science in the world has the power to exclude good sense? If we need only write in verse to be privileged in all extravagancies, for my part, I would never advise any man to meddle with prose, where he must immediately be pointed at for a coxcomb if he leaves good sense and reason never so little behind him.

I wonder extremely that the ancient poets were so scrupulous to preserve probability in the actions of men, and violated it after so abominable a manner when they come to recount the actions of the gods. Even those who have spoken of their nature more soberly than the rest could not forbear to speak extravagantly of their conduct. When they establish their being and their attributes they make them immortal, infinite, almighty, perfectly wise, and perfectly good. But at the very moment they set them a-working there is no weakness to which they do not make them stoop; there is no folly or wickedness which they do not make them commit.

We have two common sayings which appear to be directly opposite to one another, and yet I look upon both to be very probable. The one is that poetry is the language of the gods; the other, that there is not such a fool in nature as a poet.[16] Poetry that expresses with force and vigor those impetuous passions that disturb mankind, that paints the wonders of the universe in lively expressions, does elevate things purely natural, as it were above nature, by the sublimity of its thoughts and the magnificence of its discourse, which may justly enough be called the language of the gods. But when poets come once to quit this noble field of passions and wonders to speak of the gods, they abandon themselves to the caprice of their own imagination in matters which they do not understand; and their heat having no just ideas to govern it, instead of making themselves, as they vainly believe, wholly divine, they are in truth the most extravagant fools in the world. It will be no difficult matter to be convinced of this truth if we consider that this absurd and fabulous theology is equally contrary to all notions of religion and all principles of good sense. There have been some philosophers that have founded religion upon that knowledge which men may have of the deity by their natural reason. There have been law-givers too that have styled themselves the interpreters of the will of heaven to establish a religious worship which has not had reason to support it. But to make, as the poets have done, a perpetual commerce, a familiar society, and if I may use the expression, a mixture of men and gods, against religion and reason, is certainly the boldest and perhaps the most senseless thing that ever was.

It remains now to consider whether the character of a poem has virtue to rectify that of impiety and folly. Now, as I take it, we do not ascribe so much power to the secret force of any charm. That which is bad is bad for good and all; that which is extravagant can be made good sense in no respect. As for the reputation of the poet, it rectifies nothing any more than the character of the poem does. Discernment is a slave to nobody. That which is effectually bad is not at all the better for being found in the most celebrated author, and that which is just and solid is never the worse for coming from an indifferent hand. Amongst a hundred fine and lofty thoughts, a good judge will soon discover an extravagant one which one's genius threw out when it was warm and which too strong an imagination was able to maintain against unfixed reflections. On the other hand, in the course of an infinite number of extravagant things, this same judge will admire certain beauties where the mind, in spite of its impetuosity, was just and regular.

The elevation of Homer and his other noble qualities do not hinder me from taking notice of the false character of his gods, and that agreeable and judicious equality of Virgil that pleases all true judges does not conceal from me the little merit of his Aeneas. If among so many noble things which affect me in Homer and Virgil I cannot forbear to remark what is defective in them, so amongst those passages that displease me in Lucan, either for being too flat, or weary me for being too far carried on, I cannot forbear to please myself in considering the just and true grandeur of his heroes. I endeavor to relish every word in him when he expresses the secret movements of Caesar at the sight of Pompey's head; and nothing escapes me in that inimitable discourse of Labienus and Cato, where they debate whether they shall consult the oracle of Jupiter Ammon to know the destiny of the Commonwealth.

If all the ancient poets had spoken as worthily of the oracles of their gods, I should make no scruple to prefer them to the divines and philosophers of our time, and it is a passage that may serve for an example in this matter to all succeeding poets. One may see in the concourse of so many people that came to consult the oracle of Ammon what effects a public opinion can produce where zeal and superstition mingle together. One may see in Labienus a pious sensible man who to his respect for the gods joins that consideration and esteem we ought to preserve for true virtue in good men. Cato is a religious severe philosopher, weaned from all vulgar opinions, who entertains those lofty thoughts of the gods which pure undebauched reason and a truly elevated wisdom can give us of them. Everything here is poetical, everything here is consonant to sense and truth; it is not poetical upon the score of any ridiculous fiction, or for some extravagant hyperbole, but for the daring greatness and majesty of the language and for the noble elevation of the discourse. It is thus that poetry is the language of the gods and that poets are wise, and it is so much the greater wonder to find it in Lucan because it is neither to be met with in Homer or Virgil!

Pierre-Daniel Huet, Bishop of Avranches THE ORIGINAL OF ROMANCES

Though I think your curiosity very just, and that it is natural for a person who so perfectly understands the art of writing romances to be inquisitive into their original, yet I know not whether I may with equal justice undertake to satisfy that curiosity. I am without books, I have my head at present full of other matters, and I am not ignorant of the many difficulties wherewith such an inquiry must necessarily be attended. It is neither in Provence or Spain, as some have imagined, we are to trace out the beginnings of this agreeable amusement of a harmless idleness. We must search after them in countries farther off, and in the more remote recesses of antiquity. I will, notwithstanding, endeavor to comply with your desires, for that strict friendship which has been established so long between us gives you a right to demand everything of me, and takes from me the choice of refusing anything to you.

Heretofore by the word *romance* was understood not only such works as were written in prose, but more frequently those that were formed in verse. Giraldi and Pigna, his scholar, in their treatises of romances do scarce allow that name to any else, and propose Boiardo and Ariosto for models.[1] But at present the contrary acceptation prevails, and romances properly so called are fictions of love-adventures, artfully formed and delivered in prose, for the delight and instruction of the readers. I call romance a *fiction* to distinguish it from history, and a fiction of *love-adventures* because love ought to be the principal subject of a romance. It must be written in prose, to conform itself to the custom of the age; it must be contrived with art, under some certain rules, otherwise it will be a confused mass without order or beauty. The chief design of a romance, and which the writer ought in the first place to have in view, is the instruction of his reader, before whom he is to represent the reward of virtue and chastisement of vice. But forasmuch as the mind of man is naturally an enemy to instruction, against which self-love is ever ready to revolt, he must be soothed and deluded by the baits of pleasure, and the author must temper the severity of precept by the agreeableness of example till he has brought the reader insensibly to correct those faults in himself which he cannot but condemn in others. So that delight, which the ingenious romancer seems to make his chief design, is in effect no other than a medium subordinate to the principal end, the instruction of the mind and reformation of the manners; and romances are more or less regular as they come up more or less to this definition. It is only upon such that I intend my present discourse, and I am of opinion that your curiosity is with regard to such only.

I shall not therefore say anything of romances written in verse, much less of epic poems, which besides their being written in verse have several essential differences that distinguish them from romances, though in some other respects there is a great resemblance between them; and since, according to Aristotle's maxim, a poet is more to be distinguished as such by his invention than his verses, the authors of romances may be ranked among the poets. Petronius saith that poems ought to distinguish themselves [by great indirection, by the ministry of the gods] by their surprising turns and their free and hardy expressions, insomuch that they are to be considered rather as oracles proceeding from a divine impulse and spirit full of fury than as an exact regular narration.[2] Romances, on the other hand, are more simple, less elevated and metaphorical, both in the invention and expression. Poems have more of the surprising, but are always [bounded by the] probable: romances have more of the probable, and sometimes [have] something of the surprising. Poems are more regular and exact in the contrivance, but have less of matter, fewer events and episodes. On the other hand, romances have more of these because, having less of the sublime and metaphorical, they do not put the mind so much upon the stretch, but leave it in a condition to fill itself with more variety of different ideas. [Finally], poems have for their subject some action military or politic, and touch only upon love occasionally; on the other hand, love is the principal subject of romances, where war and politics are no other than incidents. I mean this of regular romances, for the greatest part of our old French, Italian, and Spanish romances have less of love and more of fighting, which inclined Giraldi to believe that the word romance is taken from a word signifying in Greek force and courage, because those books were made on purpose to magnify the strength and courage of their paladins. But Giraldi was mistaken, as I shall make appear to you in the sequel of this discourse. Neither do I comprehend under my definition of romances those histories which are notorious for their many falsities, such as that for instance of Herodotus (which however has not so many as it is generally charged withal), Hanno's voyages, the life of Apollonius written by Philostratus, and the like.[3] These writings are true in the main, and false only in some particular points, whereas romances are true in particular facts only, and false in the main. The one consists of truths mingled with some falsehoods, and the other of falsehoods mingled with some truths. I mean that truth has the ascendant in these histories, and falsehood is so prevailing a quality in romances that it will be contrary to no rule if there should not be one word of truth in the whole or in part. Aristotle saith that [that] tragedy is the most perfect whose plot is founded upon some known fact in history, because it carries a greater probability with it than that which is entirely of a new invention; and yet he does not condemn the latter, his reason for which is that though the argument be taken from history, it may nevertheless be unknown to the greatest part of the audience and consequently new to them, notwithstanding which it may prove a general entertainment. The same is to be said of romances, but with this distinction, that an entire fiction of the fable will pass easier in such pieces where the actors are of mean circumstances, as in our comical romances, than in those more lofty ones, where great princes and conquerors are the actors, and whose adventures are illustrious and remarkable, because it is not likely that such great events should have lain so long concealed and neglected by the historians; and probability, which is [not always] allowed in history, is essential in a romance.

I exclude also from the number of romances those pretended histories which are entirely false, both in the whole and in part, invented purely to supply the want of truth. Such are the imaginary originals of most nations, and even of the most barbarous. Such moreover are those gross fictions of Annius the monk of Viterbo, worthy the indignation or contempt of the learned.[4] I make the same difference between romances and those writings as there is between such who with an innocent artifice mask and disguise themselves to divert themselves whilst they are diverting others, and those abandoned wretches who assume to themselves the name and dress of some persons deceased or absent on purpose from the resemblance there is between them to lay claim to and get possession of their estates. In a word, I must likewise deny to fables a place in my definition, for a romance is the fiction of things that might have happened, but never did happen, whereas fables are of things that never were and never can be.

Having thus settled what writings they are that deserve the name of romances, I must affirm that the invention of them is owing to the Orientals, I mean to the Egyptians, Arabians, Persians, and Syrians. I do not question but you will yield me up this point when I have proved to you that most of the famous romancers of antiquity were of those countries. . . .

The Egyptian hieroglyphics serve to instance to what an excess that nation was mysterious. Everything among them was expressed by representatives, everything wore a disguise; all their religion was under a veil, nor were the vulgar suffered to receive any other knowledge of it than what was conveyed to them under the mask of fables; neither was the mask to be taken off but to those they deemed worthy to be initiated into their mysteries. Herodotus saith the Greeks borrowed from them their mythologic divinity, and recounts some stories he had been taught by the priests in Egypt, which, as credulous and as much given to fables as he was, he relates as old wives' tales, which however had something agreeable in them and tickled the curiosity of the Greeks, a people desirous to learn and great admirers of novelties. It was doubtless from these priests that Pythagoras and Plato, in their voyages to Egypt, learned to disguise their philosophy, and hide it under the shadow of mysteries.

As for the Arabians, if you read their works, you will find nothing in them but metaphors, drawn in by head and shoulders, similitudes and fictions; of this sort is their Alcoran. Mahomet saith he composed it in that manner to the end it might be more easily learnt and not easily forgotten. They have translated Aesop's fables into their language, and some of them have composed fables like them. . . . It is my opinion that we had the art of rhyming from the Arabs, and I think there is ground to believe that the Leonine verses are copied from them. For it does not appear that rhymes had met with any reputation in Europe before Tarick and Musa [5] had penetrated into Spain, but we meet with great plenty of them in the ages following, though it may be easy for me to convince you that rhyme was not utterly unknown to the ancient Romans.

The Persians have not come behind the Arabians in the art of lying agreeably. For though in the common usages of life it was reckoned most abominable among them to lie, and there was no fault they punished in their children with so much severity, yet nothing pleased them more in their books and writings, if indeed fictions can deserve the name of lies.

To prove this we need only read the fabulous adventures of their great law-giver Zoroaster. Strabo saith that the Persian schoolmasters gave their pupils precepts of morality clothed in fictions. He tells us in another place that no great credit is to be given to the ancient histories of the Persians, Medes, and Syrians, because of the inclination in their writers to fables. For observing that they among them who made it their profession to write fables were in great esteem, they thought the people would be highly delighted in reading relations false and counterfeit, provided they were written with an historical air.[6] Aesop's fables were in such high esteem among them that they claimed the author for their countryman. . . .

There are no poets that come up to the Persians in the liberty they take of lying in the lives of their saints, the origin of their religion, and in their histories. They have so disguised their histories, the true knowledge of which hath been derived to us from the Greeks and Romans, that they are not to be known; and degenerating from that laudable aversion they had heretofore to such as had recourse to lies to serve their interests, they now value themselves upon it. They are in love with poetry to excess; it is the delight of the noble and plebeian. All entertainments are imperfect where poetry is wanting, so that poets abound among them and are known by their splendid garments. Their works of gallantry and amorous stories have been highly celebrated, and discover a national genius to romances. . . .

Those fictions and parables, which remained unconsecrated in the nations before mentioned, became sanctified in Syria. The sacred penmen, accommodating themselves to the humor of the Jews, clothed the inspirations they had received from heaven in parable and allusion. The Holy Scripture is all mystical, allegorical, enigmatical. The Talmudists believe the Book of Job is nothing but a parable invented by the Hebrews. This book, that of David, the Proverbs, Ecclesiastes, the Song of Songs, and all the other sacred canticles, are so many pieces of poetry full of figures that would appear bold and extravagant in our writings, but are familiar in those of that nation. The Book of Proverbs is otherwise called the Parables, because proverbs of that kind, according to Quintilian's definition, are no other than fictions or strings of parables.[7] The Song of Songs is a dramatic piece where the passionate sentiments of the bridegroom and the bride are expressed in a manner so touching and tender that we should be charmed with them if those expressions and figures were [a little more in rapport with] our genius, or if we could divest ourselves of that unreasonable prejudice that gives us a distaste of everything that differs never so little from our own customs. Wherein we insensibly condemn ourselves, since our inconstancy will not permit us to continue long in the observance of the same customs. Our Blessed Saviour himself rarely gives any precept to the Jews but under the veil of a parable. The Talmud is stuffed with a million of fables, every one more impertinent than another. Several of the rabbins have from time to time given explanations of them, or labored to reconcile them to each other, or digested them in particular pieces, and moreover composed many poems, proverbs, and apologues. The Cypriots and Cilicians adjoining to Syria have been the authors of certain fables that have been distinguished by the names of those people respectively, and the aptness the Cilicians in particular had for lying has been exposed in one of the most ancient proverbs among the Greeks. In short, fables were in such great vogue in all those parts that according to the testimony of Lucian there were among the Arabians and Assyrians certain persons whose sole business was to explain those fables, and who from their temperate and regular manner of living enjoyed a much longer life than any others.[8]

But it is not enough to have traced out and discovered the original source of romances; it is now time to consider by what means they found a passage into Greece and Italy. . . .

The Ionians, who were originally of Attica and Peloponnesus, could not forget from whence they sprung; they maintained an uninterrupted commerce with the Grecians; they each of them sent their children from the one to the other to be educated after the custom and manners of the country, whither they were sent respectively. During this free and open communication, Greece, which of itself was naturally inclined to fables, easily learnt from the Ionians how to write romances, and soon became great proficients in the science. But for the clearer understanding of this matter, I will endeavor to recount, in due order of time, such of the Greek writers as excelled in this art.

I can meet with none of them before Alexander the Great, which makes me believe that this art had made but a small progress among them, till by the conquest of Persia they were in a condition to learn it, as it were, at the fountainhead. Clearchus of Solium, a city in Cilicia, who lived in the days of Alexander and was in like manner one of Aristotle's disciples, is the first I can find to have written books of love.[9] Nor do I know whether what he wrote was not a collection of several amorous events drawn out of the vulgar fable, like that compiled afterwards by Parthenius, under the reign of Augustus, and which is preserved down to our times.[10] . . .

I have much the same opinion of the pastorals of the sophist Longus as of the two preceding.[11] For though some learned men in these latter ages have commended them for their elegance and agreeableness, as likewise for their simplicity so proper to the subject, yet there is nothing else commendable in them besides that simplicity which however sometimes descends even to puerility and nonsense. He opens very grossly with the birth of his shepherds, and concludes his work with their nuptials. He never unravels his intrigues but by injudicious machines. Moreover he is so obscene that one must [be a little cynical] to read him without blushing. His style, for which he has been so much commended, is that for which perhaps he is the least praiseworthy; it is a style like that of a sophist, as he was, of the same stamp with that of Eustathius and Theodorus Prodromus,[12] betwixt the orator and historian, and so proper neither to the one or the other; full of metaphors and antitheses, and of those glaring figures that surprise the simple and tickle the ear without benefiting the understanding. Instead of engaging his reader by the novelty of events, the method and variety of matter, and a neat close narration which has however its proper turn and cadence, still advancing in its subject, he endeavors, as most sophists do, to delay him by descriptions foreign to the purpose. He leads him out of the high road, and whilst he exposes him to so many places where he had no business, he wearies his attention and blunts the impatience he had of arriving at the end he desired and which at first was proposed to him. I must confess I translated this romance with some pleasure in my youth, and that indeed is the only age wherein it ought to please. I will not pretend to ascertain the time wherein he lived; none of the ancients have made any mention of him, nor is there anything in him that may give ground for a conjecture, unless it be the purity of his elocution, which inclines me to think him more ancient than the two others. . . .

In the fore-mentioned catalogue I have distinguished those romances that are regular from those that are not so. I call those regular which are framed upon the rules of heroic poetry. The Grecians, by whom most arts and sciences have been brought to so great a perfection that they have been esteemed the first inventors of them, have likewise cultivated the art of romancing, and rough and unshapen as it was among the Orientals, they have worked it into a better form by confining it to the rules of the epopea and uniting in a complete body the several parts that lay without order or relation to each other in the romances that had been composed before them. Of all the Greek writers of romances beforementioned, Antonius Diogenes, Lucian, Athenagoras, Jamblicus, Heliodorus, Achilles Tatius, Eustathius, and Theodorus Prodromus are the only authors that have subjected themselves to those rules. I say nothing in this place of Lucius of Patras, nor of Damascius, whom I have not numbered in the list of romance writers. As for St. John of Damascus and Longus, they might easily have formed their works according to those rules, but they either did not know them or despised them. I know not what the three Xenophons [13] did in that respect, since we have nothing left of theirs to make any judgment upon, nor of Aristides or the rest, who with him were authors of the Milesian fables. However I believe these last observed some rules, as seems to appear from those works that have been written in imitation of them, and have been preserved down to our days, such for instance as Apuleius's *Metamorphosis*, which is regular enough.

These Milesian fables, long before they made that progress in Greece, already mentioned, conveyed themselves into Italy, where they were first entertained by the Sybarites, a people voluptuous beyond imagination; that conformity of humor which happened between them and the Milesians established between them a reciprocal communication of luxury and pleasure, and so firmly united them that Herodotus saith he never knew a better established alliance between any people whatever. From the Milesians therefore the Sybarites learnt the art of fabling, so that the Sybarite tales became as common in Italy as the Milesian were in Asia. It is hard to determine of what construction they were. Hesychius gives us to understand, in a passage that has been much corrupted, that Aesop having been in Italy, his fables grew into great reputation in that country; that improvements were made upon them; that having suffered some alterations, they were called Sybarites, and that they passed into proverbs; but he does not tell us wherein those alterations consisted.[14] Suidas thinks they were like those of Aesop, but in this he is deceived as in many other instances.[15] The old commentator upon Aristophanes saith the Sybarites introduced brutes in their fables, and that Aesop made use of men in his.[16]

This passage is certainly corrupted, for as it is plain that men were actors in Aesop's fables, it follows from thence that the Sybarites made use of brutes in theirs; and this is what the commentator saith in express terms in another place. Those of the Sybarites were diverting, and intended to

147

raise laughter in the readers. I have met with a sketch of one of them in Elian; [17] it is a story he tells us he had taken out of the histories of the Sybarites, that is to say, according to my opinion, out of their fables. You shall be a judge of it from the story itself. A Sybarite boy walking with his schoolmaster in the street met a fellow that sold dry figs, and stole one of them out of his basket; his master severely reproved him for it, but snatched the fig from him and ate it himself. These fables were not only facetious, but extremely smutty. Ovid places the *Sybaritis*, that had been composed a little before his time, in the number of the most debauched pieces. Several learned men have imagined that he thereby meant the work of Hemitheon the Sybarite, of whom Lucian speaks [18] as of a lump of lewdness. But to me there seems no ground for this imagination, for it does not appear that there was any agreement between that book of Hemitheon and the *Sybaritis*, only that both the one and the other were very lascivious, and this was common to all the fables of the Sybarites. Besides the *Sybaritis*, as has been said before, was written not long before Ovid, and it is notorious that the city of Sybaris was razed by the Crotoniats five hundred years before the birth of that poet. It is therefore most likely that the *Sybaritis* had been composed by some Roman, and so called because written in imitation of the old Sybarite fables. A certain ancient author, whose name I take to be of no moment for you to know, gives us to understand that their style was short and laconic, but that does not prove that their fables had nothing in them of the romance. . . .

If the Romans could without a blush read those fables under the Republic at a time when an austere discipline and rigidness of manners was maintained among them, it is not to be wondered at if, when the commonwealth was subjected to the will of the emperors, and everyone after their examples abandoned themselves to luxury and pleasure, their minds bcame sensible of such as the reading of romances inspired into them. . . .

Hitherto the art of romancing continued in some reputation and figure, but declined at the same time with literature and the empire, when the rugged nations of the North overwhelmed Europe with their ignorance and barbarity. Till then romances had been composed for pleasure and delight, but now fabulous histories began to prevail for want of proper materials for true ones. Thelesin, who is said to have lived about the middle of the sixth century under the reign of King Arthur, so famous in the books of chivalry, and Melkin, who was something younger, wrote the history of their country England and of King Arthur and his Round

Table.[19] Balaeus, who has given them a place in his catalogue, makes mention of them as of very fabulous authors.[20] The same thing may be said of Hunibaldus Francus, who is said to have been contemporary with Clovis, and whose history, as he calls it, is no better than a collection of lies and absurdities.[21]

And now, sir, we are got down to the celebrated piece containing the actions of Charlemagne, which has been very injudiciously ascribed to Archbishop Turpin, though he was not born till two hundred years after.[22] Pigna and some others have been so weak as to believe that romance was so called from Rheims, of which Turpin was Archbishop, because his book, as Pigna will have it, was the fountain from whence most of the romancers of Provence supplied themselves, and was, according to others, the masterpiece of romances. . . . These histories, told in a plausible manner, did not fail to please the ignorant readers, more ignorant, if possible, than their authors. So that no one was at the pains to examine into authentic records, or to be duly informed of the truth before they took upon them to write; they had their materials nearer hand, in their own head and in their own invention, and by this means history began to degenerate into romance. The Latin tongue grew as much neglected and despised in that age of ignorance as truth itself. Your poetasters, ballad-mongers, storytellers, and *jongleurs* of Provence, in short all those of that country who practised what they called the *gay science*, began in the days of Hugh Capet to romance in good earnest and to roam up and down France vending their romantic wares wherever they came, composed all in the Roman language. For at that time the Provencials were better skilled in literature and poetry than all the rest of France. This language was what the Romans had introduced with their conquests, and which, in time, was corrupted with a mixture of the old Gaulish, which had preceded, and of the Frank, or Teutonic, that succeeded it; insomuch that it was neither Latin nor Gaulish nor Frank, but a medley of them all, wherein however the Roman had the predominance, for which reason it still preserved that name to distinguish it from the particular or mother tongue of each country, whether [the French, or] the Gaulish (or Celtic) or the Aquitanic, or the Belgic; for Caesar tells us these three languages differed from each other, though Strabo saith the difference was nothing else but three different dialects upon the same common language.[23] The Spaniards put the same signification upon the word *Roman* that we do, and call their vulgar tongue *Romancé*. The Roman therefore being what was most universally understood, the Provencials wrote their stories in that language, and they were for that reason called *romances*. These authors passing thus up and down were generously paid for their pains, and well received by the great men of the country where they travelled, some of whom were so taken with them that they often stripped themselves to clothe them. However, the Provencials were not the only people who addicted themselves to that agreeable occupation, for almost all the provinces in France had their romancers too, even as far as Picardy, where they had their *sirvantois*, a sort of amorous pieces, and sometimes satirical. And from hence sprung up such an incredible number of old romances, many of which are extant in print, others are mouldering away in libraries, and the rest have been consumed by time. Even Spain itself, which by degrees grew so fertile in romances, and Italy too, borrowed the art from us. . . . "I may venture to affirm," saith [Giraldi], "that this sort of poetry had its original and beginning in France, and from thence likewise it has probably received its name. The Spaniards learnt this way of poetising from the French, and now at last it has been received by the Italians."

The late Monsieur Saumaise,[24] for whose memory I have a singular veneration, both on the account of his great learning and the friendship there was between us, imagined that Spain, having learnt of the Arabs the art of romancing, taught it the rest of Europe. To support which opinion, it must be allowed that Thelesin, Melkin, both English, and Hunibaldus Francus, who are all three said to have composed their romantic histories about the middle of the sixth century, are at least two hundred years younger than has been hitherto believed; for Count Julian's revolt and the settlement of the Arabs in Spain did not happen till the ninety-first year of the Hegira, in 712 of our Lord, and it would require some time after that for the Arabian romances to take footing in Spain and for those which it is pretended were composed by the Spaniards in imitation of them to be communicated to the rest of Europe. I am far from insisting upon the antiquity of those authors, though I have some right so to do, since the common opinion is on my side. It is very true, as I have already observed, that the Arabians were much addicted to the *gay science*, that is, to poetry, fictions, and fables. This science, which remained in its primitive roughness among them, though reformed and polished by the Greeks, was carried together with their arms into Africa when they made a conquest of that country, though it was no stranger there before; for Aristotle, and Priscian from him, make mention of the Libyan fables,[25] and the romances written by Apuleius and Martianus Capella, before-mentioned, who were both Africans, are instances of the genius of that people. . . . The Spaniards having, in course of time, received the Arabian yoke, received likewise from them their customs, and learnt, in imitation of them, to sing love verses and to celebrate the actions of great men after the manner of the bards in Gaul; but these songs, which they called *romances*, were very different from our modern romances; they were composed on purpose to be sung, and were consequently very short. There has been a collection made of several of them, some of which are so very ancient that they are hardly intelligible. Some of them have served to clear up the Spanish history and reduce events to a chronological series. Their romances, properly so called, are of a much later date; the eldest of them are posterior to our Tristans and Lancelots by several hundred years. Miguel de Cervantes, one of the finest wits that that nation ever produced, has made an excellent judicious [critique] upon them in his *Don Quixote*, wherein the curate and Master Nicholas the barber have much ado to find six among them all that deserve to be saved; the rest are delivered over to the secular arm of the chambermaid to be committed to the flames. Those which were thought worthy to be preserved are the four books of *Amadis de Gaule*, which they pronounce to be the first romance of chivalry that was ever printed in Spain, the model of the rest and the best of them all; *Palmerin of England*, supposed to have been written by a king of Portugal, and thought worthy of a box, like that of Darius, wherein Alexander kept the works of Homer; *Don Belianis, the Mirror of Chivalry*; *Tirante the White*, and *Kyrie Eleison of Montauban* (for there were such learned times wherein *Kyrie Eleison* and *Paralipomenon* were taken for some saints' names), wherein the subtleties of Madam Pleasure-of-my-Life, and the Cheats of the Widow Reposada are highly commended. But these are all of yesterday, when compared with our old romances from which they were in all likelihood modeled, as may be presumed from the conformity of the works and the neighborhood of the nations. He likewise censures romances written in verse, and some other pieces of poetry found in Don Quixote's study; but that is nothing to the present purpose.

If it be objected to me that as we have learnt from the Arabs the art of rhyming it is more than probable that we have in like manner received from the same hands the science of romance, forasmuch as most of our old romances were in rhyme, and that the custom among the French lords to give their clothes to the best versifiers, and which Marmol saith was practised by the Kings of Fez, seems to justify that assertion, I must confess that it is not impossible but that when the French borrowed their rhyme from the Arabs they at the same time learnt from them the custom of using it in romance. I will allow farther that the taste we had before for fable might be augmented and our science in romance improved, from the intercourse our vicinity to Spain and the wars with that nation have introduced between us and the Spaniards; but I do not agree that we owe to them originally this inclination, since we were possessed with it long before it was observed in Spain. . . .

It is very likely that the Italians were first induced to write romances from the example of the Provencials whilst the popes resided at Avignon; as likewise from the example of other Frenchmen, first, when the Normans, and afterwards when Charles, Earl of Anjou, brother of St. Louis, a virtuous prince, a lover of poetry, and himself a poet, carried on the war in Italy. For the Normans, as well as the rest, were dabblers in the *gay science*, and we learn from history that they sung the exploits of Roland just before they began that memorable battle wherein William the Bastard got the crown of England. All Europe was, at that time, involved in a cloud of impenetrable ignorance, though that ignorance prevailed less in France, England and Germany than in Italy, which, in those days, produced a very small number of authors, and hardly one writer of romance. Those of that country who were desirous to distinguish themselves with some tincture of knowledge came for that purpose to study in the University of Paris, the mother of sciences and nurse of the learned. St. Thomas Aquinas, St. Bonaventure, the poets Dante and Boccaccio were students there, and the President Fauchet has proved that Boccaccio has taken most of his novels out of our French romances, and that Petrarch and the other Italian poets have stolen their most beautiful passages [from] the songs of Thibaud, King of Navarre, from Gace's Brussez, from the Chatelain de Coucy, and [from] the old French romancers.[26] It was therefore, according to my opinion, during this intercourse between the two nations that the Italians learnt from us the science of romance, which they owe to us, as well as that of rhyming.

In this manner did Spain and Italy receive from us an art which was the effect of our ignorance and unpoliteness, but the fruit of politeness in the Persians, Greeks, and Ionians. In a word, as necessity compels us for the preservation of our lives to feed upon herbs and roots for want of bread, in like manner, when the knowledge of truth, which is the proper and natural food of the mind, is wanting, we support it with fiction, which is in imitation of truth. And as in the midst of plenty, to regale our taste, we sometimes quit our bread and usual food for the sake of ragouts, so when the mind is possessed of the truth it often quits the study and speculation of it to divert itself in the image of truth, which is falsehood. For the image and imitation are, according to Aristotle, sometimes more agreeable than truth itself, insomuch that two roads directly contrary, that is, ignorance and erudition, politeness and barbarity, often conduct men to one and the same end, the study of fictions, fables, and romances. From hence it is that the nations that are the most barbarous delight in romantic inventions, as those that are opposite love such as are most polite. The accounts of the originals of all the savage nations in America, and particularly those of Peru, are stuffed with fables, as are those of the Goths, which they inscribed heretofore in their ancient Runic characters upon large stones, of which I have seen some fragments in Denmark; and if we had anything remaining of the writings composed by the bards in Gaul to eternise the memory of their nation, I do not question but we should find them embellished with a multitude of fictions.

This inclination to fables, which is common to all men, is not the effect of reasoning, nor does it arise from imitation or custom; it is natural to them, and is riveted in the very frame and disposition of the soul. For the desire to learn and to know is peculiar to man, by which he is as much distinguished from other creatures as by his reason. Nay, the sparks of an imperfect rough-hewn reason are observable in some animals, but the desire of knowledge is found nowhere but in man. And this is, according to my opinion, because the faculties of our mind are of too great an extent, and of a capacity too large to be filled and satisfied with present objects, for which reason she searcheth into what is past and to come, into truth and falsehood, into imaginary spaces and even impossibilities, to find out wherewithal to exercise and satisfy those faculties. Brutes find in the objects presented to their senses sufficient to answer the powers of their mind, and go no farther; insomuch that we never observe in them that impatient thirst which incessantly incites the mind of man to search after new discoveries and [to] proportion, if it be possible, the object to the faculty, and taste therein a pleasure equal to that one finds in appeasing a violent hunger or in drinking after having been long under an impatient thirst. This is what Plato would represent to us in the fable of the marriage of Porus and Penia, that is, of riches and poverty, whose offspring, he saith, is pleasure.[27] The object is denoted by riches, which are not riches but when they are used, without which they remain unfruitful, and will never occasion the birth of pleasure. The faculty is expressed by poverty, and which is barren, and constantly attended with inquietude whilst debarred from riches; but upon their being joined, pleasure becomes the fruit of that union. This exactly squares with the disposition of our mind. Poverty, that is ignorance, is natural to it, and is continually breathing after knowledge, which is riches, and when possessed of it, that possession is attended with pleasure. But this pleasure is not always alike; it sometimes costs us a great deal of labor and pains, as when the mind applies itself to difficult speculations and abstruse sciences, whereof the subject matter is not present or obvious to our senses, and where the imagination, which works with ease, is less concerned and engaged than the understanding, whose operations are very laborious. And forasmuch as we are naturally shocked at the prospect of labor, the mind never engages in those knotty disquisitions but from the prospect of reward, or in the hope of some remote pleasure, or out of necessity. But those discoveries which engage and possess it the most effectually are such as are obtained with the least labor, wherein the imagination has the greatest share, and where the subject is such as is obvious to our senses; but more especially if those discoveries excite our passions, which give the main bias and motion to all the actions of our life. And of this sort are romances, which are to be comprehended without any great labor of the mind or the exercise of our rational faculty, and where a strong fancy will serve the turn with little or no burden to the memory. They do not raise our passions but to allay them, nor do they excite in us either fear or pity but that we may have the pleasure at [last] of seeing those escape out of the imaginary danger or distress wherein they at first had represented them. Love is not raised in us but to the end we may see those happy who are the objects of it, nor is our hatred moved but to give us the satisfaction of seeing those miserable against whom it was excited. In short, all our passions are there agreeably raised and laid. Hence it is that they who are governed more by passion than reason and act more with their imagination than understanding have a more sensible pleasure in romances; not but that the other find a pleasure in them too, but not after the same manner. These are taken with the beauties of the art and with those parts wherein the understanding was most concerned; but those, that is children and ignorants, are only touched with what strikes the imagination, and works upon their passions. They are in love with the fictions purely as such, and carry their thoughts no farther. Now fictions being narrations, that are true in appearance but false in effect, the simple, who look no farther than the outside and content themselves with the appearance of truth, rest themselves there; but they who have a deeper penetration and look into the bottom are apt to disrelish that which has only the appearance of truth. So that, in short, the first love the fiction for the sake of the appearance of truth under which it is disguised; but the later are disgusted at this imaginary truth by reason of the real falsity that is concealed under it, if that falsity is not at the same time ingenious, allegorical, and instructive, and supported by the excellency of art and invention. St. Austin saith somewhere that "those falsities which are significative and contain in them a hidden sense are not properly lies, but figurative truths, made use of by men renowned for their wisdom and sanctity, and even by our Saviour himself upon occasion."

Since therefore it is most certain that ignorance is the inexhaustible fund of falsehoods, and that the inundation of the barbarians who, issuing from the North, overran all Europe and sunk it into such an abyss of ignorance as that it was not able to recover itself out of it till about two hundred years since, is it not highly probable that the same cause produced the same effect here that it has at all times done in other places? And is it not therefore in vain to endeavor to prove that to be accidental which is manifestly natural? So that we are not to doubt but that the French, German, and English romances, with all the fables of the North, are of the country's growth, born upon the place and not transplanted thither, having no other beginning but in histories stuffed with falsehoods and written in those times of ignorance and obscurity, when men had neither industry nor curiosity enough to discover the truth, nor judgment to write it when discovered; that those histories patched up with truth and falsehoods, having been well received by the rude unpolished people, the writers were encouraged from thence to publish some that were all fiction, and those are romances. It is even the common opinion that history heretofore went by the name of romance, which word was afterwards applied to fictions; which is an invincible argument that the one arose out of the other. "Romances," [saith Pigna,] "according to the common opinion in France, were their annals, and for that reason the histories of their respective wars were published under that title likewise; whereupon others, in time, gave their writings the same name, how fabulous soever they were and foreign to truth."

Strabo, in a passage I have already cited, saith the histories of the Persians, Medes, and Syrians are not to be relied upon because the compilers of them, observing what high reputation the fabulists were in, endeavored to advance themselves likewise in the esteem of the people by giving fables the air of histories, that is, by writing romances. From whence we may conclude that the word *romance*, according to all appearance, had the same origin with us as it had heretofore among those nations.

But to return to the [trouvères] of Provence, who in France were the princes of romance: towards the end of the tenth century, their profession became so much in vogue that all the provinces in France, as has been already said, had in time their [trouvères] too. This produced in the eleventh century, and in those that succeeded, an infinite number of romances, both in prose and verse, many of which have, in spite of time, been continued down to us. Of this number were Garin le Loheran, Tristan, Lancelot du Lac, de Bertain, St. Greal, Merlin, Arthur, Perceval, Perceforet, and most of the hundred twenty-seven poets who lived before the year 1300, and upon whom the President Fauchet has written an examen. . . .

It will be sufficient to tell you that all these writings, being the fruits of ignorance, carried in them the marks of their original, and were no other than a heap of fictions bunglingly stitched one to another, and infinitely beneath that sovereign degree of art and elegance to which our nation has since raised the romance. We must confess it is a matter of wonder that at the same time that we have yielded to our neighbors the prize of epic poetry and history we should attain to such a perfection in this, as that their most finished romances come far short of the worst of ours. I am of opinion that this is owing to the politeness of our gallantry and the great liberty in which the men live with the women in France. [The women] are perfect recluses in Spain and Italy, and debarred from the men under so many obstacles that one rarely sees and seldom or never speaks to them. So that [the men] never study the art of agreeable courtship because the opportunities of putting it in practice are so rare. All their study lies in surmounting the difficulties that lie in their way to come at them; when that is done they make the best of their time without standing upon ceremony. But in France, where the ladies are left more at liberty and have no other guards upon them but their own honor, they are more impregnably secured within the bounds of that than they can be under all the locks, within all the grates, and under the care of the most vigilant duennas in Spain. This obliges the men with us to besiege in form that formidable entrenchment, and to employ so much pains and address to reduce it, that courtship is become an art in France almost unknown in other nations. It is this art which distinguishes the French romances from others, and has rendered the reading of them so bewitching that it has introduced among us a neglect of more useful studies. The ladies were the first that were taken with these allurements; they have made romances their entire study, and have so far despised that of the ancient fable and of history that they have quite laid aside those works which heretofore furnished them with their greatest ornaments. And to prevent blushing at that ignorance which they have such frequent occasions of discovering in themselves, they have found it more to their purpose to seem to despise what they do not know than to be at the pains to learn it. The men out of complaisance have followed their example. What the ladies condemn they condemn likewise, and call that pedantry which even in Malherbe's time was thought essential to politeness.[28] The succeeding poets and other [of] our French writers have been obliged to submit to this [verdict], and many of them, observing that the knowledge of antiquity was of no benefit to them, forbore studying that which they durst not put in practice. Thus a good cause has produced a very mischievous effect, and the beauty of our romances has occasioned a contempt of learning of which ignorance has been the unavoidable consequence.

I do not for this reason condemn the reading of them. The best things in the world are never without some inconveniencies, and romances [might have] worse consequences than ignorance. I know what is commonly objected to them: they deaden our devotion, they inspire us with irregular passions, and corrupt our manners. This may happen, and without doubt does happen sometimes. But what may not be perverted by a vicious inclination? Weak minds are contagious to themselves, and turn everything into poison. Upon that account, the reading of history ought to be forbidden because it affords so many pernicious examples, and mythology laid aside where transgressions are warranted from the practice of the gods themselves. A marble statue which was the object of public devotion among the heathens incited a certain young man to brutality and despair. Cherea in Terence [fortifies] himself in the prosecution of a criminal design from a painting of Jupiter, which perhaps was revered by all other spectators.[29] Small regard was had to the sobriety of manners in the generality of the Greek and old French romances, and that through the corruption of the times wherein they were written. Even *Astrea*,[30] and some other romances that succeeded, are in a degree licentious; but the romances of this age, I speak of the good ones, are so free from that imputation that there is not in them a single word or expression offensive to a chaste ear, or an action distasteful to a modest mind. If it is objected that love is therein treated after a manner so refined and insinuating that the bait of that dangerous passion is too easily swallowed by unguarded minds, I answer that it is so far from being dangerous that it is in some sort necessary for young persons to be acquainted with that passion that they may be able to shut their ears against it when it is criminal and know how to conduct themselves in it when it is innocent and honorable. This is evident from experience, which shows us that they who are the least read in love are most open to it, and that the most ignorant are the greatest cullies. Let us add to this that nothing quickens the mind so much or conduces more to the forming and finishing of it than good romances. They are silent instructors that take us up where the college left us, teaching us to speak and live after a method more edifying and persuasive than what is practised there, to whom Horace's compliment upon the *Iliad* may justly be applied, that morality is more effectually taught by them than by the precepts of the most able philosophers.[31]

Monsieur d'Urfé was the first who retrieved them from barbarity, and brought them under a regulation in his incomparable *Astrea*, a piece the most ingenious and polite of any of that kind that had appeared, and which eclipsed the glory Greece, Italy and Spain had acquired before. However, this did not discourage others who followed from entering into the same lists, or so far engrossed the esteem of the public as to leave none for so many beautiful romances as have appeared in France since his time. We cannot behold without admiration those a lady as illustrious for her modesty as her merit has published under a borrowed name, thereby generously depriving herself of a reputation so justly her due, and seeking no other recompense but what flowed from her own virtue, as if whilst she was laboring so industriously for the glory of our nation she was willing to spare our sex the shame of it. But time has done her that justice which she denied herself, and it is [now no] longer a secret that the *Illustrious Bassa*, the *Grand Cyrus*, and *Clelia* are the performances of Mademoiselle de Scudéry, so that the art of writing romances, which can justify itself against censure not only from the commendations given it by the patriarch Photinus but from the examples of those who have dealt in it may at last receive a sanction from her; and after having been cultivated by philosophers, as Apuleius and Athenagoras, by a Roman praetor, as Sisenna, by a consul, as Petronius, by a pretender to the empire, as Clodius Albinus, by a priest, as Theodorus Prodromus, by bishops, as Heliodorus and Achilles Tatius, by a Pope, as Pius II, who wrote the amours of Euryalus and Lucrece, and by a saint, as St. John of Damascus, it is at length arrived to the highest pitch of glory, by being professed by a grave and virtuous virgin.[32] As for you sir, since it is true, as I have made appear, and as Plutarch assures us, that there is no charm can captivate the soul of man so effectually as the contexture of a fable well invented and related, what success may you not promise to yourself from *Zayde*, wherein the adventures are so new and moving, and the narration so just and polite? I could wish, from the concern I have for the glory of that great monarch heaven has placed over us, that we had a history of his illustrious reign, written in a style as noble and with the same accuracy and judgment. The virtues which conduct his great actions are so heroic and that fortune which accompanies them is so surprising that posterity may doubt whether it be a history or romance.

Dominique Bouhours THE BEL ESPRIT FROM "THE CONVERSATIONS OF ARISTO AND EUGENE"

Eugene and Aristo began their walk with the reading of a work containing both prose and verse which one of their friends had recently composed. They read it attentively, as new things are always read; and after examining it at leisure they were both of the opinion that for a long time nothing had appeared which was wittier or more reasonable.

A man must be very intelligent, said Eugene, to write the kinds of works in which witticisms glitter everywhere and in which there are no paste jewels.

Intelligence alone is not enough, replied Aristo; a special kind is needed. Only the keenest wit produces masterpieces, for it is the quality which gives to excellent pieces of writing the special shape which distinguishes them from ordinary ones, and that characteristic of perfection by which new charms are always to be found in them. But everybody does not have this keen wit I am speaking of, he added, and he who counterfeits the clever man has it perhaps less than another. For there is much difference between being professionally clever and having a keen wit of a certain beauty which I can imagine.

If that beauty of wit which you imagine is a very rare thing, said Eugene, the reputation for cleverness is fairly common; it is the compliment most frequently paid in society. It even seems to me there is no quality more easily acquired. One need only be able to tell a story agreeably or turn a line of verse: a trifle gracefully said, a madrigal, a couplet for a song can often be the basis for a reputation as a wit; and you must agree that it is of these clever talkers and makers of pretty things that we are accustomed to say, He is a bel esprit.

I admit, answered Aristo, that this title has been as freely and unjustly usurped in our time as that of gentleman or marquis; and if the usurpers in the realm of letters were punished as severely as these other usurpers have been in France many people would be degraded from that rank as many have been from the nobility. Those clever gentlemen would have a hard time commanding respect for their madrigals, their jingles, and their impromptus and thus maintaining themselves in their present status; I am sure they would not find in their papers grounds for clinging to the eminence they claim. Their titles are no better than those of false nobles; the name they bear is a name floating in the air unsupported by anything substantial; they have a reputation for wit but without deserving it and without exemplifying it.

The witty man is a foolish type, said Eugene, and I don't know whether I wouldn't rather be a little stupid than to pass as what is ordinarily called clever.

All reasonable men are of your opinion, answered Aristo. Wit has been so much disparaged since its profanation through being made too common that the wittiest men object to the name and avoid being accused of it as though it were a crime. Those who are still proud of the name are not the decent people in society; indeed, they are far from being what they think they are; they are nothing less than beaux esprits, for true beauty of wit consists in a just and delicate discernment which those gentlemen do not have. That discernment shows things to be what they are in themselves, not stopping too soon, as do the common people who do not go below the surface, and not going too far like those refined intelligences which, through an excess of subtlety, evaporate in vain and chimerical imaginings.

It seems to me, interrupted Eugene, that this exquisite discernment is more closely related to common sense than to bel esprit.

True wit, answered Aristo, is inseparable from common sense, and it is a mistake to confuse it with that sort of vivacity which has nothing solid in it. One might say that judgment is the foundation for beauty of wit; or rather bel esprit is of the nature of those precious stones which are not less solid than brilliant. There is nothing more beautiful than a well-cut and well-polished diamond; it shines on every side and on every facet. *Quanta sodezza, tanto ha splendore.*[1] It is solid but brilliant matter, it dazzles but has consistency and body. The union, the mixture, the proportion of the brilliant with the solid give it all its charm and all its value. There is a symbol for bel esprit as I conceive it. It is equally brilliant and solid: it might well be defined as common sense which sparkles. For there is a kind of gloomy, bleak common sense which is hardly less the contrary of wit than is a false brilliance. The common sense I am speaking of is entirely different; it is gay, lively, full of fire, like that which is seen in the *Essays* of Montaigne and in the *Testament* of la Hoguette;[2] it proceeds from a straight and luminous intelligence and from a clear and pleasant imagination.

The just apportionment of vivacity to common sense renders the mind subtle but not vapid, brilliant but not too brilliant, quick to conceive an idea, and sound in all its judgments. With that kind of wit one thinks of things properly and expresses them as well as they have been thought. Much meaning is gathered into few words, everything is said that need be said and only that is said which must be said. The bel esprit is concerned more with things than with words; yet he does not scorn the ornaments of language, neither does he seek them out; the polish of his style does not lessen its strength, and he might be compared to those soldiers under Caesar who, for all they were clean and perfumed, were nonetheless valiant men who fought well.[3]

On the basis of what you are saying, remarked Eugene, there is not much difference between a bel esprit and a rationalist (*esprit fort*).

There is none at all, replied Aristo, if we take the latter expression in its literal meaning, a strong mind. The beauty of wit is a masculine and gallant beauty which has in it nothing soft or effeminate.

But that strength does not consist in doubting everything, in believing nothing, and in being stiff-necked before established truths. According to the remark of a Father of the Church, that kind of strength is the strength of a madman.[4] True strength consists, then, in reasoning well, in getting down to fundamental principles of knowledge and in discovering the most hidden truths. It is right for a thinker to go deeply into the subjects he treats and not to let himself be led astray by appearances. Reasons which satisfy lesser minds are not reasons for him; he always goes straight to his goal by whatever way may best lead there, without being diverted and without dawdling. His principal characteristic is to sweep other minds along in the direction he wishes them to take and to make himself master of them when he chooses. This was one of the qualities of the last Marshal Schomberg;[5] it was said of him as well of Caesar that he talked as courageously as he fought, and that his weapons were not more invincible than his arguments.

But do not imagine that the bel esprit, because he is very strong, is for that reason lacking in delicacy: he resembles Achilles in Homer and Rinaldo in Tasso whose nerves and muscles were extremely strong under a white and tender skin. His solidity and profundity do not keep him from conceiving things with finesse, nor from giving refined expression to all that he thinks. The images by which he expresses his thoughts are like those paintings which have all the technique of art and in addition what must be called a tender and graceful air which charms the connoisseur.

There are excellent minds which have no delicacy and who are proud of having none, as if delicacy were incompatible with strength. Their way of thinking and saying things has no sweetness and no attractiveness. With all their learning and all their subtlety their imaginations are in some way sombre and crude, like that Spanish painter who could make only coarse strokes and who proudly replied one day to those who criticized him for this that he preferred to be *primero en aquella grossería que secundo en delicadeza.*[6]

But men of this turn of mind, however good they may be, are not so felicitous in their works as that painter was in his. The most learned writings and even the most ingenious are judged unfavorably in our day if they are not delicately handled. Besides their solidity and their strength they must have what I shall call an agreeable and flowery quality in order to please people of good taste, and that is what gives individuality to beautiful things. To understand what I mean, remember what Plato says, that beauty is like the flower of goodness. According to that philosopher good things which do not have that flower are only good, and those which have it are really beautiful.

That is to say, added Eugene, that the bel esprit, if we define him Platonically, is a good mind in flower, like those trees which bear fruit and flowers at the same time and in which we see the maturity of autumn allied to the beauty of spring.

Col fior, maturo ha, sempre il frutto.[7]

Those fruits and flowers, Aristo went on, indicate also that happy fecundity which is so fitting in a gifted man. For myself I consider there is not less difference between sterile minds and those which are not than there is between handsome orange trees and mean growths which produce no fruit.

I doubt, interrupted Eugene, whether fertility is a sound indication of beauty of mind. It seems to me that the most fecund minds are not always the most reasonable or the most acute. Great fecundity most often degenerates into an undesirable abundance, into a profusion of false and useless thoughts; and if you examine the question carefully you will see that what you are calling a property of the bel esprit is usually no more than the effect of an unbridled imagination.

I am well aware, replied Aristo, that there is a fertility of mind similar to that of trees which, because they are too heavy-laden with fruit, bear little that is good. The fecundity I am speaking of is not of that kind. It is what I have called a happy fecundity, not only a stock of good things but one which is controlled by common sense. A real bel esprit is like those rich and wise people who live magnificently in every way, yet who nevertheless are not extravagant.

By that criterion, said Eugene, Marino would not be a bel esprit. For never has a more fertile imagination been seen, nor one less controlled, than his. You know this better than I. If he speaks of a nightingale or a rose, he says of it everything imaginable; far from rejecting what presents itself to him, he goes out of his way to seek what does not occur to him; he always exhausts his subject.

I agree, replied Aristo, and I shall also confess to you, he added laughing, that if letters patent for the bel esprit were issued as they are for the nobility I should never approve their being given to those kinds of authors who do not control their ideas or their words, and who leave nothing to be thought or said on the subjects they treat. But not all poets are as mad or as undisciplined as Marino. Some of them are wise and moderate, even among the Italians, though the only example I can give is that of Tasso.

I assure you, said Eugene, that Tasso is not always the most reasonable man in the world. Truly, it is not possible to have more genius than he has. His conceptions are noble and agreeable; his feelings are strong or delicate depending upon what the subject requires; his passions are well handled and well developed, all his comparisons are exact, all his descriptions are marvelous; but his genius sometimes carries him away; in some places he is too flowery; he trifles at rather serious junctures; he is not so respectful as Virgil of all the moral proprieties.

Yet there are in his works such great beauties, replied Aristo, that he may be pardoned these little faults. If he is a little lacking in that good sense which distinguishes Virgil from the other poets still he has an abundance of that sacred fire which makes poets. After all, whatever liberties he takes, he does not lose himself as Marino does and Ariosto.

But to go on with our discourse, he continued, a bel esprit is rich in his own resources; he finds in his own understanding what ordinary people find only in books. He studies himself and educates himself, as a learned man said of one of the greatest geniuses France has ever produced.[8] Above all he does not take over the thoughts of others; he does not steal from the ancients or from foreigners the works he gives to the public.

Yet, said Eugene, that is what most of our clever men do. They continually pillage the Greeks and the Romans, the Italians and the Spaniards; and if anyone were willing to examine their works carefully he would discover that the land of Belles Lettres is full of robbers and that Mercury, who presides over the arts and sciences, is also, and not without cause, the god of thieves, as Bartoli cleverly remarks in his *L'Uomo di lettere*.[9] For while criticizing those who steal the thoughts of others I have no desire to steal this one from its author.

While forbidding larceny to the bel esprit, Aristo went on, I do not intend to forbid him to read good books; I do not even claim that his reading ought to be useless to him. I am willing for him to imitate the great models of antiquity if only he tries to surpass them in his imitation; but I cannot allow him to do like those minor painters who limit themselves to copying the originals and who would produce nothing beautiful if the masters of the art had not done so before them.

I am also perfectly willing for him to use at certain junctures thoughts from good authors provided that he adds new beauties to them, and following the example of bees who change into honey what they take from flowers, not only that he chooses what is good in books but that besides he makes his own what he chooses, and that he turns it into something better through the usage he makes of it. This is one of the great talents of Voiture;[10] he has made himself inimitable through imitating others; he knows admirably the art of drawing the best from, and of showing off the thought of, his authors; the lines he sometimes borrows from Terence and Horace seem made for his subject and are even more beautiful in the places where he puts them than in those whence he took them, just as precious stones are more beautiful when mounted in rings than in the rocks whence they are extracted.

But do not suppose that all of the beauty of wit can be reduced to this. Besides what I have just mentioned, it demands a nature able to acquire all the artistic skills, a lofty and broad intelligence, unlimited and unsurpassed. For beauty of wit is like that of the body: little men, however well

165

formed, are not handsome, in Aristotle's opinion; at best they are only agreeable, because to have the advantage of stature is an essential part of beauty. Thus the little genius who is limited to a single thing, the maker of pretty verses who can do only that with whatever charm and decorum, is not a bel esprit, say what you will; he is really only a wit and it would be enough for him to be accepted on that footing in society.

Moreover, to be a bel esprit it is not enough to have a solid, profound, delicate, fertile, just, and universal intelligence; the mind must have besides a certain clarity which all great geniuses do not have. For some of them are naturally obscure and even affect obscurity; a large proportion of their ideas are so many enigmas and mysteries; their language is a kind of cipher which can be understood only through divination. Among modern Spaniards Gracián is one of these incomprehensible geniuses; he can rise very high, he has subtlety, strength, and common sense; but most of the time the reader doesn't know what he means as perhaps he doesn't know himself; some of his works seem made to defy understanding.

However, there ought to be neither obscurity nor confusion in what comes from a bel esprit; his thoughts and expressions must be so noble and so clear that the most intelligent of his readers admire him and the least intelligent understand him. Malherbe, who was no doubt a great genius, tried above all to give this quality of clarity to all that he wrote; and you know that when he had composed a work he read it to his servant before showing it at court in order to find out whether he had completely succeeded, believing that works of the intelligence do not achieve entire perfection if they are not filled with a certain beauty which is accessible even to the crudest of men.[11] It is plain to you, of course, that this beauty must be simple and unstudied, free of pretense and artifice, if it is to make its effect; and on that basis you can judge those writers who are not natural, who are always stilted in expression, and who try never to say anything except what surprises and dazzles.

Heavens! how you please me, said Eugene, in excluding from the company of the beaux esprits those eternal sayers of witticisms and maxims; those copiers and apes of Seneca; those Mancini, Malvezzi, and Loredans [12] who are always trying to shine through clever remarks or *vivezze d'ingegno*, as they say in their language. For to tell the truth, I cannot bear them, and I have trouble putting up with Seneca himself because of his perpetual witticisms and antitheses.

Nothing outrages common sense more than that, said Aristo, and in my opinion it is a greater defect to shine excessively than not to shine enough.

There is nothing finer than the conception you have of the bel esprit, answered Eugene. I very nearly said there is nothing finer than this picture of you, for you have, as it were, painted yourself in the picture you have just made, so much does it resemble you.

If I painted myself, said Aristo, smiling, it was so flatteringly that I do not recognize myself. But to answer you seriously, he added, I have too low an opinion of myself to believe that I am a good model of the bel esprit; I do not aspire so high and I should be ridiculous to do so.

But one must not aspire to it, said Eugene. One must not even be grateful that one is a bel esprit in order really to be one; and if I dared touch the picture you have drawn, I should add to it modesty as a last trait. It is a quality which gives relief to all the others and which is not less becoming to a bel esprit than to a pretty woman.

I am entirely of your opinion, answered Aristo, and I admit that I detest nothing so much as certain mediocrities who try very hard to be imposing. They have in their behavior, their movements, and even in the tone of their voice a quality of pride and self-sufficiency which leads one to judge that they are well satisfied with themselves. They profess never to be favorably impressed by anything and to find something to criticize in everything. Every work of literature seems to them pitiable, but on the other hand they admire all that they do themselves. In company they often take an oracular tone and decide every question highhandedly. They make a great mystery of their works perhaps from affectation, or in order to excite further the curiosity of those who want to see them, or because they judge few people capable of admiring them at their full value. Those works are hidden treasures which they show only to three or four of their admirers.

There is another class of minds, continued Eugene, who are less mysterious but who are not less convinced of their own merit. No sooner have they tossed off some trifle than they present it to everybody. They are always ready to recite their madrigals and odes in order to attract a little praise; they shamelessly praise themselves and are the first to burn incense in their own honor. However, the real bel esprit has the qualities of a real hero who never talks of what he has done. He avoids general applause, and far from pushing himself in where he is not wanted, he hides as much as he can.

I don't know, said Aristo, whether there might not be more modesty in less affectation. You have heard of that woman whom Nero loved so much, and you know that she was not very respectable. Yet, if we are to believe Tacitus, she rarely showed herself and never went out unveiled.[13]

A bel esprit ought, in my opinion, keep the temperament of Tasso's Sofronia, who was as modest as she was beautiful.

Non coprì sue bellezze, e non l'espose.[14]

He need not always keep his works a mystery, but neither must he show them everywhere; he must neither hide himself through affectation nor show himself through vanity.

Now I see, said Eugene, why the real bel esprit is so rare. Qualities as contrary as vivacity and common sense, delicacy and strength, not to mention the others, are not often found together. But I should like very much to know, he added, whence come all the qualities which make a man a bel esprit.

They come, replied Aristo, from a fortunate temperament and a certain arrangement of the organs: they are the result of a well-made and a well-proportioned head, of a well-tempered brain filled with a delicate substance, of an ardent and luminous bile made firm by melancholy and softened by the blood. The bile gives brilliance and profundity, melancholy gives good sense and solidity, the blood, charm and finesse.

I do not understand all this, said Eugene, about bile, blood and melancholy, for indeed I cannot believe that spiritual qualities more angelic than human owe what they are to what we have in common with the animals; and I do not see how the humors which stagnate in the body can be the principle of the noblest operations of the soul.

I have read in some Platonic philosopher or other, replied Aristo, that however material these humors may be they create great minds more or less as the vapors of the earth make thunder and lightning. This philosopher's idea is subtle and ingenious. I think he means that the spirits of the blood and the bile glow in the brain as a warm exhalation catches fire in a cold and damp cloud; that these glowing spirits spread through the head that *dry splendor* which according to Heraclitus makes the soul wise and intelligent; that as in corporeal things there is nothing which has less matter and more virtue, which is purer and more alive than these spirits, therefore that the flame which comes from them is the subtlest, livest and most ardent that exists in nature; that it is this flame which illumines the reason and at the same time warms the imagination; that this flame renders visible to the soul the physical shape of things and shows all things to the soul in their true light; in a word, that it is by the light of this good fire that the understanding discovers and contemplates the most hidden truths; and that it is perhaps this fire which shines in the eyes of intelligent people and distinguishes them from the stupid, whose gloomy, somber eyes sufficiently indicate that they have in their heads only a black and dark fire better suited to befog the soul than to illumine it.

Those are truly beautiful visions, said Eugene, and perhaps the daydreams of poets as much deserve belief as the ideas of those philosophers.

Even though you were to call Abelard himself a dreamer and a visionary, replied Aristo, I must tell you his idea about the differences among minds. His dear Heloïse one day put to him the question you have asked me. He answered that all men have a looking-glass in their head, and this answer was based on the words of Saint Paul [15] to the effect that we see as in a glass darkly during this life; but he added that crude minds had a dull glass and subtle minds a shining, clear one which represented objects distinctly to them. He meant that bile mixed with blood formed in the brain a kind of polished, shining surface to which melancholy served as the silver.

Whatever you may say, continued Eugene, and whatever your amorous doctor may say, I cannot make myself believe that souls borrow their light from bodies, and that beauty of mind is a perfection foreign to the spirit itself. I should rather believe that the perfection of the body depends on that of the spirit, or at least that the excellence of the spirit comes from the nobility of the soul.

I am aware that all souls are of the same kind, but that is no hindrance, if we are to believe the most reasonable philosophers, to their having special perfections which distinguish them adequately from each other, as the stars have differing degrees of clarity or differences in other qualities although they are all composed of the same matter. In truth, all reasonable souls are images of God; all are marked by the light of His countenance as the prophet says; but there exist some in which that light is better seen and in which the characteristics of its divine beauty are more deeply graven; these are the noblest and the most perfect, the most intelligent and the most ingenious. For as some figures made in wax with the same seal are clearer and better shaped than others owing to nothing but the hand that pressed down the seal, so the perfection found in some souls results from the fact that the image of God is better imprinted upon them; the greater strength of this impression makes them in some way more spiritual and more divine.

But if that is true, said Aristo, how does it come about that although the soul is incorruptible and unalterable by its nature, the mind is altered by a vapor which rises to the brain and sometimes takes away the reason?

The reason is that the noblest souls, answered Eugene, are like painters who, however skillful they may be, can do nothing without the instruments of their art. The good disposition of the organs and the special tempering of the humors do not alone make souls intelligent and ingenious, any more than delicate brushes and fine paints make excellent painters; but the organs and the humors are instruments needed by the soul if it is to act while it is in the body; once these instruments are spoiled the soul no longer acts or acts only imperfectly however perfect it may be in itself. The soul is then comparable to a good painter who has poor brushes and poor paints.

What you say is clever, interrupted Aristo, but after all, the philosophers you believe the wisest are not better founded on reason than the others; and I am very much afraid, he added laughingly, that if that nobility of soul, to which they attribute excellence of intelligence, were to be examined, the criteria by which they judge it would be found to be false. The best decision, in my opinion, is not to take sides in disputes where the truth cannot be recognized; and the most reasonable men perhaps are those who reason least about matters like that.

However that may be, Eugene continued, it is certain that nature alone does not make the bel esprit. The most fortunate native endowment must be completed by a good education and by that experience with the world which refines the intelligence and makes common sense more subtle. Thus it comes about that professional scholars are usually not beaux esprits; as they are always buried in study and have little intercourse with respectable people, their minds do not have that special politeness and that indefinable charm which they must have. Not that learning is in itself opposed to beauty of mind, but rather that the great doctors and those who know the most Greek and Latin ordinarily do not know how to use their knowledge.

It is also certain, he added, that no matter what principle such beauty comes from, there is more than one kind of bel esprit. For besides those we have mentioned up to now who excel in letters and who have acquired all the knowledge study can give, there are others who, although they have studied almost nothing except society, have all they need in order to succeed in conversation.

The characteristic of men like that is to speak well and easily and to give an entertaining twist to whatever they say; in company they always return very clever answers; they always have some subtle question to propose and some amusing story to tell with which they urge on the conversation or stimulate it when it begins to languish; once they are fairly started they say a thousand amazing things; they are skilled in witty badinage and clever chaff when the conversation is gay, but they also manage very well in serious ones; they think soundly on all subjects which are brought up and they always speak solid sense.

There is also another kind of bel esprit who can be called the diplomat or the statesman. Such a man has a clear, judicious, active intelligence suited to affairs; with one glance he looks into the heart of the matter and analyzes all its attendant circumstances and all its consequences; he finds at once all the expedients and the means by which the most difficult affairs can be handled and made to succeed. But he sees only what must be seen and only as much as he need see in order to come to a sound decision and make a reasonable choice, for it is sometimes a weakness in practical life to be too profound and too intelligent; many different points of view and different approaches dissipate the mind and often hinder execution; the time for action is spent in deliberating.

Such men are born for the government of States, for they conceive only great plans, useful to the country and glorious to the Prince; this happens especially when the Prince, convinced of their ability, their faithfulness, and their zeal, turns over to them the direction of affairs. Since they have both great intelligence and much experience they take no false measures and make no false advances. Then if fortune, which is not always in agreement with prudence, does not favor all their enterprises, they profit from their bad luck, imitating those wise steersmen who make use of contrary winds as well as of favorable ones. In negotiations they conduct themselves with great skill and in a very delicate way; first they lay bare the thoughts of him with whom they are dealing while hiding their own; they insinuate their point of view into his mind; they urge him to it on the ground of his own interest; they handle and steer him so well that he imagines he will get what he wants by agreeing with them and ends by giving what they want without even knowing he is giving. Such were Cardinal

Richelieu and Count Olivares, the two most famous ministers that France and Spain have ever had.

Those are the different characteristics of the bel esprit. These three kinds of beauty, although they are different, are occasionally found in one person. For not to mention the ancients and foreigners, Cardinal Duperron and the late Monsieur d'Avaux [16] were equally well suited to letters, to conversation, and to business; there are others among us who scarcely yield to these great men and who are equally capable of writing a work of literature, of telling a pleasant story, and of negotiating a peace treaty.

However, generally speaking, these three talents are only rarely found together. Men skilled in affairs do not ordinarily succeed in literature; but also the most polished and precise authors do not always shine in conversation. The first group have more solidity than finesse; the study of statecraft completely occupies them; they count other kinds of knowledge as nothing. The second group are too delicate and too touchy; they are almost never satisfied with what occurs to them; they almost never say anything when they are in company through thinking about what they mean to say. Since they are accustomed to sink into a brown study in order to phrase their thought well, they are most often absent-minded; they are often gloomily silent in a gay conversation, but also, since they have their heads full of their own compositions, they sometimes talk too much; they draw all the conversation to themselves and leave no chance for others to talk.

Conversational wit is a natural wit, opposed to labor and constraint; it is the opposite of learning and skill in affairs; thus we see that those who have this talent are ordinarily idlers whose principal occupation is the paying and receiving of visits. Hence, if one looks deeply into these things, it seems that these different kinds of wit are incompatible, and even that they require completely contrary natural predispositions.

Although it may seem, said Aristo then, that the bel esprit must belong to one of the various classes you have just marked out, yet he belongs to every one of those classes, for he is born ready for anything and has in himself talents such that he will succeed in whatever he wishes to undertake. The apparent diversity comes less from the nature of wit than from the subjects on which it is exercised. Great men who excel in certain things because they applied themselves to these in their youth would perhaps have succeeded equally well in others if they had brought to them as much care and application.

Dominique Bouhours

Chance, which takes a hand in the way men live and which often is the determining factor in the profession they embrace, ordinarily makes the difference we see among intelligences. Some find themselves led, I do not know how, to establish their reputation and fortune through poetry; for this they need only to have succeeded with a sonnet inspired by passion or perhaps by mere caprice; the praise which results from this is tempting bait which leads them to try a second; the high opinion one comes easily to have of oneself urges the writer on to something greater; he reads the poets, he studies the fables, he consults the masters of the art; in a word he specializes in poetry and bit by bit becomes a professional poet almost without being able to be anything else. Now if these excellent poets do not always have a talent for business or for conversation the reason is that they have taken another road from the beginning, and instead of studying politics and seeing the best people they have devoted themselves to books and writing.

The diplomatic bent is generally given pre-eminence and usually called the great talent and the great capacity, yet it does not differ from these others except by the exalted quality of its subject matter, for one cannot suggest anything more noble than to protect the interests of Princes, to enter into their most secret designs, to reconcile their differences, and to govern their lands. This is the sublimest and most glorious occupation of the mind; nothing so flatters the self-esteem, nothing better satisfies ambition than the dazzling titles of Ambassador, of Plenipotentiary, and Minister of State. Those who have been raised to these high dignities have a quality of grandeur and authority which distinguishes them from the rest of men; they are on earth what in heaven are the angels of the first order, those who approach closest to God's throne, who are illumined directly by Him and who are destined for the most important things.

However, when one examines the situation, it becomes apparent that it is chance which makes these great men by leading them sometimes into countries and into houses where by accidental and unforeseen encounters they accept employment from ambassadors and ministers. This decision requires them to concern themselves with affairs; application causes them to succeed in them and in time makes them eligible for the first offices of the State. Thus it is really chance which leads a bel esprit to play a leading part in the theater of this world while chance, too, leaves others in dust and darkness. For assuredly there are men of parts who are unknown and unused because they have no employment to show them off and to compel them to work.

I admit, said Eugene, that chance contributes much to the formation of a statesman, but it can do nothing without nature; for however favorable opportunities may be, and however industrious a man may be, few reach the dignity of Prime Minister without a talent for great affairs. For despite what you say, genius is a particular skill and a certain talent which nature gives to certain men for certain tasks. Some have it for painting and others for verse; it is not enough to have intelligence and imagination to succeed in poetry: one must be born a poet and to have that natural bent which depends neither on art nor on study and which derives in some way from inspiration.

I am of the same opinion about diplomacy and statecraft. It is not enough to be well educated and even very wise in order to succeed in it; one must have a special gift for governing other men's minds under the Prince's authority, so as to command while obeying. This has led a Spanish political writer to declare that aptitude and intelligence are the two principal causes for the advancement and the glory of a great man. *Genio y ingenio los dos ejes del lucimiento de prendas: el uno sin el otro felicidad a medias, no basta lo entendido, desease lo genial.*[17]

It is true that this natural bent, however powerful it may be, languishes as you might say, and is stifled outside the uses to which it is fitted because its development and activity require a certain subject-matter. But if we consider talent in itself, we see that it is independent of luck and fortune; it is a gift of heaven in which the earth has no part; it is this divine something which makes a bel esprit whom the providence of God has destined to the government of an Empire, which makes him, I say, naturally good and just, zealous for the glory of his prince and for the good of his country, equal to the most difficult enterprises, firm and constant in the most trying situations, impenetrable to the most piercing gaze, insensible to pleasure, indefatigable in work, free and tranquil in reverses, and always master of himself as of his affairs which, great as they are, are always subordinate to his talent.

Not that such a minister as I am imagining is limited only to affairs. Since his mind is almost infinitely broad, he has a tincture of every science; when he wishes he can even make eloquent speeches and hold his ground in an academy of beaux esprits as he does in the council of a powerful monarch; but after all, political genius is his dominant quality and his true characteristic.

I am very much pleased with that portrait of the perfect minister, said Aristo, and what pleases me most is that apparently you have not made an imaginary portrait. If I am not mistaken, your statesman is more real than Aristotle's Philosopher or Seneca's Sage; I am happy about this for the honor of our nation, for, to tell you the truth, I should be very much chagrined if France were no more important than Greece or Italy.

The Greeks and Romans, replied Eugene, are so jealous of the glory of their nation that one cannot argue about any aspect of it without quarreling with them and without having to answer for this to the bravest and cleverest men alive. For myself, he continued, laughing, since I do not like to make enemies, I prefer to yield to the Greeks and Romans and to confess in good faith that all countries are sterile in heroes when compared with ancient Greece and ancient Italy.

At least you must admit, said Aristo, that the bel esprit is found in all countries and all nations; thus, as there once were Greek and Roman beaux esprits, so there are now French, Italian, Spanish, English, even German and Russian ones.

A German or Russian bel esprit is an oddity, answered Eugene, and if there are some in the world, they must be like those spirits which never appear without causing astonishment. Cardinal Duperron once said of the Jesuit Gretser, *He is very intelligent — for a German,* as if a very intelligent German were a miracle.[18]

I allow, interrupted Aristo, that the bel esprit is rarer in cold countries because nature in those parts is drearier and more languishing so to speak.

Say rather, remarked Eugene, that the bel esprit as you have defined him is not at all compatible with the coarse temperament and the massive bodies of northern peoples.

I do not mean, he added, that all northerners are stupid; there is wit and learning in Germany and Poland as elsewhere; but all things considered, our bel esprit is unknown there, as is that art which is not learned in school and whose first rule is politeness; or if they are both known there it is only as foreigners whose language is not understood and to whom one cannot become accustomed.

I am not even sure that the Italian and Spanish beaux esprits are of the same kind as ours; of course they have some of the same qualities and characteristics, but I rather doubt whether the resemblance goes any further and whether they have precisely the character you have described. For after all this character is so suited to our nation that it cannot be found outside of France, whether because it results from some quality of the climate, or because our national spirit contributes something to it, or finally because it is the fate of the French nation to have this fine quality of mind today when other peoples do not have it.

I am astonished, answered Aristo, that a man who fears to be at odds with the Greeks and Romans should be willing so lightheartedly to have on his hands the Spaniards, the Italians, the Germans, the Poles, the Russians, and all the other nations of the earth. But joking aside, he went on, I think you are very bold to criticize all foreigners in that way. For myself, since I dislike equally the arbitrariness of settling a question and the unpleasantness of ruffling another's temper, I prefer to believe the bel esprit at home everywhere, and I have no desire to be more difficult than the satiric poet who was prepared to say that great geniuses are born everywhere.

I know that some countries are more hospitable to the things of the mind than others, that Attica was of all the nations of Greece the most fertile in beaux esprits, nor do I deny that France is at least the equal of Attica in this. But it does not follow that the other countries are as sterile as you say; after all, minds are not like gold or precious stones which nature forms only in certain places on earth; minds are to be found in cold and hot climates as well as in temperate ones and among barbarous nations as well as among civilized ones.

But if the bel esprit is to be found in all countries, said Eugene, it is certainly not found in all centuries, for some are crude and stupid, dominated by barbarism and ignorance, as was the tenth century when people were so simple-minded and so stupid that as soon as a man knew a little Greek he passed for a necromancer.

There are also centuries of the intelligence, said Aristo, and one need not be deeply versed in history and chronology to be aware that Alexander's time was fecund in beaux esprits. By Alexander's time I mean not only the period during which that famous conqueror lived but the years just before his birth and after his death. It was then that Anacreon, Socrates, Pindar, Euripides, Sophocles, Aristophanes, Isocrates, Plato, Aristotle, and Demosthenes flourished. Everybody knows that the age of Augustus was among the Romans the century of the bel esprit and of rational thought, of good authors and of good literature.

The fourth Christian century was one of the most fertile in great geniuses. For aside from Arius, who is so famous for the harm he did to Christendom, Valens, Ursacius, and Eusebius, all defenders of that heresiarch's doctrine, Julian the Apostate, and another Julian, the disciple of Pelagius, all these were bad men and good thinkers; and we might mention Themistius the Philosopher and Libanius the Sophist; there was in that century a large number of holy fathers as remarkable for the grandeur of their intelligence as for the sanctity of their lives. It is the century of Chrysostom, Jerome, Epiphanius, Ambrose, and Augustine.

How does it come about, interrupted Eugene, that one century is more or less intellectually inclined than another?

If you put that question to an astrologer, replied Aristo, he would not fail to give the responsibility to the stars, and he would probably say that the revolution and the conjunction of certain stars whose influences act to a greater or lesser degree upon the human mind are the only cause of that difference. But since I am not an astrologer, I prefer to believe it results in part from a good or a bad education, and that intelligences are subtler or coarser depending upon the degree to which they were cultivated in youth.

But would you believe that sometimes only one bel esprit is needed to civilize a whole nation? Malherbe [19] reformed the idea of poetry in France and gave us a taste for good verse. It can be said that Voiture taught us the easy and delicate way of writing which is now in fashion. Before him the would-be wit spoke only pure Balzac, and great thoughts were expressed in long words.

The rivalry which develops among certain persons and even among certain nations does much to civilize a century; ambition often has the same effect as rivalry. A thousand intelligent men spring up in a nation where intelligence is a means to success; thus in the ancient republics where a man achieved high office through his eloquence and his knowledge there were many great orators and excellent philosophers. There have always been learned men in times when princes loved knowledge.

How does it happen, do you think, that in the last century literature flourished so much in Italy if not because Lorenzo de' Medici and Leo X were so fond of it? And was it not that same fondness in Francis I which caused France in his reign to become refined and learned after having been crude and ignorant in the preceding reigns? The bent which a Prime Minister may have for a particular branch of study induces others to apply themselves to it, and so with time they will excel in it. The passion of Cardinal Richelieu for the theatre carried the Comédie Française to its highest perfection and has brought about the birth in our century of dramatic poets who almost surpass the ancients.

It seems to me, said Eugene, that times of peace also contribute a great deal to the refining of mankind, for as you know the Muses naturally love repose and silence; they cannot live in the midst of violence and noise. Beaux esprits are rare in wartime whether because war, which has in it something wild and savage, prevents minds from taking a polish or because those who have ambition turn their thoughts to weapons and choose valor as did Caesar, who, in Quintilian's opinion, might have disputed with Cicero pre-eminence in eloquence.

Periods of war, said Aristo, are not always incompatible with learning; they are sometimes very favorable not only to the grandeur of nations but also to the perfection of the mind, and without seeking foreign examples we may say that we were never more polished than while war was raging between France and Spain.

I think, he went on, that new heresies do no little to banish barbarism and ignorance; the passion on the one side to establish and defend a new doctrine, the zeal on the other to combat and destroy it urge on the two parties to study and ordinarily produce very remarkable works. For leaving old heresies aside, we perhaps owe, if it is permitted to speak in this way, we owe, I say, to recent ones some of the embellishment of our language and the polish of our century.

Could one not add, said Eugene, that nature makes an effort from time to time to produce extraordinary geniuses and then afterwards remains sterile for several centuries as if her most recent productions had exhausted her and as though she needed rest after so much labor?

One could also add, rejoined Aristo, that there is in all this a kind of doom, or to speak in a more Christian way, some disposition of Providence which is impenetrable. For this barbarism or refinement of minds passes from country to country and from century to century by ways often unknown to us. At one time a nation is crude, at another, refined. In the time of Alexander the Greeks were more productive than the Romans; in Caesar's time the Romans were more productive than the Greeks.

The last century was for Italy a century of learning and refinement; it produced more beaux esprits than the country had seen since the days of Augustus. The present century is for France what the last was for Italy;

one might say that all the intelligence and all the learning of the world are now among us and that all other nations are barbarous when compared with the French. It is not an advantage or an excellence in France to be intelligent, because everybody is. Almost everyone has had a little education, almost everyone speaks well and writes genteelly. The number of good authors and of makers of beautiful things is infinite; the number of learned academies increases every day; in short, I know of nothing more ordinary in the Kingdom than the refined good sense which used to be so rare here.

Moreover, the bel esprit is not limited to men of letters; it is found among men of the sword and persons of the highest quality who in previous reigns were generally ignorant. We have princes who can compete in wit as well as in valor with Scipio and Caesar, and I personally have the honor of knowing one [20] who in the flower of his age has all the critical discernment and the maturity it is possible to have. This young prince has many charms in his person which make him, proud as he is, the most likable man in the world. Long ago I compared him to Tasso's Rinaldo and applied to him these four lines as through the spirit of prophecy:

> L'età precorse, e la speranza; e presti
> Pareano i fior, quando n'usciro i frutti.
> S'el miri fulminar fra l'arme avvolto
> Marte lo stimi; Amor, se scopre il volto.[21]

But I shall leave aside his courage and handsomeness and speak only of his mind. However cold his face may appear he has much vivacity and fire, but this fire is not outwardly visible at all times and the vivacity is all in a subtle and penetrating intelligence which nothing escapes. He understands the shadings in everything; he judges works of literature with an admirable finesse; everything he says is just and full of good sense even when he utters trifles, for despite his wise and serious air he often takes part in witty and graceful badinage when the occasion presents itself.

He knows all the literary languages, and he has taken from learning all that a person of his quality ought to know, so that he speaks very well and in a princely way on every subject without aping the scholar and without being pretentious. You must add to this a clear and well-instructed mind which always leads him to choose the right side, a noble and lofty soul which makes him capable of anything, and finally a certain individual quality of mind which the finest bel esprit does not have.

We have besides, dukes, marquesses, and counts who are very witty and very learned, who handle the pen and the sword equally well and who know as much about planning a ballet or writing a history as about establishing a camp or lining up an army for battle. We have also duchesses, marquises, and countesses who may be the equal of the dukes, marquesses, and counts and who are real beaux esprits.

I did not suppose, interrupted Eugene, that a woman could be a bel esprit, and whatever you may say I am inclined to doubt that she can have all the qualities which are necessary really to be one. That bright flame and that good sense you spoke so well of do not result from a cold and moist complexion; the cold and moisture which make women "weak, timid, indiscreet, light, impatient and talkative" as one of our good authors has clearly shown in his *Art of Knowing Men*,[22] prevent them from having the judgment, the solidity, the strength, and the precision which bel esprit demands. That phlegm with which they are filled and which gives them their delicate coloring does not agree well with delicacy and vivacity of mind; it blunts the cutting edge of the intellect and dims its light. If you reflect on this question you will see that what is brilliant in women partakes of the nature of lightning which dazzles for a moment and which has no solidity; women shine a bit in conversation, and provided the talk be of trifles they do well; but beyond this they are not very reasonable. In a word, nothing is thinner or more limited than the female mind.

What you say is true in a general way, answered Aristo, and I admit there is a kind of contradiction between beauty of the mind and that of the body, this latter being woman's share; but that does not keep certain ones from being exceptions to the general rule. They are the ones who, as far as their minds are concerned, have none of the imperfections of their sex and to whom nature has given, it seems, a special temperament.

One may count among those privileged women the famous Grecian who invented a new kind of verse and who was called the tenth Muse;[23] the virtuous Cornelia, the mother of the Gracchi; the wise and learned Athenaïs whose merit brought her to the throne of Constantinople;[24] the illustrious Mary Stuart whose beauty, learning and virtue all Europe admired; Vittoria Colonna, Marchesa de Pesquere,[25] Isotta Nogarola,[26] Serafina Contarini,[27] Oliva Margareta Sarrochi,[28] all four Italian women; Margaret Moore[29] and Elizabeth Tanfield,[30] English; Isabel de Roseres, Spanish;[31] Catherine of Portugal, Duchess of Bragança;[32] Marguerite de Valois, sister of Francis I, who was called by the beaux esprits of her time the Tenth Muse and the Fourth Grace; Queen Margaret;[33] the Princess de Conti, daughter of Henri, Duke of Guise;[34] Mademoiselle de Gournay, whom Montaigne called his daughter and Justus Lipsius his sister; and many others who were the ornament of their country and of their time, not to mention those who are still alive.

Besides a talent for literature, an aptitude for statecraft is also found in a few women whom nature has raised above the others. There have been intelligent and able women in almost all periods who were capable of carrying on the weightiest negotiations, and a few have appeared in certain countries clear-headed enough to bear the burden of public affairs.

Aristo then told his friend all that his memory furnished him on the subject of wise princesses who have governed empires. He did not forget Pulcheria, the sister of Theodosius,[35] Blanche, the mother of Saint Louis,[36] Isabella, the wife of Ferdinand,[37] Catherine Paleologus, Duchess of Mantua and Marchesa de Montferrat, so that Eugene was obliged to confess finally that there were beaux esprits of all kinds and sorts among women.

The reflections they both made afterward on the admirable conduct of these princesses took them so far afield into history and politics that they were scarcely able to bring their conversation to an end.

Dominique Bouhours THE JE NE SAIS QUOI FROM "THE CONVERSATIONS OF ARISTO AND EUGENE"

When Aristo and Eugene had reached the place of their walk, they first gave expression to the joy they felt at passing such pleasant hours in each other's company. Eugene said: Though we may be solitary, yet I am not envious of the most agreeable society in the world.

Aristo thereupon said to his friend all those things which a warm friendship can suggest at such meetings; then, allowing his mind to rove wherever his heart might lead it, he said: It must be admitted, my dear Eugene, that there are few friendships like our own, for we can be always together and never tire of each other. Private conversations in which love plays no part are almost always tiresome when they are too frequent or when they are rather long. No matter what the esteem or the affection one may have for any gentleman, one gradually wearies of seeing only him and of speaking only to him; one even feels, in some inexplicable way, that this brings about a diminution in the feelings which his merits have caused, whether because one gradually becomes used to what at first appeared extraordinary in his person or whether through familiarity one discovers in him hidden defects which make his good qualities less estimable. Hence, for us daily to find new pleasures in our conversations, as we do, our friendship must necessarily be much stronger than ordinary ones, because, although it is virtuous, it arouses in us what love arouses in others.

In other words, added Eugene, we must be meant for each other, and there must be a rare sympathy between our minds.

What you say is very true, answered Aristo, and for myself I feel it deeply. The boredom which seizes upon me as soon as we are separated, the joy which our longest conversations give me, the slight attention I pay to learning new things and my lack of care in cultivating my old habits are apparently the effects of the great liking and those hidden inclinations which make us feel for one person an indefinable something which we do not feel for another.

From the way you speak, replied Eugene, you appear to know pretty well the nature of that indefinable something whose effects you feel.

It is something much easier to feel than to know, rejoined Aristo. It would not be indefinable if it were understood; its nature is to be incomprehensible and inexplicable.

But can we not say, Eugene responded, that it is an influence from the stars and an invisible effect of the planet which was in the ascendant when we were born?

Naturally we can say that, answered Aristo, or even that it is the tendency and instinct of the heart, that it is the most exquisite feeling of the soul for whatever makes an impression upon it, a marvelous liking and what might be called a kinship of the heart, to use the words of a Spanish wit: *un parentesco de los corazones.*

But to say that and a thousand other things is to say nothing. These feelings, these tendencies, these instincts, these likings, these kinships, are fine words which scholars have invented to delude their ignorance and to deceive others after they have been taken in themselves. One of our poets has described it better than all the philosophers; he settles the matter in a word:

> There are strong bonds of hidden, tender liking,
> Through whose sweet pow'r each lover finds his own;
> Each to each is join'd at glances' striking
> By something hidden, never to be known.

Even if that were true of the mysterious something one feels for people deep in one's heart, said Eugene, it might not be true of whatever it is that makes people pleasing, a quality which shows in their faces and which is obvious at first sight.

I assure you, said Aristo, that this latter something is as hidden and indescribable as the other. Because it is visible it is not better known or easier to define. For it is not really beauty, or a prepossessing appearance, or charming manners, or the gaiety of good humor, or brilliance of wit, because every day we meet people who have all these qualities without the faculty of being pleasing, and we see others who are very pleasant without having any agreeable qualities except the mysterious something.

Hence, the most reasonable and the most certain thing that can be said is that the greatest merit achieves nothing without it, and that it is sufficient in itself to create a very great effect. There is no advantage in being handsome, witty, gay, or what you will, if that mysterious something is lacking; all your fine qualities are as it were dead: there is nothing striking or touching about them. They are hooks without bait, pointless arrows and dull witticisms. Yet whatever defects may be found in body or soul, with this single advantage one is always pleasing, nor can one do anything wrong: the mysterious something makes everything right.

It follows from that, said Eugene, that it is a grace which brightens beauty and other natural perfections, which corrects ugliness and other natural defects, that it is a charm and an air which informs every action and every word, which has its part in the way one walks and laughs, in the tone of the voice, and even in the slightest gesture of the socially acceptable person.

But what is that grace, that charm, that air? asked Aristo. When one examines all those terms closely one ends by not making head nor tail of them, and one is forced back upon the mysterious something. One of our clever gentlemen has said of a very likable young man:

> But most of all he had a grace
> A "something" by which to surpass
> The sweetest charms of love's young face,
> A smile whose pow'r all words doth pass,
> An air distinctive and unique
> Whose secret others vainly seek.

This grace, this charm, this air are like the light which embellishes all of nature and which is seen by everybody though we do not know what it is, and so we cannot say anything more about it, to my way of thinking, except that it can neither be explained nor understood. Indeed, it is so delicate and imperceptible that it escapes the most penetrating and subtle intelligence; the human mind, which recognizes the most highly spiritual quality of the angels and the most divine quality in God, so to speak, does not recognize what is charming in a phenomenon which is both perceptible to the senses and capable of touching the heart.

If that is true, said Eugene, we must give the lie to philosophers who have always maintained that knowledge precedes love; that the will can love nothing which is unknown to the rational faculty.

They were right in their argument, said Aristo. Love is impossible without knowledge, and one always knows the loved person; that is, we may know that she is lovable, but not always know why we love her.

But if you please, interrupted Eugene, is that knowledge sufficient by which we know the person and recognize that she is lovable? Is it possible to love her and at the same time not to know what it is that makes her the object of love?

Yes, answered Aristo, and the mystery of the "certain something" consists of exactly that. Nature, like art, is careful to hide the cause of unusual impulses: we see the machine, and with pleasure, but we do not see the spring which makes it work. A woman may be pleasing to us, or inspire love at first sight without our knowing why she has this effect. You will say that in these circumstances nature sets traps for our heart so as to catch it unawares, or rather that since she knows it to be as proud and as sensitive as it is in fact, she spares it and treats it gently by hiding the dart which is to wound it.

I am inclined to think, said Eugene, that if the soul does not perceive the quality by which it is touched in such encounters the reason is that the quality acts so fast as to be imperceptible to the soul. For, as you may have noticed, anything which moves very fast is invisible. Thus arrows, bullets, cannon balls, bolts of lightning all pass before our eyes without being seen. These things are visible in themselves but the speed with which they move hides them from our sight.

That reminds me, said Aristo, of the simple-mindedness of that savage who, having been shot and not being able to understand what had wounded him, said that it was either the flame he had seen or the noise he had heard.

If stone, fire, lead, and wood, Eugene continued, become invisible through the speed with which they fly through the air, should we be amazed that the quality which at first sight makes an impression on the soul can pass unnoticed? For of all the things which move fast the fastest is the dart which wounds the heart, and the shortest of all moments, as I may say, is that in which the "mysterious something" makes its effect.

However that may be, said Aristo, it is certain that this mysterious something belongs to that class of things which are known only by the effects they produce. Our eyes witness the wonderful movements which a magnet induces in iron filings; but who can say what the power of that marvelous stone really is? The wind which shakes mountains and rocky cliffs, which destroys towns and troubles all the elements is something unseen and which has not yet been well defined. Neither have the influences which fall from the heavens and which form minerals in the depths of the earth. Let us say the same of that charm and of that peculiar fascination we are discussing: it attracts the hardest hearts, it sometimes excites violent passions in the soul, it sometimes causes very noble sentiments; but it is never known except in that way. Its importance and its advantage lie in its being hidden; it is like the source of that Egyptian river, the more famous for not having yet been discovered, or like the unknown goddess of the ancients who was adored only because she was not known.

Might one dare say, Eugene added, that it is like God Himself and that there is nothing better known nor more unknown in the world?

One can at least say this with certainty, Aristo continued, that it is one of the greatest marvels and one of the greatest mysteries of nature.

Is that not the reason, said Eugene laughing, that the most mysterious nations give it a place in everything they say? The Italians, who make a mystery of everything, use their expression *non sò che* right and left. Nothing is more usual in their poets.

Un certo non sò che
Sentesi al petto.

An indescribable sensation is felt in the
heart.

A poco a poco nacque nel mio petto
Non sò da qual radice
Com herba suol che per se stessa germini,
Un incognito affetto,
Un estranea dolcezza,
Che lascia nel fine
Un non sò che d'amaro.

Gradually there is born in my heart from unknown roots, like grass which grows of itself, an unknown love, a strange sweetness which at the end leaves behind a mysterious bitterness.

In queste voci languide risuona
Un non sò che de flebile e soave,
Ch'al cor gli serpe, ed ogni sdegno ammorza.

In these languorous words sounds something plaintive and sweet which enters secretly into his heart and calms all his rage.

Non v'e silenzio, e non v'e grido espresso,
Ma odi un non sò che roco e indistinto.

> It is not silence, nor is it a cry uttered by a
> human being, but there is audible something
> both raucous and indistinct.

Un non sò che d'inusitato e molle,
Par che nel duro petto al Re trapasse.

> Something mysterious, both rare and gentle,
> seems to pierce the king's hard heart.

Un non sò che d'insolito e confuso
Tra speranza e timor tutto m'ingombra.

> Something unwonted, a mixture of hope and
> fear, has me in its grip.

I should never finish if I tried to mention all the examples of *non sò che* which I remember. The Spaniards also have their *no sé que* which they use at all times and in all contexts, besides their *donaire* (grace) their *brio* (vigor) and their *despejo* (facility) which Gracián calls *alma de tota prenda, realce de los mismos realces, perfección de la misma perfección* (the object of all desire, splendor of all splendors, the perfection of perfection itself), and which is, according to the same author, above our thoughts and our words, *lisonjea la inteligencia, y estraña la explicación* (it deceives the intelligence and bemuses attempts at explanation).

If you took the trouble to read our books with as much care as you have read the Italians and Spaniards, said Aristo, you would find that the *je ne sais quoi* is very popular among us, and that in this we are as mysterious as our neighbors.

But to come back to what we were saying, the *je ne sais quoi* is like those beauties covered with a veil, which are the more highly prized for being less exposed to view, and to which the imagination always adds something. Hence, if by chance we were to see clearly the nature of this mysterious something which astonishes and overwhelms the heart at first glance, we should perhaps be less charmed and touched than we are; but it has not yet been unveiled and perhaps never will be since, as I have already said, once unveiled it would cease to be what it is.

Moreover, since it cannot be explained, it cannot be described either, and this is perhaps the reason why showing a person's portrait is not enough to cause her to be loved by the beholder, any more than does singing her praises, whatever romances and fables may say. The most favorable description and the most flattering portrait can produce esteem for a person and a desire to see her, but neither the one nor the other ever causes a real affection because neither the brush nor the tongue can express that mysterious something which is all-powerful.

But aside from that mysterious quality which compensates, as we have said, for natural defects and which sometimes replaces beauty, physical charm, good humor, and even intelligence, there is another which has a completely contrary effect, for it destroys, it spoils, it poisons, as you might say, the merit of those people in whom it is found.

Every day we see people who, by all the rules, ought to be very pleasant and who nevertheless are very unpleasant, like those two gentlemen well known at Court of whom it was said that they had between them more good qualities than would be needed to make four decent people, and yet they were themselves not acceptable.

We wonder sometimes why a man makes a bad impression, we ask ourselves what the reason may be, we find a thousand which indicate that he ought to make a good impression and not one which explains why he does not, except a certain disturbing quality which leads us to say in spite of ourselves: He is handsome, attractive, intelligent, but there is something about him which I dislike. Some people think that is said out of fastidiousness or caprice and is a mere pretext, yet it is a good and solid reason, although a hidden one and unknown to philosophy, and which nature alone proposes to us.

What is most astonishing to me, said Eugene, is that the same man you dislike may perhaps suit me perfectly.

There is no reason to be surprised at that, said Aristo. As there are certain mysterious qualities which are universal so that everybody is equally touched by them, so there are individual ones which affect only certain people, for these qualities are like those ghosts which are seen only in certain places and by certain people. All men have something about them which makes them attractive or unattractive at first sight, depending upon the different people who see them, and upon this are founded what we call sympathy and antipathy.

If that is true, said Eugene, we are wrong in condemning the taste or preference of another, however peculiar the taste may be and however odd the preference. We should complain of nature and not of ourselves, for we only follow her and cannot withstand her promptings in these matters.

It is true, answered Aristo, that these mysterious qualities which produce the effect of beauty or ugliness, so to speak, cause in us mysterious feelings of inclination or aversion which are beyond reason and which the will cannot control. They are impulses which forestall reflection and freedom. We can stop them in their course but we cannot prevent their arising. These feelings of liking or disliking take shape in an instant and when we are least aware of them. We love or hate at once without awareness in the mind, and, if I dare say so, without knowledge in the heart.

But do you know, he went on, that these mysterious qualities are to be found almost everywhere? The expression of the face which distinguishes one person from a hundred thousand others is such a quality, being very noticeable and yet very difficult to describe, for who has ever clearly distinguished the feaures and the lineaments in which that difference precisely resides?

An intelligent face is another mysterious phenomenon. For, if one undertakes to determine why it is that an intelligent man is usually recognizable on sight, one must conclude that it is not the breadth of his forehead, nor the brilliance or fieriness of his eyes, nor the chiseled regularity of his features, nor the form and complexion of his face, but something which results from all these things, or rather that it has nothing to do with these things at all.

There is also something mysterious in sicknesses, not only in extraordinary ones in which the masters of the healing art recognize something divine, as they themselves say, but also in the commonest ones like the fever. Those regular attacks, those chills and burning fits, those intermissions in a disease which lasts for years on end, are these not all unknown quantities? And must not the same thing be said of the ebbing and flooding of the tides, the power of the magnet and the occult qualities, as they are called by philosophers?

People of breeding usually have in their faces something noble and grand which makes them respected and which makes them recognizable in a crowd.

I agree, said Eugene, and that characteristic grandeur which God has imprinted particularly on the brow of kings distinguishes our own from all the nobles of his court. There is in his whole person an air, a mysteriously majestic quality which marks him so well that people who have

189

never seen him need not ask which is he when they see him in a tiltyard or a ballet.

And so, Aristo went on, all nature is filled

With something hidden, never to be known.

At least, Eugene added, the *je ne sais quoi* is restricted to natural phenomena for, as far as works of art are concerned, all their beauties are evident and their capacity to please is perfectly understandable.

I cannot agree, answered Aristo. The *je ne sais quoi* belongs to art as well as to nature. For, without mentioning the different manners of painters, what charms us in those excellent paintings, in those statues so nearly alive that they lack only the gift of speech, or who do not even lack that if we are to believe our eyes:

Manca il parlar, di vivo altro non chiedi;
Ne manca questo ancor, s'a gli occhi credi . . .

what charms us, I say, in such paintings and statues is an inexplicable quality. Therefore the great masters, who have discovered that only that is pleasing in nature whose attraction cannot be explained, have always tried to give charm to their works by hiding their art with great care and skill.

E quel ch'el bello, e'l caro accresce a l'opre,
L'arte che tutto fa, nulla si scopre.

> And what makes a work more beautiful and gives it greater importance is that art which does all but is nowhere to be seen.

Delicate compositions in prose and verse have something refined and genteel about them which is the source of almost all their importance and which consists in that sophisticated air, that tincture of *urbanity* which Cicero is at a loss to define. There are great beauties in Balzac's books; they are regular beauties and very pleasing; but it must be admitted that the works of Voiture, which have those secret charms, those fine and hidden graces of which we are speaking, are much more pleasing still.

Let us go further, my dear Eugene, and let us say in addition that when we examine carefully those things in this world which we most admire we see that what makes us admire them is the mysterious something which surprises us, which dazzles us, which charms us. We shall even come to see that this mysterious quality is, if it is rightly understood, the focal point of most of our passions. Besides love and hatred, which give the impetus to all the impulses of the heart, desire and hope, which fill up the whole of man's life, have practically no other foundation. For we are always desiring and hoping, because beyond the goal we have set for ourselves there is always something else to which we unceasingly aspire and which we never attain; that is why we are never satisfied with the enjoyment even of those things we have most ardently desired.

But to speak in a Christian fashion of the *je ne sais quoi*, is there not a mysterious something in us which makes us feel, despite all the weaknesses and disorders of corrupt nature, that our souls are immortal, that the grandeurs of the earth cannot satisfy us, that there is something beyond ourselves which is the goal of our desires and the centre of that felicity which we everywhere seek and never find? Do not really faithful souls recognize, as one of the Fathers of the Church says, that we were made Christians not for the goods of this life but for something of an entirely different order, which God promises to us in this life but which man cannot yet imagine?

Then, Eugene interrupted, this mysterious quality partakes of the essence of grace as well as of nature and art.

Yes, answered Aristo. Grace itself, that divine grace which has caused so much uproar in the schools and which produces such wonderful effects upon souls, that grace both strong and gentle which triumphs over hardness of heart without limiting the freedom of the will, which subjects nature by adjusting itself to her, which makes itself master of the will while leaving the will its own master, that grace, I say, what is it but a mysterious quality of a supernatural order which can be neither explained nor understood?

The Fathers of the Church have tried to define it, and they have called it "a deep and secret calling," "an impression of the spirit of God," "a divine unction," "an all-powerful gentleness," "a victorious pleasure," "a holy lust," "a covetousness for the true good"; that is to say that it is a *je ne sais quoi* which indeed makes itself felt but which cannot be explained and of which it would be better not to speak.

It is true, Aristo went on, that the *je ne sais quoi* is almost the only subject about which no books have been written and which the learned have never taken the trouble to elucidate. Lectures, dissertations and treatises have been composed on very odd subjects, but no author, as far as I know, has worked on this one.

I remember, said Eugene, reading in the *History of the French Academy* that one of the most illustrious academicians gave a speech in the Academy on the subject of the *je ne sais quoi*. However, since this speech has not been published, the world was no more illumined by it than it was before, and perhaps even if this academic discourse were to see the light we should not be much more informed than we are, the subject being one of those which have an impenetrable core and which cannot be explained other than by admiration and silence.

I am very glad, said Aristo laughing, that at last you have come to the proper conclusion and that you are satisfied to admire what at first you wanted to understand. Take my advice, he added, and let us stop here without saying anything further about a thing which continues to exist only because no one can say what it is. Besides it is time to bring our walk to an end; the sky is darkening all around us, it is starting to rain, and if we do not go in soon we shall be liable to feel the fury of the coming storm.

Dominique Bouhours THE ART OF CRITICISM, OR THE METHOD OF MAKING A RIGHT JUDGMENT UPON SUBJECTS OF WIT AND LEARNING

Dialogue I

Eudoxus and Philanthus, who manage these following dialogues, are two scholars whom their learning has not spoiled, and whose breeding is equal to their learning. Though they had pursued the same studies and knew for the most part the same things, yet their characters are widely different. Eudoxus has a true relish, and nothing pleases him in ingenious discourses which is not reasonable and natural. He loves the ancients much, especially the authors of Augustus's age, which in his opinion was the age of good sense. Cicero, Virgil, Livy, and Horace are his heroes.

As for Philanthus, what is florid and glittering charms him. The Greeks and the Romans, in his opinion, are not comparable to the Spaniards and the Italians. Among others, he admires Lope de Vega and Tasso, and his head is so full of the *Gerusalemme liberata* that he prefers it without any ceremony to the *Iliad* or the *Aeneid*. This excepted, he has wit, is an honest gentleman, and Eudoxus's friend. Their friendship, however, is no hindrance, but they often quarrel about these things. They reproach one another at every turn with their tastes, and they differ concerning every book that is published; but what differences soever they may have, yet they love each other nevertheless, and they agree so well together that they cannot live one without the other.

Eudoxus has a very pretty country house near Paris, where he goes in fine weather to take the fresh air and to enjoy the pleasures of retirement whenever his business will permit him to quit the town.

Philanthus went, as he used to do, to see him last autumn. He found him walking alone in a little grove, and reading the *Doubts Concerning the*

French Language, Proposed to the Gentlemen of the Academy By a Country Gentleman.[1]

Philanthus, who understands the tongue more by custom than rule, fell foul upon Eudoxus presently for reading it.

What business have you with that country gentleman, says he; a man as you are needs only follow his own genius to speak and to write well. I do assure you, replies Eudoxus, that a genius alone will not go far, and that one is in danger of committing a thousand faults against custom if he does not reflect upon custom itself. This country gentleman's scruples are reasonable, and the more I read them the more necessary they seem.

For my part, says Philanthus, I should rather desire his reflections upon authors' thoughts; for it seems to me to be a more necessary thing to think well than to speak well, or rather, one can neither speak nor write correctly unless his thoughts be just.[2] He promised these reflections when he told us at the end of his book that he had several other scruples about the thoughts of authors, besides those concerning the language. But he has not performed his promise, and I see plainly that this Breton is not too much a man of his word.

Since the gentlemen of the Academy gave him no solution of his first scruples, replied Eudoxus, he believed perhaps that it was to no purpose for him to propose new ones. But take notice that this place where the Low Breton seems to promise those reflections you speak of has caused me to make several which I had not made before, and that when I examined things more nearly it seemed to me that those thoughts which sometimes appear the brightest in [compositions] of wit are not always the most solid.

I am almost dead with fear, says Philanthus, interrupting him briskly, lest with reading this book of *Doubts* so much you should have learned to doubt of everything, and that this country gentleman who is scrupulously nice has communicated something of his spirit to you. It is not the provincial that I am guided by, replied Eudoxus, it is good sense which he himself takes for his rule in those things which do not perfectly depend upon custom; for one needs only consult his own reason not to approve some thoughts which almost all the world admires, as for instance that famous one of Lucan, *Victrix causa deis placuit, sed victa Catoni,*[3] which the translator of his *Pharsalia* has thus rendered: *Les dieux servent César, mais Caton suit Pompée* (The gods serve Caesar, but Cato follows Pompey).

I could be content, says Philanthus, smiling, that this should not please you; it would, said he, going on in a serious tone, be so much the worse for you.

I protest to you, replied Eudoxus, this never pleased me, and though the adorers of Lucan should owe me a spite for it, yet I would not change my opinion. But what, returned Philanthus, can be greater or finer than to set the gods on one side and Cato on the other?

The misfortune of this thought is, answered Eudoxus, that it hath only a fair outside, and when one fathoms it he will find it unreasonable at the bottom. For in short, it represents the gods at the first view fixed to the unjust side, and so Caesar's was, who sacrificed his country to his ambition, and who [presumed] to oppress the public liberty which Pompey endeavored to defend; now good sense never allows that the gods should approve of the injustice of an usurper who breaks the laws of God and man to make himself master of the world, and one that thought rightly should have forgot the gods on such an occasion, much less have brought them into play.

Besides, Cato being a good man, according to the poet's own description of him, there was no reason to oppose him to the gods, and to set him in an interest different from theirs. This is to destroy his character, to take away his virtue; for if we believe Sallust, it was a part of the Roman goodness to be zealous in the service of the immortal gods, and the Romans did not begin to neglect them till their morals began to be corrupted.[4] It is yet less reasonable to advance Cato above the gods, and by that means to raise the credit of Pompey's party, for this is what *sed victa Catoni* signifies: *But Cato followed Pompey. But* here is a mark of distinction and preference.

The truth is, this Roman was in the judgment of the Romans themselves a living image of virtue, and in everything more like the gods than men;[5] he was, if you will, a divine man. He was a man, and the poet, how much soever a pagan, how much soever a poet, could not give a man an advantage above the gods without doing injury to the religion in which he lived, so that Lucan's thought is at once both false and impious.

I do not reason so much, says Philanthus, and all your reasonings will never hinder me from esteeming Lucan's as an admirable thought. You may judge as you please, replied Eudoxus, but I cannot admire that which is not true.

But, says Philanthus, cannot this thought be thus explained? It pleased the gods that the unrighteous party should prevail over the righteous, though Cato wished otherwise. Does this shock reason? Is this not the sense of the verse? Good men every day make vows for those that are like themselves, for the success of a good cause; their vows are not always heard, and Providence sometimes turns things otherwise.

The gods declared for Caesar in the event, though Pompey's was the juster side, which Cato upheld. The *but* in the verse signifies perhaps no more than this *though*, which gives no offense to the gods, whose designs are unsearchable.

Were the poet's thoughts no more than this, replies Eudoxus, it were no great matter, and there would be no cause to cry out against it. I am sure at least that his defenders do not understand it so, and that the sense which displeases me is the very sense which they admire.

To be convinced of this, you need only remember what one of Lucan's admirers says in his reflections upon our translators. According to him, Brébeuf [6] flags sometimes, and when Lucan happily comes up to the true beauty of a thought, his translator falls very much below it; the example which this reflecter brings is that before us: *Victrix causa deis placuit, sed victa Catoni.* (The gods serve Caesar, but Cato follows Pompey.)

He maintains that the French expression does not answer the nobleness of the Latin one, and that this is misrepresenting the author's sense, because Lucan, whose mind was filled with Cato's virtues, intended to advance him above the gods when he set Cato's opinion of the merits of the cause against theirs, whereas Brébeuf turns this noble image of Cato advanced above the gods into one of Cato subject to Pompey.

I do not pretend to justify the translation, says Eudoxus, and I agree with him that it is not exact. I say only that the reflecter's censure proves what I said, that those who are fond of the Latin *Pharsalia* fancy something extraordinary in this verse, *Victrix causa deis placuit, sed victa Catoni.*

Do not refine too much, Philanthus; till just now you were of the same opinion yourself, and this new sense which you have put upon it is only an excuse to save Lucan's honor.

Be it as it will, I could have all ingenious thoughts in books of poetry or prose to be like those of a great orator whom Tully speaks of, which were as sound as they were true, as surprising as out of the way; in short, they were as natural as they were far from all that luster which has nothing in it that is not frivolous and childish.[7] For in one word, to tell you my opinion in some sort of order, truth is the first quality, and as it were the foundation of thoughts; the fairest are the faultiest, or rather those which pass for the fairest are not really so, if they want this foundation.

But tell me then, replied Philanthus, what is the exact notion of a true thought, and wherein this truth consists, without which whatever one thinks, according to you, is so imperfect and monstrous.

Thoughts, answers Eudoxus, are the images of things, as words are the images of thoughts; and generally speaking, to think is to form in oneself the picture of any object, spiritual or sensible. Now images and pictures are true no further than they resemble; so a thought is true when it represents things faithfully, and it is false when it makes them appear otherwise than they are in themselves.

I do not understand your doctrine, replies Philanthus, and I can scarce persuade myself that a witty thought should always be founded upon truth; on the contrary, I am of the opinion of a famous critic, that falsehood gives it often all its grace, and is as it were the soul of it.[8] Nay, do we not see that what strikes most in epigrams, and in other things where the wit gives all the beauty, generally turns most upon fictions, upon ambiguities, upon hyperboles, which are but so many lies?

Do not confound things, if you please, replied Eudoxus, and allow me to explain myself that I may be understood. All that appears to be false is not so, and there is a great deal of difference between fiction and falsehood; the one imitates and perfects nature in some sort, the other spoils and quite destroys it.

In truth, the fabulous world, which is the world of poets, has nothing real in it; it is altogether a work of imagination, and Parnassus, Apollo, the Muses, with the horse Pegasus, are only agreeable chimeras. But this system being once supposed, whatever is feigned within its extent passes not for falsehood amongst the learned, especially when a fiction is probable, and has some truth hidden under it.

According to the fable, for instance, flowers grow under the feet of gods and heroes, to hint, perhaps, that great men ought to spread abundance and joy everywhere. This is plausible, and has probability; so that in reading those verses of Racan upon Marie de Médicis where he bids his flock "go into the fields and take their pleasure there, making use of the happy season which the heavens had given in recompense of all these miseries, and not spare the flowers, because there would grow up enough again under Marie's feet":[9]

Paissez, chères brebis, jouissez de la joie
Que le Ciel vous envoie;
A la fin la clémence a pitié de nos pleurs.
Allez dans la campagne, allez dans la prairie;
N'épargnez point les fleurs;
Il en revient assez sous les pas de Marie.

I say in reading these verses, we find nothing *choquant* in the poet's thought; and if we allow a falsehood, yet it is an established one, which has an air of truth. So when we read in Homer that the goddesses of prayer are deformed and lame, we are not offended at it; this makes us imagine that prayer has something in itself that is mean, and that when one prays he goes not so quick as when he commands, which is as much as to say that commands are short and prayers are long. One might add that the one are fierce and haughty, the other humble and creeping.

Neither are we shocked with the fiction of the Graces being little and very low. Men hereby intended to show that prettinesses consist in little things, sometimes in a posture or a smile, sometimes in a negligent air and in something less. I say the same of all fictions that have wit in them, such as the Latin fable of the sun and the frogs which was published in the beginning of the Dutch war, and which was so well received in the world.

That is to say, answered Philanthus, interrupting him, that you would not condemn another vision of the same poet; that the stars jealous of the sun made a league against him, but that when he appeared he dispersed the conspirators and made all his enemies vanish. No, without doubt, replied Eudoxus, it is a very happy thought, and being conceived upon Parnassus according to the rules of fiction it has all the truth it can have. The fabulous system [saves] all the falsehood which these sort of thoughts have in themselves, and it is allowed, nay, it is even glorious for a poet to lie in so ingenious a manner. But then, setting the fiction aside, truth ought to be found in poetry as well as in prose. Hereby I do not pretend to take away the marvelous from poetry, which distinguishes it from the noblest and the sublimest prose; I mean only that poets ought never to destroy the essences of things when they would raise and adorn them.

In the humor you are, says Philanthus, you will not approve of what Ariosto says of one of his heroes, "that in the heat of the engagement not perceiving that he was killed, he still fought on vigorously, as dead as he was."

> Il pover'uomo che non sen'era accorto
> Andava combattendo, ed era morto.

Neither do I approve, replied Eudoxus, of what Tasso says of Argante, "He dying threatened, and he fainted not."

> Minacciava morendo, è non languia.

I give up Ariosto, says Philanthus; but I beg quarter for Tasso, and desire you to consider that a strong and fierce Saracen who had been wounded in the fight and who died of his wounds might, when he was a-dying, threaten him that gave him the fatal blow well enough. I agree with you that he might threaten him, replied Eudoxus, and even that his dying postures, that his last words, might have something in them that was fierce, proud and terrible:

> Superbi, formidabili, feroci
> Gli ultimi moti fur', l'ultime voci.

This may be, and this agrees with Argante's character: at his death he might have the same sense of things which he had when he was alive; he might call together all his spirits and what strength he had left to express [what he feels]. Sometimes men make frightful outcries before their last groans, but not to faint when they are dying, *e non languia*, is what is by no means probable. Montaigne's cannibal acts much more naturally than Tasso's Saracen.[10] For in short, if the cannibal, prisoner to his enemies, braves them even in irons, speaks reproachfully to them, spits in their faces; if in the midst of torments and at the point of death, when he has not strength to speak, he makes mouths at them to mock them, and to assure them that he is not yet overcome — there is nothing in all this which is not perfectly conformable to the genius of a fierce and resolute barbarian.

But what can be more agreeable to heroic virtue, says Philanthus, than to die without any weakness? Heroes, replies Eudoxus, have resolution in dying, have constancy when they die, but the firmness of their minds preserves not their bodies from weakness; there it is that they have no privilege. And yet the *non languia* which belongs to the body exempts Argante from this common law, and in advancing the hero destroys the man.

I am afraid, answered Philanthus, that your nicety goes too far, and that you push the criticism beyond its due bounds. I believe Tasso intended to describe Argante in a rage against Tancred, and threatening him even when he was a-dying, and so did not barely say that he died, but that his fury and his anger [in] some measure took away his faintness and made him appear vigorous.

It is pity, replies Eudoxus, that Tasso is not better explained. For my part, I tie myself to what an author speaks; I do not know how to make him speak what he never says.

After all, says Philanthus, some very grave authors are not of your opinion in the matter of that truth which you would establish and require in all ingenious thoughts. Not to speak of Macrobius and Seneca who call those things pleasant sophisms, which we term strokes of wit, and the Italians *vivezze d'ingegno*, and the Spaniards *agudezas*; Aristotle reduces almost the whole art of thinking ingeniously to the metaphor, which is a kind of fraud, and the Count Tesauro says, according to that philosopher's principles, that the subtlest and the finest thoughts are only figurative enthymemes, which equally please and impose upon the understanding.[11]

All this ought to be understood in a good sense, replies Eudoxus. What is figurative is not false, and metaphors have their truth as well as fictions. Let us call to mind what Aristotle teaches in his rhetoric, and consider his doctrine a little.[12]

When Homer says of Achilles he went like a lion, it is a comparison; but when he says of the same Achilles "This lion darted forth," it is a metaphor. In the comparison the hero is like a lion; in the metaphor the hero is a lion. The metaphor, you see, is brisker and shorter than the comparison; this represents but one object, whereas that shows us two. The metaphor confounds, as I may say, the lion with Achilles or Achilles with the lion, but there is no more falsehood in the one than in the other. These metaphorical ideas deceive no man; how little understanding soever a man has, he knows what they signify, and he must be very dull who takes these things literally. In a word, can we question that Homer called Achilles a lion for any other reason than to describe his strength, his fierceness, and his courage? And when Voiture says of the great Gustavus, "Behold the northern lion," who discovers not through this foreign image a king terrible for his valor and power throughout all the north?[13]

We may say then that metaphors are like transparent veils, through which we see what they cover, or like the habits of a masque under which the persons who are disguised are known.

How glad am I, for the sake of poets and orators, says Philanthus, that fiction and metaphor wound not that truth which you require in [works] of wit. But I am very much afraid that ambiguity and truth can never agree according to your principles. And yet it would be a pity that so many thoughts which are pretty only for their ambiguity should not be good, for instance Voiture's upon Cardinal Mazarin, whom his coachman overthrew one day in the water, "where he desires him to forgive his coachman who had driven so unfortunately, since it was his Eminence's reputation which made him rash; for he thought in overturning he could not do amiss, because it was the common report that whatever he did, in peace, in war, upon the road, or in business, he still recovered himself upon his feet."

> Prélat passant tous les prélats passés,
> Car les présents serait un peu trop dire,
> Pour Dieu rendez les péchés effacés
> De ce cocher qui vous sut mal conduire.
> S'il fut peu caut à son chemin élire,
> Votre renom le rendit téméraire.
> Il ne crut pas versant pouvoir mal faire,
> Car chacun dit que quoi que vous fassiez,
> En guerre, en paix, en voyage, en affaire,
> Vous vous trouvez toujours dessus vos pieds.

All ambiguities are not like this, answers Eudoxus, and this petition for the coachman who overthrew the cardinal pleases me better than another which I remember, wherein he desires his Eminence to pardon the afflicted coachmen, who by misfortune or carelessness tumbled him into the water. The too hardy coachman know not (says he) the history of Phaeton and his calamity. He had read no *Metamorphoses*, and he thought he need not fear making any false steps when he carried Caesar and his fortune.

> Plaise, Seigneur, plaise à votre Eminence
> Faire la paix de l'affligé cocher,
> Qui par malheur, ou bien par imprudence,
> Dessous les flots vous a fait trébucher.
> On ne lui doit ce crime reprocher.
> Le trop hardi meneur ne savait pas
> De Phaéton l'histoire et piteux cas:
> Il ne lisait *Métamorphose* aucune,
> Et ne croyait qu'on dût craindre aucun pas
> En conduisant César et sa fortune.

For if you mind, this coachman who had not read the *Metamorphoses* knew a considerable passage in Roman history. And yet I cannot see how a man who had never heard of Phaeton should be so well informed of Caesar's adventures. But that's not the thing we are now about, and I come back again to the thought of the petition you repeated. Though it be false in one sense, yet, however, it is true in another, according to the character of thoughts expressed in ambiguous terms, which have always a double sense: one proper, which is false; the other figurative, which is true. Here the proper and false sense is that the Cardinal always so recovers himself upon his feet as never to fall on the ground; the figurative and true sense is that he always so recovers himself upon his feet so that nothing overturns his designs or his fortune.

In short, what is true is always true though it be joined to that which is false. A good pistole loses none of its value when set by a false one; you have but one due to you. There are two offered to you, a good one and a bad one; make your choice; we shall see whether you understand money, and you will have the pleasure yourself to make trial of the exactness of your skill. It is much the same in this playing with words, which in reality is only a sport of the mind. Truth there is joined to falsehood, and what is very remarkable, the false carries one to the true; for from the proper sense, which is the false sense, of a quibble, one goes on to the figurative, which is the true one; this is visible in the example which you brought. When I read what Voiture says of Cardinal Mazarin, I imagine two things, as I have already told you: one false, that his feet never fail, but that he always keeps himself upon his legs; the other true, that his mind and his fortune are always in the same posture. The first brings us immediately to the second, by letting us pleasantly into the change. These ambiguities are allowable and diverting in epigrams, madrigals, masques, and other composures where the mind diverts itself.

But not to dissemble with you, there is one sort of quibbles extremely flat which men of a true relish cannot endure, because the false rules all so that the true has no share. Saint-Amant's [14] epigram upon the burning of the Palais is of this kind.

Certes l'on vit un triste jeu
Quand à Paris Dame Justice
Se mit le Palais tout en feu
Pour avoir mangé trop d'épice.[15]

> Surely there was sorry sport when at Paris Dame Justice set the Palais in a flame for having eaten too much spice.

This quatrain dazzled formerly, and there are some people still who think it extremely witty. Why, can there be anything happier or prettier?

says Philanthus, interrupting him. There can be nothing more empty or more frivolous, replies Eudoxus. These are only words in the air which have no manner of sense; it is all over false. For in one word, what is called *spice* in the Palais has no relation to burning, and the palate in a flame after eating too much pepper never leads a man to the firing of a building where justice is administered and sold, if you please.

What think you, says Philanthus, of that quibble which makes all the smartness of another of Saint-Amant's epigrams?

> Ci gît un fou nommé Pasquet,
> Qui mourut d'un coup de mousquet,
> Lorsqu'il voulut lever la crête.
> Quant à moi, je crois que le sort
> Lui mit du plomb dedans la tête
> Pour le rendre sage en sa mort.[16]

> Here lies a fool called Pasquet who died by the shot of a musket as he lifted up his head. For my part I believe that fate put all this lead into his pate to make him wise e'er he was dead.

This may be allowed in burlesque or comical writings with catches or ballads, replies Eudoxus. These are false jewels which are worn at masques and balls; it is false money which does no injury to trade when it is paid for what it is worth, but he that would have it pass for sterling would make himself very ridiculous in the company of men of sense.

Generally speaking, there is no wit in quibbling or very little; nothing costs less, or is more easily found. Ambiguity, which makes up its character, is less an ornament of discourse than a fault; and it is that which makes it insipid, especially when he who uses it thinks he speaks finely and values himself upon it. On the other side, it is not always easy to be understood: the mysterious appearance which gives it the double meaning is the occasion that a man cannot often come at the true sense without some pains, and when he is come at it he is sorry for his labor; he thinks himself cheated, and I cannot tell but that what he feels at such a time is a sort of vexation for having searched so long to find nothing.

All these reasons sink the credit of pure quibbles very low with men of good sense. I say pure quibbles: for all figures which contain a double sense have every one in its kind their beauties and graces which make them valuable, though they have something in them of the quibble. One single example will make you understand what I mean. Martial tells Domitian, "The people of your empire speak several languages, yet they have but one language when they say that you are the true father of your country." [17] Here are two senses, as you see, and two senses which make an antithesis: speak several languages and have but one language. They are both true as they are severally taken, and one destroys not the other. On the contrary they agree very well, and from the union of these two opposite senses there arises something, I can't tell what, which is ingenious, founded upon the ambiguous word *vox* in Latin and *language* in English. Several smart things in epigrams and a great many jests and witty repartees affect us only because of the double sense which is found in them, and these are properly those thoughts which Macrobius and Seneca call agreeable sophisms.

As far as I see, says Philanthus, truth has a larger extent than I imagined, since it may agree with equivocal expressions in matters of wit; there is nothing now to be done but to reconcile it to hyperboles, and I would very willingly know your opinion about them.

The bare original of the word, replies Eudoxus, decides the thing in general. Whatever is excessive is vicious, even in virtue, which ceases to be virtue when it comes to extremities, and keeps no longer within bounds. So likewise, thoughts which turn upon an hyperbole are all false in themselves, and deserve to have no place in reasonable discourses unless the hyperbole be of a particular kind, or that such qualifications are admitted which moderate its excess; for some hyperboles are less bold than others, and go not beyond their bounds,[18] though they are above common belief. There are others naturalized, as I may say, by custom, which are so established that they have nothing *choquant*. Homer calls Nireus beauty itself,[19] and Martial says that Zoilus is not vicious, but vice itself.[20] We say daily when we are speaking of a very wise and virtuous person, "He is wisdom, he is virtue itself." We say also after the Greeks and Romans, "She is whiter than snow. He goes faster than the wind." These hyperboles, according to Quintilian, lie without deceiving; or, as Seneca says,[21] they bring the mind to truth by a lie, by causing it to comprehend what they signify when they express anything in such a manner as seems to make it incredible.

Those therefore which are prepared and brought on by little and little never shock the minds of the readers or the audience. They even gain belief, I know not how, as Hermogenes says, and the falsest things they propose become at least probable. We have a noted example in Homer. He does not say at once that Polyphemus tore off the top of a mountain; that would scarce have appeared credible. He disposes the reader by his description of that Cyclops, whom he sets forth as a person of an enormous stature, and then gives him strength equal to his height when he makes him carry the body of a great tree for a club and stop the mouth of his cave with a large rock. Besides, he makes him eat more meat at a meal than would serve several men; and at last he adds that Neptune was his father. After all these preparations, when the poet comes to say that Polyphemus tore off the top of a mountain the action does not seem so strange. Nothing seems impossible to a man who is the son of the god of the sea, and who is not made like ordinary men.

There are other ways of qualifying an hyperbole, and which give it even an air of probability. Virgil says that to have seen Antony's and Augustus's fleets at the Battle of Actium, one would have thought they had been the Cyclades floating in the sea.[22] And Florus,[23] speaking of the expedition with which the Romans built a great number of ships in the first Punic War, says that the ships did not seem to have been made by workmen, but the trees seemed to be turned into ships by the gods. They do not say that the vessels were floating islands, or that the trees were turned into ships; they say only that one would think it was so, and that they seemed to be so. This precaution serves for a passport to an hyperbole, as I may say, and makes it allowable even in prose. "For whatever is excused before it is spoke is always favorably hearkened to, be it as uncredible as it will."[24]

Nicolas Boileau-Despréaux

L'Art poétique

the French text

with

a translation and adaptation

by Sir William Soame and John Dryden

The Art of Poetry

Nicolas Boileau-Despréaux L'ART POETIQUE

CHANT I

C'est en vain qu'au Parnasse un téméraire auteur
Pense de l'art des vers atteindre la hauteur:
S'il ne sent point du ciel l'influence secrète,
Si son astre en naissant ne l'a formé poëte,
Dans son génie étroit il est toujours captif: [1]
Pour lui Phébus est sourd, et Pégase est rétif.
O vous donc qui, brûlant d'une ardeur périlleuse,
Courez du bel esprit la carrière épineuse,
N'allez pas sur des vers sans fruit vous consumer,
10   Ni prendre pour génie un amour de rimer:
Craignez d'un vain plaisir les trompeuses amorces,
Et consultez longtemps votre esprit et vos forces.
La nature, fertile en esprits excellens,
Sait entre les auteurs partager les talens: [2]
L'un peut tracer en vers une amoureuse flamme;
L'autre d'un trait plaisant aiguiser l'épigramme;
Malherbe d'un héros peut vanter les exploits; [4]
Racan, chanter Philis, les bergers et les bois: [6]
Mais souvent un esprit qui se flatte et qui s'aime
20   Méconnoît son génie, et s'ignore soi-même.
Ainsi tel [8] autrefois qu'on vit avec Faret [9]
Charbonner de ses vers les murs d'un cabaret,
S'en va, mal à propos, d'une voix insolente,
Chanter du peuple hébreu la fuite triomphante,
Et, poursuivant Moïse au travers des déserts,
Court avec Pharaon se noyer dans les mers.

Sir William Soame and *John Dryden* THE ART OF

POETRY

CANTO I

    Rash author, 'tis a vain presumptuous crime
To undertake the sacred art of rhyme;
If at thy birth the stars that ruled thy sense
Shone not with a poetic influence,
In thy strait genius thou wilt still be bound,
Find Phœbus deaf, and Pegasus unsound.[1]
You, then, that burn with a desire to try
The dangerous course of charming poetry,
Forbear in fruitless verse to lose your time,
Or take for genius the desire of rhyme;   10
Fear the allurements of a specious bait,
And well consider your own force and weight.
    Nature abounds in wits of every kind,
And for each author can a talent find: [2]
One may in verse describe an amorous flame,
Another sharpen a short epigram;
Waller a hero's mighty acts extol,[3]
Spenser sing Rosalind in pastoral.[5]
But authors that themselves too much esteem
Lose their own genius, and mistake their theme: 20
Thus in times past Dubartas vainly writ,[7]
Alloying sacred truth with trifling wit,
Impertinently, and without delight,
Described the Israelites' triumphant flight,
And following Moses o'er the sandy plain,
Perished with Pharaoh in th' Arabian main.

209

Quelque sujet qu'on traite, ou plaisant, ou sublime,
Que toujours le bon sens s'accorde avec la rime:
L'un l'autre vainement ils semblent se haïr;
30   La rime est une esclave, et ne doit qu'obéir.
Lorsqu'à la bien chercher d'abord on s'évertue,
L'esprit à la trouver aisément s'habitue;
Au joug de la raison sans peine elle fléchit,
Et, loin de la gêner, la sert et l'enrichit.
Mais lorsqu'on la néglige, elle devient rebelle,[10]
Et pour la rattraper le sens court après elle.
Aimez donc la raison: que toujours vos écrits
Empruntent d'elle seule et leur lustre et leur prix.[11]
La plupart, emportés d'une fougue insensée,
40   Toujours loin du droit sens vont chercher leur pensée:
Ils croiroient s'abaisser, dans leurs vers monstrueux,
S'ils pensoient ce qu'un autre a pu penser comme eux.
Evitons ces excès: laissons à l'Italie
De tous ces faux brillans l'éclatante folie.[12]
Tout doit tendre au bon sens: mais, pour y parvenir,
Le chemin est glissant et pénible à tenir;
Pour peu qu'on s'en écarte, aussitôt l'on se noie.
La raison pour marcher n'a souvent qu'une voie.
Un auteur quelque fois trop plein de son objet
50   Jamais sans l'épuiser n'abandonne un sujet.
S'il rencontre un palais, il m'en dépeint la face;
Il me promène après de terrasse en terrasse;
Ici s'offre un perron; là règne un corridor,
Là ce balcon s'enferme en un balustre d'or.
Il compte des plafonds les ronds at les ovales;
«Ce ne sont que festons, ce ne sont qu'astragales».[13]
Je saute vingt feuillets pour en trouver la fin,
Et je me sauve à peine au travers du jardin.
Fuyez de ces auteurs l'abondance stérile,
60   Et ne vous chargez point d'un détail inutile.
Tout ce qu'on dit de trop est fade et rebutant;
L'esprit rassasié le rejette à l'instant.
Qui ne sait se borner ne sut jamais écrire.
Souvent la peur d'un mal nous conduit dans un pire.

Whate'er you write of pleasant or sublime,
Always let sense accompany your rhyme.
Falsely they seem each other to oppose—
Rhyme must be made with reason's laws to close;　　　　30
And when to conquer her you bend your force,
The mind will triumph in the noble course;
To reason's yoke she quickly will incline,
Which, far from hurting, renders her divine; [10]
But if neglected, will as easily stray,
And master reason, which she should obey.
Love reason then; and let whate'er you write
Borrow from her its beauty, force, and light.[11]
　　Most writers, mounted on a resty muse,
Extravagant and senseless objects choose;　　　　40
They think they err, if in their verse they fall
On any thought that's plain or natural.
Fly this excess; and let Italians be
Vain authors of false glittering poetry.[12]
All ought to aim at sense; but most in vain
Strive the hard pass and slippery path to gain;
You drown if to the right or left you stray;
Reason to go has often but one way.
　　Sometimes an author, fond of his own thought,
Pursues his object till it's overwrought:　　　　50
If he describes a house, he shows the face,
And after walks you round from place to place;
Here is a vista, there the doors unfold,
Balconies here are balustered with gold;
Then counts the rounds and ovals in the halls,
"The festoons, friezes, and the astragals"; [13]
Tired with his tedious pomp, away I run,
And skip o'er twenty pages to be gone.
Of such descriptions the vain folly see,
And shun their barren superfluity.　　　　60
All that is needless carefully avoid;
The mind once satisfied is quickly cloyed.
He cannot write who knows not to give o'er;
To mend one fault he makes a hundred more:

211

Un vers étoit trop foible, et vous le rendez dur;
J'évite d'être long, et je deviens obscur;
L'un n'est point trop fardé, mais sa muse est trop nue;
L'autre a peur de ramper, il se perd dans la nue.
Voulez-vous du public mériter les amours,
70 Sans cesse en écrivant variez vos discours.
Un style trop égal et toujours uniforme
En vain brille à nos yeux, il faut qu'il nous endorme
On lit peu ces auteurs, nés pour nous ennuyer,
Qui toujours sur un ton semblent psalmodier.
Heureux qui, dans ses vers, sait d'une voix légère
Passer du grave au doux, du plaisant au sévère!
Son livre, aimé du ciel, et chéri des lecteurs,
Est souvent chez Barbin entouré d'acheteurs.[14]
Quoi que vous écriviez, évitez la bassesse:
80 Le style le moins noble a pourtant sa noblesse.
Au mépris du bon sens, le burlesque effronté [15]
Trompa les yeux d'abord, plut par sa nouveauté;
On ne vit plus en vers que pointes triviales;
Le Parnasse parla le langage des halles;
La licence à rimer alors n'eut plus de frein;
Apollon travesti devint un Tabarin.[16]
Cette contagion infecta les provinces,
Du clerc et du bourgeois passa jusques aux princes;
Le plus mauvais plaisant eut ses approbateurs;
90 Et, jusqu'à d'Assoucy, tout trouva des lecteurs.[18]
Mais de ce style enfin la cour désabusée
Dédaigna de ces vers l'extravagance aisée,
Distingua le naïf du plat et du bouffon,
Et laissa la province admirer le Typhon.[20]
Que ce style jamais ne souille votre ouvrage.
Imitons de Marot l'élégant badinage,[22]
Et laissons le burlesque aux plaisans du pont Neuf.[23]
Mais n'allez point aussi, sur les pas de Brébeuf,
Même en une Pharsale, entasser sur les rives,
100 «De morts et de mourans cent montagnes plaintives.» [24]
Prenez mieux votre ton. Soyez simple avec art,
Sublime sans orgueil, agréable sans fard.

212

A verse was weak, you turn it much too strong,
And grow obscure for fear you should be long.
Some are not gaudy, but are flat and dry;
Not to be low, another soars too high.
Would you of every one deserve the praise?
In writing, vary your discourse and phrase;   70
A frozen style, that neither ebbs nor flows,
Instead of pleasing, makes us gape and doze.
Those tedious authors are esteemed by none,
Who tire us, humming the same heavy tone.
Happy who in his verse can gently steer
From grave to light, from pleasant to severe;
His works will be admired wherever found,
And oft with buyers will be compassed round.
In all you write be neither low nor vile;
The meanest theme may have a proper style.   80
The dull burlesque appeared with impudence,
And pleased by novelty in spite of sense.
All, except trivial points, grew out of date;
Parnassus spoke the cant of Billingsgate;
Boundless and mad, disordered rhyme was seen;
Disguised Apollo changed to Harlequin.
This plague, which first in country towns began,
Cities and kingdoms quickly overran;
The dullest scribblers some admirers found,
And the *Mock Tempest* [17] was a while renowned.   90
But this low stuff the town at last despised,
And scorned the folly that they once had prized,
Distinguished dull from natural and plain,
And left the villages to Flecknoe's reign.[19]
Let not so mean a style your muse debase,
But learn from Butler the buffooning grace,[21]
And let burlesque in ballads be employed.
Yet noisy bombast carefully avoid,
Nor think to raise, though on Pharsalia's plain,
"Millions of mourning mountains of the slain"; [24]   100
Nor, with Dubartas, "bridle up the floods,
And periwig with wool the baldpate woods." [25]

N'offrez rien au lecteur que ce qui peut lui plaire.
Ayez pour la cadence une oreille sévère:
Que toujours dans vos vers le sens coupant les mots,
Suspende l'hémistiche, en marque le repos.
Gardez qu'une voyelle à courir trop hâtée
Ne soit d'une voyelle en son chemin heurtée.
Il est un heureux choix de mots harmonieux.
110   Fuyez des mauvais sons le concours odieux:
Le vers le mieux rempli, la plus noble pensée
Ne peut plaire à l'esprit quand l'oreille est blessée.
   Durant les premiers ans du Parnasse françois [26]
Le caprice tout seul faisoit toutes les lois.
La rime, au bout des mots assemblés sans mesure,
Tenoit lieu d'ornemens, de nombre et de césure.
Villon [28] sut le premier dans ces siècles grossiers
Débrouiller l'art confus de nos vieux romanciers.[29]
Marot bientôt après fit fleurir les ballades,[30]
120   Tourna des triolets, rima des mascarades,
A des refrains réglés asservit les rondeaux,
Et montra pour rimer des chemins tout nouveaux.
Ronsard,[32] qui le suivit par une autre méthode,
Réglant tout, brouilla tout, fit un art à sa mode,
Et toutefois longtemps eut un heureux destin.
Mais sa muse, en françois parlant grec et latin,
Vit dans l'âge suivant, par un retour grotesque,
Tomber de ses grands mots le faste pédantesque.
Ce poëte orgueilleux, trébuché de si haut,
130   Rendit plus retenus Desportes et Bertaut.[34]
   Enfin Malherbe vint, et, le premier en France,
Fit sentir dans les vers une juste cadence,
D'un mot mis en sa place enseigna le pouvoir,
Et réduisit la muse aux règles du devoir.[36]
Par ce sage écrivain la langue réparée
N'offrit plus rien de rude à l'oreille épurée.
Les stances avec grâce apprirent à tomber,
Et le vers sur le vers n'osa plus enjamber.
Tout reconnut ses lois; et ce guide fidèle
140   Aux auteurs de ce temps sert encor de modèle.

Choose a just style. Be grave without constraint,
Great without pride, and lovely without paint.
    Write what your reader may be pleased to hear,
And for the measure have a careful ear;
On easy numbers fix your happy choice;
Of jarring sounds avoid the odious noise;
The fullest verse, and the most labored sense,
Displease us if the ear once take offense.   110
    Our ancient verse, as homely as the times,
Was rude, unmeasured, only tagged with rhymes:
Number and cadence, that have since been shown,
To those unpolished writers were unknown.
Fairfax was he who in that darker age
By his just rules restrained poetic rage; [27]
Spenser did next in pastorals excel,
And taught the noble art of writing well,
To stricter rules the stanza did restrain,
And found for poetry a richer vein.   120
Then Davenant came, who with a new-found art
Changed all, spoiled all, and had his way apart; [31]
His haughty muse all others did despise,
And thought in triumph to bear off the prize,
Till the sharp-sighted critics of the times
In their *Mock Gondibert* exposed his rhymes,[33]
The laurels he pretended did refuse,
And dashed the hopes of his aspiring muse.
This headstrong writer, falling from on high,
Made following authors take less liberty.   130
    Waller came last, but was the first whose art
Just weight and measure did to verse impart,[35]
That of a well-placed word could teach the force,
And showed for poetry a nobler course.
His happy genius did our tongue refine,
And easy words with pleasing numbers join;
His verses to good method did apply,
And changed harsh discord to soft harmony.
All owned his laws, which, long approved and tried,
To present authors now may be a guide.   140

Marchez donc sur ses pas; aimez sa pureté,
Et de son tour heureux imitez la clarté.
Si le sens de vos vers tarde à se faire entendre,
Mon esprit aussitôt commence à se détendre,
Et, de vos vains discours prompt à se détacher,
Ne suit point un auteur qu'il faut toujours chercher.

Il est certains esprits dont les sombres pensées
Sont d'un nuage épais toujours embarrassées;
Le jour de la raison ne le sauroit percer.
150   Avant donc que d'écrire apprenez à penser.
Selon que notre idée est plus ou moins obscure,
L'expression la suit, ou moins nette, ou plus pure.
Ce que l'on conçoit bien s'énonce clairement,
Et les mots pour le dire arrivent aisément.[37]

Surtout, qu'en vos écrits la langue révérée
Dans vos plus grands excès vous soit toujours sacrée.
En vain vous me frappez d'un son mélodieux,
Si le terme est impropre, ou le tour vicieux;
Mon esprit n'admet point un pompeux barbarisme,
160   Ni d'un vers ampoulé l'orgueilleux solécisme.
Sans la langue, en un mot, l'auteur le plus divin
Est toujours, quoi qu'il fasse, un méchant écrivain.

Travaillez à loisir, quelque ordre qui vous presse,
Et ne vous piquez point d'une folle vitesse;
Un style si rapide, et qui court en rimant,
Marque moins trop d'esprit, que peu de jugement.
J'aime mieux un ruisseau qui sur la molle arène
Dans un pré plein de fleurs lentement se promène,
Qu'un torrent débordé qui, d'un cours orageux,
170   Roule, plein de gravier, sur un terrain fangeux.
Hâtez-vous lentement,[38] et, sans perdre courage,
Vingt fois sur le métier remettez votre ouvrage:
Polissez-le sans cesse et le repolissez;
Ajoutez quelquefois, et souvent effacez.

C'est peu qu'en un ouvrage où les fautes fourmillent,
Des traits d'esprit semés de temps en temps pétillent.
Il faut que chaque chose y soit mise en son lieu;
Que le début, la fin répondent au milieu;

216

Tread boldly in his steps, secure from fear,
And be, like him, in your expressions clear.
If in your verse you drag, and sense delay,
My patience tires, my fancy goes astray,
And from your vain discourse I turn my mind,
Nor search an author troublesome to find.

There is a kind of writer pleased with sound,
Whose fustian head with clouds is compassed round;
No reason can disperse them with its light.
Learn then to think ere you pretend to write;   150
As your idea is clear or else obscure,
The expression follows perfect or impure.
What we conceive with ease we can express;
Words to the notions flow with readiness.[37]

Observe the language well in all you write,
And swerve not from it in your loftiest flight.
The smoothest verse and the exactest sense
Displease us, if ill English give offense;
A barbarous phrase no reader can approve,
Nor bombast, noise, or affectation love.   160
In short, without pure language, what you write
Can never yield us profit or delight.

Take time for thinking; never work in haste;
And value not yourself for writing fast.
A rapid poem, with such fury writ,
Shows want of judgment, not abounding wit.
More pleased we are to see a river lead
His gentle streams along a flowery mead,
Than from high banks to hear loud torrents roar,
With foamy waters on a muddy shore.   170
Gently make haste,[38] of labor not afraid;
A hundred times consider what you've said;
Polish, repolish, every color lay,
And sometimes add, but oftener take away.

'Tis not enough, when swarming faults are writ,
That here and there are scattered sparks of wit;
Each object must be fixed in the due place,
And differing parts have corresponding grace;

217

Que d'un art délicat les pièces assorties
180   N'y forment qu'un seul tout de diverses parties;
Que jamais du sujet le discours s'écartant
N'aille chercher trop loin quelque mot éclatant.
    Craignez-vous pour vos vers la censure publique?
Soyez-vous à vous-même un sévère critique.
L'ignorance toujours est prête à s'admirer.
Faites-vous des amis prompts à vous censurer:
Qu'ils soient de vos écrits les confidens sincères,
Et de tous vos défauts les zélés adversaires.
    Dépouillez devant eux l'arrogance d'auteur;
190   Mais sachez de l'ami discerner le flatteur:
Tel vous semble applaudir, qui vous raille et vous joue.
Aimez qu'on vous conseille et non pas qu'on vous loue.[39]
    Un flatteur aussitôt cherche à se récrier:
Chaque vers qu'il entend le fait extasier.
Tout est charmant, divin: aucun mot ne le blesse;
Il trépigne de joie, il pleure de tendresse;
Il vous comble partout d'éloges fastueux:
La vérité n'a point cet air impétueux.
    Un sage ami, toujours rigoureux, inflexible,
200   Sur vos fautes jamais ne vous laisse paisible:
Il ne pardonne point les endroits négligés,
Il renvoie en leur lieu les vers mal arrangés,
Il réprime des mots l'ambitieuse emphase;
Ici le sens le choque, et plus loin c'est la phrase.
Votre construction semble un peu s'obscurcir;
Ce terme est équivoque, il le faut éclaircir.
C'est ainsi que vous parle un ami véritable.
    Mais souvent sur ses vers un auteur intraitable
A les protéger tous se croit intéressé,
210   Et d'abord prend en main le droit de l'offensé.
De ce vers, direz-vous, l'expression est basse, —
Ah! monsieur, pour ce vers je vous demande grâce,
Répondra-t-il d'abord. — Ce mot me semble froid;
Je le retrancherois. — C'est le plus bel endroit! —
Ce tour ne me plaît pas. — Tout le monde l'admire.
Ainsi toujours constant à ne se point dédire,

Till, by a curious art disposed, we find
One perfect whole of all the pieces joined.   180
Keep to your subject close in all you say,
Nor for a sounding sentence ever stray.
   The public censure for your writings fear,
And to yourself be critic most severe.
Fantastic wits their darling follies love;
But find you faithful friends that will reprove,
That on your works may look with careful eyes,
And of your faults be zealous enemies.
Lay by an author's pride and vanity,
And from a friend a flatterer descry,   190
Who seems to like, but means not what he says;
Embrace true counsel, but suspect false praise.[39]
   A sycophant will everything admire;
Each verse, each sentence, sets his soul on fire;
All is divine! there's not a word amiss!
He shakes with joy, and weeps with tenderness;
He overpowers you with his mighty praise.
Truth never moves in those impetuous ways.
   A faithful friend is careful of your fame,
And freely will your heedless errors blame;   200
He cannot pardon a neglected line,
But verse to rule and order will confine,
Reproves of words the too-affected noise:
"Here the sense flags, and repetition cloys;
Your fancy tires, and your discourse grows vain,
Your terms improper; make them just and plain."
Thus 'tis a faithful friend will freedom use.
   But authors partial to their darling muse
Think to protect it they have just pretense,
And at your friendly counsel take offense.   210
Said you of this, that the expression's flat?
"You servant, sir, you must excuse me that,"
He answers you.—"This word has here no grace,
Pray leave it out."—"That, sir, 's the proper'st place."—
"This turn I like not."—" 'Tis approved by all."
Thus, resolute not from a fault to fall,

Qu'un mot dans son ouvrage ait paru vous blesser,
C'est un titre chez lui pour ne point l'effacer.
Cependant, à l'entendre, il chérit la critique;
220   Vous avez sur ses vers un pouvoir despotique,
Mais tout ce beau discours dont il vient vous flatter
N'est rien qu'un piége adroit pour vous les réciter.
Aussitôt il vous quitte; et, content de sa muse,
S'en va chercher ailleurs quelque fat qu'il abuse:
Car souvent il en trouve: ainsi qu'en sots auteurs,
Notre siècle est fertile en sots admirateurs;
Et, sans ceux que fournit la ville et la province,
Il en est chez le duc, il en est chez le prince.
L'ouvrage le plus plat a, chez les courtisans,
230   De tout temps recontré de zélés partisans;
Et, pour finir enfin par un trait de satire,
Un sot trouve toujours un plus sot qui l'admire.

CHANT II

Telle qu'une bergère, au plus beau jour de fête,
De superbes rubis ne charge point sa tête,
Et, sans mêler à l'or l'éclat des diamans,
Cueille en un champ voisin ses plus beaux ornemens;
Telle, aimable en son air, mais humble dans son style,
Doit éclater sans pompe une élégante idylle.
Son tour simple et naïf n'a rien de fastueux,
Et n'aime point l'orgueil d'un vers présomptueux.
Il faut que sa douceur flatte, chatouille, éveille,
10   Et jamais de grands mots n'épouvante l'oreille.
Mais souvent dans ce style un rimeur aux abois

If there's a syllable of which you doubt,
'Tis a sure reason not to blot it out.
Yet still he says you may his faults confute,
And over him your power is absolute.   220
But of his feigned humility take heed;
'Tis a bait laid to make you hear him read.
And when he leaves you, happy in his Muse,
Restless he runs some other to abuse,
And often finds; for in our scribbling times
No fool can want a sot to praise his rhymes.
The flattest work has ever in the court
Met with some zealous ass for its support;
And in all times a forward, scribbling fop
Has found some greater fool to cry him up.   230

CANTO II

As a fair nymph, when rising from her bed,
With sparkling diamonds dresses not her head,
But without gold, or pearl, or costly scents,
Gathers from neighboring fields her ornaments;
Such, lovely in its dress, but plain withal,
Ought to appear a perfect Pastoral.
Its humble method nothing has of fierce,
But hates the rattling of a lofty verse;
There native beauty pleases and excites,
And never with harsh sounds the ear affrights.   10
   But in this style a poet often spent,

Jette là, de dépit, la flûte et le hautbois;
Et, follement pompeux, dans sa verve indiscrète,
Au milieu d'une églogue entonne la trompette.
De peur de l'écouter, Pan fuit dans les roseaux,
Et les Nymphes, d'effroi, se cachent sous les eaux.
Au contraire cet autre, abject en son langage,
Fait parler ses bergers comme on parle au village.
Ses vers plats et grossiers, dépouillés d'agrément,
20   Toujours baisent la terre, et rampent tristement:
On diroit que Ronsard, sur ses pipeaux rustiques,
Vient encor fredonner ses idylles gothiques,
Et changer, sans respect de l'oreille et du son,
Lycidas en Pierrot, et Philis en Toinon.[1]
Entre ces deux excès la route est difficile.
Suivez, pour la trouver, Théocrite et Virgile: [2]
Que leurs tendres écrits, par les Grâces dictés,
Ne quittent point vos mains, jour et nuit feuilletés.
Seuls, dans leurs doctes vers, ils pourront vous apprendre
30   Par quel art sans bassesse un auteur peut descendre;
Chanter Flore, les champs, Pomone, les vergers;
Au combat de la flûte animer deux bergers,
Des plaisirs de l'amour vanter la douce amorce;
Changer Narcisse en fleur, couvrir Daphné d'écorce;
Et par quel art encor l'églogue quelquefois
Rend dignes d'un consul la campagne et les bois.[3]
Telle est de ce poëme et la force et la grâce.

    D'un ton un peu plus haut, mais pourtant sans audace,
La plaintive élégie, en longs habits de deuil,
40   Sait, les cheveux épars, gémir sur un cercueil.
Elle peint des amans la joie et la tristesse;
Flatte, menace, irrite, apaise une maîtresse.
Mais, pour bien exprimer ces caprices heureux,
C'est peu d'être poëte, il faut être amoureux.
    Je hais ces vains auteurs, dont la muse forcée
M'entretient de ses feux, toujours froide et glacée.
Qui s'affligent par art, et, fous de sens rassis,
S'érigent pour rimer, en amoureux transis.
Leurs transports les plus doux ne sont que phrases vaines.

In rage throws by his rural instrument,
And vainly, when disordered thoughts abound,
Amidst the eclogue makes the trumpet sound;
Pan flies alarmed into the neighboring woods,
And frighted naiads dive into the floods.

   Opposed to this, another, low in style,
Makes shepherds speak a language base and vile;
His writings, flat and heavy, without sound,
Kissing the earth and creeping on the ground;   20
You'd swear that Randal, in his rustic strains,
Again was quavering to the country swains,
And changing, without care of sound or dress,
Strephon and Phyllis into Tom and Bess.[1]

   'Twixt these extremes 'tis hard to keep the right;
For guides take Virgil and read Theocrite; [2]
Be their just writings, by the gods inspired,
Your constant pattern, practiced and admired.
By them alone you'll easily comprehend
How poets without shame may condescend   30
To sing of gardens, fields, of flowers and fruit,
To stir up shepherds and to tune the flute;
Of love's rewards to tell the happy hour,
Daphne a tree, Narcissus make a flower,
And by what means the eclogue yet has power
To make the woods worthy a conqueror; [3]
This of their writings is the grace and flight;
Their risings lofty, yet not out of sight.

   The Elegy, that loves a mournful style,
With unbound hair weeps at a funeral pile;   40
It paints the lover's torments and delights,
A mistress flatters, threatens, and invites;
But well these raptures if you'll make us see,
You must know love, as well as poetry.

   I hate those lukewarm authors, whose forced fire
In a cold style describes a hot desire;
That sigh by rule and, raging in cold blood,
Their sluggish muse whip to an amorous mood.
Their feigned transports appear but flat and vain;

223

50   Ils ne savent jamais que se charger de chaînes,
Que bénir leur martyre, adorer leur prison,
Et faire quereller les sens et la raison.
Ce n'étoit pas jadis sur ce ton ridicule
Qu'Amour dictoit les vers que soupiroit Tibulle,
Ou que, du tendre Ovide animant les doux sons,[4]
Il donnoit de son art les charmantes leçons.
Il faut que le coeur seul parle dans l'élégie.
    L'ode, avec plus d'éclat, et non moins d'énergie,
Elevant jusqu'au ciel son vol ambitieux,
60   Entretient dans ses vers commerce avec les dieux.
Aux athlètes dans Pise [5] elle ouvre la barrière,
Chante un vainqueur poudreux au bout de la carrière,
Mène Achille sanglant au bord du Simoïs,[6]
Ou fait fléchir l'Escaut sous le joug de Louis.[8]
Tantôt comme une abeille ardente à son ouvrage,
Elle s'en va de fleurs dépouiller le rivage;
Elle peint les festins, les danses et les ris;
Vante un baiser cueilli sur les lèvres d'Iris,
«Qui mollement résiste, et, par un doux caprice,
70   Quelquefois le refuse, afin qu'on le ravisse.» [9]
Son style impétueux souvent marche au hasard.
Chez elle un beau désordre est un effet de l'art.
    Loin ces rimeurs craintifs dont l'esprit flegmatique
Garde dans ses fureurs un ordre didactique;
Qui, chantant d'un héros les progrès éclatans,
Maigres historiens, suivront l'ordre des temps.
Ils n'osent un moment perdre un sujet de vue,
Pour prendre Dôle, il faut que Lille soit rendue;
Et que leur vers exact, ainsi que Mézerai,
80   Ait fait déjà tomber les remparts de Courtrai.[10]
Apollon de son feu leur fut toujours avare.
On dit, à ce propos, qu'un jour ce dieu bizarre,
Voulant pousser à bout tous les rimeurs françois,
Inventa du sonnet les rigoureuses lois;
Voulut qu'en deux quatrains de mesure pareille
La rime avec deux sons frappât huit fois l'oreille;
Et qu'ensuite six vers artistement rangés

They always sigh, and always hug their chain,   50
Adore their prison and their sufferings bless,
Make sense and reason quarrel as they please.
'Twas not of old in this affected tone
That smooth Tibullus made his amorous moan,
Nor Ovid, when, instructed from above,[4]
By nature's rule he taught the art of love.
The heart in elegies forms the discourse.
   The Ode is bolder and has greater force:
Mounting to heaven in her ambitious flight,
Amongst the gods and heroes takes delight;   60
Of Pisa's [5] wrestlers tells the sinewy force,
And sings the dusty conqueror's glorious course;
To Simois' streams does fierce Achilles bring,[6]
And makes the Ganges bow to Britain's king.[7]
Sometimes she flies like an industrious bee,
And robs the flowers by nature's chemistry,
Describes the shepherd's dances, feasts, and bliss,
And boasts from Phyllis to surprise a kiss,
"When gently she resists with feigned remorse,
That what she grants may seem to be by force." [9]   70
Her generous style at random oft will part,
And by a brave disorder shows her art.
   Unlike those fearful poets, whose cold rhyme
In all their raptures keeps exactest time;
That sing th' illustrious hero's mighty praise
(Lean writers!) by the terms of weeks and days,
And dare not from least circumstances part,
But take all towns by strictest rules of art.
Apollo drives those fops from his abode;
And some have said that once the humorous god   80
Resolving all such scribblers to confound,
For the short Sonnet ordered this strict bound,
Set rules for the just measure and the time,
The easy running and alternate rhyme;
But, above all, those licenses denied
Which in these writings the lame sense supplied,
Forbade a useless line should find a place,

225

Fussent en deux tercets par le sens partagés.[11]
Surtout de ce poëme il bannit la licence:
90   Lui-même en mesura le nombre et la cadence;
Défendit qu'un vers foible y pût jamais entrer,
Ni qu'un mot déjà mis osât s'y remontrer.
Du reste il l'enrichit d'une beauté suprême:
Un sonnet sans défauts vaut seul un long poëme.
Mais en vain mille auteurs y pensent arriver;
Et cet heureux phénix est encore à trouver.
A peine dans Gombaut, Maynard et Malleville,
En peut-on admirer deux ou trois entre mille:
Le reste, aussi peu lu que ceux de Pelletier
100   N'a fait de chez Sercy, qu'un saut chez l'épicier.[12]
Pour enfermer son sens dans la borne prescrite,
La mesure est toujours trop longue et trop petite.
    L'épigramme, plus libre en son tour plus borné,
N'est souvent qu'un bon mot de deux rimes orné.
Jadis de nos auteurs les pointes [13] ignorées
Furent de l'Italie en nos vers attirées.
Le vulgaire, ébloui de leur faux agrément,
A ce nouvel appât courut avidement.
La faveur du public excitant leur audace,
110   Leur nombre impétueux inonda le Parnasse.
Le madrigal [14] d'abord en fut enveloppé;
Le sonnet orgueilleux lui-même en fut frappé:
La tragédie [15] en fit ses plus chères délices;
L'élégie en orna ses douloureux caprices;
Un héros sur la scène eut soin de s'en parer,
Et sans pointe un amant n'osa plus soupirer:
On vit tous les bergers, dans leurs plaintes nouvelles,
Fidèles à la pointe encor plus qu'à leurs belles;
Chaque mot eut toujours deux visages divers:
120   La prose la reçut aussi bien que les vers;
L'avocat au palais en hérissa son style,
Et le docteur en chaire en sema l'Evangile.[16]
    La raison outragée enfin ouvrit les yeux,
La chassa pour jamais des discours sérieux;
Et, dans tous ces écrits la déclarant infâme,

226

Or a repeated word appear with grace.
A faultless sonnet, finished thus, would be
Worth tedious volumes of loose poetry.   90
A hundred scribbling authors, without ground,
Believe they have this only phœnix found,
When yet the exactest scarce have two or three,
Among whole tomes, from faults and censure free;
The rest, but little read, regarded less,
Are shoveled to the pastry from the press.
Closing the sense within the measured time,
'Tis hard to fit the reason to the rhyme.

The Epigram, with little art composed,
Is one good sentence in a distich closed.   100
These points [13] that by Italians first were prized,
Our ancient authors knew not, or despised;
The vulgar, dazzled with their glaring light,
To their false pleasures quickly they invite;
But public favor so increased their pride,
They overwhelmed Parnassus with their tide.
The Madrigal [14] at first was overcome,
And the proud Sonnet fell by the same doom;
With these grave Tragedy adorned her flights,
And mournful Elegy her funeral rites;   110
A hero never failed them on the stage,
Without his point a lover durst not rage;
The amorous shepherds took more care to prove
True to their point, than faithful to their love.
Each word, like Janus, had a double face,
And prose, as well as verse, allowed it place;
The lawyer with conceits adorned his speech,
The parson without quibbling could not preach.

At last affronted reason looked about,
And from all serious matters shut them out,   120
Declared that none should use them without shame,
Except a scattering in the epigram—
Provided that by art, and in due time,
They turned upon the thought, and not the rhyme.
Thus in all parts disorders did abate;

Par grâce lui laissa l'entrée en l'épigramme,
Pourvu que sa finesse, éclatant à propos,
Roulât sur la pensée, et non pas sur les mots.
Ainsi de toutes parts les désordres cessèrent.
130 Toutefois à la cour les Turlupins restèrent,[17]
Insipides plaisans, bouffons infortunés,
D'un jeu de mots grossier partisans surannés.
Ce n'est pas quelquefois qu'une muse un peu fine
Sur un mot, en passant, ne joue et ne badine,
Et d'un sens détourné n'abuse avec succès;
Mais fuyez sur ce point un ridicule excès,
Et n'allez pas toujours d'une pointe frivole
Aiguiser par la queue une épigramme folle.
 Tout poëme est brilliant de sa propre beauté.
140 Le rondeau, né gaulois, a la naïveté.
La ballade, asservie à ses vieilles maximes,
Souvent doit tout son lustre au caprice des rimes.
Le madrigal, plus simple et plus noble en son tour,
Respire la douceur, la tendresse et l'amour.
 L'ardeur de se montrer, et non pas de médire,
Arma la Vérité du vers de la satire.
Lucile le premier osa la faire voir,[19]
Aux vices des Romains présenta le miroir,
Vengea l'humble vertu, de la richesse altière,
150 Et l'honnête homme à pied, du faquin en litière.
Horace à cette aigreur mêla son enjoûment;
On ne fut plus ni fat ni sot impunément;
Et malheur à tout nom, qui, propre à la censure,
Put entrer dans un vers sans rompre la mesure!
Perse, en ses vers obscurs, mais serrés et pressans,
Affecta d'enfermer moins de mots que de sens.[20]
Juvénal, élevé dans les cris de l'école,
Poussa jusqu'à l'excès sa mordante hyperbole.
Ses ouvrages, tout pleins d'affreuses vérités,
160 Etincellent pourtant de sublimes beautés;
Soit que, sur un écrit arrivé de Caprée,
Il brise de Séjan la statue adorée;
Soit qu'il fasse au conseil courir les sénateurs,

Yet quibblers in the court had leave to prate,
Insipid jesters and unpleasant fools,
A corporation of dull punning drolls.
'Tis not but that sometimes a dextrous muse
May with advantage a turned sense abuse, 130
And on a word may trifle with address;
But above all avoid the fond excess,
And think not, when your verse and sense are lame,
With a dull point to tag your epigram.
　　Each poem his perfection has apart:
The British Round [18] in plainness shows his art;
The Ballad, though the pride of ancient time,
Has often nothing but his humorous rhyme;
The Madrigal may softer passions move,
And breathe the tender ecstasies of love. 140
　　Desire to show itself, and not to wrong,
Armed Virtue first with Satire in its tongue.
Lucilius was the man who, bravely bold,[19]
To Roman vices did this mirror hold,
Protected humble goodness from reproach,
Showed worth on foot, and rascals in the coach.
Horace his pleasing wit to this did add,
And none uncensured could be fool or mad;
Unhappy was that wretch whose name might be
Squared to the rules of their sharp poetry. 150
Persius obscure, but full of sense and wit,
Affected brevity in all he writ.[20]
And Juvenal, learn'd as those times could be,
Too far did stretch his sharp hyperbole;
Though horrid truths through all his labors shine,
In what he writes there's something of divine.
Whether he blames the Caprean debauch,
Or of Sejanus' fall tells the approach,
Or that he makes the trembling senate come
To the stern tyrant to receive their doom, 160
Or Roman vice in coarsest habits shows,
And paints an empress reeking from the stews,
In all he writes appears a noble fire.[21]

229

D'un tyran soupçonneux pâles adulateurs;
Ou que, poussant à bout la luxure latine,
Aux portefaix de Rome il vende Messaline,
Ses écrits pleins de feu partout brillent aux yeux.[21]
   De ces maîtres savans disciple ingénieux,
Régnier seul parmi nous formé sur leurs modèles,
170   Dans son vieux style encore a des grâces nouvelles.[22]
Heureux, si ses discours, craints du chaste lecteur,
Ne se sentoient des lieux où fréquentoit l'auteur,
Et si, du son hardi de ses rimes cyniques,
Il n'alarmoit souvent les oreilles pudiques!
Le latin, dans les mots, brave l'honnêteté:
Mais le lecteur françois veut être respecté;
Du moindre sens impur la liberté l'outrage,
Si la pudeur des mots n'en adoucit l'image.
Je veux dans la satire un esprit de candeur,
180   Et fuis un effronté qui prêche la pudeur.
   D'un trait de ce poëme en bons mots si fertile,
Le François, né malin, forma le vaudeville,[23]
Agréable indiscret, qui, conduit par le chant,
Passe de bouche en bouche et s'accroît en marchant.
La liberté françoise en ses vers se déploie.
Cet enfant de plaisir veut naître dans la joie.
Toutefois n'allez pas, goguenard dangereux,
Faire Dieu le sujet d'un badinage affreux.
A la fin tous ces jeux que l'athéisme élève,
190   Conduisent tristement le plaisant à la Grève.[25]
Il faut, même en chansons, du bon sens et de l'art.
Mais pourtant on a vu le vin et le hasard
Inspirer quelquefois une muse grossière,
Et fournir, sans génie, un couplet à Linière.[26]
Mais pour un vain bonheur qui vous a fait rimer,
Gardez qu'un sot orgueil ne vous vienne enfumer.
Souvent l'auteur altier de quelque chansonnette
Au même instant prend droit de se croire poëte:
Il ne dormira plus qu'il n'ait fait un sonnet;
200   Il met tous les matins six impromptus au net.
Encore est-ce un miracle, en ses vagues furies,

To follow such a master then desire.
   Chaucer alone, fixed on this solid base,
In his old style conserves a modern grace;
Too happy, if the freedom of his rhymes
Offended not the method of our times.
The Latin writers decency neglect,
But modern readers challenge our respect,   170
And at immodest writings take offense,
If clean expression cover not the sense.
I love sharp satire, from obsceneness free,
Not impudence that preaches modesty.
   Our English, who in malice never fail,
Hence in Lampoons and Libels learnt to rail;
Pleasant detraction, that by singing goes
From mouth to mouth, and as it marches grows!
Our freedom in our poetry we see,
That child of joy begot by liberty.   180
But, vain blasphemer, tremble when you choose
God for the subject of your impious muse;
At last those jests which libertines invent
Bring the lewd author to just punishment.
Ev'n in a song there must be art and sense;
Yet sometimes we have seen that wine or chance
Has warmed cold brains, and given dull writers mettle,
And furnished out a scene for Mr. S – – .[24]
But for one lucky hit that made thee please,
Let not thy folly grow to a disease,   190
Nor think thyself a wit; for in our age
If a warm fancy does some fop engage,
He neither eats nor sleeps till he has writ,
But plagues the world with his adulterate wit.
Nay 'tis a wonder if, in his dire rage,
He prints not his dull follies for the stage,
And, in the front of all his senseless plays,
Makes David Loggan crown his head with bays.[27]

231

Si bientôt, imprimant ses sottes rêveries,
Il ne se fait graver au-devant du recueil,
Couronné de lauriers par la main de Nanteuil.[28]

CHANT III

    Il n'est point de serpent ni de monstre odieux,
Qui, par l'art imité, ne puisse plaire aux yeux:
D'un pinceau délicat l'artifice agréable
Du plus affreux objet fait un objet aimable.
Ainsi, pour nous charmer, la Tragédie en pleurs
D'Œdipe tout sanglant fit parler les douleurs,
D'Oreste parricide exprima les alarmes,
Et, pour nous divertir, nous arracha des larmes.
    Vous donc, qui d'un beau feu pour le théâtre épris,

10   Venez en vers pompeux y disputer le prix,
Voulez-vous sur la scène étaler des ouvrages
Où tout Paris en foule apporte ses suffrages,
Et qui, toujours plus beaux, plus ils sont regardés,
Soient au bout de vingt ans encor redemandés?
Que dans tous vos discours la passion émue
Aille chercher le coeur, l'échauffe et le remue.
Si d'un beau mouvement l'agréable fureur
Souvent ne nous remplit d'une douce terreur
Ou n'excite en notre âme une pitié charmante,[1]

20   En vain vous étalez une scène savante:
Vos froids raisonnemens ne feront qu'attiédir
Un spectateur toujours paresseux d'applaudir,
Et qui, des vains efforts de votre rhétorique
Justement fatigué, s'endort ou vous critique.

232

CANTO III

There's not a monster bred beneath the sky
But, well-disposed by art, may please the eye;
A curious workman, by his skill divine,
From an ill object makes a good design.
Thus, to delight us, Tragedy, in tears
For Œdipus, provokes our hopes and fears;
For parricide Orestes asks relief,
And, to increase our pleasure, causes grief.
    You, then, that in this noble art would rise,
Come, and in lofty verse dispute the prize.   10
Would you upon the stage acquire renown,
And for your judges summon all the town?
Would you your works forever should remain,
And after ages past be sought again?
In all you write observe with care and art
To move the passions and incline the heart.
If, in a labored act, the pleasing rage
Cannot our hopes and fears by turns engage,
Nor in our mind a feeling pity raise,[1]
In vain with learned scenes you fill your plays;   20
Your cold discourse can never move the mind
Of a stern critic, naturally unkind,
Who, justly tired with your pedantic flight,
Or falls asleep or censures all you write.

Le secret est d'abord de plaire et de toucher: [2]
Inventez des ressorts qui puissent m'attacher.
Que dès les premiers vers l'action préparée
Sans peine du sujet aplanisse l'entrée.
Je me ris d'un acteur qui, lent à s'exprimer,
30 De ce qu'il veut, d'abord ne sait pas m'informer,
Et qui, débrouillant mal une pénible intrigue,
D'un divertissement me fait une fatigue.
J'aimerois mieux encor qu'il déclinât son nom,
Et dît: Je suis Oreste ou bien Agamemnon,
Que d'aller, par un tas de confuses merveilles
Sans rien dire à l'esprit, étourdir les oreilles:
Le sujet n'est jamais assez tôt expliqué.[3]
 Que le lieu de la scène y soit fixe et marqué.
Un rimeur, sans péril, delà les Pyrénées,
40 Sur la scène en un jour renferme des années.
Là souvent le héros d'un spectacle grossier,
Enfant au premier acte, est barbon au dernier.[4]
Mais nous, que la raison à ses règles engage,
Nous voulons qu'avec art l'action se ménage;
Qu'en un lieu, qu'en un jour, un seul fait accompli
Tienne jusqu'à la fin le théâtre rempli.[5]
 Jamais au spectateur n'offrez rien d'incroyable:
Le vrai peut quelquefois n'être pas vraisemblable.[6]
Une merveille absurde est pour moi sans appas:
50 L'esprit n'est point ému de ce qu'il ne croit pas.
Ce qu'on ne doit point voir, qu'un récit nous l'expose:
Les yeux en le voyant saisiront mieux la chose;
Mais il est des objets que l'art judicieux
Doit offrir à l'oreille et reculer des yeux.
 Que le trouble, toujours croissant de scène en scène,
A son comble arrivé se débrouille sans peine.
L'esprit ne se sent point plus vivement frappé,
Que lorsqu'en un sujet d'intrigue enveloppé,
D'un secret tout à coup la vérité connue
60 Change tout, donne à tout une face imprévue.[7]
 La tragédie, informe et grossière en naissant,
N'étoit qu'un simple choeur où chacun en dansant,

The secret is, attention first to gain,
To move our minds and then to entertain,[2]
That, from the very opening of the scenes,
The first may show us what the author means.
   I'm tired to see an actor on the stage
That knows not whether he's to laugh or rage;   30
Who, an intrigue unraveling in vain,
Instead of pleasing keeps my mind in pain.
I'd rather much the nauseous dunce should say
Downright, "My name is Hector in the play,"
Than with a mass of miracles, ill-joined,
Confound my ears, and not instruct my mind.
The subject's never soon enough expressed.
   Your place of action must be fixed, and rest.
A Spanish poet may with good event
In one day's space whole ages represent;   40
There oft the hero of a wandering stage
Begins a child, and ends the play of age.[4]
But we, that are by reason's rules confined,
Will that with art the poem be designed,
That unity of action, time, and place
Keep the stage full, and all our labors grace.[5]
   Write not what cannot be with ease conceived;
Some truths may be too strong to be believed.[6]
A foolish wonder cannot entertain;
My mind's not moved if your discourse be vain.   50
You may relate what would offend the eye;
Seeing indeed would better satisfy,
But there are objects that a curious art
Hides from the eyes, yet offers to the heart.
   The mind is most agreeably surprised,
When a well-woven subject, long disguised,
You on a sudden artfully unfold,
And give the whole another face and mold.[7]
   At first the Tragedy was void of art,
A song, where each man danced and sung his part,   60
And of god Bacchus roaring out the praise,
Sought a good vintage for their jolly days;

Et du dieu des raisins entonnant les louanges,
S'efforçoit d'attirer de fertiles vendanges.
Là, le vin et la joie éveillant les esprits,
Du plus habile chantre un bouc étoit le prix.
Thespis fut le premier qui, barbouillé de lie,
Promena par les bourgs cette heureuse folie;
Et, d'acteurs mal ornés chargeant un tombereau,
70   Amusa les passans d'un spectacle nouveau.
Eschyle dans le choeur jeta les personnages,
D'un masque plus honnête habilla les visages,
Sur les ais d'un théâtre en public exhaussé,
Fit paroître l'acteur d'un brodequin [8] chaussé.
Sophocle enfin, donnant l'essor à son génie,
Accrut encor la pompe, augmenta l'harmonie,
Intéressa le choeur dans toute l'action,
Des vers trop raboteux polit l'expression,
Lui donna chez les Grecs cette hauteur divine
80   Où jamais n'atteignit la foiblesse latine.
    Chez nos dévots aïeux le théâtre abhorré
Fut longtemps dans la France un plaisir ignoré.
De pélerins, dit-on, une troupe grossière
En public à Paris y monta la première;
Et, sottement zéléé en sa simplicité,
Joua les Saints, la Vierge et Dieu, par piété.
Le savoir, à la fin dissipant l'ignorance,
Fit voir de ce projet la dévote imprudence.
On chassa ces docteurs prêchans sans mission: [9]
90   On vit renaître Hector, Andromaque, Ilion.
Seulement, les acteurs laissant le masque antique,
Le violon tint lieu de choeur et de musique.[10]
    Bientôt l'amour, fertile en tendres sentimens,
S'empara du théâtre, ainsi que des romans.
De cette passion la sensible peinture
Est pour aller au coeur la route la plus sûre.
Peignez donc, j'y consens, les héros amoureux;
Mais ne m'en formez pas des bergers doucereux:
Qu'Achille aime autrement que Thyrsis et Philène;
100   N'allez pas d'un Cyrus nous faire un Artamène.[11]

Then wine and joy were seen in each man's eyes,
And a fat goat was the best singer's prize.
Thespis was first, who, all besmeared with lee,
Began this pleasure for posterity,
And with his carted actors and a song
Amused the people as he passed along.
Next Æschylus the different persons placed,
And with a better mask his players graced,   70
Upon a theatre his verse expressed,
And showed his hero with a buskin dressed.
Then Sophocles, the genius of his age,
Increased the pomp and beauty of the stage,
Engaged the Chorus song in every part,
And polished rugged verse by rules of art;
He in the Greek did those perfections gain
Which the weak Latin never could attain.

  Our pious fathers, in their priest-rid age,
As impious and profane abhorred the stage.   80
A troop of silly pilgrims, as 'tis said,
Foolishly zealous, scandalously played,
Instead of heroes and of love's complaints,
The angels, God, the Virgin, and the saints.
At last right reason did his laws reveal,
And showed the folly of their ill-placed zeal,
Silenced those nonconformists of the age,
And raised the lawful heroes of the stage; [9]
Only th' Athenian mask was laid aside,
And Chorus by the music was supplied.[10]   90

  Ingenious love, inventive in new arts,
Mingled in plays, and quickly touched our hearts;
This passion never could resistance find,
But knows the shortest passage to the mind.
Paint then, I'm pleased my hero be in love;
But let him not like a tame shepherd move;
Let not Achilles be like Thyrsis seen,
Or for a Cyrus show an Artamene; [11]
That, struggling oft, his passions we may find
The frailty, not the virtue of his mind.   100

Et que l'amour, souvent de remords combattu,
Paroisse une foiblesse et non une vertu.
   Des héros de roman fuyez les petitesses: [12]
Toutefois aux grands coeurs donnez quelques foiblesses.
Achille déplairoit, moins bouillant et moins prompt:
J'aime à lui voir verser des pleurs pour un affront.
A ces petits défauts marqués dans sa peinture,
L'esprit avec plaisir reconnoît la nature.
Qu'il soit sur ce modèle en vos écrits tracé:
110 Qu'Agamemnon soit fier, superbe, intéressé;
Que pour ses dieux Enée ait un respect austère;
Conservez à chacun son propre caractère.
Des siècles, des pays, étudiez les moeurs.
Les climats font souvent les diverses humeurs.
Gardez donc de donner, ainsi que dans Clélie,[13]
L'air, ni l'esprit françois à l'antique Italie;
Et, sous des noms romains faisant notre portrait,
Peindre Caton galant et Brutus dameret.
Dans un roman frivole aisément tout s'excuse;
120 C'est assez qu'en courant la fiction amuse;
Trop de rigueur alors seroit hors de saison:
Mais la scène demande une exacte raison,
L'étroite bienséance y veut être gardée.
   D'un nouveau personnage inventez-vous l'idée?
Qu'en tout avec soi-même il se montre d'accord,
Et qu'il soit jusqu'au bout tel qu'on l'a vu d'abord.
   Souvent, sans y penser, un écrivain qui s'aime,
Forme tous ses héros semblables à soi-même:
Tout a l'humeur gasconne en un auteur gascon;
130 Calprenède et Juba parlent du même ton.[15]
   La nature est en nous plus diverse et plus sage;
Chaque passion parle un différent langage:
La colère est superbe et veut des mots altiers;
L'abattement s'explique en des termes moins fiers.
   Que devant Troie en flamme Hécube désolée
Ne vienne pas pousser une plainte ampoulée,
Ni sans raison décrire en quel affreux pays,
Par sept bouches l'Euxin reçoit le Tanaïs.[16]

Of romance heroes shun the low design; [12]
Yet to great hearts some human frailties join.
Achilles must with Homer's heart engage—
For an affront I'm pleased to see him rage.
Those little failings in your hero's heart
Show that of man and nature he has part.
To leave known rules you cannot be allowed;
Make Agamemnon covetous and proud,
Æneas in religious rites austere;
Keep to each man his proper character.   110
Of countries and of times the humors know;
From different climates different customs grow.
And strive to shun their fault who vainly dress
An antique hero like a modern ass,
Who make old Romans like our English move,
Show Cato sparkish, or make Brutus love.
In a romance those errors are excused;
There 'tis enough that, reading, we're amused.
Rules too severe would there be useless found;
But the strict scene must have a juster bound.   120
Exact decorum we must always find.
    If then you form some hero in your mind,
Be sure your image with itself agree;
For what he first appears he still must be.
    Affected wits will naturally incline
To paint their figures by their own design;
Your bully poets bully heroes write;
Chapman in *Bussy D'Ambois* took delight,
And thought perfection was to huff and fight.[14]
    Wise nature by variety does please;   130
Clothe differing passions in a differing dress:
Bold anger in rough haughty words appears;
Sorrow is humble and dissolves in tears.
    Make not your Hecuba with fury rage,
And show a ranting grief upon the stage,
Or tell in vain how the rough Tanais bore
His sevenfold waters to the Euxine Shore.[16]
These swollen expressions, this affected noise,

Tous ces pompeux amas d'expressions frivoles
140   Sont d'un déclamateur amoureux des paroles.
Il faut dans la douleur que vous vous abaissiez.
Pour me tirer des pleurs, il faut que vous pleuriez.
Ces grands mots dont alors l'acteur emplit sa bouche
Ne partent point d'un coeur que sa misère touche.
Le théâtre, fertile en censeurs pointilleux,
Chez nous pour se produire est un champ périlleux.
Un auteur n'y fait pas de faciles conquêtes;
Il trouve à le siffler des bouches toujours prêtes.
Chacun le peut traiter de fat et d'ignorant;
150   C'est un droit qu'à la porte on achète en entrant.
Il faut qu'en cent façons, pour plaire, il se replie;
Que tantôt il s'élève, et tantôt s'humilie;
Qu'en nobles sentimens il soit partout fécond;
Qu'il soit aisé, solide, agréable, profond;
Que de traits surprenans sans cesse il nous réveille;
Qu'il coure dans ses vers de merveille en merveille;
Et que tout ce qu'il dit, facile à retenir,
De son ouvrage en nous laisse un long souvenir.
Ainsi la Tragédie agit, marche, et s'explique.
160   D'un air plus grand encor la poésie épique,
Dans le vaste récit d'une longue action,
Se soutient par la fable, et vit de fiction.
Là pour nous enchanter tout est mis en usage;
Tout prend un corps, une âme, un esprit, un visage.
Chaque vertu devient une divinité:
Minerve est la prudence, et Vénus la beauté.
Ce n'est plus la vapeur qui produit le tonnerre,
C'est Jupiter armé pour effrayer la terre;
Un orage terrible aux yeux des matelots,
170   C'est Neptune en courroux qui gourmande les flots;
Echo n'est plus un son qui dans l'air retentisse,
C'est une nymphe en pleurs qui se plaint de Narcisse.
Ainsi, dans cet amas de nobles fictions,
Le poëte s'égaye en mille inventions,
Orne, élève, embellit, agrandit toutes choses,
Et trouve sous sa main des fleurs toujours écloses.

Shows like some pedant that declaims to boys.
In sorrow you must softer methods keep,   140
And, to excite our tears, yourself must weep.
Those noisy words with which ill plays abound
Come not from hearts that are in sadness drowned.
   The theatre for a young poet's rhymes
Is a bold venture in our knowing times.
An author cannot easily purchase fame;
Critics are always apt to hiss and blame.
You may be judged by every ass in town—
The privilege is bought for half-a-crown.
To please, you must a hundred changes try,   150
Sometimes be humble, then must soar on high,
In noble thoughts must everywhere abound,
Be easy, pleasant, solid, and profound;
To these you must surprising touches join,
And show us a new wonder in each line;
That all, in a just method well-designed,
May leave a strong impression in the mind.
These are the arts that tragedy maintain.
   But the Heroic claims a loftier strain.
In the narration of some great design   160
Invention, art, and fable all must join;
Here fiction must employ its utmost grace;
All must assume a body, mind, and face.
Each virtue a divinity is seen:
Prudence is Pallas, Beauty Paphos' queen;
'Tis not a cloud from whence swift lightnings fly,
But Jupiter that thunders from the sky;
Nor a rough storm that gives the sailor pain,
But angry Neptune plowing up the main;
Echo's no more an empty airy sound,   170
But a fair nymph that weeps her lover drowned.
Thus in the endless treasure of his mind
The poet does a thousand figures find,
Around the work his ornaments he pours,
And strews with lavish hand his opening flowers.
'Tis not a wonder if a tempest bore

Qu'Enée et ses vaisseaux, par le vent écartés,
Soient aux bords africains d'un orage emportés;
Ce n'est qu'une aventure ordinaire et commune,
180   Qu'un coup peu surprenant des traits de la fortune.
Mais que Junon, constante en son aversion,
Poursuive sur les flots les restes d'Ilion;
Qu'Eole, en sa faveur, les chassant d'Italie,
Ouvre aux vents mutinés les prisons d'Eolie;
Que Neptune en courroux s'élevant sur la mer,
D'un mot calme les flots, mette la paix dans l'air,
Délivre les vaisseaux, des syrtes les arrache; [17]
C'est là ce qui surprend, frappe, saisit, attache.
Sans tous ces ornemens le vers tombe en langueur,
190   La poésie est morte, ou rampe sans vigueur;
Le poëte n'est plus qu'un orateur timide,
Qu'un froid historien d'une fable insipide.
     C'est donc bien vainement que nos auteurs déçus,[18]
Bannissant de leurs vers ces ornemens reçus,
Pensent faire agir Dieu, ses saints et ses prophètes,
Comme ces dieux éclos du cerveau des poëtes;
Mettent à chaque pas le lecteur en enfer;
N'offrent rien qu'Astaroth, Belzébuth, Lucifer.
De la foi d'un chrétien les mystères terribles
200   D'ornemens égayés ne sont point susceptibles:
L'Evangile à l'esprit n'offre de tous côtés
Que pénitence à faire, et tourmens mérités;
Et de vos fictions le mélange coupable
Même à ses vérités donne l'air de la fable.
Et quel objet enfin à présenter aux yeux
Que le diable toujours hurlant contre les cieux,
Qui de votre héros veut rabaisser la gloire,
Et souvent avec Dieu balance la victoire! [19]
     Le Tasse, dira-t-on, l'a fait avec succès.
210   Je ne veux point ici lui faire son procès:
Mais, quoi que notre siècle à sa gloire publie,
Il n'eût point de son livre illustré l'Italie,
Si son sage héros, toujours en oraison,
N'eût fait que mettre enfin Satan à la raison;

The Trojan fleet against the Libyan shore;
From faithless fortune this is no surprise,
For every day 'tis common to our eyes.
But angry Juno, that she might destroy   180
And overwhelm the rest of ruined Troy;
That Æolus, with the fierce goddess joined,
Opened the hollow prisons of the wind;
Till angry Neptune, looking o'er the main,
Rebukes the tempest, calms the waves again,
Their vessels from the dangerous quicksands steers—[17]
These are the springs that move our hopes and fears.
Without these ornaments before our eyes
The unsinewed poem languishes and dies,
Your poet in his art will always fail,   190
And tell you but a dull insipid tale.
    In vain have our mistaken authors tried [18]
These ancient ornaments to lay aside,
Thinking our God, and prophets that he sent,
Might act like those the poets did invent,
To fright poor readers in each line with hell,
And talk of Satan, Ashtaroth, and Bel.
The mysteries which Christians must believe
Disdain such shifting pageants to receive;
The Gospel offers nothing to our thoughts   200
But penitence, or punishment for faults;
And mingling falsehoods with those mysteries
Would make our sacred truths appear like lies.
Besides, what pleasure can it be to hear
The howlings of repining Lucifer,
Whose rage at your imagined hero flies,
And oft with God himself disputes the prize? [19]
    Tasso, you'll say, has done it with applause.
It is not here I mean to judge his cause;
Yet though our age has so extolled his name,   210
His works had never gained immortal fame
If holy Godfrey in his ecstasies
Had only conquered Satan on his knees,
If Tancred and Armida's pleasing form

243

Et si Renaud, Argant, Tancrède et sa maîtresse
N'eussent de son sujet égayé la tristesse.
  Ce n'est pas que j'approuve, en un sujet chrétien,
Un auteur follement idolâtre et païen.[20]
Mais, dans une profane et riante peinture,
220 De n'oser de la fable employer la figure,
De chasser les Tritons de l'empire des eaux,
D'ôter à Pan sa flûte, aux Parques leurs ciseaux,
D'empêcher que Caron, dans la fatale barque
Ainsi que le berger ne passe le monarque:
C'est d'un scrupule vain s'alarmer sottement,
Et vouloir aux lecteurs plaire sans agrément.
  Bientôt ils défendront de peindre la Prudence,
De donner à Thémis ni bandeau ni balance,
De figurer aux yeux la Guerre au front d'airain;
230 Ou le Temps qui s'enfuit une horloge à la main;
Et partout des discours, comme une idolâtrie,
Dans leur faux zèle, iront chasser l'allégorie.
  Laissons-les s'applaudir de leur pieuse erreur;
Mais, pour nous, bannissons une vaine terreur,
Et, fabuleux chrétiens, n'allons point dans nos songes
Du Dieu de vérité faire un dieu de mensonges.
  La fable offre à l'esprit mille agrémens divers:
Là tous les noms heureux semblent nés pour les vers,
Ulysse, Agamemnon, Oreste, Idoménée,
240 Hélène, Ménélas, Pâris, Hector, Enée.
O le plaisant projet d'un poëte ignorant,
Qui de tant de héros va choisir Childebrand! [21]
D'un seul nom quelquefois le son dur ou bizarre
Rend un poëme entier, ou burlesque ou barbare.
  Voulez-vous longtemps plaire, et jamais ne lasser?
Faites choix d'un héros propre à m'intéresser,
En valeur éclatant, en vertus magnifique:
Qu'en lui, jusqu'aux défauts, tout se montre héroïque;
Que ses faits surprenans soient dignes d'être ouïs;
250 Qu'il soit tel que César, Alexandre, ou Louis
Non tel que Polynice et son perfide frère.[22]
On s'ennuie aux exploits d'un conquérant vulgaire.

244

Did not his melancholy theme adorn.
    'Tis not that Christian poems ought to be
Filled with the fictions of idolatry; [20]
But in a common subject, to reject
The gods, and heathen ornaments neglect,
To banish Tritons who the seas invade,   220
To take Pan's whistle, or the Fates degrade,
To hinder Charon in his leaky boat,
To pass the shepherd with the man of note,
Is with vain scruples to disturb your mind,
And search perfection you can never find.
As well they may forbid us to present
Prudence or Justice for an ornament,
To paint old Janus with his front of brass,
And take from Time his scythe, his wings, and glass,
And everywhere, as 'twere idolatry,   230
Banish descriptions from our poetry.
Leave them their pious follies to pursue,
But let our reason such vain fears subdue,
And let us not, amongst our vanities,
Of the true God create a god of lies.
    In fable we a thousand pleasures see,
And the smooth names seem made for poetry:
As *Hector, Alexander, Helen, Phyllis,*
Ulysses, Agamemnon, and *Achilles.*
In such a crowd, the poet were to blame   240
To choose *King Chilperic* for his hero's name.
Sometimes the name, being well or ill applied,
Will the whole fortune of your work decide.
    Would you your reader never should be tired?
Choose some great hero, fit to be admired,
In courage signal, and in virtue bright;
Let even his very failings give delight;
Let his great actions our attention bind,
Like Cæsar or like Scipio frame his mind,
And not like Œdipus his perjured race;   250
A common conqueror is a theme too base.
Choose not your tale of accidents too full,

N'offrez point un sujet d'incidens trop chargé.
Le seul courroux d'Achille, avec art ménagé,
Remplit abondamment une Iliade entière.
Souvent trop d'abondance appauvrit la matière.
    Soyez vif et pressé dans vos narrations;
Soyez riche et pompeux [23] dans vos descriptions.
C'est là qu'il faut des vers étaler l'élégance.
260   N'y présentez jamais de basse circonstance.
N'imitez pas ce fou, qui, décrivant les mers
Et peignant, au milieu de leurs flots entr'ouverts,
L'Hébreu sauvé du joug de ses injustes maîtres,
Met, pour les voir passer, les poissons aux fenêtres,[24]
Peint le petit enfant qui va, saute, revient,
«Et joyeux à sa mère offre un caillou qu'il tient.»
Sur de trop vains objets c'est arrêter la vue.
Donnez à votre ouvrage une juste étendue.
    Que le début soit simple et n'ait rien d'affecté.
270   N'allez pas dès l'abord, sur Pégase monté,
Crier à vos lecteurs, d'une voix de tonnerre:
«Je chante le vainqueur des vainqueurs de la terre.» [25]
Que produira l'auteur après tous ces grands cris?
La montagne en travail enfante une souris,
Oh! que j'aime bien mieux cet auteur plein d'adresse
Qui, sans faire d'abord de si haute promesse,
Me dit d'un ton aisé, doux, simple, harmonieux:
«Je chante les combats, et cet homme pieux
«Qui, des bords phrygiens conduit dans l'Ausonie,
280   «Le premier aborda les champs de Lavinie!» [26]
Sa muse en arrivant ne met pas tout en feu,
Et pour donner beaucoup, ne nous promet que peu.
Bientôt vous la verrez, prodiguant les miracles,
Du destin des Latins prononcer les oracles,
De Styx et d'Achéron peindre les noirs torrens,
Et déjà les Césars dans l'Elysée errans.
    De figures sans nombre égayez votre ouvrage;
Que tout y fasse aux yeux une riante image:
On peut être à la fois et pompeux et plaisant;
290   Et je hais un sublime ennuyeux et pesant.

Too much variety may make it dull.
Achilles' rage alone, when wrought with skill,
Abundantly does a whole *Iliad* fill.

    Be your narration lively, short, and smart;
In your descriptions show your noblest art—
There 'tis your poetry may be employed;
Yet you must trivial accidents avoid.
Nor imitate that fool who, to describe   260
The wonderous marches of the chosen tribe,
Placed on the sides, to see their armies pass,
The fishes staring through the liquid glass; [24]
Described a child who, with his little hand,
Picked up the shining pebbles from the sand.
Such objects are too mean to stay our sight;
Allow your work a just and nobler flight.

    Be your beginning plain; and take good heed
Too soon you mount not on the airy steed.
Nor tell your reader, in a thundering verse,   270
"I sing the conqueror of the universe." [25]
What can an author after this produce?
The laboring mountain must bring forth a mouse.
Much better are we pleased with his address
Who, without making such vast promises,
Says in an easier style and plainer sense,
"I sing the combats of that pious prince
Who from the Phrygian coast his armies bore,
And landed first on the Lavinian shore." [26]
His opening muse sets not the world on fire,   280
And yet performs more than we can require.
Quickly you'll hear him celebrate the fame
And future glory of the Roman name,
Of Styx and Acheron describe the floods,
And Cæsars wandering in the Elysian woods.

    With figures numberless your story grace,
And everything in beauteous colors trace;
At once you may be pleasing and sublime.
I hate a heavy melancholy rhyme;
I'd rather read Orlando's comic tale [27]   290

247

J'aime mieux Arioste et ses fables comiques,[27]
Que ces auteurs toujours froids et mélancoliques,
Qui dans leur sombre humeur se croiroient faire affront
Si les Grâces jamais leur déridoient le front.
   On diroit que pour plaire, instruit par la nature,
Homère ait à Vénus dérobé sa ceinture.[28]
Son livre est d'agrémens un fertile trésor :
Tout ce qu'il a touché se convertit en or.
Tout reçoit dans ses mains une nouvelle grâce ;
300   Partout il divertit et jamais il ne lasse.
Une heureuse chaleur anime ses discours :
Il ne s'égare point en de trop longs détours.
Sans garder dans ses vers un ordre méthodique,
Son sujet de soi-même et s'arrange et s'explique ;
Tout, sans faire d'apprêts, s'y prépare aisément :
Chaque vers, chaque mot court à l'événement.
Aimez donc ses écrits, mais d'un amour sincère ;
C'est avoir profité que de savoir s'y plaire.
   Un poëme excellent, où tout marche et se suit,
310   N'est pas de ces travaux qu'un caprice produit :
Il veut du temps, des soins ; et ce pénible ouvrage
Jamais d'un écolier ne fut l'apprentissage.
Mais souvent parmi nous un poëte sans art,[29]
Qu'un beau feu quelquefois échauffa par hasard,
Enflant d'un vain orgueil son esprit chimérique,
Fièrement prend en main la trompette héroïque :
Sa muse déréglée, en ses vers vagabonds,
Ne s'élève jamais que par sauts et par bonds :
Et son feu, dépourvu de sens et de lecture,
320   S'éteint à chaque pas faute de nourriture.
Mais en vain le public, prompt à le mépriser,
De son mérite faux le veut désabuser ;
Lui-même, applaudissant à son maigre génie,
Se donne par ses mains l'encens qu'on lui dénie :
Virgile, au prix de lui, n'a point d'invention ;
Homère n'entend point la noble fiction.
Si contre cet arrêt le siècle se rebelle,
A la postérité d'abord il en appelle.

248

Than a dull author always stiff and stale,
Who thinks himself dishonored in his style
If on his works the Graces do but smile.
   'Tis said that Homer, matchless in his art,
Stole Venus' girdle to engage the heart.[28]
His works indeed vast treasures do unfold,
And whatsoe'er he touches turns to gold;
All in his hands new beauty does acquire;
He always pleases, and can never tire.
A happy warmth he everywhere may boast,   300
Nor is he in too long digressions lost;
His verses without rule a method find,
And of themselves appear in order joined;
All without trouble answers his intent;
Each syllable is tending to th' event.
Let his example your endeavors raise;
To love his writings is a kind of praise.
   A poem where we all perfections find
Is not the work of a fantastic mind;
There must be care, and time, and skill, and pains,   310
Not the first heat of inexperienced brains.
Yet sometimes artless poets,[29] when the rage
Of a warm fancy does their minds engage,
Puffed with vain pride, presume they understand,
And boldly take the trumpet in their hand;
Their fustian muse each accident confounds,
Nor can she fly, but rise by leaps and bounds;
Till, their small stock of learning quickly spent,
Their poem dies for want of nourishment.
In vain mankind the hot-brained fool decries,   320
No branding censures can unveil his eyes;
With impudence the laurel they invade,
Resolved to like the monsters they have made.
Virgil, compared to them, is flat and dry,
And Homer understood not poetry.
Against their merit if this age rebel,
To future times for justice they appeal.
But, waiting till mankind shall do them right,

Mais attendant qu'ici le bon sens de retour
330   Ramène triomphans ses ouvrages au jour,
Leur tas, au magasin, cachés à la luminère,
Combattent tristement les vers et la poussière.
Laissons-les donc entre eux s'escrimer en repos,
Et, sans nous égarer, suivons notre propos.
    Des succès fortunés du spectacle tragique
Dans Athènes naquit la comédie antique.
Là le Grec, né moqueur, par mille jeux plaisans,
Distilla le venin de ses traits médisans.
Aux accès insolens d'une bouffonne joie,
340   La sagesse, l'esprit, l'honneur, furent en proie.
On vit, par le public un poëte avoué
S'enrichir aux dépens du mérite joué;
Et Socrate par lui, dans «un choeur de Nuées,» [30]
D'un vil amas de peuple attirer les huées.
Enfin de la licence on arrêta le cours:
Le magistrat, des lois emprunta le secours,
Et, rendant par édit les poëtes plus sages,
Défendit de marquer les noms et les visages.
Le théâtre perdit son antique fureur;
350   La comédie apprit à rire sans aigreur,
Sans fiel et sans venin sut instruire et reprendre,
Et plut innocemment dans les vers de Ménandre.[31]
Chacun, peint avec art dans ce nouveau miroir,
S'y vit avec plaisir, ou crut ne s'y point voir:
L'avare, des premiers, rit du tableau fidèle
D'un avare souvent tracé sur son modèle;
Et mille fois un fat, finement exprimé,
Méconnut le portrait sur lui-même formé.
    Que la nature donc soit votre étude unique,[32]
360   Auteurs qui prétendez aux honneurs du comique.
Quiconque voit bien l'homme, et d'un esprit profond,
De tant de coeurs cachés a pénétré le fond;
Qui sait bien ce que c'est qu'un prodigue, un avare,
Un honnête homme, un fat, un jaloux, un bizarre,
Sur une scène heureuse il peut les étaler,
Et les faire à nos yeux vivre, agir et parler.

250

And bring their works triumphantly to light,
Neglected heaps we in bye-corners lay, 330
Where they become to worms and moths a prey;
Forgot, in dust and cobwebs let them rest,
Whilst we return from whence we first digressed.
 The great success which tragic writers found
In Athens first the comedy renowned.
Th' abusive Grecian there, by pleasing ways,
Dispersed his natural malice in his plays;
Wisdom and virtue, honor, wit, and sense,
Were subject to buffooning insolence;
Poets were publicly approved and sought, 340
That vice extolled and virtue set at naught;
A Socrates himself, in that loose age,
Was made the pastime of a scoffing stage.[30]
At last the public took in hand the cause,
And cured this madness by the power of laws,
Forbade, at any time or any place,
To name the person or describe the face.
The stage its ancient fury thus let fall,
And comedy diverted without gall,
By mild reproofs recovered minds diseased, 350
And, sparing persons, innocently pleased.[31]
Each one was nicely shown in this new glass,
And smiled to think he was not meant the ass.
A miser oft would laugh at first, to find
A faithful draught of his own sordid mind;
And fops were with such care and cunning writ,
They liked the piece for which themselves did sit.
 You, then, that would the comic laurels wear,
To study nature [32] be your only care.
Whoe'er knows man, and by a curious art 360
Discerns the hidden secrets of the heart;
He who observes, and naturally can paint
The jealous fool, the fawning sycophant,
A sober wit, an enterprising ass,
A humorous Otter,[33] or a Hudibras,
May safely in those noble lists engage,

251

Présentez-en partout les images naïves;
Que chacun y soit peint des couleurs les plus vives.
La nature, féconde en bizarres portraits,
370   Dans chaque âme est marquée à de différens traits;
Un geste la découvre, un rien la fait paroître:
Mais tout esprit n'a pas des yeux pour la connoître.
    Le temps, qui change tout, change aussi nos humeurs.
Chaque âge a ses plaisirs, son esprit et ses moeurs.
Un jeune homme, toujours bouillant dans ses caprices,
Est prompt à recevoir l'impression des vices;
Est vain dans ses discours, volage en ses désirs,
Rétif à la censure, et fou dans les plaisirs.
L'âge viril, plus mûr, inspire un air plus sage,
380   Se pousse auprès des grands, s'intrigue, se ménage,
Contre les coups du sort songe à se maintenir,
Et loin dans le présent regarde l'avenir.
La vieillesse chagrine incessamment amasse;
Garde, non pas pour soi, les trésors qu'elle entasse;
Marche en tous ses desseins d'un pas lent et glacé;
Toujours plaint le présent et vante le passé;
Inhabile aux plaisirs dont la jeunesse abuse,
Blâme en eux les douceurs que l'âge lui refuse.
Ne faites point parler vos acteurs au hasard,
390   Un vieillard en jeune homme, un jeune homme en vieillard.
    Etudiez la cour et connoissez la ville;
L'une et l'autre est toujours en modèles fertile.[34]
C'est par là que Molière, illustrant ses écrits,
Peut-être de son art eût remporté le prix,
Si, moins ami du peuple, en ses doctes peintures,
Il n'eût point fait souvent grimacer ses figures,
Quitté, pour le bouffon, l'agréable et le fin,
Et sans honte à Térence allié Tabarin.[35]
Dans ce sac ridicule où Scapin s'enveloppe,
400   Je ne reconnois plus l'auteur du Misanthrope.[36]
    Le comique, ennemi des soupirs et des pleurs,
N'admet point en ses vers de tragiques douleurs;
Mais son emploi n'est pas d'aller, dans une place,
De mots sales et bas charmer la populace.

And make them act and speak upon the stage.
Strive to be natural in all you write,
And paint with colors that may please the sight.
Nature in various figures does abound,   370
And in each mind are different humors found.
A glance, a touch, discovers to the wise,
But every man has not discerning eyes.
    All-changing time does also change the mind,
And different ages different pleasures find.
Youth, hot and furious, cannot brook delay,
By flattering vice is easily led away;
Vain in discourse, inconstant in desire,
In censure rash, in pleasures all on fire.
The manly age does steadier thoughts enjoy;   380
Power and ambition do his soul employ;
Against the turns of fate he sets his mind,
And by the past the future hopes to find.
Decrepit age, still adding to his stores,
For others heaps the treasure he adores,
In all his actions keeps a frozen pace,
Past times extols, the present to debase;
Incapable of pleasures youth abuse,
In others blames what age does him refuse.
Your actors must by reason be controlled;   390
Let young men speak like young, old men like old.
    Observe the town and study well the court,
For thither various characters resort.
Thus 'twas great Jonson purchased his renown,
And in his art had borne away the crown,
If, less desirous of the people's praise,
He had not with low farce debased his plays,
Mixing dull buffoonry with wit refined,
And Harlequin with noble Terence joined.[35]
When in the *Fox* I see the tortoise hissed,[37]   400
I lose the author of the *Alchemist.*
    The comic wit, born with a smiling air,
Must tragic grief and pompous verse forbear;
Yet may he not, as on a market-place,

Il faut que ses acteurs badinent noblement; [38]
Que son noeud bien formé se dénoue aisément;
Que l'action marchant où la raison la guide,
Ne se perde jamais dans une scène vide;
Que son style humble et doux se relève à propos;
410   Que ses discours, partout fertiles en bons mots,
Soient pleins de passions finement maniées,
Et les scènes toujours l'une à l'autre liées.
Aux dépens du bon sens gardez de plaisanter:
Jamais de la nature il ne faut s'écarter.
Contemplez de quel air un père dans Térence [39]
Vient d'un fils amoureux gourmander l'imprudence;
De quel air cet amant écoute ses leçons,
Et court chez sa maîtresse oublier ces chansons.
Ce n'est pas un portrait, une image semblable;
420   C'est un amant, un fils, un père véritable.
    J'aime sur le théâtre un agréable auteur
Qui, sans se diffamer aux yeux du spectateur,
Plaît par la raison seule, et jamais ne la choque.
Mais pour un faux plaisant, à grossière équivoque,
Qui, pour me divertir, n'a que la saleté,
Qu'il s'en aille, s'il veut, sur deux tréteaux monté,
Amusant le pont Neuf de ses sornettes fades,
Aux laquais assemblés jouer ses mascarades. [40]

CHANT IV

Dans Florence jadis vivoit un médecin,
Savant hâbleur, dit-on, et célèbre assassin. [1]
Lui seul y fit longtemps la publique misère:

With bawdy jests amuse the populace.
With well-bred conversation you must please,[38]
And your intrigue unravelled be with ease;
Your action still should reason's rules obey,
Nor in an empty scene may lose its way.
Your humble style must sometimes gently rise,   410
And your discourse sententious be and wise;
The passions must to nature be confined,
And scenes to scenes with artful weaving joined.
Your wit must not unseasonably play,
But follow business, never lead the way.
Observe how Terence does this error shun: [39]
A careful father chides his amorous son;
Then see that son, whom no advice can move,
Forget those orders, and pursue his love!
'Tis not a well-drawn picture we discover;   420
'Tis a true son, a father, and a lover.
   I like an author that reforms the age,
And keeps the right decorum of the stage,
That always pleases by just reason's rule;
But for a tedious droll, a quibbling fool,
Who with low nauseous bawdry fills his plays,
Let him be gone, and on two trestles raise
Some Smithfield stage, where he may act his pranks,
And make Jack-Puddings speak to mountebanks.[41]

CANTO IV

   In Florence dwelt a doctor of renown,
The scourge of God, and terror of the town,
Who all the cant of physic had by heart,

255

Là le fils orphelin lui redemande un père:
Ici le frère pleure un frère empoisonné.
L'un meurt vide de sang, l'autre plein de séné; [2]
Le rhume à son aspect se change en pleurésie.
Et par lui la migraine est bientôt frénésie.
Il quitte enfin la ville, en tous lieux détesté.
10   De tous ses amis morts un seul ami resté
Le mène en sa maison de superbe structure:
C'étoit un riche abbé, fou de l'architecture.
Le médecin d'abord semble né dans cet art.
Dejà de bâtimens parle comme Mansart: [3]
D'un salon qu'on élève il condamne la face;
Au vestibule obscur il marque une autre place;
Approuve l'escalier tourné d'autre façon,
Son ami le conçoit et mande son maçon.
Le maçon vient, écoute, approuve et se corrige.
20   Enfin, pour abréger un si plaisant prodige,
Notre assassin renonce à son art inhumain;
Et désormais, la règle et l'équerre à la main,
Laissant de Galien la science suspecte,
De méchant médecin devient bon architecte. [5]
    Son exemple est pour nous un précepte excellent.
Soyez plutôt maçon, si c'est votre talent,
Ouvrier estimé dans un art nécessaire,
Qu'écrivain du commun et poëte vulgaire.
Il est dans tout autre art des degrés différens.
30   On peut avec honneur remplir les seconds rangs;
Mais dans l'art dangereux de rimer et d'écrire,
Il n'est point de degrés du médiocre au pire.
Qui dit froid écrivain dit détestable auteur.
Boyer est à Pinchêne égal pour le lecteur;
On ne lit guère plus Rampale et Mesnardière,
Que Magnon, du Souhait, Corbin et La Morlière. [7]
Un fou du moins fait rire, et peut nous égayer;
Mais un froid écrivain ne sait rien qu'ennuyer.
J'aime mieux Bergerac et sa burlesque audace
40   Que ces vers où Motin nous morfond et nous glace. [9]
    Ne vous enivrez point des éloges flatteurs

And never murdered but by rules of art.[1]
The public mischief was his private gain:
Children their slaughtered parents sought in vain;
A brother here his poisoned brother wept;
Some bloodless died, and some by opium slept; [2]
Colds, at his presence, would to frenzies turn,
And agues like malignant fevers burn.   10
Hated, at last, his practice gives him o'er;
One friend, unkilled by drugs, of all his store,
In his new country-house affords him place
('Twas a rich abbot, and a building ass).
Here first the doctor's talent came in play;
He seems inspired and talks like Wren or May; [4]
Of this new portico condemns the face,
And turns the entrance to a better place,
Designs the staircase at the other end.
His friend approves, does for his mason send;   20
He comes; the doctor's arguments prevail.
In short, to finish this our humorous tale,
He Galen's dangerous science does reject,
And from ill doctor turns good architect.[5]

   In this example we may have our part:
Rather be mason ('tis a useful art)
Than a dull poet; for that trade accursed
Admits no mean betwixt the best and worst.
In other sciences, without disgrace,
A candidate may fill a second place,   30
But poetry no medium can admit,
No reader suffers an indifferent wit;
The ruined stationers against him bawl,
And Herringman degrades him from his stall.[6]
Burlesque at least our laughter may excite,
But a cold writer never can delight.
The *Counter-scuffle* has more wit and art
Than the stiff formal style of *Gondibert*.[8]

   Be not affected with that empty praise
Which your vain flatterers will sometimes raise,   40
And, when you read, with ecstasy will say,

Qu'un amas quelquefois de vains admirateurs
Vous donne en ces Réduits, prompts à crier merveille!
Tel écrit récité se soutint à l'oreille,
Qui, dans l'impression au grand jour se montrant,
Ne soutient pas des yeux le regard pénétrant.[11]
On sait de cent auteurs l'aventure tragique:
Et Gombaud tant loué garde encor la boutique.[12]
    Ecoutez tout le monde, assidu consultant:
50   Un fat quelquefois ouvre un avis important.
Quelques vers toutefois qu'Apollon vous inspire,
En tous lieux aussitôt ne courez pas les lire.
Gardez-vous d'imiter ce rimeur furieux,
Qui, de ses vains écrits lecteur harmonieux,
Aborde en récitant quiconque le salue,
Et poursuit de ses vers les passans dans la rue.
Il n'est temple si saint, des anges respecté,
Qui soit contre sa muse un lieu de sûreté.[13]
    Je vous l'ai déjà dit, aimez qu'on vous censure,
60   Et, souple à la raison, corrigez sans murmure.
Mais ne vous rendez pas dès qu'un sot vous reprend.
Souvent dans son orgueil un subtil ignorant
Par d'injustes dégoûts combat toute une pièce,
Blâme des plus beaux vers la noble hardiesse.
On a beau réfuter ses vains raisonnemens:
Son esprit se complaît dans ses faux jugemens;
Et sa foible raison, de clarté dépourvue,
Pense que rien n'échappe à sa débile vue.
Ses conseils sont à craindre; et, si vous les croyez,
70   Pensant fuir un écueil, souvent vous vous noyez.
    Faites choix d'un censeur solide et salutaire,
Que la raison conduise et le savoir éclaire,
Et dont le crayon sûr d'abord aille chercher
L'endroit que l'on sent foible, et qu'on se veut cacher.
Lui seul éclaircira vos doutes ridicules,
De votre esprit tremblant lèvera les scrupules.
C'est lui qui vous dira par quel transport heureux,
Quelquefois dans sa course un esprit vigoureux,
Trop reserré par l'art, sort des règles prescrites,

258

"The finished piece! the admirable play!"—
Which, when exposed to censure and to light,
Cannot endure a critic's piercing sight.
A hundred authors' fates have been foretold,
And Shadwell's works are printed, but not sold.[10]
　　Hear all the world; consider every thought;
A fool by chance may stumble on a fault.
Yet, when Apollo does your muse inspire,
Be not impatient to expose your fire;　　　　　　　50
Nor imitate the Settles of our times,
Those tuneful readers of their own dull rhymes,
Who seize on all th' acquaintance they can meet,
And stop the passengers that walk the street;
There is no sanctuary you can choose
For a defense from their pursuing muse.[13]
　　I've said before, be patient when they blame;
To alter for the better is no shame.
Yet yield not to a fool's impertinence:
Sometimes conceited sceptics, void of sense,　　　60
By their false taste condemn some finished part,
And blame the noblest flights of wit and art.
In vain their fond opinions you deride;
With their loved follies they are satisfied,
And their weak judgment, void of sense and light,
Thinks nothing can escape their feeble sight.
Their dangerous counsels do not cure, but wound;
To shun the storm they run your verse aground,
And thinking to escape a rock, are drowned.
　　Choose a sure judge to censure what you write,　70
Whose reason leads, and knowledge gives you light,
Whose steady hand will prove your faithful guide,
And touch the darling follies you would hide.
He, in your doubts, will carefully advise,
And clear the mist before your feeble eyes.
'Tis he will tell you to what noble height
A generous muse may sometimes take her flight;
When, too much fettered with the rules of art,
May from her stricter bounds and limits part.[14]

259

80   Et de l'art même apprend à franchir leurs limites.[14]
Mais ce parfait censeur se trouve rarement:
Tel excelle à rimer qui juge sottement;
Tel s'est fait par ses vers distinguer dans la ville,
Qui jamais de Lucain n'a distingué Virgile.[15]
    Auteurs, prêtez l'oreille à mes instructions.
Voulez-vous faire aimer vos riches fictions?
Qu'en savantes leçons votre muse fertile
Partout joigne au plaisant le solide et l'utile.
Un lecteur sage fuit un vain amusement,
90   Et veut mettre à profit son divertissement.
    Que votre âme et vos moeurs, peintes dans vos ouvrages,
N'offrent jamais de vous que de nobles images.
Je ne puis estimer ces dangereux auteurs
Qui, de l'honneur, en vers, infâmes déserteurs,
Trahissant la vertu sur un papier coupable,
Aux yeux de leurs lecteurs rendent le vice aimable.
    Je ne suis pas pourtant de ces tristes esprits
Qui, bannissant l'amour de tous chastes écrits,
D'un si riche ornement veulent priver la scène,
100   Traitent d'empoisonneurs et Rodrigue et Chimène.[16]
L'amour le moins honnête, exprimé chastement,
N'excite point en nous de honteux mouvement.
Didon a beau gémir, et m'étaler ses charmes; [17]
Je condamne sa faute en partageant ses larmes.
Un auteur vertueux, dans ses vers innocens,
Ne corrompt point le coeur en chatouillant les sens;
Son feu n'allume point de criminelle flamme.
Aimez donc la vertu, nourrissez-en votre âme:
En vain l'esprit est plein d'une noble vigueur;
110   Le vers se sent toujours des bassesses du coeur.
    Fuyez surtout, fuyez ces basses jalousies,
Des vulgaires esprits malignes frénésies.
Un sublime écrivain n'en peut être infecté;
C'est un vice qui suit la médiocrite.
Du mérite éclatant cette sombre rivale
Contre lui chez les grands incessamment cabale,
Et, sur les pieds en vain tâchant de se hausser,

But such a perfect judge is hard to see, 80
And every rhymer knows not poetry;
Nay, some there are for writing verse extolled,
Who know not Lucan's dross from Virgil's gold.[15]
    Would you in this great art acquire renown?
Authors, observe the rules I here lay down.
In prudent lessons everywhere abound;
With pleasant join the useful and the sound:
A sober reader a vain tale will slight;
He seeks as well instruction as delight.
    Let all your thoughts to virtue be confined, 90
Still offering nobler figures to our mind.
I like not those loose writers who employ
Their guilty muse good manners to destroy,
Who with false colors still deceive our eyes
And show us vice dressed in a fair disguise.
    Yet do I not their sullen muse approve
Who from all modest writings banish love,
That strip the playhouse of its chief intrigue
And make a murderer of Roderigue.[16]
The lighest love, if decently expressed, 100
Will raise no vicious motions in our breast.
Dido in vain may weep, and ask relief; [17]
I blame her folly whilst I share her grief.
A virtuous author, in his charming art,
To please the sense needs not corrupt the heart;
His heat will never cause a guilty fire.
To follow virtue then be your desire.
In vain your art and vigor are expressed;
The obscene expression shows the infected breast.
    But, above all, base jealousies avoid, 110
In which detracting poets are employed.
A noble wit dares liberally commend,
And scorns to grudge at his deserving friend.
Base rivals, who true wit and merit hate,
Caballing still against it with the great,
Maliciously aspire to gain renown
By standing up, and pulling others down.

Pour s'égaler à lui, cherche à le rabaisser.

Ne descendons jamais dans ces lâches intrigues:

120 N'allons point à l'honneur par de honteuses brigues.

Que les vers ne soient pas votre éternel emploi.

Cultivez vos amis, soyez homme de foi:

C'est peu d'être agréable et charmant dans un livre,

Il faut savoir encore et converser et vivre.[18]

Travaillez pour la gloire, et qu'un sordide gain

Ne soit jamais l'objet d'un illustre écrivain.

Je sais qu'un noble esprit peut, sans honte et sans crime,

Tirer de son travail un tribut légitime;

Mais je ne puis souffrir ces auteurs renommés,

130 Qui, dégoûtés de gloire et d'argent affamés,

Mettent leur Apollon aux gages d'un libraire,

Et font d'un art divin un métier mercenaire.[19]

Avant que la raison, s'expliquant par la voix,

Eût instruit les humains, eût enseigné les lois,

Tous les hommes suivoient la grossière nature,

Dispersés dans les bois couroient à la pâture:

La force tenoit lieu de droit et d'équité;

Le meurtre s'exerçoit avec impunité.

Mais du discours enfin l'harmonieuse adresse

140 De ces sauvages moeurs adoucit la rudesse,

Rassembla les humains dans les forêts épars,

Enferma les cités de murs et de remparts,

De l'aspect du supplice effraya l'insolence,

Et sous l'appui des lois mit la foible innocence.

Cet ordre fut, dit-on, le fruit des premiers vers.

De là sont nés ces bruits reçus dans l'univers,

Qu'aux accens dont Orphée emplit les monts de Thrace,

Les tigres amollis dépouilloient leur audace;

Qu'aux accords d'Amphion les pierres se mouvoient,

150 Et sur les murs thébains en ordre s'élevoient.

L'harmonie en naissant produisit ces miracles.

Depuis, le ciel en vers fit parler les oracles;

Du sein d'un prêtre ému d'une divine horreur,

Apollon par des vers exhala sa fureur.

Bientôt, ressuscitant les héros des vieux âges,

Never debase yourself by treacherous ways,
Nor by such abject methods seek for praise.
    Let not your only business be to write;   120
Be virtuous, just, and in your friends delight.
'Tis not enough your poems be admired;
But strive your conversation be desired.[18]
    Write for immortal fame, nor ever choose
Gold for the object of a generous muse.
I know a noble wit may, without crime,
Receive a lawful tribute for his time,
Yet I abhor those writers who despise
Their honor, and alone their profits prize,
Who their Apollo basely will degrade,   130
And of a noble science make a trade.[19]
    Before kind reason did her light display,
And government taught mortals to obey,
Men, like wild beasts, did nature's laws pursue:
They fed on herbs, and drink from rivers drew;
Their brutal force, on lust and rapine bent,
Committed murders without punishment.
Reason at last, by her all-conquering arts,
Reduced these savages, and tuned their hearts,
Mankind from bogs, and woods, and caverns calls,   140
And towns and cities fortifies with walls;
Thus fear of justice made proud rapine cease,
And sheltered innocence by laws and peace.
    These benefits from poets we received;
From whence are raised those fictions since believed,
That Orpheus, by his soft harmonious strains,
Tamed the fierce tigers of the Thracian plains;
Amphion's notes, by their melodious powers,
Drew rocks and woods, and raised the Theban towers.
These miracles from numbers did arise;   150
Since which, in verse heaven taught his mysteries,
And by a priest possessed with rage divine
Apollo spoke from his prophetic shrine.[20]
Soon after, Homer the old heroes praised,
And noble minds by great examples raised;

Homère aux grands exploits anima les courages.
Hésiode à son tour, par d'utiles leçons,
Des champs trop paresseux vint hâter les moissons.[21]
En mille écrits fameux la sagesse tracée
160   Fut, à l'aide des vers, aux mortels annoncée;
Et partout des esprits ses préceptes vainqueurs,
Introduits par l'oreille entrèrent dans les coeurs.
Pour tant d'heureux bienfaits, les Muses révérées
Furent d'un juste encens dans la Grèce honorées,
Et leur art, attirant le culte des mortels,
A sa gloire en cent lieux vit dresser des autels.
    Mais enfin l'indigence amenant la bassesse,
Le Parnasse oublia sa première noblesse.
Un vil amour du gain, infectant les esprits,
170   De mensonges grossiers souilla tous les écrits;
Et partout, enfantant mille ouvrages frivoles,
Trafiqua du discours, et vendit les paroles.
Ne vous flétrissez point par un vice si bas.
Si l'or seul a pour vous d'invincibles appas,
Fuyez ces lieux charmans qu'arrose le Permesse: [22]
Ce n'est point sur ses bords qu'habite la richesse,
Aux plus savans auteurs, comme aux plus grands guerriers,
Apollon ne promet qu'un nom et des lauriers.
    Mais quoi! dans la disette une muse affamée
180   Ne peut pas, dira-t-on, subsister de fumée;
Un auteur qui, pressé d'un besoin importun,
Le soir entend crier ses entrailles à jeun,
Goûte peu d'Hélicon les douces promenades: [23]
Horace a bu son soûl quand il voit les Ménades,[24]
Et, libre du souci qui trouble Colletet,[25]
N'attend pas, pour dîner, le succès d'un sonnet.
    Il est vrai: mais enfin cette affreuse disgrâce
Rarement parmi nous afflige le Parnasse.
Et que craindre en ce siècle, où toujours les beaux-arts
190   D'un astre favorable éprouvent les regards,
Où d'un prince éclairé la sage prévoyance
Fait partout au mérite ignorer l'indigence?
    Muses, dictez sa gloire à tous vos nourrissons.[26]

Then Hesiod did his Grecian swains incline
To till the fields, and prune the bounteous vine.[21]
Thus useful rules were, by the poet's aid,
In easy numbers to rude men conveyed,
And pleasingly their precepts did impart,   160
First charmed the ear, and then engaged the heart;
The Muses thus their reputation raised,
And with just gratitude in Greece were praised.
With pleasure mortals did their wonders see,
And sacrificed to their divinity.
    But want, at last, base flattery entertained,
And old Parnassus with this vice was stained;
Desire of gain dazzling the poets' eyes,
Their works were filled with fulsome flatteries;
Thus needy wits a vile revenue made,   170
And verse became a mercenary trade.
Debase not with so mean a vice thy art;
If gold must be the idol of thy heart,
Fly, fly th' unfruitful Heliconian strand! [22]
Those streams are not enriched with golden sand;
Great wits, as well as warriors, only gain
Laurels and honors for their toil and pain.
    But what? an author cannot live on fame,
Or pay a reckoning with a lofty name:
A poet to whom fortune is unkind,   180
Who when he goes to bed has hardly dined,
Takes little pleasure in Parnassus' dreams,
Nor relishes the Heliconian streams; [23]
Horace had ease and plenty when he writ,[24]
And, free from cares for money or for meat,
Did not expect his dinner from his wit.
    'Tis true; but verse is cherished by the great,
And now none famish who deserve to eat.
What can we fear when virtue, arts, and sense,
Receive the stars' propitious influence,   190
When a sharp-sighted prince, by early grants,
Rewards your merits, and prevents your wants?
    Sing then his glory, celebrate his fame; [26]

Som nom vaut mieux pour eux que toutes vos leçons.
Que Corneille, pour lui rallumant son audace,
Soit encor le Corneille et du Cid et d'Horace;
Que Racine, enfantant des miracles nouveaux,
De ses héros sur lui forme tous les tableaux;
Que de son nom, chanté par la bouche des belles,
200   Benserade en tous lieux amuse les ruelles; [28]
Que Segrais dans l'églogue en charme les forêts; [29]
Que pour lui l'épigramme aiguise tous ses traits.
Mais quel heureux auteur, dans une autre Enéide,
Aux bords du Rhin tremblant conduira cet Alcide? [30]
Quelle savante lyre, au bruit de ses exploits,
Fera marcher encor les rochers et les bois;
Chantera le Batave, éperdu dans l'orage,
Soi-même se noyant pour sortir du naufrage,[31]
Dira les bataillons sous Mastricht enterrés
210   Dans ces affreux assauts du soleil éclairés? [32]
    Mais tandis que je parle une gloire nouvelle
Vers ce vainqueur rapide aux Alpes vous appelle.
Déjà Dôle et Salins sous le joug ont ployé;
Besançon fume encor sur son roc foudroyé.[34]
Où sont ces grands guerriers dont les fatales ligues
Devoient à ce torrent opposer tant de digues?
Est-ce encore en fuyant qu'ils pensent l'arrêter,
Fiers du honteux honneur d'avoir su l'éviter? [35]
Que de remparts détruits! Que de villes forcées!
220   Que de moissons de gloire en courant amassées!
    Auteurs, pour les chanter, redoublez vos transports:
Le sujet ne veut pas de vulgaires efforts.
    Pour moi, qui, jusqu'ici nourri dans la satire,
N'ose encore manier la trompette et la lyre,
Vous me verrez pourtant, dans ce champ glorieux,
Vous animer du moins de la voix et des yeux;
Vous offrir ces leçons que ma muse au Parnasse,
Rapporta jeune encor du commerce d'Horace; [37]
Seconder votre ardeur, échauffer vos esprits,
230   Et vous montrer de loin la couronne et le prix.
Mais aussi pardonnez, si, plein de ce beau zèle,

Your noblest theme is his immortal name.
Let mighty Spenser raise his reverend head,
Cowley and Denham start up from the dead,
Waller his age renew, and offerings bring;
Our monarch's praise let bright-eyed virgins sing;
Let Dryden with new rules our stage refine,[27]
And his great models form by this design.   200
But where's a second Virgil, to rehearse
Our hero's glories in his epic verse?
What Orpheus sing his triumphs o'er the main,
And make the hills and forests move again;
Show his bold fleet on the Batavian shore,
And Holland trembling as his cannons roar; [31]
Paint Europe's balance in his steady hand,
Whilst the two worlds in expectation stand
Of peace or war, that wait on his command?
But, as I speak, new glories strike my eyes,[33]   210
Glories which heaven itself does give and prize,
Blessings of peace; that with their milder rays
Adorn his reign and bring Saturnian days.
Now let rebellion, discord, vice, and rage,
That have in patriots' forms debauched our age,
Vanish with all the ministers of hell;
His rays their poisonous vapors shall dispel.
'Tis he alone our safety did create,
His own firm soul secured the nation's fate,
Opposed to all the *boutefeus* [36] of the State.   220
Authors, for him your great endeavors raise;
The loftiest numbers will but reach his praise.
For me, whose verse in satire has been bred,
And never durst heroic measures tread—
Yet you shall see me in that famous field,
With eyes and voice my best assistance yield;
Offer you lessons that my infant muse
Learnt when she Horace for her guide did choose; [37]
Second your zeal with wishes, heart, and eyes;
And afar off hold up the glorious prize.   230
But pardon too, if, zealous for the right,

De tous vos pas fameux, observateur fidèle,
Quelquefois du bon or je sépare le faux,
Et des auteurs grossiers j'attaque les défauts;
Censeur un peu fâcheux, mais souvent nécessaire,
Plus enclin à blâmer que savant à bien faire.[38]

A strict observer of each noble flight,
From the fine gold I separate th' allay,
And show how hasty writers sometimes stray;
Apter to blame, than knowing how to mend;
A sharp, but yet a necessary friend.

Nicolas Boileau-Despréaux SELECTIONS FROM THE

PREFACE TO HIS TRANSLATION OF LONGINUS

The little treatise a translation of which I now present to the public is a small piece which escaped the wreck that befell several other books composed by Longinus. However, it is not come down to us entire, for though the volume might not at first be very large, there are several places defective in what remains, and the Treatise of the Passions, which the author wrote of in a book by itself, to serve as a sequel to this, is quite lost. Nevertheless, as disfigured as it is, there is enough still to give us a very great idea of the author and make us heartily sorry for the loss of his other writings, the number of which was not small. Suidas [1] reckons up nine, but the titles of them are only left us, and those too confusedly. They were all pieces of criticism and certainly we can never sufficiently grieve for the loss of these excellent originals, which, if we judge of them by this, must have been so many master-pieces of good sense, learning, and eloquence. Eloquence I say, because Longinus was not satisfied with giving us, like Aristotle and Hermo-genes, dry precepts without any manner of ornament. He would not commit the same fault he laid to the charge of Cecilius,[2] who, says he, wrote of the sublime in a low style; for when he treats of the beauties of elocution, he makes use of all its graces; he often employs the figure he teaches and, in talking of the sublime, is himself most sublime. How-ever, he does it so apropos and with such art that one cannot accuse him anywhere of going once out of the didactic style. This is what has got his book such a great reputation among the learned, who have all looked upon it as one of the most precious remains of antiquity on the subject of rhetoric. Casaubon [3] calls it the Golden Book, to show the value of this little piece, which, as little as it is, may be put in the balance with the greatest volumes.

. . . . .

Nicolas Boileau-Despréaux

By this we may perceive Longinus was not only an able rhetorician, like Quintilian and Hermogenes, but a philosopher worthy to be put in comparison with the Socrateses and Catos. There is nothing in his book which is not agreeable to this character. The man of honor is to be seen everywhere in it, and there is something in the sentiments which shows not only a sublime wit, but a soul elevated very much above what is common; wherefore I do not repent that I have employed some time in endeavoring to explain and make clear this excellent work, which, I may say, has hitherto been understood but by a very few, even of the learned.

. . . . .

I would, if I could, excuse the faults that may have escaped me in this French translation by those in the Latin, though I have done my best to make mine as exact as it could be made. To say truth, I have not met with a few difficulties. It is easy for a Latin translator to rid himself of a troublesome business, even in those places that he does not understand. He need only translate the Greek word for word, and put such in his translation as may at least be supposed to be intelligible, for the reader, who very often has no conception of the matter, will rather take it upon himself than imagine the ignorance was in the translator. It is not the same thing with translations in a vulgar language: everything the reader does not understand he calls nonsense, and the translator alone is accountable for it; the very author's faults are laid to his charge, and he must in some places rectify him without daring to leave him in any. As little as this volume of Longinus may be, I cannot think I have made a mean present to the public if I have given it a good translation in our tongue. I have spared neither for care nor pains; however, the reader is not to expect here a timorous version confined servilely to Longinus's words; though I obliged myself never to break the rules of a true translation in any one place, yet I took honest liberty, especially in the passages quoted by him. I thought I was not bound to give a mere translation of Longinus, but a treatise on the sublime that might be useful to the world. After all, there may perhaps be some persons who will be so far from approving of my version that they will not spare even the original. I expect that there will be several who will except against Longinus's authority, who will condemn what he approves and approve what he condemns; such

271

certainly is the treatment he ought to expect from the greatest part of the judges of our times. These men accustomed to the depravity and extravagance of modern poets, who admire nothing but what they do not understand, do not suppose that an author can have an elevated genius unless he flies entirely out of sight in his writings; these little wits, I say, will not be very much touched with the flights of the Homers, the bold strokes of the Platos and Demostheneses; they may often seek after the sublime in the sublime, and perhaps laugh at the exclamations [that] Longinus sometimes makes on passages which, though very sublime, are nevertheless simple and natural, and rather seize the soul than dazzle the eyes. Whatever assurance these gentlemen may have of the clearness of their understandings, I beg they would consider that this is not the work of a learner but the masterpiece of one of the greatest critics of antiquity—that if they do not find out the beauty of those passages, it may as well be occasioned by the weakness of their sight as by the little luster that shines in them; or, let the worst happen that can, I advise them to accuse the translation, since it is but too true that I have neither attained, nor could attain, to the perfection of those excellent originals, and I declare readily beforehand, if there are any faults, they could come from nobody but me.

The only thing that remains to be said to finish this Preface is to explain what Longinus means by the sublime, for as he wrote on this subject after Cecilius, who had wasted almost all his works in showing what the sublime was, he did not think it necessary for him to enter upon the explanation of a thing which had been but too much discussed already. It must be observed then that by the sublime he does not mean what the orators call the *sublime style,* but something *extraordinary* and *marvelous* that strikes us in a discourse and makes it elevate, ravish, and transport us. The *sublime style* requires always great words, but the *sublime* may be found in a thought only, or in a figure or turn of expression. A thing may be in the *sublime style,* and yet not be *sublime,* that is, have nothing *extraordinary* nor *surprising* in it: as for example, "The Sovereign Arbiter of nature with one word only formed the light"; this is in the *sublime style,* and yet is far from being *sublime,* because there is nothing very marvelous in it, and which might not be easily thought and expressed on that occasion by anyone. But, "God said, 'Let there be light, and there was light,' " is an extraordinary turn of expression which so well denotes the obedience of the creature to the orders of the Creator that it is truly sublime, and has something divine in it; therefore by the *sublime* in Longinus must be understood that which is *extraordinary, surprising,* and as I have translated it, *marvelous* in discourse.

I have quoted those words out of Genesis as an expression the most proper of any to put my thoughts in a true light, and made use of it the more willingly because this very expression is cited with applause by Longinus himself, who under the darkness of paganism could not but perceive something divine in those words of the Scripture. What then shall we say of one of the most learned men of our age, who, having the advantage of the Gospel light, did not find out the beauty of this passage, but has presumed to advance in a book he wrote in defense of the Christian religion that Longinus was mistaken in thinking these words sublime; [4] however I have the satisfaction to find there are persons [5] of as profound erudition of another opinion. The translators of the first book of Genesis in their Preface, among several other excellent proofs that that book was dictated by the Holy Ghost, have mentioned this passage of Longinus to show how much Christians ought to be convinced of a truth so clear that a pagan himself could not help being sensible of its power by the light of reason only.

. . . . .

[1701]

In all my other editions I let this Preface pass as it was in the first impression about twenty years ago, and added nothing to it; but now as I revised the proofs and had prepared them to be returned to the printer, I thought it might not perhaps be amiss, the better to explain what Longinus means by the word *sublime,* to add some other example, which I have met with elsewhere, to that I quoted out of the Bible. While I was thinking of it this came happily into my mind; it is taken out of Monsieur Corneille's *Horace.* In this tragedy, the three first acts of which are in my mind the masterpiece of that illustrious writer, a woman who had been present at the combat of the three Horatii with the Curatii, but went away from the place too soon and had not seen the end of it, came too hastily to old Horace, their father, and told him two of his sons were killed, and the third finding he was not able to make any resistance afterwards fled; upon which this old Roman, full of love to his country, without mourning for the death of his two

273

sons who had died so gloriously, grieved only for the shameful flight of the last, who, says he, by so base an action had fixed an eternal stain on the name of Horace; and their sister, who was present, saying to him, "What would you have had him do against three?" he replied briskly, "Die!" A short answer; yet there is nobody who hears the word *die* but is sensible of the heroic grandeur contained in it, which expression is the more sublime for being so simple and natural—and because we see that the old hero speaks from the very bottom of his soul. If instead of "Die!" he had said, "Let him follow the example of his brethren, or sacrifice his life to the interest and glory of his country," a great deal of the force of his answer had been lost, for it is even the simplicity of it that makes the dignity. Such things as these are what Longinus calls the sublime, and such things as these that he would have admired in Corneille had he been his contemporary, much more than those big words with which Ptolemy fills his mouth at the beginning of the death of Pompey, to aggravate the vain circumstances of a rout which he did not see.

Nicolas Boileau-Despréaux REFLECTION VII FROM
"CRITICAL REFLECTIONS ON . . . LONGINUS"

"We must think what judgment posterity will pass upon our writings."
—Longinus

Indeed there is nothing but the approbation of posterity that can establish the true merit of writings. Whatever noise a writer makes in his lifetime, whatever applause is given him, we cannot, for all that, infallibly conclude that his writings are excellent. A false brilliant, a newness of style, a fashionable turn of wit, may set a value upon them; and perhaps in the next age people's eyes will be open, and they will despise what the present admires. We have a good example of this in Ronsard and his imitators, as du Bellay, du Bartas, Desportes, who in the preceding age were the admiration of all the world, and now nobody will read them.

The same thing befell some of the Roman authors, as Nævius, Livy, and Ennius,[6] who in Horace's time, as we learn from that poet, had still abundance of admirers. We must not imagine that the fall of these authors, as well French as Latin, was occasioned by the alteration of the language of their country. The true cause of it was their not rising in those tongues to that point of solidity and perfection without which no works will be lasting and always valuable. As for instance, the Latin tongue in which Cicero and Virgil wrote was very much altered in Quintilian's time, and as much more in Aulus Gellius's;[7] however, Cicero and Virgil were then more esteemed than even in their own time, because they had, as it were, fixed the language by their writings, having attained the point of perfection I have been speaking of.

Wherefore it is not the antiquity of Ronsard's words and expressions that has cried down Ronsard; it is because it was perceived all at once that what was taken for beauties in him were not beauties. Bertaut, Malherbe, Distingendes, and Racan,[8] who came after him, contributed very much towards this discovery, and hit on the true genius of the French language in the serious kind. For the tongue was so far from being in its maturity in Ronsard's time, as Pasquier [9] erroneously imagined, that it was not then even out of its infancy. On the contrary the true turn of the epigram, rondeau, and natural epistles was found out before Ronsard by Marot, Saint-Gelais,[10] and others, whose works in this kind are not only not fallen into contempt, but are now generally esteemed, insomuch that to hit upon the natural air of the French tongue recourse is often had to their style; and it is that which made the famous Monsieur de La Fontaine succeed as he has done.

But when writers have been admired a great many ages, and condemned only by persons of a whimsical taste (for there will always be depraved tastes), there is not only rashness but madness in doubting the merit of such authors. If you do not see the beauties of their works, it must not be concluded there are none, but that you are blind and have no taste. The bulk of mankind will not always be mistaken in their judgment of writers and writings. It is not now a matter of dispute whether Homer, Plato, Cicero, Virgil are wonderful men or not; it is incontestable, since twenty ages have agreed in it. All that we are to inquire into now is in what they are wonderful, and why so many ages admired them. And you must find out a way to know it or renounce the belles lettres, for which you ought to believe you have neither taste nor genius, since you are not sensible of what so many men have been sensible of before you.

When I say this, it is with a supposition that you understand the language these authors wrote in. For if you do not understand it, and have not made it familiar to you, I do not find fault with you for not perceiving the beauties, I only blame you for speaking of them. And in this Monsieur Perrault [11] can never be too much condemned, who, not understanding Homer's language, charges him so boldly with the errors of his translators, and tells all mankind, that have for so many ages admired the works of this great poet, "You have admired trifles." It is as if a man born blind should run about the streets crying, "Gentlemen, I know the sun that you see seems very beautiful, but I, who never saw it, declare to you that it is very ugly."

To return to what I am about. Since it is posterity only that sets a

276

true value upon all writings, you must not, as admirable as you may take a modern writer to be, presently put him on a level with those writers who have been admired a great many ages, because one cannot be sure his works will pass with glory to the next. Indeed, without going far for examples, how many authors have we seen admired in our age whose glory is vanished in a very few years? How were Balzac's [12] works esteemed thirty years ago? He was not talked of only as the most eloquent man of his time, but as the only eloquent. He had, it is true, wonderful qualities; it may be said of him, no man ever understood his own tongue better than he, nor the propriety of words, nor the just measure of periods. This is a commendation nobody still denies him; yet all on a sudden it was perceived the art about which he employed himself all his lifetime was the art he knew least of, I mean that of writing a letter. For though his are full of wit and things are admirably well said everywhere, yet we observe in them the two vices the most opposite to the epistolary kind—affectation and puffiness; and he will no more be forgiven the vicious care he has taken to say things quite otherwise than other men said them, so that the verse which Maynard [13] made formerly in his praise is now every day retorted upon him:

There's not a mortal that can talk like him.

However, he is still read by some persons; but nobody dares imitate his style—those who have done it having been laughed at by all the world.

We might instance another example, more illustrious than Balzac. Corneille, of all our poets, was he who in our age made most noise; and it was thought there would never be a poet again in France worthy of being compared to him. Indeed there has not been one of a more lofty genius, nor [one] who has written more; yet all his present merit, having been put by time into a sort of crucible, is brought down to eight or nine theatrical pieces which are admired and are, as it were, the noon of his poetry, of which the morning and evening were worth nothing. Besides in this small number of plays there are not only a pretty many faults in the language, but we begin to find out abundance of places that are declamations only and were not formerly found out by anyone. By which means it is not taken ill if we compare Monsieur Racine with him, and there are a great many who prefer him to Corneille. Posterity will judge which of the two is most valuable, for I am satisfied the writings of both the one and the other will be transmitted to future ages. But till then neither the one nor the other ought to be put into a parallel with Euripides and Sophocles, because their works have not yet the seal to them which the works of Sophocles and Euripides have: I mean the approbation of several ages.

Notwithstanding what I have said, it must not be imagined that in the number of writers approved by all ages I would include those authors who are indeed ancient but never acquired above an ordinary reputation: as Lycophron, Nonnius, Silius Italicus,[14] the author of the tragedies attributed to Seneca, and several others, to whom many modern writers may not only be compared but, in my opinion, are justly preferable. In this high rank I place only the few admirable authors whose names alone are a panegyric: as Homer, Plato, Cicero, Virgil, etc. And I do not measure my esteem of them by the time their works have lasted, but by the time they have been admired. Abundance of people ought to be cautioned of this, lest they should give into what our censor would insinuate—that we only praise the ancients and condemn the moderns because the one are ancients and the other moderns—which is not at all true, there being a great many ancients whom we do not admire and a great many moderns whom all the world extol. The antiquity of a writer is a certain sign of his merit; but the antique and constant admiration which his works have always been in is a sure and infallible proof that they ought to be admired.

René Rapin REFLECTIONS ON ARISTOTLE'S TREATISE

OF POESY (Book I: In General)

I

The true value of poetry is ordinarily so little known that scarce ever is made a true judgment of it. It is the talent of wits only that are above the common rank to esteem of it according to its merit, and one cannot consider how Alexander, Scipio, Julius Caesar, Augustus, and all the great men of antiquity have been affected therewith without conceiving a noble idea of it. In effect, poesy, of all arts, is the most perfect: for the perfection of other arts is limited, but this of poesy has no bounds; to be excellent therein one must know all things. But this value will best appear by giving a particular of the qualities necessary for a poet.

II

He must have a genius extraordinary; great natural gifts; a wit just, fruitful, piercing, solid, universal; an understanding clean and distinct; an imagination neat and pleasant; an elevation of soul that depends not on art nor study, and which is purely a gift of heaven, and must be sustained by a lively sense and vivacity; a great judgment to consider wisely of things, and a vivacity to express them with that grace and abundance which gives them beauty. But as judgment without wit is cold and heavy, so wit without judgment is blind and extravagant. Hence it is that Lucan often in his *Pharsalia* grows flat for want of wit. And Ovid in his *Metamorphoses* sometimes loses himself through his defect of judgment. Ariosto has too much flame; Dante has none at all. Boccaccio's wit is just but not copious; the Cavalier Marino is luxuriant, but wants that justness. For in fine, to accomplish a poet is required a temperament of wit and of fancy, of strength and of sweetness, of penetration and of delicacy, and above all things he must have a sovereign eloquence and a profound capacity. These are the qualities that must concur together to form the genius of a poet and sustain his character.

III

But the first injustice that poets suffer is that commonly what is merely the effect of fancy is mistaken for wit. Thus an ignorant person shall start up and be thought a poet in the world for a lucky hit in a song or catch, where is only the empty flash of an imagination heated perhaps by a debauch, and nothing of that celestial fire which only is the portion of an extraordinary genius. "One must be careful," saith Horace, "of profaning that name by bestowing it without distinction on all those who undertake to versify. For," saith he, "there must be a greatness of soul, and something divine in the spirit. There must be lofty expressions, and noble thoughts, and an air of majesty to deserve that name." [1] A sonnet, ode, elegy, epigram, and those little kind of verses that often make so much noise in the world are ordinarily no more than the mere productions of imagination; a superficial wit with a little conversation of the world is capable of these things. True poetry requires other qualifications; a genius for war or for business comes nothing near it. A little phlegm, with a competency of experience, may fit a man for an important negotiation, and an opportunity well managed, joined with a little hazard, may make the success of a battle, and all the good fortune of a campaign; but to excite these emotions of the soul and transports of admiration that are expected from poetry, all the wit that the soul of man is capable of is scarce sufficient.

VI

One may be an orator without the natural gift of eloquence, because art may supply that defect; but no man can be a poet without a genius, the want of which no art or industry is capable to repair. This genius is that celestial fire intended by the fable, which enlarges and heightens the soul and makes it express things with a lofty air. Happy is he to whom nature has made this present; by this he is raised above himself, whereas others are always low and creeping, and never speak but what is mean and common. He that hath a genius appears a poet on the smallest subjects by the turn he gives them and the noble manner in which he expresses himself. This character the French gave their Monsieur Racan;[2] but in truth where shall we find all these qualities I have mentioned? Where is that sparkling wit and that solid judgment? that flame and that phlegm? that rapture and that moderation which constitute that genius we inquire after? It is the little wits always who think they versify the best; the greatest poets are the most modest. . . .

VII

It is not easily decided what the nature and what precisely is the end of this art; the interpreters of Aristotle differ in their opinions. Some will have the end to be delight, and that it is on this account it labors to move the passions, all whose motions are delightful, because nothing is more sweet to the soul than agitation; it pleases itself in changing the objects to satisfy the immensity of its desires. It is true, delight is the end poetry aims at, but not the principal end, as others pretend. In effect, poetry, being an art, ought to be profitable by the quality of its own nature and by the essential subordination that all arts should have to polity, whose end in general is the public good. This is the judgment of Aristotle and of Horace, his chief interpreter.

VIII

After all, since the design of poetry is to delight, it omits nothing that may contribute thereto; it is to this intent that it makes use of numbers and harmony, which are naturally delightful, and animates its discourse with more lively draughts and more strong expressions than are allowed in prose, and does affranchize itself from that constraint and reservedness that is ordinary with orators, and permits a great liberty to imagination, and makes frequent images of what is most agreeable in nature; and never speaks but with figures, to give a greater luster to the discourse; and is noble in its ideas, sublime in the expressions, bold in the words, passionate in the motions, and takes pleasure in relating extraordinary adventures to give the most common and natural things a fabulous gloss, to render them more admirable and heighten truth by fiction. It is finally for this that it employs whatever art has that is pleasant, because its end is to delight. [Empedocles and Lucretius, who used not this art in their poems (as Homer and Virgil did), are not true poets.] Homer is delightful even in the description of Laertes' swineherd's lodge in his *Odyssey*, and Virgil in the dung and thistles in his *Georgics* as he expresses himself, for everything becomes beautiful and flowery in the hands of a poet who hath a genius.

281

IX

However, the principal end of poesy is to profit, not only by refreshing the mind to render it more capable of the ordinary functions and by assuaging the troubles of the soul with its harmony and all the elegancies of expression, but furthermore, by purging the manners with wholesome instructions which it professes to administer to human kind; for virtue being naturally austere by the constraint it imposes on the heart in repressing the desires, morality, which undertakes to regulate the motions of the heart by its precepts, ought to make itself delightful that it may be listened to, which can by no means be so happily effected as by poetry. It is by this that morality, in curing the maladies of men, makes use of the same artifice that physicians have recourse to in the sickness of children: they mingle honey with the medicine to take off the bitterness. The principal design therefore of this art is to render pleasant that which is wholesome, in which it is more wise than other arts, which endeavor to profit without any care to please. Eloquence itself by its most passionate discourse is not always capable to persuade men to virtue with that success as poetry, because men are more sensible and sooner impressed upon by what is pleasant than by reason. For this cause, all poetry that tends to the corruption of manners is irregular and vicious, and poets are to be looked on as a public contagion whose morals are not pure; and it is these dissolute and debauched poets that Plato banished his commonwealth. And true it is that the petty wits only are ordinarily subject to say what is impious or obscene. Homer and Virgil were never guilty in this kind; they were sweet and virtuous as philosophers. The Muses of true poets are as chaste as Vestals.

X

For no other end is poetry delightful than that it may be profitable. Pleasure is only the means by which the profit is conveyed, and all poetry, when it is perfect, ought of necessity to be a public lesson of good manners for the instruction of the world. Heroic poesy proposes the example of great virtues and great vices to excite men to abhor these and to be in love with the other. It gives us an esteem for Achilles in Homer, and contempt for Thersites; it begets in us a veneration for the piety of Aeneas in Virgil and horror for the profaneness of Mezentius. Tragedy rectifies the use of passions by moderating our fear and our pity, which are obstacles of virtue; it lets men see that vice never escapes unpunished when it represents Aegisthus in the *Electra* of Sophocles, punished after the ten years' enjoyment of his crime. It teaches us that the favors of fortune and the grandeurs of the world are not always true goods when it shows on the theatre a queen so unhappy as Hecuba, deploring with that pathetic air her misfortunes, in Euripides. Comedy, which is an image of common conversation, corrects the public vices by letting us see how ridiculous they are in particulars. Aristophanes does not mock at the foolish vanity of Praxagora (in his *Parliament of Women*) but to cure the vanity of the other Athenian women; and it was only to teach the Roman soldiers in what consisted true valor that Plautus exposed in public the extravagance of false bravery in his braggadoccio captain in that comedy of *The Glorious Soldier*.

XI

But because poetry is only profitable so far as it is delightful, it is of greatest importance in this art to please; the only certain way to please is by rules. These therefore are to be established that a poet may not be left to confound all things, imitating those extravagances which Horace so much blames — that is to say, by joining things naturally incompatible, "mixing tigers with lambs, birds with serpents, to make one body of different species, and thereby authorize fancies more indigested than the dreams of sick men;" [3] for unless a man adhere to principles, he is obnoxious to all extravagances and absurdities imaginable; unless he go by rule, he slips at every step towards wit, and falls into errors as often as he sets out. Into what enormities hath Petrarch run in his *Africa*, Ariosto in his *Orlando Furioso*, Cavalier Marino in his *Adone*, and all the other Italians who were ignorant of Aristotle's rules and followed no other guides but their own genius and capricious fancy. Truth is, the wits of Italy were so prepossessed in favor of the romantic poetry of Pulci, Boiardo, and Ariosto that they regarded no other rules than what the heat of their genius inspired. The first Italian poet who let the world see that the art was not altogether unknown to him was Giorgio Trissino,[4] in his poem of Italy delivered from the Goths under the pontificates of Leo X and Clement VIII. . . .

XII

Aristotle drew the platform of these rules from the poems of Homer and other poets of his time by the reflections he had a long time made on their works. I pretend not by a long discourse to justify the necessity, the justness, and the truth of these rules, nor to make an history of Aristotle's treatise of poesy, or examine whether it is complete, which many others have done; all these things I suppose. Only I affirm that these rules well considered, one shall find them made only to reduce nature into method, to trace it step by step, and not suffer the least mark of it to escape us. It is only by these rules that the verisimility in fictions is maintained which is the soul of poesy. For unless there be the unity of place, of time, and of the action in the great poems, there can be no verisimility. In fine, it is by these rules that all becomes just, proportionate, and natural, for they are founded upon good sense and sound reason rather than on authority and example. Horace's book *Of Poetry*, which is but an interpretation of that of Aristotle, discovers sufficiently the necessity of being subject to rules by the ridiculous absurdities one is apt to fall into who follows only his fancy; for though poesy be the effect of fancy, yet if this fancy be not regulated it is a mere caprice, not capable of producing anything reasonable.

XIII

But if the genius must indispensably be subjected to the servitude of rules, it will not easily be decided whether art or nature contributes more to poetry; it is one of those questions unresolved which might be proper for a declamation, and the decision is of small importance. It suffices that we know both the one and the other are of that moment that none can attain to any sovereign perfection in poetry if he be defective in either. So that both (saith Horace) must mutually assist each other and conspire to make a poet accomplished. But though nature be of little value without the help of art, yet we may approve of Quintilian's opinion, who believed that art did less contribute to that perfection than nature.[5] And by the comparison that Longinus makes betwixt Apollonius and Homer, Eratosthenes and Archilocus, Bacchilides and Pindar, Ion and Sophocles, the former of all which never transgressed against the rules of art whereas these others did, it appears that the advantage of wit is always preferred before that of art.[6]

XVI

Nothing can more contribute to this perfection than a judgment proportioned to the wit, for the greater that the wit is and the more strength and vigor that the imagination has to form these ideas that enrich poesy, the more wisdom and discretion is requisite to moderate that heat and govern its natural fury. For reason ought to be much stronger than the fancy to discern how far the transports may be carried. It is a great talent to forbear speaking all one thinks and to leave something for others to employ their thoughts. It is not ordinarily known how far matters should be carried; a man of an accomplished genius stops regularly where he ought to stop, and retrenches boldly what ought to be omitted. It is a great fault not to leave a thing when it is well, for which Apelles so much blamed Protogenes.[7] This moderation is the character of a great wit; the vulgar understand it not, and (whatever is alleged to the contrary) never any save Homer and Virgil had the discretion to leave a thing when it was well.

XVIII

The art of poetry in general comprehends the matters of which a poet treats and the manner in which he handles them; the invention, the contrivance, the design, the proportion and symmetry of parts, the general disposition of matters, and whatever regards the invention belong to the matters of which this art ought to treat. The fable, the manners, the sentiments, the words, the figures, the numbers, the harmony, the versification regard the manner in which the matters are to be handled. So that the art is, as it were, the instrument of the genius, because it contains essentially all the different parts which are employed in the management. So that those who are furnished with a naked wit only, and who, to be great poets, rely principally on their fancy, as Cavalier Marino among the Italians, Théophile among the French; and those likewise who place the essence of poetry in big and pompous words, as Statius among the Latins and Du Bartas among the French, are much mistaken in their account when they aspire to the glory of poetry by such feeble means.

XIX

Among the particulars of this art, the subject and design ought to have the first place because it is, as it were, the first production of the wit, and the design in a poem is what they call the *ordonnance* in a picture. The great painters only are capable of a great design in their draughts, such as Raphael, a Giulio Romano, a Poussin, and only great poets are capable of a great subject in their poetry. An indifferent wit may form a vast design in his imagination, but it must be an extraordinary genius that can work this design, and fashion it according to justness and proportion. For it is necessary that the same spirit reign throughout, that all contribute to the same end, and that all the parts bear a secret relation to each other; all depend on this relation and alliance, and this general design is nothing else but the form which a poet gives to his work. This also is the most difficult part, being the effect of an accomplished judgment; and because judgment is not the ordinary talent of the French, it is generally in the contrivance of their design that their poets are defective, and nothing is more rare among them than a design that is great, just, and well conceived. They pretend to be more happy in the talents of wit and fancy, as likewise the Italians. The most perfect design of all modern poems is that of Tasso; nothing more complete has appeared in Italy, though great faults are in the conduct of it. And the most judicious, the most admirable, the most perfect design of all antiquity is that of Virgil in his *Aeneid*; all there is great and noble, all proportionable to the subject, which is the establishment of the empire of Rome, to the hero, who is Aeneas, to the glory of Augustus and the Romans, for whom it was composed. Nothing is weak or defective in the execution; all there is happy, all is just, all is perfect. But the sovereign perfection of a design, in the opinion of Horace, is to be simple, and that all turn on the same center. Which is so true that even in little things, that is to say, in an eclogue, elegy, song, or epigram, and in the meanest compositions, there ought to be a just cast, and that all of it turn on the same point. Ovid did much violence to himself to unite his *Metamorphoses* and close them in one design, in which he was not altogether so happy as afterwards in his elegies, where wellnigh always one may find a certain turn which binds the design and makes thereof a work that is just by the dependence and relation of its parts. In this the ancient poets were always more exact than the modern, for most of the modern express their thoughts higgle-piggle, without any order or connection. If there be design, it is never with that scrupulous unity which is the principal virtue that should be predominant to make it just and complete. I know there are a kind of works which, by the quality of their character, ought to be writ with a free air, without other design than that of writing things naturally and without constraint; such are the hymns of Orpheus, Homer, Callimachus; and such are certain odes of Pindar, Anacreon, and Horace, that have no other rule but enthusiasm; and such likewise are the most part of the elegies of Tibullus and Propertius. But it must be granted that these are not the best and most beautiful, and who reflects on the elegies of Ovid shall always there perceive a secret turn which makes the design; and this is ordinarily the principal beauty in these little works

of verse, as may be seen in most epigrams of the *Anthology*, in those of
Catullus, in the correct odes of Horace, and in the phaleusiacs of Bonnefons,[8] who within this last age has writ in Latin verse with all the softness
and delicacy possible. Thus every sort of poesy ought to have its proportionable design — a great design in great poems, and in little, a little design. But of this the ordinary wits know nothing; their works, which generally are mere productions of imagination, have scarcely any design,
unless it be by chance. It must be the work of an accomplished genius to
close his thoughts in a design, whence results an agreement and proportion
of parts that makes the harmony perfect.

XXI

Aristotle divides the fable, which serves for argument to a poem, into
simple and compound. The simple is that which hath no change of fortune, as is the *Prometheus* of Aeschylus and the *Hercules* of Seneca. The
compound fable is that which hath a turn from bad fortune to good, or
from good to bad, as the *Oedipus* of Sophocles. And the contrivance of
each fable must have two parts, the intrigue and the discovery. The intrigue embroils matters, casting troubles and confusion among the affairs.
The discovery remits all into a calm again. Whatever goes before the
change of fortune is called the intrigue; all that makes the change or follows
it is the discovery. The intrigue in the *Andromache* of Euripides is that
this princess, after she had lost Hector, her husband, and seen her father
Priam murdered, the chief city of his kingdom burnt, became a slave to
Neoptolemus. Hermione, the wife of this prince, pricked with jealousy
against Andromache, was minded to kill her. Menelaus, father of Hermione, causes her with her son Astyanax to be dragged to execution; this
is the intrigue. Now she is rescued from death by Tethys and Peleus, who
prefer the son to be king of the Molosians, and the mother to be queen
by a marriage with Helenus; this is the discovery. And every fable must
have these two parts to be the subject of a just poem. Thus Aeneas,
chased from his country, spoiled of all that he possessed, beaten by tempests, wandering from coast to coast, destitute of all succors, persecuted
by Juno and the other deities of her cabal, after all these disgraces became
the founder of the greatest monarchy in the world. This is the fable of the
Aeneid with its intrigue and its discovery. And it is to be observed that
only by this change of fortune the fable pleases and has its effect, in which

the simple fable is defective, in Aristotle's opinion, because it wants variety.

XXIII

The admirable is all that which is against the ordinary course of nature. The probable is whatever suits with common opinion. The changing of Niobe into a stone is an event that holds of the admirable; yet this becomes probable when a deity, to whose power this change was possible, is engaged. Aeneas, in the twelfth book of the *Aeneid*, lifts by himself a stone that ten men could scarce remove; this prodigy is made probable by the assistance of the gods that took his part against Turnus. But most part of those that make verse, by too great a passion they have to create admiration, take not sufficient care to temper it with probability. Against this rock most ordinarily fall the poets, who are too easily carried to say incredible things that they may be admirable. . . .

XXIV

Besides that probability serves to give credit to whatever poesy has the most fabulous, it serves also to give to whatever the poet saith a greater luster and air of perfection than truth itself can do, though probability is but the copy. For truth represents things only as they are, but probability renders them as they ought to be. Truth is wellnigh always defective by the mixture of particular conditions that compose it. Nothing is brought into the world that is not remote from the perfection of its idea from the very birth. Originals and models are to be searched for in probability and in the universal principles of things, where nothing that is material and singular enters to corrupt them. For this reason the portraits of history are less perfect than the portraits of poesy, and Sophocles, who in his tragedies represents men as they ought to be, is, in the opinion of Aristotle, to be preferred before Euripides, who represents men as really they are; and Horace makes less account of the lessons of Crantor and Chrysippus for the manners than of those of Homer.[9]

XXV

After the design or fable, Aristotle places the manners for the second part; he calls the manners the cause of the action, for it is from these that a man begins to act. Achilles retires from the Grecian army in Homer because he is discontent. Aeneas in Virgil carries his gods into Italy because he is pious. Medea kills her children in Seneca because she is revengeful; so the manners are, as it were, the first springs of all human actions. The painter draws faces by their features, but the poet represents the minds of men by their manners, and the most general rule for painting the manners is to exhibit every person in his proper character: a slave, with base thoughts and servile inclinations; a prince, with a liberal heart and air of majesty; a soldier, fierce, insolent, surly, inconstant; an old man, covetous, wary, jealous. It is in describing the manners that Terence triumphed over all the poets of his time, in Varro's opinion, for his persons are never found out of their characters. He observes their manners in all the niceties and rigors of decorum, which Homer himself has not always done, as some pretend. Longinus cannot endure the wounds, the adulteries, the hatred, and all the other weaknesses to which he makes the gods obnoxious, contrary to their character. Philostratus finds much to object against his portraits, but Justin Martyr excuses him, alleging that he took these notions from Orpheus, and that he had followed the opinion that publicly prevailed in those days. However it be, it may be granted that Homer has not treated the gods with all the respect due to their condition. Aristotle condemns Euripides for introducing Melanippa to speak too much like a philosopher of the sect of Anaxagoras, whose opinions were then new in his time.[10] Theon the Sophist cannot endure the unseasonable discourses of Hecuba on her misfortunes, in the same author. Sophocles makes Oedipus too weak and low-spirited in his exile after he had bestowed on him that character of constancy and resolution before his disgrace. Seneca, for his part, knows nothing of the manners. He is a fine speaker who is eternally uttering pretty sayings, but is in no wise natural in what he speaks, and whatever persons he makes to speak, they always have the mien of actors. The Angelica of Ariosto is too immodest. The Armida of Tasso is too free and impudent. These two poets rob women of their character, which is modesty. Rinaldo is soft and effeminate in the one, Orlando is too tender and passionate in the other. These weaknesses in no wise agree with heroes; they are degraded from the nobleness of their condition to make them guilty of folly. The sovereign rule for treating of manners is to copy them after nature, and above all to study well the heart of man to know how to distinguish all its motions. It is this which none are acquainted with. The heart of man is an abyss, where none can sound the bottom; it is a mystery which the most quick-sighted cannot pierce into, and in which the most cunning are mistaken. At the worst the poet is obliged to speak of manners according to the common opinion. Ajax must be represented grim, as Sophocles; Polyxena and Iphigenia generous, as Euripides has represented them. Finally, the manners must be proportionable to the age, to the sex, to the quality, to the employment, and to the fortune of the persons; and it is particularly in the second book of Aristotle's *Rhetoric* and in Horace's book *Of Poetry* that this secret may be learned. Whatever agrees not with his principles is false. Nothing tolerable can be performed in poetry without this knowledge, and with it all becomes admirable. And Horace, in that place of his book *Of Poetry* [153 sqq.] where he makes distinction of ages to draw their portraits, affirms that it is only by the "representation of manners" that any can have success on the stage, for there all is frivolous if the manners be not observed.

XXVI

The third part of the art consists in the thoughts or sentiments, which are properly the expressions of the manners as words are the expressions of the thoughts. Their office, saith Aristotle, is to approve or dislike, to stir or to calm the passions, to magnify or diminish things. . . . Thoughts must not only be comfortable to the persons to whom they are given, but likewise to the subject treated of; that is to say, on great subjects are required great thoughts, as those of Evadne in the *Suppliants* of Euripides. There this queen, after the death of her husband Capaneus, may be seen to express all the extremity of her grief by force of a sorrow the most generous that ever was; her affliction oppresses her without extorting from her one word that betrays anything of weakness. The Greek poets are full of these great thoughts, and it is much by this greatness of their sentiments that they are particularly signalized in their works. Demetrius and Longinus perpetually propose them for models to those who study the sublime style, and it is in these great originals that our modern poets ought to consult nature, to learn how to raise their wits and be lofty. We may flatter ourselves with our wit and the genius of our (the French) nation, but our soul is not enough exalted to frame great ideas; we are busied with petty subjects, and by that means it is that we prove so cold in the great, and that in our works scarce appears any shadow of that sublime poesy of which the ancient poets have left such excellent models, and above all Homer and Virgil. For great poetry must be animated and sustained by great thoughts and great sentiments; but these we ordinarily want, either because our wit is too much limited, or because we take not care to exercise on important matters. Thus we are low on high subjects. For example, how feeble are we when we speak of the conquests of a king! Our poets make their expressions swell to supply the want of noble sentiments, but it is not only the greatness of the subjects and the thoughts that give this air of majesty to poetry; there is likewise required lofty words and noble expressions.

XXVII

The last part is the expression and whatever regards the language; it must have five qualities to have all the perfection poetry demands: it must be apt, clear, natural, splendid, and numerous. The language must in the first place be apt, and have nothing impure or barbarous. For though one may speak what is great, noble, and admirable, all is despicable and odious if the purity be wanting; the greatest thoughts in the world have not any grace if the construction be defective. This purity of writing is of late so strongly established among the French that he must be very hardy that will make verse in an age so delicate, unless he understand the tongue perfectly. Secondly, the language must be clear that it may be intelligible, for one of the greatest faults in discourse is obscurity. In this Camoëns, whom the Portuguese call their Virgil, is extremely blamable, for his verses are so obscure that they may pass for mysteries, and the thoughts of Dante are so profound that much art is required to dive into them. Poetry demands a more clear air and what is less incomprehensible. The third quality is that it be natural, without affectation, according to rules of decorum and good sense. Studied phrases, a too florid style, fine words, terms strained and remote, and all extraordinary expressions are insupportable to the true poesy; only simplicity pleases, provided it be sustained with greatness and majesty. But this simplicity is not known except by great souls; the little wits understand nothing of it. It is the masterpiece of poesy, and the character of Homer and Virgil. The ignorant hunt after wit and fine thoughts because they are ignorant. The language must be lofty and splendid, which is the fourth quality. For the common and ordinary terms are not proper for a poet; he must use words that partake nothing of the base and vulgar; they must be noble and magnificent, the expressions strong, the colors lively, the draughts bold. His discourse must be such as may equal the greatness of the ideas of a workman who

291

is the creator of his work. The fifth quality is that it be numerous, to uphold that greatness and air of majesty which reigns throughout in poesy, and to express all the force and dignity of the great things it speaks. Terms that go off roundly from the mouth and that fill the ears are sufficient to render all admirable, as poesy requires. But this is not enough that the expressions be stately and great; there must likewise be heat and vehemence, and above all, there must shine throughout the discourse a certain grace and delicacy which makes the principal ornament and most universal beauty.

XXIX

The loftiness of expression is so important that for the attaining it it is not enough to propose Homer and Virgil; it must be searched in Pindar, in Sophocles, in Euripides, and it must be had in grave and serious subjects that of themselves are capable to furnish with great thoughts, as the great thoughts are capable to furnish with noble expressions. "But the way to heighten discourse," saith Aristotle, "is to make good use of metaphors, and to understand perfectly their nature, that they may not be abused." [11] And he adds in the same place that this discernment is the mark of an excellent wit. And because, as saith Quintilian,[12] this loftiness which is aimed at by the boldness of a metaphor is dangerous, insomuch that it comes nigh to rashness, Aristotle must be consulted on this matter to employ them with discretion, as Virgil has done, who, treating of bees in the fourth book of his *Georgics*, that he might heighten the meanness of his subject, speaks not of them but in metaphorical terms — of a court, of legions, of armies, of combats, pitched fields, kings, captains, soldiers — and by this admirable art forms a noble image of the lowest subject, for after all, they are still but flies. Finally, the poet must above all things know what eloquence has of art and method for the use of figures, for it is only by the figures that he gives force to the passions, luster to the discourses, weight to the reasons, and makes delightful all he speaks. It is only by the most lively figures of eloquence that all the emotions of the soul become fervent and passionate. Nature must be the only guide that can be proposed in the use of these figures and metaphors, and must therefore be well understood that it may be traced and followed without mistake; for no portraits can be drawn that have resemblance without it, and all the images that poetry employs in expressing itself are false unless they be natural.

René Rapin

XXX

But this sublime style is the rock to the mean wits; they fly out in too vast and boisterous terms from what is natural when they endeavor to be high and lofty. For this haughty and pompous kind of speech becomes vain and cold if not supported with great thoughts, and the great words that are indiscreetly affected to heighten the discourse for the most part only make a noise. . . . For the most essential virtue of speech, next to the clearness and perspicuity, is that it be chaste and modest, as Demetrius Phalerius observes.[13] There must be, saith he, a proportion betwixt the words and the things; and nothing is more ridiculous than to handle a frivolous subject in a sublime style, for whatsoever is disproportionate is altogether false or at the least is trifling and childish. [It is for this that Socrates reproaches the Sophist Gorgias Leontinus], whom he pleasantly plays upon for affecting to speak petty things with a great and solemn mien.[14] Most French poets fall into this vice for want of genius; their verses, where logic is much neglected, most commonly are either pedantry or nonsense. . . .

XXXI

Of late some have fallen into another extremity by a too scrupulous care of purity of language: they have begun to take from poesy all its nerves and all its majesty by a too timorous reservedness and false modesty, which some thought to make the character of the French tongue by robbing it of all those wise and judicious boldnesses that poesy demands. They would retrench without reason the use of metaphors and of all those figures that give life and luster to the expressions, and study to confine all the excellency of this admirable art within the bounds of a pure and correct discourse without exposing it to the danger of any high and bold flight. The gust of the age, which loved purity, the women, who naturally are modest, the court, which then had scarce any commerce with the great men of antiquity, through their ordinary antipathy to learning and the general ignorance in the persons of quality, gave reputation to this way of writing. But nothing more authorized it than the verses of Voiture and Sarasin, the *Metamorphosis of the Eyes of Phillis into Stars, The Temple of Death*, the eclogues of Lane, and some other works of that character that came abroad at that time with a success which distinguished them from the vulgar.[15] In this way they were polite and writ good sense, and it agreed with the gust of the age and was followed. And who succeeded therein would make a new kind of refinement in poetry, as if the art consisted only in the purity and exactness of language. This indeed pleased well, and was much to the advantage of women that had a mind to be tampering and writing in verse; they found it their concern to give vogue to this kind of writing, of which they were as capable as the most part of men, for all the secret was no more but to make some little easy verses, in which they were content if they could close some kind of delicateness of sweet and passionate thoughts, which they made the essence of poetry. The ill fortune is, Horace was not of their mind. "It is not enough," saith he, "to write with purity to make a poet; he must have other qualities." . . .[16]

XXXVI

. . . But that I may not repeat what hath been said in the twenty-fifth Reflection, I proceed to the passions, which give no less grace to poetry than the manners, when the poet has found the art to make them move by their natural springs. Without the passions all is cold and flat in the discourse, saith Quintilian,[17] for they are, as it were, the soul and life of it; but the secret is to express them according to the several estates and different degrees from their birth. And in this distinction consists all the delicacy wherewith the passions are to be handled to give them that character which renders them admirable by the secret motions they impress on the soul. Hecuba in Euripides falls into a swound on the stage, the better to express all the weight of her sorrow that could not be represented by words. But Achilles appears with too much calmness and tranquillity at the sacrifice of Iphigenia, designed for him in marriage by Agamemnon; his grief has expressions too little suiting to the natural impetuosity of his heart. Clytemnestra much better preserves her character; she discovers all the passion of a mother in the loss of a daughter so lovely as was this unfortunate princess, whom they were about to sacrifice to appease the gods. And Agamemnon generously lays aside the tenderness of a father to take, as he ought, the sentiments of a king; he neglected his own interest to provide for the public. Seneca, so little natural as he is, omits not to have of these strokes that distinguish the passion, as that of Phaedra in the second act of his *Hippolytus*; for she affects a negligence of her person, and considered it as not very proper to please a hunter, who hated ornament and neatness. It is finally this exact distinction of the different degrees of passion that is of most effect in poetry. For this gives the draught of nature, and is the most infallible spring for moving the soul, but it is good to observe that the most ardent and lively passions become cold and dead if they be not well managed or be not in their place. The poet must judge when there must be a calm and when there must be trouble, for nothing is more ridiculous than passion out of season. But it is not enough to move a passion by a notable incident; there must be art to conduct it so far as it should go. For by a passion that is imperfect and abortive the soul of the spectator may be shaken, but this is not enough; it must be ravished.

XXXVII

Besides the graces that poetry finds in displaying the manners and the passions, there is a certain I know not what in the numbers, which is understood by few, and notwithstanding gives great delight in poetry. Homer hath excelled generally all the poets by this art, whether the nature of his language was favorable to him by the variety in the numbers and by the noble sound of the words, or that the delicacy of his ear made him perceive this grace, whereof the other poets of his time were not sensible; for his verse sound the most harmoniously that can be imagined. Athenaeus pretends that nothing is more proper to be sung than the verses of Homer, so natural is the harmony of them.[18] It is true I never read this poet or hear him read, but I feel what is found in a battle when the trumpets are heard. . . .

XXXIX

Besides all the rules taken from Aristotle, there remains one mentioned by Horace, to which all the other rules must be subject as to the most essential, which is the decorum, without which the other rules of poetry are false, it being the most solid foundation of that probability so essential to this art.[19] Because it is only by the decorum that this probability gains its effect; all becomes probable where the decorum is strictly preserved in all circumstances. One ordinarily transgresses this rule, either by confounding the serious with the pleasant, as Pulci has done in his poem of *Morgante*; or by giving manners disproportionate to the condition of the persons, as Guarini has done to his shepherds, which are too polite, in like manner as those of Ronsard are too gross; or because no regard is had to make the wonderful adventures probable, whereof Ariosto is guilty in his *Orlando*; or that a due preparation is not made for the great events by a natural conduct, in which Bernardo Tasso transgressed in his poem of *Amadis* and in his *Floridante*; or by want of care to sustain the characters of persons, as Théophile in his tragedy of *Pyramus and Thisbe*; or by following rather a capricious genius than nature, as Lope de Vega, who gives his wit too much swing, and is ever foisting in his own fancies on all occasions; or by want of modesty, as Dante, who invokes his own wit for his deity; and as Boccaccio, who is perpetually speaking of himself; or by saying everything indifferently without shame, as Cavalier Marino in his *Adone*. Finally, whatever is against the rules of time, of manners, of thoughts, of expression, is contrary to the decorum, which is the most universal of all the rules.

René Rapin REFLECTIONS ON ARISTOTLE'S TREATISE

OF POESY (Book II: In Particular)

II

The epic poem is that which is the greatest and most noble in poesy; it is the greatest work that human wit is capable of. All the nobleness and all the elevation of the most perfect genius can hardly suffice to form one such as is requisite for an heroic poet; the difficulty of finding together fancy and judgment, heat of imagination and sobriety of reason, precipitation of spirit and solidity of mind, causes the rareness of this character and of this happy temperament which makes a poet accomplished; it requires great images and yet a greater wit to form them. Finally, there must be a judgment so solid, a discernment so exquisite, such perfect knowledge of the language in which he writes, such obstinate study, profound meditation, vast capacity, that scarce whole ages can produce one genius fit for an epic poem. And it is an enterprise so bold that it cannot fall into a wise man's thoughts but affright him. Yet how many poets have we seen of late days who, without capacity and without study, have dared to undertake these sort of poems, having no other foundation for all but the only heat of their imagination and some briskness of spirit.

VII

The unity of the action, however simple and scrupulous it ought to be, is no enemy to those delights which naturally arise from variety when the variety is attended with that order and that proportion which makes uniformity, as one palace may contain the various ornaments of architecture and a great diversity of parts, provided it be built in the same order and after the same design. This variety hath a large field in heroic poesy; the enterprises of war, the treaties of peace, embassies, negotiations, voyages, councils, debates, building of palaces and towns, manners, passions, unexpected discoveries, unforeseen and surprising revolutions, and the different images of all that happens in the life of great men, may there be employed, so be that all go to the same end; without this order, the most beautiful figures become monstrous, and like those extravagances that Horace taxes as ridiculous in the beginning of his book *Of Poetry*.

X

The principal character of an heroic poem consists in the narration; it is in this that it is opposed to the dramatic, which consists altogether in the action. But as nothing is more difficult than to relate things as one ought, the poet must employ all his art to succeed herein. The qualities a narration must have to be perfect are these: it must be short and succinct, that nothing may be idle, flat, or tedious; it must be lively, quick, and delightful, that it may have nothing but what is attractive; finally, it must be simple and natural, but it is a great art to know how to relate things simply and yet the simplicity not appear. The most ordinary graces of a narration must come from the figures, the transitions, and from all those delicate turns that carry the reader from one thing to another without his regarding it; and in this chiefly consists all the artifice of the narration. It must never pour out all the matter, that some place may always be left for the natural reflections of the reader; it must likewise avoid the particulars and the length of affected description. Homer, great speaker as he is, amuses not himself, says Lucian, to discourse of the torments of the unhappy in Hell when Ulysses descended thither, though this was a fair occasion for him.[20] But the poet, when he is judicious, makes no descriptions but to clear the matters, and never to show his wit. Finally, the narration must be delightsome, not only by the variety of things it relates, but likewise by the variety of the numbers. It is this variety that makes the Greek versification more harmonious and more proper for narration than the Latin, and though Tasso has been successful enough in the narrations of his poem, and likewise Ariosto, who to me seems more natural than he, yet the pauses and interruptions to which the Italian poesy is subjected by the stanzas do weaken, methinks, and enervate that force and vigor which makes one part of the character of heroic verse. That monotony of the Alexandrine verse, which can suffer no difference nor any variety of numbers, seems to me likewise a great weakness in the French poetry. And though the vigor of the verse might be sustained either by the great subjects or by an extraordinary genius and wit above the common rate, yet this sort of verse will grow tedious and irksome in a long poem. For the rest, one shall scarce ever meet with narrations that are continued with the same force and the same spirit except in Homer and Virgil. It is true the narration of the death of Polyxena in the *Hecuba* of Euripides is the most lively and most moving in the world, and that of Tecmessa in the *Ajax* of Sophocles is the most tender and most passionate that can be imagined. It is by these great models that a poet must learn to be pathetical in what he relates without amusing himself to make subtle and witty narrations by ridiculous affectations. In the other Greek and Latin poets are found only some imperfect essays of narrations. He among the moderns who has the best genius to sustain all the nobleness of a narration in heroic verse is Hierom Vida, Bishop of Alba, in his poem on the death of Jesus Christ,[21] and if sometimes he fell not into low expressions and harshnesses like those of Lucretius, his style had been incomparable. Scaliger objects against the long narrations which Homer makes his heroes speak in the heat and fury of a battle; in effect this is neither natural nor probable. Neither can I approve the descriptions of Alcina's palace in Ariosto, nor of Armida's in Tasso, no more than the particulars of the pleasant things which both of them mix in their narrations; hereby they degenerate from their character, and show a kind of puerility that is in no wise conformable to the gravity of an heroic poem, where all ought to be majestic.

XIII

Finally, the sovereign perfection of an epic poem, in the opinion of Aristotle, consists in the just proportion of all the parts. The marvelous of tragedy consists in the pathetical style; but the marvelous of an heroic poem is that perfect connection, that just agreement and the admirable relation that the parts of this great work have each to other, as the perfection of a great palace consists in the uniformity of design and in the proportion of parts. It is this symmetry that Horace so much commends in the beginning of his book *Of Poetry*, where he taxes the ridiculousness of the extravagant disproportions in the picture he speaks of, and which he compares to the prodigious adventures of dolphins in the forests and wild boars in the sea, and all the other images he so much blames because disproportionable to the subject. And this proportion that Aristotle demands is not only in the quantity of the parts, but likewise in the quality. In which point Tasso is very faulty, who mixes in his poem the light character with the serious, and all the force and majesty of heroic with the softness and delicacy of the eclogue and lyric poesy. For the shepherd's adventures with Herminia in the seventh canto, and the letters of her lover's name which she carved on the bark of bays and beeches, the moan she made to the trees and rocks, the purling streams, the embroidered meadows, the singing of birds, in which the poet himself took so much pleasure, the enchanted wood in the thirteenth canto, the songs of Armida in the fourteenth to inspire Rinaldo with love, the caresses this sorceress made him, the description of her palace where nothing is breathed but softness and effeminacy, and those other affected descriptions have nothing of that grave and majestic character which is proper for heroic verse. It is thus that Sannazarius in his poem *De Partu Virginis* has injudiciously mingled the fables of paganism with the mysteries of Christian religion, as also Camoëns,[22] who speaks without discretion of Venus and Bacchus and the other profane deities in a Christian poem. It is not sufficient that all be grand and magnificent in an epic poem; all must be just, uniform, proportionable in the different parts that compose it.

XVII

Tragedy, of all parts of poesy, is that which Aristotle has most discussed, and where he appears most exact. He alleges that tragedy is a public lecture, without comparison more instructive than philosophy, because it teaches the mind by the sense, and rectifies the passions by the passions themselves in calming by their emotion the troubles they excite in the heart. The philosopher had observed two important faults in man to be regulated, pride and hardness of heart, and he found for both vices a cure in tragedy. For it makes man modest by representing the great masters of the earth humbled, and it makes him tender and merciful by showing him on the theatre the strange accidents of life and the unforeseen disgraces to which the most important persons are subject. But because man is naturally timorous and compassionate, he may fall into another extreme, to be either too fearful or too full of pity; the too much fear may shake the constancy of mind, and the too great compassion may enfeeble the equity. It is the business of tragedy to regulate these two weaknesses; it prepares and arms him against disgraces by showing them so frequent in the most considerable persons, and he shall cease to fear ordinary accidents when he sees such extraordinary happen to the highest part of mankind. But as the end of tragedy is to teach men not to fear too weakly the common misfortunes, and manage their fear, it makes account also to teach them to

René Rapin

spare their compassion for objects that deserve it. For there is an injustice in being moved at the afflictions of those who deserve to be miserable. One may see without pity Clytemnestra slain by her son Orestes in Aeschylus, because she had cut the throat of Agamemnon, her husband, and one cannot see Hippolytus die by the plot of his stepmother Phaedra in Euripides without compassion, because he died not but for being chaste and virtuous. This to me seems, in short, the design of tragedy according to the system of Aristotle, which to me appears admirable but which has not been explained as it ought by his interpreters; they have not, it may seem, sufficiently understood the mystery to unfold it well.

XVIII

But it is not enough that tragedy be furnished with all the most moving and terrible adventures that history can afford, to stir in the heart those motions it pretends, to the end it may cure the mind of those vain fears that may annoy it, and those childish compassions that may soften it. It is also necessary, says the philosopher, that every poet employ these great objects of terror and pity as the two most powerful springs in art to produce that pleasure which tragedy may yield. And this pleasure which is properly of the mind consists in the agitation of the soul moved by the passions. Tragedy cannot be delightful to the spectator unless he become sensible to all that is represented; he must enter into all the different thoughts of the actors, interest himself in their adventures, fear, hope, afflict himself, and rejoice with them. The theatre is dull and languid when it ceases to produce these motions in the soul of those that stand by. But as of all passions fear and pity are those that make the strongest impressions on the heart of man by the natural disposition he has of being afraid and of being mollified, Aristotle has chosen these amongst the rest, to move more powerfully the soul by the tender sentiments they cause when the heart admits and is pierced by them. In effect, when the soul is shaken by motions so natural and so humane, all the impressions it feels become delightful; its trouble pleases, and the emotion it finds is a kind of charm to it which does cast it into a sweet and profound meditation and which insensibly does engage it in all the interests that are managed on the theatre. It is then that the heart yields itself over to all the objects that are proposed, that all images strike it, that it espouses the sentiments of all those that speak, and becomes susceptible of all the passions that are presented because it is moved. And in this agitation consists all the pleasure that one is capable to receive from tragedy, for the spirit of man does please itself with the different situations caused by the different objects and the various passions that are represented.

XX

Modern tragedy turns on other principles; the genius of our (the French) nation is not strong enough to sustain an action on the theatre by moving only terror and pity. These are machines that will not play as they ought but by great thoughts and noble expressions, of which we are not indeed altogether so capable as the Greeks. Perhaps our nation, which is naturally gallant, has been obliged by the necessity of our character to frame for ourselves a new system of tragedy to suit with our humor. The Greeks, who were popular estates and who hated monarchy, took delight in their spectacles to see kings humbled and high fortunes cast down because the exaltation grieved them. The English, our neighbors, love blood in their sports by the quality of their temperament. These are *insulaires*, separated from the rest of men; we are more humane. Gallantry moreover agrees with our manners, and our poets believed that they could not succeed well on the theatre but by sweet and tender sentiments; in which, perhaps, they had some reason, for, in effect, the passions represented become deformed and insipid unless they are founded on sentiments conformable to those of the spectator. It is this that obliges our poets to stand up so strongly for the privilege of gallantry on the theatre, and to bend all their subjects to love and tenderness, the rather to please the women, who have made themselves judges of these divertissements and usurped the right to pass sentence. And some besides have suffered themselves to be prepossessed and led by the Spaniards, who make all their cavaliers amorous. It is by them that tragedy began to degenerate, [that we have slowly become accustomed to seeing] heroes on the theatre smitten with another love than that of glory, and that by degrees all the great men of antiquity have lost their characters in our hands. It is likewise perhaps by this gallantry that our age would devise a color to excuse the feebleness of our wit, not being able to sustain always the same action by the greatness of words and thoughts. However it be; for I am not hardy enough to declare myself against the public; it is to degrade tragedy from that majesty which is proper to it to mingle in it love, which is of a character always light, and little suitable to that gravity of which tragedy makes profession. Hence it proceeds that these tragedies mixed with gallantries never make such admirable impressions on the spirit as did those of Sophocles and Euripides, for all the bowels were moved by the great objects of terror and pity which they proposed. It is likewise for this that the reputation of our modern tragedies so soon decays, and yield but small delight at two years' end; whereas the Greek please yet to those that have a good taste, after two thousand years, because what is not grave and serious on the theatre, though it give delight at present, after a short time grows distasteful and unpleasant, and because what is not proper for great thoughts and great figures in tragedy cannot support itself. The ancients who perceived this did not interweave their gallantry and love save in comedy. For love is of a character that always degenerates from that heroic air of which tragedy must never divest itself. And nothing to me shows so mean and senseless as for one to amuse himself with whining about frivolous kindnesses when he may be admirable by great and noble thoughts and sublime expressions. But I dare not presume so far on my own capacity and credit to oppose myself of my own head against a usage so established. I must be content modestly to propose my doubts, and that may serve to exercise the wits in an age that only wants matter. But to end this reflection with a touch of Christianism, I am persuaded that the innocence of the theatre might be better preserved according to the idea of the ancient tragedy, because the new is become too effeminate by the softness of latter ages; and the Prince de Conti,[23] who signalized his zeal against the modern tragedy by his treatise on that subject, would, without doubt, have allowed the ancient, because that has nothing that may seem dangerous.

XXV

Comedy is an image of common life; its end is to show on the stage the faults of particulars in order to amend the faults of the public, and to correct the people through a fear of being rendered ridiculous. So that which is most proper to excite laughter is that which is most essential to comedy. One may be ridiculous in words or ridiculous in things. There is an honest laughter, and a buffoon laughter. It is merely a gift of nature to make everything ridiculous. For all the actions of human life have their fair and their wrong side, their serious and their ridiculous. But Aristotle, who gives precepts to make men weep, leaves none to make them laugh. This proceeds purely from the genius; art and method have little to do with it; it is the work of nature alone. The Spaniards have a genius to discern the ridiculous of things much better than the French, and the Italians, who are naturally comedians, express it better; their tongue is more proper for it by a drolling tone peculiar to them. The French may be capable of it when their language has attained its perfection. Finally, that pleasant turn, that gaiety which can sustain the delicacy of his character without falling into coldness nor into buffoonery, that fine raillery which is the flower of wit, is the talent which comedy demands. But it must always be observed that the true ridiculous of art, for the entertainment on the theatre, ought to be no other but the copy of the ridiculous that is found in nature. Comedy is as it should be when the spectator believes himself [to be in the midst of a group of neighbors or among members of a family instead of in a theatre, and when] he there sees nothing but what he sees in the world. . . .

XXVII

The eclogue is the most considerable of the little poems; it is an image of the life of shepherds. Therefore the matter is low, and nothing great is in the genius of it; its business is to describe the loves, the sports, the piques, the jealousies, the disputes, the quarrels, the intrigues, the passions, the adventures, and all the little affairs of shepherds. So that its character must be simple, the wit easy, the expression common; it must have nothing that is exquisite, neither in the thoughts, nor in the words, nor in any fashions of speech; in which the Italians, who have writ in this kind of verse, have been mistaken, for they always aim at being witty, and to say things too finely. The true character of the eclogue is simplicity and modesty. Its figures are sweet, the passions tender, the motions easy, and though sometimes it may be passionate and have little transports and little despairs, yet it never rises so high as to be fierce or violent; its narrations are short, descriptions little, the thoughts ingenious, the manners innocent, the language pure, the verse flowing, the expressions plain, and all the discourse natural, for this is not a great talker that loves to make a noise. . . .

XXX

The ode ought to have as much nobleness, elevation, and transport as the eclogue has of simplicity and modesty. It is not only the wit that heightens it, but likewise the matter. For its use is to sing the praises of the gods and to celebrate the illustrious actions of great men, so it requires to sustain all the majesty of its character an exalted nature, a great wit, a daring fancy, an expression noble and sparkling, yet pure and correct. All the briskness and life which art has by its figures is not sufficient to heighten the ode so far as its character requires. But the reading alone of Pindar is more capable to inspire this genius than all my reflections. . . .

XXXII

It remains to speak of the madrigal, the rondelay, the sonnet, the ballad, and all the other little verse that are the invention of these latter ages; but as a little fancy may suffice to be successful in these kind of works without any genius, I shall not amuse myself in making reflections on the method that is to be observed in composing them. Not but that he who has a genius would have a much different success, either by a more happy turn he gives to what he writes, or by a more lively air, or by more natural beauties, or finally, by more delicate fashions of speech; and generally, the genius makes the greatest distinction in whatsoever work a man undertakes. The character of the smaller verse and of all the little works of poesy requires that they be natural, together with a delicacy; for, seeing the little subjects afford no beauty of themselves, the wit of the poet must supply that want out of its own stock. . . .

XXXIV

Finally, to conclude with a touch of morality. Since the reputation of being modest is more worth than that of making verses, were I to make any, I would never forsake honesty nor modesty. For if nothing renders men more ridiculous than the kind opinion they conceive of themselves and of their performances, the poets are yet more ridiculous than other men when their vanity rises from the difficulty of succeeding well in their mystery. But if I made verse better than another, I would not force any man to find them good; I would not have a greater opinion of myself though all the world applauded them, nor should the success blind me. Amongst the praises that were bestowed on me, I could not persuade myself to suffer those where appeared ought of favor, and I would impose silence on them who, in commending me, spoke further than my conscience, to save myself from that ridiculousness which some vain spirits fall into who would have praises and admirations eternally for everything they do. I would employ all my reason and all my wit to gain more docility and more submission to the advice my friends should give me; I would borrow their lights to supply the weakness of mine; and I would listen to all the world, that I might not be ignorant of any of my faults. In the praises that I gave to those I found worthy, I would be so conscientious that for no interest whatsoever would I speak against my opinion, and there should never enter into anything that went from my hands any of those mercenary glances which so greatly debase the character of a poet. Lastly, I would rid myself of all the ridiculous vanities to which those who make verse are ordinarily obnoxious, and by this prudent conduct I would endeavor to destroy those fripperies which by custom are said of a profession that might continue honorable, were it only exercised by men of honorable principles.

René Le Bossu TREATISE OF THE EPICK POEM

Book I, Chapter 2

The fables of poets were originally employed in representing the Divine Nature according to the notion then conceived of it. This sublime subject occasioned the first poets to be called divines, and poetry the language of the gods. They divided the divine attributes into so many persons because the infirmity of a human mind cannot sufficiently conceive or explain so much power and action in a simplicity so great and indivisible as that of God. And, perhaps, they were also jealous of the advantages they reaped from such excellent and exalted learning, and of which they thought the vulgar part of mankind was not worthy.

They could not describe the operations of this almighty Cause without speaking at the same time of its effects; so that to divinity they added physiology, and treated of both without quitting the umbrages of their allegorical expressions.

But man being the chief and most noble of all that God produced, and nothing being so proper or more useful to poets than this subject, they added it to the former, and treated of the doctrine of morality after the same manner as they did that of divinity and philosophy; and from morality thus treated is formed that kind of poem and fable which we call epic.

The poets did the same in morality that the divines had done in divinity. But that infinite variety of the actions and operations of the Divine Nature (to which our understanding bears so small a proportion) did, as it were, force them upon dividing the single idea of the only one God into several persons, under the different names of Jupiter, Juno, Neptune, and the rest.

And on the other hand, the nature of moral philosophy being such as never to treat of things in particular but in general, the epic poets were obliged to unite in one single idea, in one and the same person and in an action which appeared singular, all that looked like it in different persons and in various actions which might be thus contained as so many species under their genus.

The presence of the Deity and the care such an august cause is to be supposed to take about any action obliges the poet to represent this action as great, important, and managed by kings and princes. It obliges him likewise to think and speak in an elevated way above the vulgar, and in a style that may in some sort keep up the character of the divine persons he introduces. To this end serve the poetical and figurative expression and the majesty of the heroic verse.

But all this, being divine and surprising, may quite ruin all probability; therefore the poet should take a peculiar care as to that point, since his chief aim is to instruct, and without probability any action is less likely to persuade.

Lastly, since precepts ought to be concise to be the more easily conceived and less oppress the memory, and since nothing can be more effectual to this end than proposing one single idea and collecting all things so well together as to be present to our minds all at once, therefore the poets have reduced all to one single action, under one and the same design, and in a body whose members and parts should be homogeneous.

Book I, Chapter 3

What we have observed of the nature of the epic poem gives us a just idea of it, and we may define it thus:

The epic poem is a discourse invented by art to form the manners by such instructions as are disguised under the allegories of some one important action, which is related in verse after a probable, diverting, and surprising manner.

Book I, Chapter 8

In every design which a man deliberately undertakes, the end he proposes is the first thing in his mind, and that by which he governs the whole work and all its parts; thus, since the end of the epic poem is to regulate the manners, it is with this first view the poet ought to begin.

But there is a great difference between the philosophical and the poetical doctrine of manners. The schoolmen content themselves with treating of virtues and vices in general; the instructions they give are proper for all states of people and for all ages. But the poet has a nearer regard to his own country and the necessities of his own nation. With this design he makes choice of some piece of morality, the most proper and just he can imagine; and in order to press this home, he makes less use of the force of reasoning than of the power of insinuation, accommodating himself to the particular customs and inclinations of those who are to be the subject, or the readers, of his work.

Let us now see how Homer has acquitted himself in all these respects.

He saw the Grecians, for whom he designed his poem, were divided into as many states as they had capital cities. Each was a body politic apart, and had its form of government independent from all the rest. And yet these distinct states were very often obliged to unite together in one body against their common enemies. These were two very different sorts of government, such as could not be comprehended in one maxim or morality and in one single poem.

The poet, therefore, has made two distinct fables of them. The one is for Greece in general, united into one body but composed of parts independent on each other, and the other for each particular state considered as they were in time of peace, without the former circumstances and the necessity of being united.

As for the first sort of government, in the union or rather in the confederacy of many independent states experience has always made it appear that nothing so much causes success as a due subordination and a right understanding among the chief commanders. And on the other hand, the inevitable ruin of such confederacies proceeds from the heats, jealousies, and ambition of the different leaders and the discontents of submitting to a single general. All sort of states, and in particular the Grecians, had dearly experienced this truth. So that the most useful and necessary instructions that could be given them was to lay before their eyes the loss which both the people and the princes must of necessity suffer by the ambition, discord, and obstinacy of the latter.

Homer then has taken for the foundation of his fable this great truth, that a misunderstanding between princes is the ruin of their own states. "I sing," says he, "the anger of Achilles, so pernicious to the Grecians, and the cause of many heroes' deaths, occasioned by the discord and separation of Agamemnon and that prince."

But that this truth may be completely and fully known, there is need of a second to support it. It is necessary in such a design not only to represent the confederate states at first disagreeing among themselves and from thence unfortunate, but to show the same states afterwards reconciled and united and of consequence victorious.

Let us now see how he has joined all these in one general action.

Several princes independent of one another were united against a common enemy. The person whom they had elected their general offers an affront to the most valiant of all the confederates. This offended prince is so far provoked as to relinquish the union and obstinately refuse to fight for the common cause. This misunderstanding gives the enemy such an advantage that the allies are very near quitting their design with dishonor. He himself who made the separation is not exempt from sharing the misfortune which he brought upon his party. For having permitted his intimate friend to succor them in a great necessity, this friend is killed by the enemy's general. Thus the contending princes, being both made wiser at their own cost, are reconciled and unite again; then this valiant prince not only obtains the victory in the public cause, but revenges his private wrongs by killing with his own hands the author of the death of his friend.

This is the first platform of the poem, and the fiction which reduces into one important and universal action all the particulars upon which it turns.

In the next place it must be rendered probable by the circumstances of times, places, and persons. Some persons must be found out, already known by history or otherwise, whom we may with probability make the actors and personages of this fable. Homer has made choice of the siege of Troy, and feigned that this action happened there. To a phantom of his brain, whom he would paint valiant and choleric, he has given the name of Achilles; that of Agamemnon, to his general; that of Hector, to the enemy's commander; and so, to the rest.

Besides, he was obliged to accommodate himself to the manners, customs, and genius of the Greeks his auditors, the better to make them attend to the instruction of his poem, and to gain their approbation by praising them so that they might the better forgive him the representation of their own faults in some of his chief personages. He admirably discharges all these duties by making these brave princes and those victorious people all Grecians and the fathers of those he had a mind to commend.

But not being content, in a work of such a length, to propose only the principal point of the moral, and to fill up the rest with useless ornaments and foreign incidents, he extends this moral by all its necessary consequences. As for instance in the subject before us it is not enough to know that a good understanding ought always to be maintained among confederates, it is likewise of equal importance that, if there happens any division, care must be taken to keep it secret from the enemy, that their ignorance of this advantage may prevent their making use of it. And in the second place, when their concord is but counterfeit and only in appearance, one should never press the enemy too closely, for this would discover the weakness which we ought to conceal from them.

The episode of Patroclus most admirably furnishes us with these two instructions. For when he appeared in the arms of Achilles, the Trojans, who took him for that prince now reconciled and united to the confederates, immediately gave ground, and quitted the advantages they had before over the Greeks. But Patroclus, who should have been contented with this success, presses upon Hector too boldly, and, by obliging him to fight, soon discovers that it was not the true Achilles who was clad in his armor, but a hero of much inferior prowess. So that Hector kills him and regains those advantages which the Trojans had lost on the opinion that Achilles was reconciled.

Book I, Chapter 10

The *Odyssey* was not designed, like the *Iliad*, for the instruction of all the states of Greece joined in one body, but for each state in particular. As a state is composed of two parts, the head which commands and the members which obey, there are instructions requisite for both, to teach the one to govern and the others to submit to government.

There are two virtues necessary to one in authority: prudence to order, and care to see his orders put in execution. The prudence of a politician is not acquired but by a long experience in all sorts of business, and by an acquaintance with all the different forms of governments and states. The care of the administration suffers not him that has the government to rely upon others, but requires his own presence, and kings who are absent from their states are in danger of losing them, and give occasion to great disorders and confusion.

These two points may be easily united in one and the same man. A king forsakes his kingdom to visit the courts of several princes, where he learns the manners and customs of different nations. From hence there naturally arises a vast number of incidents, of dangers, and of adventures, very useful for a political institution. On the other side, this absence gives way to the disorders which happen in his own kingdom, and which end not till his return, whose presence only can re-establish all things. Thus the absence of a king has the same effects in this fable as the division of the princes had in the former.

The subjects have scarce any need but of one general maxim, which is to suffer themselves to be governed and to obey faithfully, whatever reason they may imagine against the orders they receive. It is easy to join this instruction with the other by bestowing on this wise and industrious prince such subjects as in his absence would rather follow their own judgment than his commands, and by demonstrating the misfortunes which this disobedience draws upon them, the evil consequences which almost infallibly attend these particular notions, which are entirely different from the general idea of him who ought to govern.

But as it was necessary that the princes in the *Iliad* should be choleric and quarrelsome, so it is necessary in the fable of the *Odyssey* that the chief person should be sage and prudent. This raises a difficulty in the fiction, because this person ought to be absent for the two reasons aforementioned, which are essential to the fable and which constitute the principal aim of it; but he cannot absent himself without offending against another maxim of equal importance, viz., that a king should upon no account leave his country.

It is true there are sometimes such necessities as sufficiently excuse the prudence of a politician in this point. But such a necessity is a thing important enough of itself to supply matter for another poem, and this multiplication of the action would be vicious. To prevent which, in the first place, this necessity and the departure of the hero must be disjoined from the poem; and in the second place, the hero having been obliged to absent himself for a reason antecedent to the action and placed distinct from the fable, he ought not so far to embrace this opportunity of instructing himself as to absent himself voluntarily from his own government. For at this rate, his absence would be merely voluntary, and one might with reason lay to his charge all the disorders which might arise.

Thus in the constitution of the fable he ought not to take for his action and for the foundation of his poem the departure of a prince from his own country nor his voluntary stay in any other place, but his return, and this return retarded against his will. This is the first idea Homer gives us of it. His hero appears at first in a desolate island, sitting upon the side of the sea, which, with tears in his eyes, he looks upon as the obstacle which had so long opposed his return and detained him from revisiting his own dear country.

And lastly, since this forced delay might more naturally and usually happen to such as make voyages by sea, Homer has judiciously made choice of a prince whose kingdom was in an island.

Let us see then how he has feigned all this action, making his hero a person in years, because years are requisite to instruct a man in prudence and policy.

A prince had been obliged to forsake his native country and to head an army of his subjects in a foreign expedition. Having gloriously performed this enterprise, he was marching home again, and conducting his subjects to his own state. But spite of all the attempts with which his eagerness to return had inspired him, he was stopped by the way by tempests for several years, and cast upon several countries differing from each other in manners and government. In these dangers his companions, not always following his orders, perished through their own fault. The grandees of his country strangely abuse his absence, and raise no small disorders at home. They consume his estate, conspire to destroy his son, would constrain his queen to accept of one of them for her husband, and indulge themselves in all violence, so much the more because they were persuaded he would never return. But at last he returns, and discovering himself only to his son and some others who had continued firm to him, he is an eye-witness of the insolence of his enemies, punishes them according to their deserts, and restores to his island that tranquillity and repose to which they had been strangers during his absence.

As the truth which serves for foundation to this fiction is that the absence of a person from his own home or his neglect of his own affairs is the cause of great disorders, so the principal point of the action, and the most essential one, is the absence of the hero. This fills almost all the poem. For not only this real absence lasted several years, but even when the hero returned he does not discover himself; and this prudent disguise, from whence he reaped so much advantage, has the same effect upon the authors of the disorders, and all others who knew him not, as his real absence had before, so that he is absent as to them till the very moment of their punishment.

After the poet had thus composed his fable and joined the fiction to the truth, he then makes choice of Ulysses, the king of the isle of Ithaca, to maintain the character of his chief personage, and bestowed the rest upon Telemachus, Penelope, Antinous, and others, whom he calls by what names he pleases.

I shall not here insist upon the many excellent advices which are so many parts and natural consequences of the fundamental truth, and which the poet very dexterously lays down in those fictions which are the episodes and members of the entire action. Such for instance are these advices: not to intrude oneself into the mysteries of government which the prince keeps secret; (this is represented to us by the winds shut up in a bullhide, which the miserable companions of Ulysses would needs be so foolish as to pry into); not to suffer oneself to be led away by the seeming charms of an idle and inactive life, to which the Sirens' song invited; not to suffer oneself to be sensualized by pleasures, like those who were changed into brutes by Circe; and a great many other points of morality necessary for all sorts of people.

This poem is more useful to the people than the *Iliad*, where the subjects suffer rather by the ill conduct of their princes than through their own miscarriages. But in the *Odyssey* it is not the fault of Ulysses that is the ruin of his subjects. This wise prince leaves untried no method to make them partakers of the benefit of his return. Thus the poet in the *Iliad* says he sings the anger of Achilles, which had caused the death of so many Grecians, and, on the contrary, in the *Odyssey* he tells his readers that the subjects perished through their own fault.

Book I, Chapter 16

Aristotle bestows great encomiums on Homer for the simplicity of his design because he has included in one single part all that happened at the siege of Troy. And to this he opposes the ignorance of some poets who imagined that the unity of the fable or action was sufficiently preserved by the unity of the hero, and who composed their Theseids, Heraclids, and the like, wherein they only heaped up in one poem everything that happened to one personage.

Book I, Chapter 17

He finds fault with those poets who were for reducing the unity of the fable into the unity of the hero, because one man may have performed several adventures which it is impossible to reduce under any one [general and] simple head. This reducing of all things to unity and simplicity is what Horace likewise makes his first rule.

Denique sit quod vis simplex dumtaxat, et unum [1]

314

According to these rules, it will be allowable to make use of several fables, or (to speak more correctly) of several incidents, which may be divided into several fables provided they are so ordered that the unity of the fable be not spoiled. This liberty is still greater in the epic poem, because it is of a larger extent and ought to be entire and complete.

I will explain myself more distinctly by the practice of Homer.

No doubt but one might make four distinct fables out of these four following instructions.

I. Division between those of the same party exposes them entirely to their enemies.

II. Conceal your weakness, and you will be dreaded as much as if you had none of those imperfections of which they are ignorant.

III. When your strength is only feigned and founded only in the opinion of others, never venture so far as if your strength was real.

IV. The more you agree together, the less hurt can your enemies do you.

It is plain, I say, that each of these particular maxims might serve for the groundwork of a fiction, and one might make four distinct fables out of them. May one not, then, put all these into one single epopea? Not unless one single fable can be made out of all. The poet indeed may have so much skill as to unite all into one body as members and parts, each of which taken asunder would be imperfect; and if he joins them so, as that this conjunction shall be no hindrance at all to the unity and regular simplicity of the fable. This is what Homer has done with such success in the composition of the *Iliad*.

1. The division between Achilles and his allies tended to the ruin of their designs. 2. Patroclus comes to their relief in the armor of this hero, and Hector retreats. 3. But this young man, pushing the advantage which his disguise gave him too far, ventures to engage with Hector himself; but not being master of Achilles's strength (whom he only represented in outward appearance) he is killed, and by this means leaves the Grecian affairs in the same disorder from which, in that disguise, he came to free them. 4. Achilles, provoked at the death of his friend, is reconciled, and revenges his loss by the death of Hector. These various incidents being thus united do not make different actions and fables, but are only the uncomplete and unfinished parts of one and the same action and fable, which alone, when taken thus complexly, can be said to be complete and entire;

and all these maxims of the moral are easily reduced into these two parts, which, in my opinion, cannot be separated without enervating the force of both. The two parts are these, that a right understanding is the preservation, and discord the destruction, of states.

Though then the poet has made use of two parts in his poems, each of which might have served for a fable, as we have observed, yet this multiplication cannot be called a vicious and irregular polymythia, contrary to the necessary unity and simplicity of the fable; but it gives the fable another qualification altogether necessary and regular, namely, its perfection and finishing stroke.

Book II, Chapter 1

The action of a poem is the subject which the poet undertakes, proposes, and builds upon. So that the moral and the instructions, which are the end of the epic poem, are not the matter of it. Those the poets leave in their allegorical and figurative obscurity. They only give notice at the exordium that they sing some action: the revenge of Achilles, the return of Ulysses, etc.

Since then the action is the matter of a fable, it is evident that whatever incidents are essential to the fable or constitute a part of it are necessary also to the action and are parts of the epic matter, none of which ought to be omitted. Such, for instance, are the contention of Agamemnon and Achilles, the slaughter Hector makes in the Grecian army, the reunion of the Greek princes, and lastly, the resettlement and victory which was the consequence of that reunion.

Book II, Chapter 7

There are four qualifications in the epic action: the first is its unity, the second its integrity, the third its importance, the fourth its duration.

The unity of the epic action, as well as the unity of the fable, does not consist either in the unity of the hero or in the unity of time; three things, I suppose, are necessary to it. The first is to make use of no episode but what arises from the very platform and foundation of the action, and is as it were a natural member of the body. The second is exactly to unite these episodes and these members with one another. And the third is never to finish any episode so as it may seem to be an entire action, but to let each episode still appear in its own particular nature as the member of a body and as a part of itself not complete.

Book II, Chapter 9

Aristotle not only says that the epic action should be one, but adds that it should be entire, perfect, and complete, and for this purpose ought to have a beginning, a middle, and an end. These three parts of a whole are too generally and universally denoted by the words *beginning, middle* and *end*; we may interpret them more precisely and say that the causes and designs of an action are the beginning, that the effects of these causes and the difficulties that are met with in the execution of these designs are the middle, and that the unraveling and resolution of these difficulties are the end.

Book II, Chapter 11

Homer's design in the *Iliad* is to relate the anger and revenge of Achilles. The beginning of this action is the change of Achilles from a calm to a passionate temper. The middle is the effects of his passion, and all the illustrious deaths it is the cause of. The end of the same action is the return of Achilles to his calmness of temper again. All was quiet in the Grecian camp, when Agamemnon, their general, provokes Apollo against them, whom he was willing to appease afterwards at the cost and prejudice of Achilles, who had no part in his fault. This then is an exact beginning; it supposes nothing before, and requires after it the effects of this anger. Achilles revenges himself, and that is an exact middle: it supposes before it the anger of Achilles; this revenge is the effect of it. Then this middle requires after it the effects of this revenge, which is the satisfaction of Achilles; for the revenge had not been complete unless Achilles had been satisfied. By this means the poet makes his hero, after he was glutted by the mischief he had done to Agamemnon, by the death of Hector, and the honor he did his friend by insulting over his murderer; he makes him, I say, to be moved by the tears and misfortunes of King Priam. We see him as calm at the end of the poem, during the funeral of Hector, as he was at the beginning of the poem, whilst the plague raged among the Grecians. This end is just, since the calmness of temper Achilles re-enjoyed is only an effect of the revenge which ought to have preceded; and after this nobody expects any more of his anger. Thus has Homer been very exact in the beginning, middle and end of the action he made choice of for the subject of his *Iliad*.

His design in the *Odyssey* was to describe the return of Ulysses from the siege of Troy and his arrival at Ithaca. He opens this poem with the complaints of Minerva against Neptune, who opposed the return of this hero, and against Calypso, who detained him in an island from Ithaca. Is this a beginning? No; doubtless the reader would know why Neptune is displeased with Ulysses, and how this prince came to be with Calypso. He would know how he came from Troy thither. The poet answers his demands out of the mouth of Ulysses himself, who relates these things and begins the action by the recital of his travels from the city of Troy. It signifies little whether the beginning of the action be the beginning of the poem. The beginning of this action is that which happens to Ulysses when, upon his leaving Troy, he bends his course for Ithaca. The middle comprehends all the misfortunes he endured and all the disorders of his own government. The end is the reinstating of this hero in the peaceable possession of his kingdom, where he was acknowledged by his son, his wife, his father, and several others. The poet was sensible he should have ended ill had he gone no farther than the death of these princes who were the rivals and enemies of Ulysses, because the reader might have looked for some revenge which the subjects of these princes might have taken on him who had killed their sovereign; but this danger over, and the people vanquished and quieted, there was nothing more to be expected. The poem and the action have all their parts and no more.

Book II, Chapter 12

But the order of the *Odyssey* differs from that of the *Iliad* in that the poem does not begin with the beginning of the action.

The causes of the action are also what the poet is obliged to give an account of. There are three sorts of causes: the humors, the interests, and the designs of men; and these different causes of an action are likewise often the causes of one another, every man taking up those interests in which his humor engages him and forming those designs to which his humor and interest incline him. Of all these the poet ought to inform his readers, and render them conspicuous in his principal personages.

Homer has ingeniously begun his *Odyssey* with the transactions at Ithaca during the absence of Ulysses. If he had begun with the travels of his hero, he would scarce have spoken of anyone else, and a man might have read a great deal of the poem without conceiving the least idea of Telemachus, Penelope, or her suitors, who had so great a share in the action; but in the beginning he has pitched upon, besides these personages whom he discovers, he represents Ulysses in his full length, and from the very first opening one sees the interest which the gods take in the action.

The skill and care of the same poet may be seen likewise in inducing his personages in the first book of his *Iliad*, where he discovers the humors, the interests, and the designs of Agamemnon, Achilles, Hector, Ulysses, and several others, and even of the deities. And in his second he makes a review of the Grecian and Trojan armies, which is full evidence that all we have here said is very necessary.

Book II, Chapter 13

As these causes are the beginning of the action, the opposite designs against that of the hero are the middle of it, and form that difficulty or intrigue which makes up the greatest part of the poem; the solution or unraveling commences when the reader begins to see that difficulty removed and the doubts cleared up. Homer has divided each of his poems into two parts, and has put a particular intrigue and the solution of it into each part.

The first part of the *Iliad* is the anger of Achilles, who is for revenging himself upon Agamemnon by the means of Hector and the Trojans. The intrigue comprehends the three days' fight which happened in the absence of Achilles, and it consists on one side in the resistance of Agamemnon and the Grecians and on the other in the revengeful and inexorable humor of Achilles, which would not suffer him to be reconciled. The loss of the Grecians and the despair of Agamemnon prepare for a solution by the satisfaction which the incensed hero received from it. The death of Patroclus, joined to the offers of Agamemnon, which of itself had proved ineffectual, remove this difficulty, and make the unraveling of the first part.

This death is likewise the beginning of the second part, since it puts Achilles upon the design of revenging himself on Hector. But the design of Hector is opposite to that of Achilles; this Trojan is valiant, and resolved to stand on his own defense. This valor and resolution of Hector are on his part the cause of the intrigue. All the endeavors Achilles used to meet with Hector and be the death of him, and the contrary endeavors of the Trojan to keep out of his reach and defend himself, are the intrigue, which comprehends the battle of the last day. The unraveling begins at the death of Hector; and besides that, it contains the insulting of Achilles over his body, the honors he paid to Patroclus, and the entreaties of King Priam. The regrets of this king and the other Trojans in the sorrowful obsequies they paid to Hector's body end the unraveling; they justify the satisfaction of Achilles, and demonstrate his tranquillity.

The first part of the *Odyssey* is the return of Ulysses into Ithaca. Neptune opposes it by raising tempests, and this makes the intrigue. The unraveling is the arrival of Ulysses upon his own island, where Neptune could offer him no farther injury. The second part is the reinstating this hero in his own government. The princes that are his rivals oppose him, and this is a fresh intrigue; the solution of it begins at their deaths, and is completed as soon as the Ithacans were appeased.

These two parts in the *Odyssey* have not one common intrigue. The anger of Achilles forms both the intrigues in the *Iliad*, and it is so far the matter of this epopea that the very beginning and end of this poem depend on the beginning and end of this anger. But let the desire Achilles had to revenge himself and the desire Ulysses had to return to his own country be never so near allied, yet we cannot place them under one and the same notion; for that desire of Ulysses is not a passion that begins and ends in the poem with the action: it is a natural habit; nor does the poet propose it for his subject as he does the anger of Achilles. . . .

Book II, Chapter 14

We have already observed what is meant by the intrigue and the unraveling thereof; let us now say something of the manner of forming both. These two should arise naturally out of the very essence and subject of the poem, and are to be deduced from thence. Their conduct is so exact and natural that it seems as if their action had presented them with whatever they inserted without putting themselves to the trouble of a farther inquiry.

What is more usual and natural to warriors than anger, heat, passion, and impatience of bearing the least affront or disrespect? This is what forms the intrigue of the *Iliad*, and everything we read there is nothing else but the effect of this humor and these passions.

What more natural and usual obstacle to those who take voyages than the sea, the winds, and the storms? Homer makes this the intrigue of the first part of the *Odyssey*, and for the second he makes use of almost the infallible effect of the long absence of a master whose return is quite despaired of, viz., the insolence of his servants and neighbors, the danger of his son and wife, and the sequestration of his estate. Besides, an absence of almost twenty years, and the insupportable fatigues joined to the age of which Ulysses then was, might induce him to believe that he should not be owned by those who thought him dead and whose interest it was to have him really so. Therefore if he had presently declared who he was and had called himself Ulysses, they would easily have destroyed him as an impostor before he had an opportunity to make himself known.

There could be nothing more natural nor more necessary than this ingenious disguise, to which the advantages his enemies had taken of his absence had reduced him, and to which his long misfortunes had inured him. This allowed him an opportunity, without hazarding anything, of taking the best measures he could against those persons who could not so much as mistrust any harm from him. This way was afforded him by the very nature of his action to execute his designs and overcome the obstacles it cast before him. And it is this contest between the prudence and the dissimulation of a single man on one hand and the ungovernable insolence of so many rivals on the other which constitutes the intrigue of the second part of the *Odyssey*.

Book II, Chapter 15

If the plot or intrigue must be natural and such as springs from the very subject, as has been already urged, then the winding up of the plot by a more sure claim must have this qualification and be a probable consequence of all that went before. As this is what the readers regard more than the rest, so should the poet be more exact in it. This is the end of the poem and the last impression that is to be stamped upon them.

We shall find this in the *Odyssey*. Ulysses by a tempest is cast upon the island of the Phaeacians, to whom he discovers himself and desires they would favor his return to his own country, which was not very far distant. One cannot see any reason why the king of this island should refuse such a reasonable request to a hero whom he seemed to have in great esteem. The Phaeacians, indeed, had heard him tell the story of his adventures, and in this fabulous recital consisted all the advantage they could derive from his presence; for the art of war which they admired in him, his undauntedness under dangers, his indefatigable patience and other virtues, were such as these islanders were not used to. All their talent lay in singing and dancing and whatsoever was charming in a quiet life. And here we see how dexterously Homer prepares the incidents he makes use of. These people could do no less for the account with which Ulysses had so much entertained them than afford him a ship and a safe convoy, which was of little expense or trouble to them.

When he arrived, his long absence and the travels which had disfigured him made him altogether unknown, and the danger he would have incurred had he discovered himself too soon forced him to a disguise. Lastly, this disguise gave him an opportunity of surprising those young suitors, who for several years together had been accustomed to nothing but to sleep well and fare daintily.

It was from these examples that Aristotle drew this rule, that whatever concludes the poem should so spring from the very constitution of the fable as if it were a necessary or at least a probable consequence.

Book II, Chapter 18

The time of the epic action is not fixed like that of the dramatic poem; it is much longer, for an uninterrupted duration is much more necessary in an action which one sees and is present at than in one which we only read or hear repeated. Besides, tragedy is fuller of passion, and consequently of such a violence as cannot admit of so long a duration.

The *Iliad* containing an action of anger and violence, the poet allows it but a short time, about forty days. The design of the *Odyssey* required another conduct: the character of the hero is prudence and long-suffering; therefore the time of its duration is much longer, above eight years.

Book III, Chapter 9

The passions of tragedy are different from those of the epic poem. In the former, terror and pity have the chief place; the passion that seems most peculiar to epic poetry is admiration.

Besides this admiration, which in general distinguishes the epic poem from the dramatic, each epic poem has likewise some peculiar passion which distinguishes it in particular from other epic poems, and constitutes a kind of singular and individual difference between these poems of the same species. These singular passions correspond to the character of the hero. Anger and terror reign throughout the *Iliad* because Achilles is angry and the most terrible of all men. The *Aeneid* has all soft and tender passions, because that is the character of Aeneas. The prudence, wisdom, and constancy of Ulysses do not allow him either of these extremes; therefore the poet does not permit one of them to be predominant in the *Odyssey*. He confines himself to admiration only, which he carries to an higher pitch than in the *Iliad*, and it is upon this account that he introduces a great many more machines in the *Odyssey* into the body of the action than are to be seen in the actions of the other two poems.

Jean de La Bruyère OF POLITE LEARNING FROM

"CHARACTERS"

We are come too late, after above seven thousand years that there have been men, and men have thought, to say anything which has not been said already. The finest and most beautiful thoughts concerning manners are carried away before us, and we can do nothing now but glean after the ancients and the most ingenious of the moderns.

We must only endeavor to think and speak justly ourselves, without aiming to bring others over to our taste and sentiments. We shall find that too great an enterprise.

To make a book is like making a pendulum: a man must have experience as well as wit to succeed in it. A certain magistrate arriving by his merit to the first dignities of the gown thought himself qualified for everything; he printed a treatise of morality and published himself a coxcomb.

It is not so easy to raise a reputation by a complete work as to make an indifferent one valued by a reputation already acquired.

A satire or a libel when it is handed privately from one to another with strict charge of secrecy, if it is but mean in itself, passes for wonderful; the printing it would ruin its reputation.

Take away from most of our moral essays the advertisement to the reader, the epistle dedicatory, the preface, the table, and the commendatory verses, there will seldom be enough left to deserve the name of a book.

Several things are insupportable if they are but indifferent, as poetry, music, painting, and public speeches.

It is the worst punishment in the world to hear a dull declamation delivered with pomp and solemnity, and bad verses rehearsed with the emphasis of a wretched poet.

Some poets in their dramatic pieces are fond of big words and sounding verses, which seem strong, elevated, and sublime. The people stare, gape, and hear them greedily; they are transported at what they fancy is rare, and where they understand least are sure to admire most; they scarce allow themselves time to breathe, and are loath to be interrupted by claps or applauses. When I was young I imagined these places were clear and intelligible to the actors, the pit, boxes, and galleries; that the authors understood them, and that I was in the wrong to know nothing of the matter after much attention. But I am now undeceived.

There never was seen any piece excellent in its kind that was the joint labor of several men; Homer writ his *Iliad*, Virgil his *Aeneid*, Livy his *Decades*, and Cicero his *Orations*.

As there is in nature, so there is in art a point of perfection. He who is sensible of it and is touched with it has a good taste; he who is not sensible of it, but is wavering, has a vicious taste. Since, then, there is a good and a bad taste, we may with reason dispute the difference.

Everyone has more fire than judgment, or rather there are few men of wit who are good critics.

The lives of heroes have enriched history, and history has adorned the actions of heroes; and thus it is difficult to tell who are most indebted, the historians to those who furnished them with such noble materials or the great men to their historians.

It is a sorry commendation that is made up of a heap of epithets; it is actions and the manner of relating them which speak a man's praise.

The chief art of an author consists in making good definitions, good pictures. Moses, Homer, Plato, Virgil, and Horace excel other writers mostly in their expressions and images. Truth is the best guide to make a man write forcibly, naturally, and delicately.

We should do by style as we have done by architecture, banish entirely the Gothic order, which the barbarians introduced in their palaces and temples, and recall the Doric, Ionic, and Corinthian. Let what we see in the ruins of ancient Rome and old Greece shine in our porticoes and peristyles, and become modern, since we cannot arrive to perfection, or, if possible, surpass the ancients in building or writing but by imitating them.

How many ages were lost in ignorance before men could come back to the taste of the ancients in the arts and sciences, or recover at last the simple and the natural.

We nourish ourselves by the ancients and ingenious moderns; we draw from them as much as we can, and, at their expense, in the end become authors. Then we quickly think we can walk alone and without help; we oppose our benefactors and treat them like those children who, grown pert and strong with the milk they have sucked, turn themselves against their nurses.

It is the practice of a modern wit to prove the ancients inferior to us by two ways, reason and example. He takes the reason from his particular opinion and the example from his writings.

He confesses the ancients, as unequal and incorrect as they are, have a great many good lines; he cites them, and they appear so fine that they ruin his criticisms.

Some learned men declare in favor of the ancients against the moderns. But we are afraid they judge in their own cause, and so many of their works are made after the model of antiquity that we except against their authority.

An author should be fond of reading his works to those who know how to correct and esteem them.

He that will not be corrected nor advised in his writings is a pedant.

An author ought to receive with equal modesty the praises and the criticisms which are passed on his productions.

Amongst all the different expressions which can render any one of our thoughts, there is but one good. We are not always so fortunate as to hit upon it in writing or speaking; however, it is true that it exists, that all the rest are weak and will not satisfy a man of sense who would make himself understood.

A good author who writes with care, when he meets with the expression he has searched after for some time without knowing it, finds it at last the most simple and the most natural, and fancies it ought to have presented itself to him at first without search or inquiry.

Those who write by humor are frequently subject to revise their works and give them new touches. And as their humors are never fixed, but vary on every slight occasion, they quickly spoil their writings by new expressions and terms which they like better than the former.

The same true sense which makes an author write a great many good things tells him that there are not enough to deserve reading.

A man of little sense is ravished with himself, and thinks his writings divine; a man of good sense is harder to be pleased, and would only be reasonable.

One, says Aristus, engaged me to read my book to Zoilus. I read it; he was satisfied, and before he had leisure to dislike it, he commended it coldly in my presence. Since that, he takes no notice on it, nor says a word in its favor. However, I excuse him; I desire no more of an author, and even pity him the hearing so many fine things which were not his own making.

Such as by their circumstances are free from the jealousies of an author have other cares and passions to distract them and make them cold towards another man's conceptions. It is difficult to find a person whose fortune and good humor put him in a condition to taste all the pleasure a complete piece can give him.

The pleasure of criticizing takes away the pleasure of being sensibly charmed with very fine productions.

Many men who perceive the beauties of a manuscript when they hear it read will not declare themselves in its favor till they see what success it has in the world when it is printed, and what character the ingenious give it. They will not hazard their votes before its fortune is made, and they are carried away with the crowd or engaged by the multitude. Then they are very forward to publish how early they were in their approbation, and how glad they are to find the world is of their opinion.

These men lose a fair opportunity to convince us that they are persons of capacity and insight, that they make a true judgment, and distinguish an excellent thing from one that is good. A fine piece falls into their hands, the author's first work, before he has got a name, or they are yet prepossessed in his behalf; he has not endeavored to make his court to the great men by flattering their writings; neither is it required that they should proclaim to please some man of quality or topping wit who has declared himself in its favor, "This is a masterpiece. Human wit never went so far. We will judge of nobody's opinion but in proportion to what thoughts he has of this book." Extravagant and offensive expressions, which smell of the pension or the abbey, [1] and are injurious to what is really commendable. Why did they not profess it by themselves? When they might have been alone in their praises, why did they not then commend it? It is true, at last they cry aloud, "It is an admirable book," when the whole kingdom has approved it; when foreigners as well as their own countrymen are fond of it; when it is printed all over Europe, translated into all languages; in short, when it is too late, and the author is not obliged to them for their applauses.

Some of them read a book, collect certain lines which they do not understand, and rob them of their value by what they put in of their own. Yet these lines, so broken and disguised that they are indeed their proper style and thoughts, they expose to censure, maintain them to be bad, and as they cite them the world readily agrees with them. But the passage they pretend to quote is never the worse for their injustice.

"Well," says one, "what's your opinion of Hermedorus's book?" "That it is bad," replies Anthimus. "That it is bad? What d'ye mean, sir?" "That it is bad," continues he; "at least it deserves not the character people give it." "Have you read it?" "No," says Anthimus, "but Fulvia and Melania have condemned it without reading, and I am a friend to Fulvia and Melania."

Arsenes from the altitudes of his understanding contemplates mankind, and at the distance from whence he beholds them seems affrighted at their littleness. He is commended, exalted, and mounted to the skies by certain persons who have reciprocally covenanted to admire one another. Contented with his own merit, he fancies he has as much wit as he wants, and more than he ever will have. Thus employed by his high thoughts, and full of sublime ideas, he scarcely finds time to pronounce the sacred oracles. He is elevated by his character above human judgments, and leaves it for common souls to value a common and uniform life, being answerable for his inconstancy to none but his particular friends who have resolved to idolize him. For this reason, they only know how to judge or think; they only know how to write, and it is only in them a duty. As for other pieces, however received in the world or universally liked by men of honor and worth, he is so far from approving them that he never condescends to read them, and is incapable of being corrected by this picture, which will not be so happy as to reach him.

Theocrines is very well acquainted with what is trivial and unprofitable. He is less profound than methodical. He is the abstract of disdain, and seems continually laughing in himself at such as he thinks despise him. By chance I once read him something of mine. He heard it out with impatience; he cried presently, "Is it done?" and then talked of his own. "But what said he of yours," say you? "I have told you already, sir, he talked of his own."

The most accomplished piece which the age has produced would fail under the hands of the critics and censurers if the author would hearken to their objections and allow them to throw out what is not to their satisfaction.

Experience tells us, if there are ten persons who would blot a thought or an expression out of a book, there are a like number who would oppose it. These will allege, "For what would you suppress that thought? It is new, fine, and handsomely expressed." Those, on the contrary, affirm it should be omitted; at least they would have given it another turn. "In your work," says one, "there is a term exceedingly witty; it points out your meaning very naturally." "Methinks," says another, "that word is too bold, and yet does not signify so much as you would have it." It is the same word and the same line these critics differ so much about, and yet they are all judges, or pass for such amongst their acquaintance. What then shall an author do but follow the advice of those who approve it?

A serious author is not obliged to trouble his head with all the extravagant banters and bad jests which are thrown on him, or to be concerned at the impertinent constructions which a sort of men may make on some passages of his writings; neither ought he to give himself the trouble to suppress them. He is convinced that if a man is never so exact in his manner of writing, the dull raillery and wretched buffoonry of certain worthless people are unavoidable, since they make use of the best things only to turn them into ridicule.[2]

There is a prodigious difference between a fine piece and one that is regular and perfect. I question if there is anything to be found in the last kind, it being less difficult for a rare genius to hit upon the great and sublime than to avoid all errors. The *Cid* at its first appearance was universally admired. It lived in spite of policy or power, which attempted in vain to destroy it. The wits, who were otherwise divided in their sentiments, united in favor of this tragedy. The persons of quality and the common people agreed to keep it in their memory; they were beforehand with the actors in rehearsing it at the theatre. The *Cid,* in short, is one of the finest poems which can be made, and one of the best critiques which ever was written on any subject is that on the *Cid*.[3]

Capys sets up for a judge of style, and fancies he writes like Bouhours [and] Rabutin; he opposes himself to the voice of the people, and says all alone Damis is not a good author. However, Damis gives way to the multitude, and affirms ingenuously with the public that Capys is a dull writer.[4]

It is the business of a newsmonger to inform us when a book is to be published, for whom it is printed, for Cramoisy or for whom else, in what character, how bound and what paper, how many of them are gone off, and at what sign the bookseller lives. This is his duty; it is foolish in him to pretend to be a critic.

The highest reach of a newsmonger is an empty reasoning on policy and vain conjectures on the public management.

Boevius [5] lies down at night in great tranquillity at some false news which dies before morning, and he is obliged to abandon it as soon as he awakes.

The philosopher wastes his life in observing men and exposing foppery and vice; he gives his thoughts no other turn than what serves to set a truth he has found out in a proper light, that it may make the impression he designs. He has little of the vanity of an author, and yet some readers think they do very well by him if they say with a magisterial air they have read his book and there is some sense in it. But he returns them their praises, having other ends than bare applause in his sweating so much and breaking his rest. He has higher aims, and acts by a more elevated policy; he requires from mankind a greater and more extraordinary success than commendation or even rewards. He expects amendment and reformation.

A fool reads a book and understands nothing in it; a little wit reads it and is presently master of all without exception; a man of sense sometimes does not comprehend it entirely: he distinguishes what is clear from what is obscure, whilst the beaux esprits will have those passages dark which are not, and cannot understand what is really intelligible.

An author endeavors in vain to make himself admired by his productions. A fool may sometimes admire him, but then he is a fool. And a man of sense has in him the seeds of all truth and opinions; nothing is new to him. He admires little, it being his province chiefly to approve.

I question if it is possible to find in letters of wit a better manner, more agreeableness, and a finer style than we see in Balzac's and Voiture's.[6] It is true they are void of those sentiments which have since taken among us, and were invented by the ladies. That sex excels ours in this kind of writing. Those expressions and graces flow from them which are in us the effect of tedious labor and troublesome inquiry. They are happy in their terms, and place them so justly that everyone presently lights upon their meaning. As familiar as they are, yet they have the charm of novelty, and seem only designed for the use they put them to. They only can express a whole sentence in a single word, and render a delicate thought in a turn altogether as delicate. We find in all their letters an inimitable connection continued through the whole very naturally and always bounded by good

sense. If the ladies were more correct, I might affirm that they have produced some letters the best written of anything in our language.

Terence wanted nothing but warmth; with what purity, exactness, politeness, elegance, and characters are his plays adorned! Molière wanted
nothing but to avoid jargon and to write purely. What fire, what naivety,
what a source of good pleasantry, what imitation of manners, what images,
what a flail of ridicule are in his comedies! What a man could we make of
these two comedians!

I have read Malherbe and Théophile.[7] They both understood nature,
with this difference: the first in a plain, uniform style discovered at once
something noble, fine, simple, and natural like a good painter or a true
historian; the other, without choice or exactness, with a free and uneven
pen, sometimes loaden with descriptions, grows heavy in particulars and
gives you an anatomy, and sometimes he feigns, exaggerates, and goes so
much beyond the natural truth that he makes a romance.

Ronsard[8] and Balzac have each in their kind good and bad things,
enough to form after them very great men in verse or prose.

Marot[9] by his turn and style seems to have written since Ronsard. There
is little difference between the first and us but the alteration of a few
words.

Ronsard and his contemporaries were more prejudicial than serviceable
to style. They kept it back in the way to perfection and exposed it to the
danger of being always defective. It is surprising that Marot's works, which
are so easy and natural, had not taught Ronsard, otherwise full of rapture
and enthusiasm, to make a greater poet than Marot or himself, and that
on the contrary Belleau, Jodelle, and Saint-Gelais were so soon followed
by a Racan and a Malherbe;[10] or that our language ere it was scarce corrupted should be so quickly recovered.

Marot and Rabelais are inexcusable for scattering so much ribaldry in
their writings; they had both genius and wit enough to have omitted it
without striving to please such as would rather meet matter of laughter
than admiration in an author. Rabelais is incomprehensible. His book is
an inexplicable enigma, a mere chimera; it has a woman's face, with the
feet and tail of a serpent or some beast more deformed. It is a monstrous
collection of political and ingenious morality, with a mixture of beastli-
ness. Where it is bad it is abominable and fit for the diversion of the rabble,
and where it is good it is exquisite, and may entertain the most delicate.

Two writers in their works have condemned Montaigne. I confess he sometimes exposes himself to censure, but neither of these gentlemen will allow him to have anything valuable. One of them thinks too little to taste an author who thinks a great deal, and the other thinks too subtly to be pleased with what is natural.

A grave, serious, and scrupulous style will live a long while. Amyot and Coëffeteau are read, and who else of their contemporaries? [11] Balzac for his phrase and expression is less old than Voiture. But if the wit, genius, and manner of the last is not modern nor so conformable to our present writers, it is because they can more easily neglect than imitate him, and that the few who followed could never overtake him.

The *Mercure galant* [12] is a trifle, next to nothing, and there are [a good many works like it]; however, the author has had the good luck to live well by his invention, and there have been fops always ready to take off an impression of his foolish book. Whence we may perceive it is the ignorance of the people's judgment which makes men sometimes fearful to venture abroad a great many dull pieces.

An opera is the sketch of some magnificent show, of which it serves to give one an idea.

I wonder how an opera, with all its charge and music, should yet so suddenly tire me.

There are some places in an opera which make us desire more, and others that dispose us to wish it all over, according as we are pleased or offended with the scenes, the action, and the things represented.

An opera is not nowadays a poem, it is verses; nor a show, since machines have disappeared by the dexterous management of Amphion and his race. It is a concert of voices assisted by instruments. We are cheated by those who tell us machines are the amusements of children and proper only for puppet plays. It increases and embellishes the fiction, and keeps the spectators in that sweet illusion which is the highest pleasure of the theatre, especially where it has a mixture of the marvelous. There is no need of wings or cars or metamorphoses; but it is, however, the design of an opera and its representation to hold the mind, the eye, and the ear in an equal enchantment.[13]

The critics, or such as would be thought so, will ever have the decisive voice at all public sights. They canton and divide themselves into parties, pushed on of both sides by a particular interest opposite to that of the public or equity, admiring only such a poem or such a piece of music, and condemning all the rest. They are sometimes so warm in their prejudices that they are at a loss how to defend them, and injure the reputation of their cabal by their visible injustices and partiality. These men discourage the poets and musicians by a thousand contradictions, retarding the progress of the arts and sciences, depriving several masters of the fruit they would draw from emulation, and the world of many excellent performances.

What's the reason that we laugh so freely and are ashamed to weep at the theatre? Is nature less subject to be softened by pity than to burst forth at what is comical? Is it the alteration of our looks that prevents us? It is as great in an extraordinary laughter as in the most bitter weeping and we turn away our faces to laugh as well as to weep in the presence of people of quality, or such as we respect. Is it our backwardness to be thought tender or to show any emotion at a false subject where we fancy we are made cullies? Without naming some grave men or persons of sound judgments who think there is as much weakness shown in laughing excessively as in weeping, what is it that we look for at a tragedy? Is it to laugh? Does not truth reign there as lively by its images as in a comedy? And does not the soul imagine things true in either kind before it suffers itself to be moved? Or is it so easy to be pleased that verisimility is not necessary towards it? If not, we must suppose it is the natural effect of a good tragedy to make us weep freely in sight of the whole audience without any other trouble than drying our eyes and wiping our faces. It being no more ridiculous to be seen weeping than to be heard to laugh by the whole theatre, on the contrary we then conclude there was something acted very pleasantly and to the life, and the restraint a man puts on himself to hide his tears by an affected grimace plainly demonstrates that he ought not to resist the main design of a tragedy, but give way to his passions, and discover them as openly and with as much confidence as at a comedy. Besides, when we have been so patient as to sit out a whole play we should be less ashamed to weep at the theatre than to sit there three hours for nothing.

It is not sufficient that the manners of the theatre ought not to be bad; they should be decent and instructive. Some things are so low, so mean, so dull and insignificant in themselves, that the poet is not permitted to write nor the audience to be diverted by them. The peasant or the drunkard may furnish out some scenes for a farce-maker; they must never enter into true comedy, for since such characters cannot answer the main end, they should not be the main action of the play. Perhaps you will say they are natural. So is a whistling lackey, or a sick man on his closet-stool. By the same rule you may bring them on the stage, or the drunkard snoring and vomiting;

is there anything more natural? It is the property of a beau to rise late, to pass the best part of the day at his toilet, to adjust himself at his glass, to be perfumed and powdered, to put on his patches, to receive and answer his *billets*. When this part is brought on the stage, if it is continued two or three acts it may be the more natural and conformable to the original, but it is the more dull and insipid.

Plays and romances, in my opinion, may be made as useful as they are prejudicial to such as read them. There are so many great examples of constancy, virtue, tenderness, and disinterest, so many fine and perfect characters, that when a young person turns his prospect thence on everything about him and finds nothing but unworthy objects, very much below what he [has just been] admiring, I wonder how he can be guilty of the least [interest in] them.

Corneille cannot be equalled where he is excellent; he is then an original and unimitable, but he is unequal. His first plays are dry and languishing, and gave us no reason to hope he would afterwards rise to such a height, and his last plays make us wonder he could fall from it. In some of his best pieces there are unpardonable faults against the manners, the action is embarrassed with the declamatory style, there are such negligences in the verse and expression that we can hardly comprehend how so great a man could be guilty of them. The most eminent thing in him is his sublime wit, though he is very happy sometimes in his verses, and generally in the conduct of his plays, where he often ventures against the rules of the ancients. He is admirable in unraveling his plots, and in this does not always subject himself to the judgment of the Greeks or their great simplicity. On the contrary, he loads the scene with events, and most commonly comes off with success. He is above all to be admired for his great variety and the little agreement we find in his designs amongst the great number of poems he composed. In Racine's plays there are more likenesses; they lead more to the same thing. But he is even and everywhere supported, as well in the design and conduct of his pieces, which are just, regular, full of good sense, and natural, as for the versification, which is rich in rhymes, elegant, numerous, harmonious, and correct. He is an exact imitator of the ancients, whom he follows religiously in the simplicity of action. He wants not the sublime and the marvelous, and where it is proper he is ever master of the moving and the pathetic as well as his predecessor Corneille. Where can we find greater tenderness than is diffused through the *Cid*, *Polyeucte*, and *Horace*? What greatness of soul is there in Mithradate, Porus, and Burrhus! [14] They were both well acquainted with horror and pity, the favorite passions of the ancients, which the poets are fond of exciting on the theatre, as Oreste in the *Andromaque* of Racine, the Phèdre of the same author, and the *Oedipe* and the *Horace* of Corneille sufficiently prove. If I may be allowed to make a comparison or to show the talent of both the one and the other as it is to be discovered in their writings, I should probably say that Corneille reigns over us by his characters and ideas; Racine's are more conformable to our own. The one paints men as they ought to be; the other describes them as they are. There is in the first more of what we admire and ought to imitate, and in the second more of what we know in others and approve in ourselves. Corneille elevates, surprises, triumphs, and instructs. Racine pleases, affects, moves, and penetrates. The former works on us by what is fine, noble, and commanding. The latter insinuates himself into us by the delicacy of his passions. One is full of maxims, rules, and precepts, the other of opinions and judgments; we are engaged more at Corneille's pieces, at Racine's more softened and concerned. Corneille is more moral, Racine more natural. The one seems to imitate Sophocles, the other Euripides.

Some persons have a faculty of speaking alone and a long time, joined with extravagant gestures, a loud voice, and strong lungs: this the people call eloquence. Pedants never admit [eloquence] but in public orations, and cannot distinguish [it from] a heap of figures, the use of [big] words, and the roundness of periods.

Logic is the art to make truth prevalent, and eloquence a gift of the soul that renders one master of the sense and hearts of other men, by which we persuade and inspire them with what we please.

Eloquence may be found in all discourses and all kinds of writings; it is rarely where we seek it, and sometimes where it is least expected.

Eloquence is to the sublime what the whole is to its part.

What is the sublime? We talk much about it, but nobody pretends to define it. Is it in itself a figure? Is it composed of one or more figures? Does the sublime enter into all sorts of writing, or are great subjects only capable of it? [Can anything shine in eclogues but] a fine wit and a natural simplicity, [or] in familiar letters and conversation [anything but] a great delicacy; or rather [are not the natural and the delicate] the sublime of those works where they make the perfection? What is this sublime, and in what does it consist?

Synonyms are several dictions or phrases that signify the same thing.

335

An antithesis is the opposition of two truths which give light to each other. A metaphor or comparison borrows from a strange thing the natural and sensible image of a true one. An hyperbole expresses things above truth to reclaim the mind that it may the better understand it. The sublime paints nothing but the truth, only in a noble subject it paints it all entire in its causes and effects. It is the expression or image most worthy the dignity of the truth it treats of. Little wits cannot find the simple expression, and use synonyms. Young men are dazzled with the luster of antitheses, and generally make use of them. True wits, who would be exact in their images, are for metaphors and comparisons. Quick wits, full of fire and vast imagination, carry themselves above rules or justice, and are never satisfied without an hyperbole. As for the sublime, [even among the great geniuses only the most elevated are capable of it].

Everyone who would write purely should put himself in the place of his readers, examine his own work as a thing that is new to him, which he never read before, where he is not at all concerned; and the author must submit to the critic. He should not suppose another man will understand them himself but forasmuch as they are in themselves really intelligible.

An author should not only endeavor to make himself understood; he must strive to inform us of such things as deserve it. He ought, it is true, to have pure language and a chaste expression, but they ought also to express lively, noble, and solid thoughts, full of good sense and sound reason. He prostitutes chastity and clearness of style who wastes it on some frivolous, puerile, dull, and common subject, having neither spirit, fire, nor novelty, where the reader may perhaps easily find out the meaning of the author, but he is much more certain to be tired with his productions.

If we aim to be profound in certain writings, if we affect a polite turn and sometimes too much delicacy, it is merely for the good opinion we have of our readers.

We have this disadvantage in reading books written by men of party and cabal: we seldom meet with the truth in them. Actions are there disguised; the reasons of both sides are not alleged with all their force nor with an entire exactness. He who has the greatest patience must read an abundance of hard, injurious reflections on the gravest men, with whom the writer has some personal quarrel about a point of doctrine or matter of controversy. These books are particular in this, that they deserve not the prodigious sale they find at their first appearance, nor the profound oblivion that attends them afterwards. When the fury and division of these authors cease, they are forgotten, like an almanac out of date.

It is the glory and merit of some men to write well, and of others not to write at all. For this last twenty years we have been regular in our writings. We have faithfully observed constructions and enriched our language with new words, thrown off the yoke of Latinism, and reduced our style to a pure French phrase. We have almost found again the numbers which Malherbe and Balzac hit upon first and so many authors after them suffered to be lost. We have, in short, brought into our discourses all the order and clearness they are capable of, and this will insensibly lead us at last to add wit.

There are some artists and skillful men whose genius is as vast as the art or science they profess. They restore with interest, by their contrivance and invention, what they borrow from its principals. They frequently break through the rules of art to ennoble it, and thwart the common roads if they don't conduct them to what is great and extraordinary. They go alone; they leave their company a long way behind, whilst they are by themselves mounting high and penetrating far into the secrets of their profession, emboldened by their success and encouraged by the advantages they draw from their irregularity, whilst men of ordinary, soft, and moderate parts, as they can never reach them, so they never admire them; they can't comprehend, and much less imitate them. They live peaceably within the compass of their own sphere, aiming at a certain point, which makes the bounds of their insight and capacity. They go no farther because they feel nothing beyond it. They are at best but the first of a second class, and excellent in mediocrity.

I may venture to call certain wits inferior or subaltern; they seem as if they were born only to collect, register, and raise magazines out of the productions of other geniuses. They are plagiaries, translators, or compilers. They never think, but tell you what other men have thought; and as the good choice of thoughts proceeds from invention, having none of their own, they are seldom just in their collections, but choose rather to make them large than excellent. They know nothing of what they learn, and learn what the rest of the world are unwilling to know: a vain and useless science, neither agreeable nor profitable in commerce or conversation. Like false money, it has no currency, for we are at once surprised with these coxcombs' reading and tired with their company and writings. However, the great ones and the vulgar mistake them for men of learning; but wise men know very well what they are, and rank them with the pedants.

Criticism is commonly a trade, not a science; it requires more health than wit, more labor than capacity, and habit than genius. If a person pretends to it who has less discernment than reading, he will be at a loss where to exercise himself, and corrupt his own judgment as well as his readers'.

I advise an author born only to copy, who in extreme modesty works after another man, to choose for his patterns such writings as are full of wit, imagination, and even good learning; if he does not understand his originals, he may at least come at them and read them. He ought, on the contrary, to avoid as he would destruction any desire to imitate those who write by humor, who speak from their hearts, which inspired them with figures and terms, and draw, if I may say it, from their very entrails what they express on their paper. These are dangerous models, and will infallibly make him write meanly, dully, and ridiculously. Besides, I should laugh at a man who would seriously endeavor to speak in my tone of voice or be like me in the face.

A man born a Christian and a Frenchman is confined in satire. Some subjects are forbidden him by the greatness of their quality; others are too low, but he is obliged frequently to fall on them to ease him of his resentment, and by this means he raises them in the beauties of his style and genius.

Everyone should avoid imitating [. . .] a vain, puerile style; a man may be sometimes bold in his expressions, use transpositions and anything which paints his subject to the life, pitying those who are not sensible of the pleasure there is in this liberty to such as understand it.

He who regards nothing more in his works than the taste of the age has a greater value for his person than his writings. He should always aim at perfection, and, though his contemporaries refuse him justice, posterity will give it him.

We must never put a jest in the wrong place; it offends instead of pleasing, and vitiates our own judgments as well as other men's. The ridicule is only proper when it comes in with a good grace, and in a manner which both pleases and instructs.

"Horace and Boileau have said such a thing before you." I take your word for it, but I said it as my own; and may not I think a just thought after them, as others may do the same after me?

Bernard Le Bovier de Fontenelle OF PASTORALS

Of all kinds of poetry the pastoral is probably the most ancient, as the keeping of flocks was one of the first employments which men took up. It is very likely that these primitive shepherds, amidst the tranquility and leisure which they enjoyed, bethought themselves of singing their pleasures and their loves; and then their flocks, the woods, the springs, and all those objects that were most familiar to them, naturally came into the subject of their songs. They lived in great plenty after their way, without any control by superior power, being in a manner the kings of their own flocks, and I do not doubt but that a certain joy and openness of heart that generally attends plenty and liberty induced them to sing and to make verses. Society in time was brought to perfection, or [perhaps] declined and was perverted, and men took up employments that seemed to them of greater consequence. More weighty affairs filled their minds; towns and cities were built everywhere, and mighty states at last were founded and established. Then those who lived in the country became slaves to those who dwelt in cities, and the pastoral life, being grown the lot of the most wretched sort of people, no longer inspired any delightful thought.

To please others in ingenious compositions, men ought to be in a condition to free themselves from pressing want, and their minds ought to be refined through a long use of civil society. Now a pastoral life has always wanted one of these two circumstances: the primitive shepherds, of whom we have spoken, lived indeed in plenty enough, but in their times the world had not yet had leisure to grow polite. The following ages might have produced something more refined, but the shepherds of those days were too poor and dejected, so that the country way of living and the poetry of shepherds must needs have been always very homely and artless.

And indeed nothing is more certain than that no real shepherds can be altogether like those of Theocritus. Can anyone think that it is natural for shepherds to say like his:

> Gods! When she view'd, how strong was the surprise!
> Her soul took fire, and sparkled through her eyes!
> How did her passions, how her fury move!
> How soon she plung'd into th'abyss of love!

Let the following passages be examined:

> O that, to crown what e'er my wish can crave,
> I were that bee which flies into your cave!
> There softly through your garland would I creep,
> And steal a kiss when you are fast asleep!

> I know what love is now, a cruel god,
> A tigress bore and nursed him in a wood,
> A cruel god, he shoots through ev'ry vein —

> The fair Calistris, as my goats I drove,
> With apples pelts me, and still murmurs love.

> The pastures flourish, and the flocks improve,
> All smiles, so soon as here resorts my love;
> But oh! when e'er the dear one leaves the place,
> At once there fade the shepherds and the grass.

> Ye gods, I wish not heaps of gold refin'd,
> Nor rapid swiftness to outstrip the wind;
> But let me sit and sing by yonder rock,
> Clasp thee, my dear, and view my feeding flock.

I am of opinion that there will be found in these expressions more beauty and more delicacy of imagination than real shepherds have.

But I don't know how Theocritus, having sometimes raised his shepherds in so pleasing a manner above their native genius, could let them so very often fall to it again. I wonder he did not perceive it was fit that a certain gross clownishness, which is always very unbecoming, should be omitted. When Daphnis in the First Idyllium is ready to die for love, and a great number of deities are come to visit him, in the midst of that honorable company he is reproved for being like the goatherds, who envy the pleasure of their copulating goats and are jealous of them; and it is most certain that the terms used by Theocritus to represent this are much of the kind of the idea which they give.

> Ah Daphnis, loose and wanton in thy love!
> A herdsman thought, thou dost a goatherd prove:
> A goatherd, when he sees the kids at rut,
> Sits down and grieves that he's not born a goat.

Thus, when you see the virgins dance, you grieve
Because refus'd, and now disdain to live.

In another idyllium the goatherd Comatas and the herdsman Laco contend about some theft which they had committed against each other; Comatas stole Laco's pipe, and Laco had stolen the skin which Comatas used to wear to cover himself withal, so that he had left him bare. They rail at each other, and vent their passion in reviling and abusive words, which might become a couple of Grecians, but certainly are not over civil; and then, after a gentle item which one of them gives the other of smelling rank, they both sing for a wager, the one having challenged the other to that musical fight, though it should rather have been to a rubbers at fisticuffs, considering what went before; and what seems the more odd is that whereas they begun with gross taunts and ill language, now they are going to sing against each other, they affect an uncommon niceness concerning the choice of a place where they are to sing, each proposing one, of which he makes a florid description. For my part, I have a much-a-do to believe that all this is very well set together. Their songs are as oddly diversified; for among the things that relate to their amours and that are pretty, Comatas puts Laco in mind of a beating which he bestowed upon him, and Laco answers him that he does not remember it, but that he has not forgot how Comatas was bound and soundly lashed by his master Eumaras. I do not fancy that those who say that Venus, the Graces, and Cupid composed Theocritus's idyllia will pretend that they had a hand in these passages.

There are some other places in Theocritus that are not altogether so low which yet are not very entertaining, because they barely treat of country matters. His Fourth Idyllium is wholly of this kind. The subject of it is only a certain Aegon, who, being gone to the Olympic Games, has left his herds to one Corydon. Battus tells the trustee that the herds are in a pitiful condition since Aegon left them. Corydon answers that he does his best, that he drives them to the best pastures he knows, and feeds them at a rack of hay. Battus says that Aegon's pipe is spoiled and mouldy in his absence; Corydon replies that it is not so, that Aegon when he went gave it him, and that he is a notable piper. Then Battus desires Corydon to pull a thorn out of his foot, and the other having advised him never to walk over mountains without his shoes, the idyllium presently concludes, a thing which those who are not conversant with antiquity would scarce have believed possible.

When in a pastoral strife one says, "Ho! My goats go on the brow of yonder hill"; and the other answers, "Go, my sheep, feed on to the eastward"; or, "I hate the brush-tailed fox, which comes at night and devours our grapes"; and the other, "I hate the beetles that eat the figs"; or, when one says, "I have made myself a bed with cow's skins near a cool stream,"

> And there I value summer's burning heats
> No more than children do their father's threats,
> Their mother's kind complaints, etc.

And the other answers, "I live in a large shady cave, where"

> Soft chitterlings afford me pleasing food
> And when the winter comes I'm stor'd with wood;
> So that I value cold no more, not I,
> Than toothless men do nuts when pap is by.

May not these discourses be thought too clownish, and fitter to be spoken by real country fellows than by such shepherds as are introduced in eclogues?

Virgil, who, having had the example of Theocritus before his eyes, has had an opportunity to outdo him, hath made his shepherds more polite and agreeable. Anyone who compares his Third Eclogue with that of Laco and Comatas in Theocritus will easily find how well he could rectify and surpass what he did imitate; not but that he still somewhat too much resembles Theocritus when he loses some time in making his pastors say,

> [Graze not too near the banks, my jolly sheep:
> The ground is false; the running streams are deep:
> See, they have caught the father of the flock,
> Who dries his fleece upon the neighboring rock.] [1]

And

> Kids from the river drive, and fling your hook;
> Anon I'll wash them in the shallow brook.

And

> Boys, drive to shades when milk is drained by heat;
> In vain the milkmaid strokes an empty teat.

All this is the less pleasing, considering that it comes after some tender things which are very pretty and genteel, and which have made the reader the more unfit to relish such things as altogether relate to the country.

Calpurnius, a writer of eclogues who lived almost three hundred years after Virgil,[2] and whose works however are not wholly destitute of beauty, seems to have been sorry that Virgil did express but with the words *novi-*

mus et qui te[3] those injurious terms with which Laco and Comatas treat one another in Theocritus, though after all it had yet been better had Virgil wholly suppressed that short hint. Calpurnius has judged this passage worthy a larger extent, and therefore wrote an eclogue which is made up of nothing but those invectives with which two shepherds ready to sing for a prize, ply each other with a great deal of fury, till the shepherd who was to be their judge is so affrighted that he runs away and leaves them. A very fine conclusion!

But no author ever made his shepherds so clownish as J. Baptista Mantuanus,[4] a Latin poet, who lived in the foregoing age and who has been compared to Virgil, though he has indeed nothing common with him besides his being of Mantua. The shepherd Faustus, describing his mistress, says that she had a good big bloated red face, and that, though she was almost blind of an eye, he thought her more beautiful than Diana. It were impossible to guess what precaution another shepherd takes before he begins a discourse of considerable length. And who knows but that our modern Mantuan valued himself mightily upon having copied nature most faithfully in those passages?

I therefore am of opinion that pastoral poetry cannot be very charming if it is as low and clownish as shepherds naturally are, or if it precisely runs upon nothing but rural matters. For to hear one speak of sheep and goats and of the care that ought to be taken of those animals has nothing which in itself can please us; what is pleasing is the idea of quietness, which is inseparable from a pastoral life. Let a shepherd say, "My sheep are in good case, I conduct them to the best pastures, they feed on nothing but the best grass," and let him say this in the best verse in the world, I am sure that your imagination will not be very much delighted with it. But let him say, "How free from anxious cares is my life! In what a quiet state I pass my days! All my desires rise no higher than that I may see my flocks in a thriving condition, and the pastures wholesome and pleasing; I envy no man's happiness, etc." You perceive that this begins to become more agreeable. The reason of it is that the idea runs no longer immediately upon country affairs, but upon the little share of care which shepherds undergo, and upon the quietness and leisure which they enjoy, and, what is the chiefest point, upon the cheapness of their happiness.

For all men would be happy, and that too at any easy rate. A quiet pleasure is the common object of all their passions, and we are all controlled by a certain laziness. Even those who are most stirring are not precisely such for business' sake, or because they love to be in action, but because they cannot easily satisfy themselves.

Ambition, as it is too much an enemy to this natural laziness, is neither a general passion nor very delicious. A considerable part of mankind is not ambitious; many have begun to be such but by the means of some undertakings and ties that have determined them before they seriously reflected on what they did, and that have made them unfit ever to return to calmer inclinations; and even those who have most ambition do often complain of the cares which it exacts and the pains that attend it. The reason of this is that the native laziness of which we were speaking is not wholly suppressed, though it has been sacrificed to that presumptuous tyrant of the mind; it proved the weakest, and could not overbalance its rival, yet it still subsists and continually opposes the motions of ambition. Now no man can be happy while he is divided by two warring inclinations.

However, I do not say that men can relish a state of absolute laziness and idleness; no, they must have some motion, some agitation; but it must be such a motion and agitation as may be reconciled, if possible, to the kind of laziness that possesses them; and this is most happily to be found in love, provided it be taken in a certain manner. It must neither be a hot, jealous, touchy, furious, desperate love, but tender, pure, simple, delicate, faithful, and, that it may preserve itself in this state, attended with hopes. Then the heart is taken up but not disturbed; we have cares but no uneasinesses; we are moved but not torn; and this soft motion is just such as the love of rest and our native laziness can bear it.

Besides, it is most certain that love is the most general and the most agreeable of all the passions. So in the state of life which we have now described there is a concurrence of the two strongest passions, laziness and love, which thus are both satisfied at once; and that we may be as happy as it is possible we should by the passions, it is necessary that all those by which we are moved agree together in us.

This is properly what we conceive of a pastoral life. For it admits of no ambition, nor of anything that moves the heart with too much violence; therefore our laziness has cause to be contented. But this way of living, by reason of its idleness and tranquillity, creates love more easily than any other, or at least indulges it more. But after all, what love! A love more innocent because the mind is not so dangerously refined, more assiduous because those who feel it are not diverted by any other passions, more full of discretion because they hardly have any acquaintance with vanity, more faithful because, with a vivacity of imagination less used, they have also less uneasiness, less distaste, and less fickleness; that is to say, in short, a love purged of whatever the excesses of human fancy have sophisticated it with.[5]

This considered, it is not to be admired why the pictures which are drawn of a pastoral life have always something so very smiling in them, and indulge our fancies more than the pompous description of a splendid court, and of all the magnificence that can shine there. A court gives us no idea but of toilsome and constrained pleasures. For, as we have observed, the idea is all in all.[6] Could the scene of this quiet life, with no other business but love, be placed anywhere but in the country, so that no goats nor sheep should be brought in, I fancy it would be never the worse, for the goats and sheep add nothing to its felicity; but as the scene must lie either in the country or in towns, it seems more reasonable to choose the first.

As the pastoral life is the most idle of all others, it is also the most fit to be the groundwork of those ingenious representations of which we are speaking. So that no ploughmen, reapers, vine-dressers, or huntsmen can by any means be so properly introduced in eclogues as shepherds; which confirms what I said, that what makes this kind of poetry please is not its giving an image of a country life, but rather the idea which it gives of the tranquillity and innocence of that life.

Yet there is an idyllium of Battus and Milo, two reapers in Theocritus, which has beauties. Milo asks Battus why he does not reap as fast as he used to do. He answers that he is in love, and then sings something that is very pretty about the woman that he loves. But Milo laughs at him, and tells him he is a fool for being so idle as to be in love; that this is not an employment fit for one who works for food; and that, to divert himself and excite one another to work, he should sing some songs which he denotes to him, and which altogether relate to the harvest. I must needs own that I do not so well like this conclusion. For I would not be drawn from a pleasing and soft idea to another that is low and without charms.

Sannazarius has introduced none but fishermen in his eclogues, [7] and I always perceive when I read those piscatory poems that the idea I have of fishermen's hard and toilsome way of living shocks me. I don't know what moved him to bring in fishermen instead of shepherds, who were in possession of the eclogue time out of mind; but had the fishermen been in possession of it, it had been necessary to put the shepherds in their place. For singing and above all an idle life becomes none but shepherds. Besides, methinks it is prettier and more genteel to send flowers or fruit to one's mistress than send her oysters, as Sannazarius's Lyco doth to his.

It is true that Theocritus hath an idyllium of two fishermen, but it doth not seem to me so beautiful as to have deserved to tempt any man to write one of that kind. The subject of it is this: two old fishermen had but sparingly supped together in a wretched little thatched house by the seaside. One of them wakes his bedfellow to tell him he had just dreamt that he was catching a golden fish, and the other answers him that he might starve [even] though he had really caught such a one. Was this worth writing an eclogue!

However, though none but shepherds were introduced in eclogues, it is impossible but that the life of shepherds, which after all is yet very clownish, must lessen and debase their wit, and hinder their being as ingenious, nice, and full of gallantry as they are commonly represented in pastorals. The famous Lord d'Urfé's *L'Astrée* seems a less fabulous romance than *Amadis de Gaule*; [8] yet I fancy that in the main it is as incredible as to the politeness and graces of his shepherds as *Amadis* can be as to all its enchantments, all its fairies, and the extravagance of its adventures. How comes it then that pastorals please in spite of the falsity of the characters, which ought always to shock us? Could we be pleased with seeing some courtiers represented as having a clownishness which should resemble that of real shepherds as much as the gallantry which shepherds have in pastorals resembles that of courtiers? No, doubtless; but indeed that character of the shepherds is not false after all, if we look upon it one way. For we do not mind the meanness of the concerns that are their real employment, but the little trouble those concerns bring. This meanness would wholly exclude ornaments and gallantry, but on the other hand the quiet state promotes them; and it is only on that tranquillity that whatever pleases in a pastoral life is grounded.

Our imagination is not to be pleased without truth, but it is not very hard to please it, for often it is satisfied with a kind of half truth. Let it see only the half of a thing, but let that half be shown in a lively manner, then it will hardly bethink itself that you hide from it the other half; and you may thus deceive it as long as you please, since all the while it imagines that this single moiety, with the thoughts of which it is taken up, is the whole thing. The illusion and at the same time the pleasingness of pastorals therefore consists in exposing to the eye only the tranquility of a shepherd's life, and in dissembling or concealing its meanness, as also in showing only its innocence and hiding its miseries; so that I do not comprehend why Theocritus dwelt so much upon its miseries and clownishness.

If those who are resolved to find no faults in the ancients tell us that Theocritus had a mind to draw nature just such as it is, I hope that according to those principles we shall have some idyllia of porters or watermen discoursing together of their particular concerns, which will be every whit as good as some idyllia of shepherds speaking of nothing but their goats or their cows.

The business is not purely to describe; we must describe such objects as are delightful. When the quiet that reigns in the country, and the simplicity and tenderness which [are] discovered there in making love, are represented to me, my imagination, moved and affected with these pleasing ideas, is fond of a shepherd's life; but though the vile and low employments of shepherds were described to me with all the exactness possible, I should never be taken with them, and my imagination would not in the least be touched. The chief advantage of poetry consists in representing to us in a lively manner the things that concern us, and in striking strongly a heart which is pleased with being moved.

Here's enough and perhaps too much against these shepherds of Theocritus, and those who, like them, have too much of the shepherd in them. What we have left of Moschus and Bion in the pastoral kind makes me extremely lament what we have lost of theirs. They have no manner of rusticity, but rather a great deal of delicacy and grace, and some ideas wholly new and pleasing. They are accused of being too florid, and I do not deny but that they may be said to be such in some few places; yet I don't know why the critics are more inclined to excuse Theocritus's clownishness than Moschus and Bion's elegancy; methinks they should have done the contrary. Is it not that Virgil has prejudiced everyone for Theocritus, having done to no other the honor of imitating and copying him? Or is it not rather than the learned have a taste [accustomed to disdaining] what is delicate and genteel? Whatever it is, I find that all their favor is for Theocritus, and that they have resolved to dub him prince of the bucolic poets.

The moderns have not often been guilty of making their shepherds thus clownish. The author of *L'Astrée*, in that romance which otherwise is full of admirable things, has rather run into the other extreme. Some of his shepherds are absolutely drawn such as they ought to have been, but some others, if I am not mistaken, might better have been placed in *Le Grand Cyrus* or in *Cléopâtre*. These shepherds often seem to me courtiers disguised in a pastoral dress, and ill mimics of what they would imitate; sometimes they appear to me most cavilling sophisters. For though none but Sylvandre has studied in the school of the Massilians, there are some others who happen to be as full of subtlety as himself, though I don't comprehend how they could even but understand him, not having like him took their degrees in the Massilian schools.

It does not belong to shepherds to speak of all sorts of matters, and when a poet has a mind to raise his style, he may make use of other persons. When Virgil desired to give a pompous description of the imaginary return of the Golden Age, which he promises to the world at the birth of Pollio's son, he should not have excited the pastoral muses to leave their natural strain and raise their voices to a pitch which they can never reach; his business was to have left them, and have addressed himself to some others. Yet I do not know after all if it had not been better to have kept to the pastoral muses, for he might have given a pleasing description of the good which the return of peace was ready to cause in the country; and this, methinks, had been as acceptable at least as all those incomprehensible wonders which he borrows of the Cumaean Sibyl, this new race of men which is to descend from heaven, these grapes which are to grow on briars, and these lambs whose native fleece is to be of a scarlet or crimson hue to save mankind the trouble of dyeing the wool. He might have flattered Pollio more agreeably with things that might have seemed more consistent with it, at least to the party concerned; for praise is seldom thought such by those on whom it is lavished.

Shall I dare to say that Calpurnius, an author much inferior to Virgil, seems to have handled a subject of the same nature much more to the purpose? Take notice that I only speak of the design or fable, and not at all of the style. He brings in two shepherds, who to be screened from the sun's sultry heat shelter themselves in a cave, where they find some verses written with the god Faunus's own hand, which contain a prophecy about the happiness which the Roman Empire is to enjoy under the Emperor Carus. According to the duty of a pastoral poet, he dwells sufficiently on the prosperity and plenty that relates to the country, and then proceeds to higher matters, because, as he makes a god speak, he has a right to do so; but he brings in nothing like the Sibyl's prophecies.

It is pity that Virgil did not write the verses of this piece; neither had there been need to have had them all written by him.

Virgil makes Phoebus say to him at the beginning of his Sixth Eclogue that a shepherd ought not to sing kings nor wars, but to stick to his flocks, and such subjects as only require a plain style. Without doubt Phoebus's counsel was very good, but I cannot imagine how Virgil could forget it so much as to fall a-singing, immediately after, the original of the world and the framing of the universe according to Epicurus's system, which was a great deal worse than to sing kings and wars. I must needs own that I cannot in the least tell what to make of this piece; I do not understand what is the design, nor what coherence there is between the several parts of it. For after these philosophical notions we have the fables of Hylas and Pasiphae and of Phaeton's sisters, which have no manner of relation to them; and in the middle of these fables, which are all borrowed from very remote times, we have Cornelius Gallus, Virgil's contemporary, and the honors which he receives on Parnassus; after which we presently come to the fables of Scylla and Philomela. It is honest Silenus that gives all this fine medley, and, as Virgil tells us that according to his laudable custom he had taken a hearty carouse the day before, I am afraid the fumes were hardly yet got out of his head.

Here let me once more take the freedom to own that I like better the design of an eclogue of this kind by Nemesianus, [9] an author who was Calpurnius's contemporary, and who is not altogether to be despised. Some shepherds, finding Pan asleep, try to play on his pipe; but as a mortal can make a god's pipe yield only a very unpleasing sound, Pan is awaked by it, and tells them that if they are for songs he'll gratify them presently. With this he sings to them something of the history of Bacchus, and dwells on the first vintage that ever was made, of which he gives a description which seems to me very agreeable. This design is more regular than that of Virgil's Silenus, and the verses also are pretty good.

The moderns have been often guilty of handling high subjects in their eclogues. The French poet Ronsard has given us in his the praises of princes and of France, and almost all that looks like bucolic in them is his calling Henry II Henriot [or Harry], Charles IX Carlin [or Charlie], and Queen Catharine de Medicis Catin [or Kate]. It is true that he owns that he did not follow the rules, but it had been better to have done it, and thus have avoided the ridicule which the disproportion that is between the subject and the form of the work produces. Hence it happens that in his first eclogue it falls to the lot of the shepherdess Margot to sing the elegy of Turnebus, Budaeus, and Vatable, [10] the greatest men of their age for Greek and Hebrew, but with whom certainly Peg ought not have been acquainted.

Because shepherds look well in some kinds of poetry, many writers prostitute them to every subject. They are often made to sing the praises of kings in the sublimest style the poet can write, and provided he has but talked of oaten pipes, meads, and plains, fern or grass, streams or valleys, he thinks he has written an eclogue. When shepherds praise a hero they should praise him shepherd-like, and I do not doubt but that this would be very ingenious and taking; but it would require some art, and the shortest cut, it seems, is to make the shepherds speak the common dialect of praise, which is very big and lofty indeed, but very common, and consequently easy enough of conscience.

Allegorical eclogues also are not very easy. J. B. Mantuanus, who was a Carmelite friar, has one in which two shepherds dispute, the one representing a Carmelite friar who is of that party of the order which they call *the strict observance*, and the other of that which they call the *mitigated*. The famous Bembus is their judge, and it is worth observing that he prudently makes them lay down their crooks lest they fall together by the ears.

Now though in the main our Mantuan has pretty well kept the allegory, it is too ridiculous to find the controversy between these two sorts of Carmelitans handled ecloguewise.

Yet I had rather see a shepherd represent one of these than have him act the Epicurean and say impious things; it is what happens sometimes to some of Mantuanus's shepherds, though they are very clownish, and he himself was of a religious order. Amyntas, one of them, in an angry fit which makes him rail against the laws and virtue merely because he is in love, says that men are great fools to feed themselves up with a fancy of being taken up to heaven after their death, and he adds that the most that is like to happen then is that they may chance to transmigrate into some birds and so flutter up and down through the air. In vain to make this excusable, our friar says that Amyntas had lived a long time in town; and as much in vain Badius his commentator — for as much a modern as Mantuanus is, he has one, and as bigoted and hot for his author as those of the ancients — in vain, I say, he takes from thence an opportunity to make this rare reflection, that love causes us to doubt of matters of faith. It is certain that these errors, which ought to be detested by all those who have heard of them, ought not to be known, much less mentioned by shepherds.

To make amends, sometimes our Mantuan makes his shepherds mighty godly. In one of his eclogues you have a catalogue of all the Virgin Mary's holidays; in another an apparition of the Virgin, who promises a shepherd that when he shall have passed his life on Mount Carmel she'll take him to a more pleasant place, and will make him dwell in heaven with the dryads and hamadryads, a sort of new-fashioned saints whom we did not yet know in heaven.

Such gross and inexcusable indecencies may be easily avoided in the character of shepherds, but there are some that are not so observable, of which some writers cannot so easily be freed: it is the making their shepherds speak too wittily. Sometimes even those of the Marquess de Racan [11] are guilty of this, though they generally use to be very reserved in that point. As for the Italian authors, they are also so full of false and pointed thoughts that we must resolve, right or wrong, to give them leave to indulge themselves in that darling style of theirs, as natural to them as their mother tongue. They never take the pains to make their shepherds speak in a pastoral style, but make use of as bold and exaggerated figures, and are as full of conceits in that sort of poetry, as they are in others.

Father Bouhours, in his excellent treatise *Of the Manner of Thinking Justly in Ingenious Composures*, finds fault with Tasso's Sylvia, who, seeing the reflection of her face in a fountain and adorning herself with flowers, tells them she does not wear them to mend her beauty, but to lessen them and disgrace them by being placed near her brighter charms. Our judicious critic thinks this thought too full of affectation, and not natural enough for a shepherdess, and none can refuse their assent to this criticism, which is the result of a very delicate taste. But when this is done, let none give themselves the trouble of reading Guarini's, Bonarelli's, and Marini's pastoral poetry with a design to find anything in them truly pastoral, for Sylvia's thought is one of the most unaffected and simple things in the world, if compared to most of those of which these authors are full. [12]

And indeed Tasso's *Amynta* is the best thing that Italy has produced in the pastoral kind, and has certainly very great beauties; even the passage of Sylvia, except what we have observed in it, is one of the most ingenious and best-described things I ever read, and we ought to own ourselves extremely obliged to an Italian author for not having been more prodigal of pointed thoughts. [13]

Monsieur de Segrais, whose works are the most excellent pattern we have of pastoral poetry, owns himself that he did not always keep exactly to the style which it requires. [14] He says that he has sometimes been obliged to humor the genius of this age, which delights in figures and glittering things. But this must be said on his behalf, that he only condescended to follow this method after he had sufficiently proved that he could when he pleased perfectly hit the true beauties of pastoral. After all, none can well tell which is the taste or genius of this age; it is not determined either what is good or bad, but seems wavering sometimes on this and sometimes on that side. So I believe that, since there is still a hazard to be run whatever side we take, it were better to follow the rules and true ideas of things.

Between the usual clownishness of Theocritus's shepherds and the too much wit of most of our modern shepherds, a certain medium should be kept, but it is so far from being easily followed in the performance that it is even difficult to denote it. The shepherds ought to have wit, and it ought to be fine and genteel too, for they could not please without it; but they ought to have that wit only in a certain degree, otherwise they are no more shepherds. I'll endeavor to determine this degree, and adventure to give my notion of it.

The men who have the most wit and those who have but an indifferent share of it do not differ so much in the sense which they have of things as they do in their manner of expressing it. The passions, amidst all the disturbance which they cause, are attended by a kind of light which they impart almost equally to all those whom they possess. There is a certain penetration, certain ideas, which, without any regard to the difference of the minds, are always found in men in whatever concerns and affects them. But these passions, at the same time that they in a manner inform the mind of all men alike, do not enable them to speak equally well. Those whose mind is more refined, more capacious, and more improved by study or conversation do, while they express their sentiments, add something that hath the air of a reflection, and that is not inspired by the passion alone; whereas the others speak their minds more simply, and add in a manner nothing that is foreign. Any ordinary man will easily say, "I so passionately desired that my mistress might be faithful that I believed her such"; but it only belongs to a refined wit, as the Duke de la Rochefoucauld, to say, "My understanding was fooled by my will," or, "My reason was cullied by my desire [l'esprit a été en moi la dupe du coeur]." The sense is the same, the penetration equal, but the expression is so different that one would almost think it is no more the same thing.

We take no less pleasure in finding a sentiment expressed simply than in a more thoughtlike and elaborate manner, provided it be always equally fine. Nay, the simple way of expressing it ought to please more, because it occasions a kind of gentle surprise and a final admiration. We are amazed to find something that is fine and delicate in common and unaffected terms; and on that account the more the thing is fine without ceasing to be natural, and the expression common without being low, the deeper we ought to be struck.

Admiration and surprise are so powerful that they can even raise the value of things beyond their intrinsic worth. All Paris has lavished exclamations of admiration on the Siamese ambassadors for their ingenious sayings.[15] Now had some Spanish or English ambassadors spoken the same things, nobody would have minded it. This happened because we wrongfully supposed that some men who came from the remotest part of the world, of a tawny complexion, dressed otherwise than we are, and till then esteemed barbarians by those of Europe, were not to be endowed with common sense; and we were very much surprised to find they had it, so that the least thing they said filled us with admiration, an admiration which after all was injurious enough to those gentlemen.

The same happens of our shepherds, for we are the more pleasingly struck with finding them thinking finely in their simple style because we the least expected it.

Another thing that suits with the pastoral style is to run only on actions, and never almost on reflections. Those who have a middling share of wit, or a wit but little improved by a converse with polite books or persons, use to discourse only of those particular things of which they have had a sense, while others, raising themselves higher, reduce all things into general ideas. The minds of the latter have worked and reflected upon their sentiments and experiments; it happens that what they have seen hath led them to what they have not seen; whereas those of an inferior order, not pursuing their ideas beyond what they have a sense of, it may happen that what resembles it most may still be new to them. Hence proceeds the insatiable desire of the multitude to see the same objects, and their admiring always almost the same things.

A consequence of this disposition of mind is the adding to the things that are related any circumstances, whether useful or not. This happens because the mind has been extremely struck with the particular action, and with all that attended it. Contrary to this a great genius, despising all these petty circumstances, fixes on what is most essential in things, which commonly may be related without the circumstances.

It is truer than it seems that in such composures wherein passion is to be described it is better to imitate the way of speaking used by men of indifferent capacity than the style of more refined wits. I must own that thus there is little related besides actions, and we do not rise to reflections, but nothing is more graceful than actions so displayed as to bring their reflection along with them. Such is this admirable touch in Virgil: "Galatea throws an apple at me, then runs to hide herself behind the willows, and first would be perceived." The shepherd does not tell you what is Galatea's design, though he is fully sensible of it; but the action has made a deep, pleasing impression on his mind, and according as he represents it, it is impossible but you must guess its meaning. Now the mind is delighted with sensible ideas because it easily admits of them, and it loves to penetrate, provided it be without effort; whether it be that it loves to act but to a certain degree, or that a little penetration indulges its vanity. So the mind hath the double pleasure, first of getting an easy idea, then of penetrating, whenever such cases as that of Galatea are laid before it. The action and in a manner the soul of the action all at once strike the eyes of the mind; it can see nothing more in the matter, nor more quickly; neither can it ever be put to less expense.

In Virgil's Second Eclogue, Corydon, to commend his pipe, tells us that Damaetas gave it him when he died, and said to him, "Thou art the second master it hath had," and Amyntas was jealous because it was not bequeathed him. All these circumstances are altogether pastoral. It might not perhaps be disagreeable to bring in a shepherd who is puzzled in the midst of his story, and who finds some difficulty in recovering himself; but this would require some art in the management.

There are no persons whom it becomes better to lengthen a little their narrations with circumstances than lovers. They ought not indeed to be absolutely needless or too far-fetched, for this would be tedious, though it may be natural enough; but those that have but a half relation to the action which is talked of, and that show more passion than they are considerable, can never fail to please. So when, in one of Monsieur de Segrais's eclogues, a shepherdess says,

> The songs which Lysis and Menalcas sing
> Please ev'ry swain, and make the valleys ring;
> But I like better those which near this tree
> My jealous shepherd lately made for me.

The circumstance of the [tree] is pretty only as it had been needless for any other but a lover. According to our idea of shepherds, tales and narrations become them very well; but for them to make speeches such as those in *L'Astrée*, full of general reflections and chains of arguments, is a thing which I do not think their character allows.

It is not amiss to make them give descriptions, provided they be not very long. That of the cup which the goatherd promises to Thyrsis in Theocritus's first idyllium somewhat exceeds the bounds. Yet, according to that example, Ronsard and Belleau, his contemporary, have made some that are yet longer. When their shepherds are about describing a basket, a goat, or a blackbird, which they make the prize of a pastoral combat, they never have done. Not that their descriptions are sometimes without great beauties, and are writ without admirable art; far from this, they have too much of it for shepherds.

Vida, a Latin poet of the last age and of great reputation, in his eclogue of Nicé, whom I take to be Vittoria Colonna, the Marquess of Pescario's widow, brings in the shepherd Damon giving a description of a rush basket which he is to make for her. He says that he will represent in it Davalos, that is the marquess, dying, and grieved that he does not die in battle; some kings, captains, and nymphs in tears about him, Nicé praying the gods in vain, Nicé fainting away at the news of Davalos's death, and with difficulty recovering her senses by the means of the water which her women throw on her face; and he adds that he would have expressed many complaints and moans if they could be expressed on rush. Here are a great many things to be showed on a basket! Neither do I relate them all; but I cannot tell how all this can be expressed on rush, nor how Damon, who owns he cannot express on it the complaints of Nicé is not at a loss to display on it the marquess's grief for dying in his bed. I shrewdly suspect that Achilles's shield is the original from which this basket has been imitated.

I find that Virgil has used similitudes very often in his pastoral discourses. These similitudes are very properly brought in to supply the place of those trivial comparisons, and principally of those clownish proverbial sayings, which real shepherds use almost continually. But as there is nothing more easily to be imitated than this way of using similitudes, it is what Virgil hath been most copied in. We find in all your writers of eclogues, nothing more common than shepherdesses who exceed all others as much "as lofty pines o'ertop the lowly reed, or highest oaks the humblest shrubs exceed"; we see nothing but the cruelty of ungrateful shepherdesses who are to a shepherd "what frosts or storms are to the tenderest flowers, like hail to rip'ning corn, etc." I think all this old and worn threadbare at this time of day, and to say the truth on it, it is no great pity. Similitudes naturally are not very proper for passion, and shepherds should only use them when they find it difficult to express themselves otherwise; then they would have a very great beauty; but I know but very few of that kind.

Thus we have pretty near discovered the pitch of wit which shepherds ought to have, and the style they should use. It is methinks with eclogues as with those dresses which are worn at masques or balls; they are of much finer stuff than those which real shepherds usually wear; nay, they are even adorned with ribbands and points, and are only made after the country cut. In the same manner the thoughts which are the subject matter of eclogues ought to be finer and more delicate than those of real shepherds, but they must have the most simple and most rural dress possible.

Not but that we ought to use both simplicity and a country-like plainness even in the thoughts, but we ought to take notice that this simplicity and country-like plainness only exclude your excessive delicacy in the thoughts, like that of the refined wits in courts and cities, and not the light which nature and the passions bestow of themselves; otherwise the poet would degenerate and run into childish talk that would beget laughter rather than admiration. Something of this kind is pleasant enough in one of Rémi Belleau's eclogues, where a young shepherd, having stolen a kiss from a pretty shepherdess, says to her,

> I've kissed some new-fawned kids, like other swains,
> I've kissed the sucking calf, which in our plains
> Young Colin gave me; but this kiss, I swear,
> Is sweeter much than all those kisses were.

Yet such a childishness seems more pardonable in this young shepherd than in the Cyclops Polyphemus. In Theocritus's idyllium that bears his name, and which is fine, he is thinking how to be revenged on his mother, a sea nymph, because she never took care to make Galatea, another sea nymph, have a kindness for his giantship; so he says to his mistress that he'll tell his mother, to make her mad, that he has a pain in his head and in his thighs.

It is hard to imagine that, ugly as he was, his mother could dote on him so much as to be very much concerned to hear the poor little urchin have those petty ills, or that the clownish giant could invent so gentle a revenge; his character is better kept when he promises his mistress to make her a present of a litter of cubs or young bears, which he breeds for her in his cave. And now that I speak of bears, I would gladly know why Daphnis when he is going to die bids adieu to the bears, the lions, and the wolves, as well as to the fair fountain Arethuse, and to the silver streams of Sicily. Methinks a man does not often use to regret the loss of such company.

I have but one remark more to make, which hath no manner of connection with those that go before. It is concerning those eclogues which have a burthen much like those in ballads, that is, a verse or two repeated several times. I need not say that we ought to place those repeated verses in such parts of the eclogue as may require, or at least bear such a verse to interlard them; but it may not be amiss to observe that all the art that Theocritus hath used in an idyllium of this kind was only to take this burthen and scatter it up and down through his idyllium, right or wrong, without the least regard to the sense of the places where he inserted it, nay, without even so much as respecting some of the phrases which he made no difficulty to split in two.

I have here spoken with a great deal of freedom of Theocritus and Virgil, notwithstanding they are ancients, and I do not doubt but that I shall be esteemed one of the profane by those pedants who profess a kind of religion which consists in worshipping the ancients. It is true, however, that I have often commended Virgil and Theocritus, but yet I have not always praised them; much less have I said, like the superstitious, that even their faults (if they had any) were beautiful; neither have I strained all the natural light of reason to justify them. I have partly approved and partly censured them, as if they have been some living authors whom I saw every day, and there lies the sacrilege! [16]

Bernard Le Bovier de Fontenelle A DIGRESSION

ON THE ANCIENTS AND THE MODERNS

Once the whole question of the pre-eminence of the ancients and moderns is properly understood, it boils down to knowing whether the trees which used to be seen in the countryside were taller than those of today.[17] If they were, Homer, Plato, Demosthenes cannot be equaled in these latter centuries; but if our trees are as tall as those of former times, then we can equal Homer, Plato, and Demosthenes.

Let us explain this paradox. If the ancients were more intelligent than we, the reason must be that brains in those days were better arranged, made of firmer or more delicate fibers, and filled with more animal spirits;[18] but why should the brains of those days have been better arranged? Trees too, then, would have been taller and more beautiful; for if Nature was then younger and more vigorous, trees as well as human brains must have felt the effect of that vigor and youth.

The admirers of the ancients ought to be very careful when they tell us that the ancients are the sources of good taste and reason as well as of knowledge destined to illuminate all other men; that one is intelligent only in proportion as one admires them; and that Nature wore herself out in producing those great originals; for in fact these admirers make the ancients of another species from ourselves, and science is not in agreement with all these fine phrases. Nature has at hand a certain clay which is always the same and which she unendingly turns and twists into a thousand different shapes, thus forming men, animals, and plants; and certainly she did not shape Plato, Demosthenes, or Homer from finer or better-prepared clay than she used for our philosophers, orators, and poets of today. As to our minds, which are not of a material nature, I am concerned here only with their connection with the brain (which is material) and which by its varying arrangements produces the differences between one man and another.

But if trees are equally tall in all centuries they are not so in all countries. Similar differences occur also among minds. The various ideas are like plants or flowers which do not flourish equally in all climates.[19] Perhaps French soil is not suitable for Egyptian lines of thought as it is not for their palm trees; and not to go so far afield, perhaps orange trees, which do not grow so well here as in Italy, are an indication that in Italy there is a certain kind of mind which does not have its exact equal in France. In any case it is sure that through the connection and reciprocal interdependence which exist among the parts of the material world, the differences of climate, whose effect is observable in plants, must produce some effect on human brains as well.[20]

However, this effect is smaller and less obvious because art and culture work more successfully on brains than on the land, which is of a harder and less manipulable substance. Thus the thoughts of one country can be more easily carried to another than its plants, and we would not have as much difficulty in capturing the Italian genius in our literary works as we would have in raising orange trees.

It is ordinarily said that there is more diversity among minds than among faces. I am not so sure. Faces, merely because they look at each other, do not come to look like each other; but minds develop resemblances as a result of reciprocal contacts. Thus minds, which naturally would differ as much as faces, come to differ less.

The ease with which minds use each other for models produces the result that nations do not persevere in whatever habits of thought they derive from their climate. The reading of Greek books produces in us proportionately the same effect as if we were to marry Greek women. It is certain that after many alliances of this kind the blood of Greece and that of France would be changed and the facial expression peculiar to each of the two nations would be somewhat altered.

What is more, since it is not possible to judge which climates are the most favorable for the mind, and since they all apparently have complementary advantages and disadvantages, and since those climates which of themselves would give a higher degree of liveliness would also produce less precision (and so on for the other pairs of good and bad qualities), it follows that the differences between climates must be counted for nothing provided minds are otherwise equally cultivated. At the very most one might think that the torrid zone and the two frigid zones are not well adapted to learning.[21] Up to the present day education has not gone farther than Egypt and Mauritania in one direction and Sweden in the other; perhaps it is not by chance that learning has been restricted to the area between the Atlas Mountains and the Baltic Sea; but we do not know whether these are the limits which nature has set for it or whether we may hope some day to see great Negro or Lapp authors.

However that may be, the main question concerning the ancients and the moderns now seems to me resolved. Centuries do not put any natural differences among men. The climate of Greece or Italy and that of France are too much alike to be the cause of a perceptible difference between the Greeks and the Romans and ourselves. Even if some such difference existed it would be very easy to eliminate, and after all would be no more to their advantage than to ours. So we are now all perfectly equal, ancients and moderns, Greeks, Romans, and Frenchmen.

I cannot guarantee that this reasoning will seem convincing to everybody. If I had used the great tricks of eloquence, if I had balanced facts of history favorable to the moderns with facts of history favorable to the ancients, and passages praising the ones with passages praising the others, if I had called "obstinate pedants" those who call us "ignorant and superficial thinkers"; and if according to the code established among men of letters I had given back exactly insult for insult to the partisans of the ancients, perhaps my proofs would have been more to the common taste; but it seemed to me that if the business were gone about that way it would never end, and after many fine declamations on either side we should be amazed to see that we had not advanced one step. I thought it would be quicker to consult science on this question, for science has the secret of shortening many of the disputes which rhetoric makes endless.

On this subject, for instance, after we have recognized the equality existing between the ancients and ourselves, there remains no further difficulty. It is obvious that all the differences, whatever they may be, must be caused by exterior circumstances, such as the historical moment, the government, and the state of things in general.

"The ancients discovered everything"; on this point their partisans triumph. "Therefore they were much more intelligent than we"; not at all, but they were ahead of us. I should be just as willing to see them praised for having drunk first the waters of our rivers and for us to be blamed because we drink only what they left. If we had been in their place we would have done the discovering; if they were in ours, they would add to what has already been discovered. There is no great mystery about that.

Bernard Le Bovier de Fontenelle

I am not speaking here of the discoveries brought about by chance and for which credit may perhaps be given to the stupidest man in the world; I am concerned only with those discoveries which required thought and some mental effort. It is sure that the crudest of these were reserved for the greatest geniuses, and that all Archimedes could have done in the earliest ages would have been to invent the plough. Archimedes living in another century burns the Roman fleet with mirrors — if indeed that is not just a tale.

A man concerned to utter specious and brilliant remarks would maintain to the glory of the moderns that the mind need not make a great effort for first discoveries, and that Nature seems herself to lead us to them; but more effort is needed to add to them and a still greater effort in proportion to the amount already added because the subject is more nearly exhausted and what remains in it to be discovered is less apparent to the naked eye. Perhaps the admirers of the ancients would not neglect a line of reasoning as good as that if it favored their side, but I admit in all good faith that it is not very solid.

It is true that to add to earlier discoveries often requires a greater effort of mind than the original discoveries did, but one is in a much more advantageous position to make the effort. The mind has already been enlightened by the very discoveries one has before one's eyes; we have conceptions borrowed from others which can be added to those we form ourselves; and if we surpass the first discoverer, he himself has helped us to do so; thus he still has a share in the glory of our work, and if he withdrew what belongs to him we should have nothing more left than he.

So far do I carry the equity with which I consider this point that I give the ancients credit for numberless false ideas they had, for faults of logic they committed, and for foolish statements they made. In the nature of things it is not given to us to arrive quickly at a reasonable opinion on anything; we must first wander about for a long time and pass through many kinds of mistakes and many kinds of irrelevancies. It seems now that it would always have been easy to conceive the idea that the whole working of nature is explained by the shapes and movements of various bodies; however, before arriving at that point we had first to try the ideas of Plato, the numbers of Pythagoras, and the qualities of Aristotle; only when these had been recognized as false were we driven to accept the correct theory. I say we were driven to it, for in fact no other remained, and it seems that we avoided the truth as long as we could. We are grateful to the ancients

361

for having worn out most of the false ideas conceivable; it was absolutely necessary to pay to ignorance and error the tribute the ancients paid, and we ought not to be harsh toward those who discharged this debt for us. The same thing is true of various subjects about which we would say foolish things if they had not already been said and, so to speak, preempted; however there still are occasionally moderns who return to them, perhaps because these things have not yet been said as many times as necessary. Thus, enlightened by the ideas of the ancients and by their very mistakes, we might be expected to surpass them. If we only equaled them we should be far inferior to them by nature; we should barely be men compared with them.

However, if the moderns are to be able to improve continually on the ancients, the fields in which they are working must be of a kind which allows progress. Eloquence and poetry require only a certain number of rather narrow ideas as compared with other arts, and they depend for their effect primarily upon the liveliness of the imagination. Now mankind could easily amass in a few centuries a small number of ideas, and liveliness of imagination has no need of a long sequence of experiences nor of many rules before it reaches the furthest perfection of which it is capable. But science, medicine, mathematics, are composed of numberless ideas and depend upon precision of thought which improves with extreme slowness; sometimes indeed these studies must be helped by experiences which chance alone brings forth and which it does not produce at the desired place. It is obvious that all this is endless and that the last physicists or mathematicians will naturally have to be the ablest.

And in fact, the most important aspect of philosophy, and that which is applicable not only to philosophy but to everything, I mean the way we think, has been very much improved in this century. I doubt that many will be able to understand the remark I am about to make; nevertheless I shall make it for the sake of those who understand the problem of philosophical thought; and I may boast that it is evidence of courage to expose oneself for the sake of truth to the criticisms of all the others, whose number is assuredly not negligible. No matter what the subject is, the ancients rarely reason with absolute correctness. Often mere expediency, petty similarities, frivolous witticisms, or vague and confused discourse pass among them for proofs; therefore, it cost them very little effort to prove anything. However, what an ancient could prove in all frivolity would cause a good deal of trouble nowadays to a modern, for are we not much more rigorous in the matter of reasoning? Reasoning must be intelligible, it must be exact, it must be conclusive. Scholars are cunning enough to pick out the slightest ambiguity in ideas or in words; they are harsh enough to condemn the cleverest thing in the world if it does not bear on the point. Before Descartes reasoning was done more comfortably; past centuries are very fortunate not to have had that man. It is he, as I believe, who introduced this new method of reasoning which is much more estimable than his philosophy itself, for of that a considerable part has been shown to be false or uncertain according to the very rules he taught us. In sum, there now reigns not only in our good scientific and philosophical works but also in those on religion, ethics, and criticism a precision and an exactness which have scarcely been known until now.

I am even convinced that these will be carried yet further. A few arguments in the style of the ancients still slip into our best books, but we shall be the ancients some day, and will it not be just for our posterity in its turn to rectify our mistakes and to go beyond us, especially in the technique of reasoning which is a science in itself and the most difficult as well as the least cultivated of all?

As far as eloquence and poetry are concerned, since these are the subject of the principal dispute between the ancients and the moderns although they are not very important in themselves, I think the ancients may have attained perfection in them because, as I have said, such perfection can be achieved in a few centuries, and I do not know exactly how many are necessary. I say that the Greeks and the Romans may have been excellent poets and orators, but were they? Clarification of this point would require an endless discussion which, however just and exact it might be, would never satisfy the partisans of the ancients. How can one debate with them? They have resolved to excuse all the faults of the ancients. What am I saying, to "excuse" them? They are determined to admire those faults above all else. This is the particular characteristic of textual commentators, the most superstitious of all the groups which are swayed by the cult of antiquity. What charming ladies would not be happy to inspire in their lovers a passion as intense and as tender as that which a Greek or Roman author inspires in his respectful commentator?

Nevertheless I shall say something more precise about the eloquence and the poetry of the ancients, not that I am unaware of the danger which lurks in such a declaration, but because it seems to me that the slight authority I have and the little attention people will pay to my opinions set me at liberty to say whatever I want. I think eloquence was further developed among the ancients than poetry, and that Demosthenes and Cicero are more perfect in their art than Homer and Virgil in theirs. I see an entirely natural reason for this. Eloquence was the key to success in the Greek and Roman republics, and it was as advantageous to be born with the talent for speaking well as it would be today to be born with an income of a million a year. Poetry, on the other hand, was good for nothing, as it has always been under all kinds of governments; that failing is of the essence of poetry. I think too that in both poetry and eloquence the Greeks are inferior to the Romans. I shall make an exception for one kind of poetry wherein the Romans have nothing to compare with the Greeks; I am, of course, speaking of tragedy. To my individual taste Cicero is better than Demosthenes, Virgil than Theocritus and Homer, Horace than Pindar, Livy and Tacitus than all the Greek historians.

In the light of the theory we established at the beginning, this order is a natural one. The Romans were modern compared to the Greeks, but since eloquence and poetry are rather limited there must have been a time when they were carried to their ultimate perfection; I hold that for eloquence and for history that time was the century of Augustus. I cannot imagine anything surpassing Cicero and Livy. Not that they do not have their faults, but I do not believe it is possible to have fewer faults with so many great qualities, and, as everyone knows, this is the only way in which men may be described as perfect in anything.

Virgil's is the most beautiful versification in the world; perhaps, however, it would not have been harmed if he had had the leisure to touch it up a little. There are great passages in the *Aeneid* of a finished beauty which I do not think will ever be surpassed. Insofar as the structure of the poem as a whole is concerned, or the manner of handling events or of producing agreeable surprises, or the nobility of the characters or the variety of the incidents, I shall not be surprised if Virgil is far surpassed; our novels, which are prose poems, have already shown the possibility of outdoing him.

My intention is not to go into critical detail; I merely wish to point out that since the ancients were able to achieve ultimate perfection in certain things and not in others, we ought, in gauging their success, to show no respect for their great names nor have any indulgence for their faults; we ought, instead, to treat them as though they were moderns. We must be capable of saying, or of hearing others say without blinking the fact, that there are irrelevancies in Homer or in Pindar; we must make bold to believe that mortal eyes can see faults in these great geniuses; we must be able to accept a comparison between Cicero or Demosthenes and a man with a French name, perhaps even a commoner's name: this will require a great, a prodigious effort of the reason!

In this connection I cannot keep from laughing at the ridiculousness of men. Prejudice for prejudice, it would be more reasonable to favor the moderns than the ancients. Naturally the moderns have outdone the ancients: prepossession in their favor is thus well founded. What are, on the other hand, the foundations of prejudice in favor of the ancients? Their names, which sound better in our ears because they are Greek or Latin; the reputation they had of being the greatest men of their century; the number of their admirers, which is very great because it has had time to grow through a long period of years. Taking all that into consideration, it would still be better to be prejudiced in favor of the moderns, but mankind, not content to abandon reason for prejudices, often chooses among these the ones which are the most unreasonable.

Once we have decided that the ancients have reached the point of perfection in something, let us be satisfied to say they cannot be surpassed, but let us not say they cannot be equaled, as their admirers are very prone to do. Why should we not equal them? As men we always have the right to aspire to do so. Is it not odd that we need to prick up our courage on this point and that we, whose vanity is often based on nothing solid, should sometimes show a humility no less insecure? It is thus certain that no manifestation of the ridiculous will be spared us.

No doubt Nature still remembers well how she shaped the head of Cicero and Livy. In every century she produces men fit to be great men, but the historical moment does not always let them use their talents. Inundations of barbarians, governments either wholly opposed or generally unfavorable to the sciences and the arts, prejudices and imaginings which can take endlessly different forms, as in China the respect for dead bodies which prevents all dissections, universal wars — phenomena such as these often put ignorance and bad taste into the saddle, and for a long time. Add to these all the various turns which personal fortune can take, and you will see how vainly Nature sows Ciceros and Virgils in this world, and how rare it must be that some of them, so to speak, yield their fruit. It is said that Heaven, in bringing forth great kings, brings forth also great poets to sing their praises and fine historians to set down their lives. At least this much of that is true: in all periods the historians and the poets are ready, and princes need only want to set them to work.

The barbarous centuries which followed that of Augustus and preceded this one provide the partisans of the ancients with that one among their arguments which seems most sound. How does it happen, they say, that in those centuries ignorance was so thick and so deep? Because the Greeks and Romans were not known in those times and were no longer read; but from the moment that men again perceived those excellent models reason and good taste were reborn. That is true, and yet it proves nothing. If a man having a good start in learning and in literature happened to fall ill of a disease which led him to forget them, would it be right to say that he had become unable to learn them? No, for he could pick them up again at will, beginning with their most elementary aspects. If a medicine suddenly gave him back his memory he would be spared a great deal of trouble, for he would find himself in possession of all he had known before; and to go on he would have only to start again where he had left off. The reading of ancient authors [they say] dissipated the ignorance and barbarism of earlier centuries. I am sure it did. It brought back to us, all of a sudden, ideas of the good and the beautiful which we should otherwise have been a long time in conceiving, but which we would have arrived at in the end without the help of the Greeks and Romans if we had thought diligently enough. And where should we have found them? Where the ancients did. Even the ancients, before they found them, groped about for a long time.

The comparison we have just made between the men of all periods and an individual man may be extended to the whole question of the ancients and the moderns. A cultivated intelligence is composed, so to speak, of all the intelligences of preceding centuries; one intelligence only has been cultivated during all that time. Thus Mankind, which has lived from the beginning of the world to the present day, has had a childhood, during which he concerned himself only with the most pressing needs of life; and a youth, during which he succeeded rather well in the things of the imagination such as poetry and eloquence, and when he even began to think, but with less soundness than enthusiasm. He is now in the prime of life and reasons more forcefully and more incisively than ever; but he would be much farther advanced if the passion of war had not occupied him for a long time and filled him with scorn for that learning to which he has at last returned.

It is a shame not to be able to carry to the end a comparison which is going so well; but I am forced to admit that mankind will never have an old age; in each century men will be able to do the things proper to youth as they will more and more those which are suited to the prime of life; that is to say, to leave the allegory, that mankind will never degenerate, and the sound views of all subsequent thinkers will forever be added to the existing stock.

That endlessly growing stock of ideas to be followed up, of rules to be carried out, also continually increases the difficulty of all branches of the sciences and the arts; but on the other hand, gains are made which compensate for these difficulties. I can best explain by examples. In Homer's time it was a great wonder that a man was able to subject his speech to rhythm, to long and short syllables, and at the same time to make of it something reasonable. Poets were given endless license, and the public was only too glad to have verses at all. Homer might speak five different languages in one line; he might use the Doric dialect when the Ionian was not suitable; if neither suited, he could use the Attic, the Eolic, or the common tongue, that is to say, speak Picard, Gascon, Norman, Breton, and plain French at the same time. He could lengthen a word if it was too short or shorten it if it was too long; nobody found anything to criticize in such procedures. This odd mixture of languages, this outlandish gathering of disfigured words, was the speech of the gods; at least it certainly was not that of men. Bit by bit the ridiculousness of such poetic license was recognized. One by one permissible variants were excluded, and at the present time poets, despoiled of their former privileges, are reduced to speaking in a natural manner. It would seem that the task has grown harder and the difficulty of making verses greater. No, for our minds are enriched with many poetic ideas supplied by our study of the ancients; we are guided by the many rules and reflections which have been made concerning the poetic art, and since Homer lacked all those aids he was justly compensated by the broad poetic license he was allowed. To tell the truth, however, I think his condition better than ours; compensation in these matters is never exact.

Mathematics and physics are sciences whose yoke grows daily heavier on all who practice them; in the end we would be compelled to give up except that methods are improving at the same time; the same intelligence which brings disciplines nearer to perfection by adding new aspects to them also perfects and abridges the manner of learning them and provides new means with which to grasp the wider range which science has. A scientist in our day knows ten times as much as a scientist of the time of Augustus, but he has had ten times as many opportunities of becoming a scientist.

I should like to paint Nature with scales in her hand, like Justice, to indicate how she weighs and measures out almost equally whatever she distributes among men, happiness, talent, the advantages and disadvantages of different social stations, the facilities and difficulties associated with the things of the mind.

By virtue of these compensations we can hope to be excessively admired in the centuries to come just as we are little valued today in our own. Efforts will be made to find in our works beauties we did not claim to put there. An indefensible mistake, recognized as such by the author himself today, will find defenders of an invincible courage; and Heaven only knows with what scorn they will treat, in comparison with us, the thinkers of those times, who may well be Red Indians. So the same prejudice abases us at one time only to exalt us at another; so we are first its victim and then its god; it all makes a rather amusing game which one can follow with indifferent eyes.

I can even carry prediction still further. Once the Romans were moderns and complained of the stubbornness with which the Greeks were admired, they being then the ancients. The difference of time between them disappears in our eyes because of the great distance at which we find ourselves from them; they are both ancients for us, and we have no scruples in ordinarily preferring the Romans to the Greeks, because as between ancients and ancients there is no harm in preferring one to the other; but as between ancients and moderns it would be a great scandal for the moderns to win. We need only be patient, and after a long succession of centuries we shall become the contemporaries of the Greeks and Romans; it is easy to foresee that then nobody will hesitate to prefer us openly to them in many things. The best works of Sophocles, of Euripides, of Aristophanes will not stand up before *Cinna, Horace, Ariane, Le Misanthrope,* and many other tragedies and comedies of the great period; for we must honestly admit that the great period has been ended for several years. I do not think that *Théagène et Chariclée,* or *Clitophon et Leucippe* will ever be compared to *Cyrus,* to *L'Astrée,* to *Zaïde,* or to *La Princesse de Clèves.*[22] There are even new literary types such as amatory letters, tales, operas, in each of which we have an excellent author [23] and with which antiquity provides nothing for comparison; apparently posterity will not surpass us in these. Let the new types be represented only by popular ballads, a kind of writing which is very ephemeral and to which we do not pay great attention; it must be admitted that we have an enormous number of them, all filled with fire and wit. I maintain that if they had been known to Anacreon, he would have sung them rather than most of his own. We see by the example of many works of poetry that versification can be just as noble today as it ever was, and at the same time more precise and exact. I intend to omit details and I shall not dwell any longer on our riches; but I am convinced we are like great lords who do not always take the trouble to keep an accurate account of all their possessions, and who are unaware of some of them.

If the great men of this century had charitable feelings toward posterity, they would warn it not to admire them too much, but always to aspire to equal them at least. Nothing so limits progress, nothing narrows the mind so much as excessive admiration of the ancients. When the authority of Aristotle was unquestioned, when truth was sought only in his enigmatic writings and never in Nature, not only did philosophy not advance at all, but it fell into an abyss of nonsense and unintelligible ideas whence it was rescued only with great difficulty. Aristotle has never made one true philosopher, but he has stifled many who might have become philosophers if they had been allowed. And the worst is that once a fancy of that kind is established among men it lasts for a long time; whole centuries are needed for recovery from it, even after its preposterousness has been recognized. If some day we should become equally stubborn about Descartes and put him in Aristotle's place very much the same bad effect would result.

However, I must keep nothing back, and so I shall say that I am not at all sure posterity will count as one of our merits the two or three thousand years which one day will separate it from us as we do the time that separates the Greeks and Romans from ourselves. In all probability reason will have made progress and the generality of men will be freed from the crude prejudice in favor of the old. Perhaps that prejudice will not last much longer; perhaps at this moment we admire the ancients vainly and are never to be similarly admired ourselves. That would be somewhat unfortunate.

If after all I have just said I am not excused for having dared to attack the ancients in the *Discourse on the Eclogue*, it must be that such an attack is an unpardonable crime. I shall therefore say no more about it. I shall add only that if I have shocked past centuries by my criticism of the eclogues of the ancients, I very much fear that I shall not please this century by my own. Aside from the defects they contain, they always present a tender, delicate, diligent love which is faithful to the point of superstition; and from all that I hear, this century is ill chosen for the painting of such perfect love.

NOTES AND INDEX

Notes

The following are some of the chief works, in English and French, on literary criticism in seventeenth-century France.

Adams, Henry H., and Baxter Hathaway, *Dramatic Essays of the Neoclassic Age*, New York, 1950.

Borgerhoff, E. B. O. E., *The Freedom of French Classicism*, Princeton, 1950.

Clark, A. F. B., *Boileau and the French Classical Critics in England (1660–1830)*, Paris, 1925.

Clark, Barrett H., *European Theories of the Drama*, New York, 1947.

Kern, Edith G., *The Influence of Heinsius and Vossius upon French Dramatic Theory*, Baltimore, 1949.

Lancaster, H. C., *A History of French Dramatic Literature in the Seventeenth Century*, Baltimore, 1929–1942.

Morrissette, Bruce A., "French Criticism: Seventeenth Century," in Joseph T. Shipley, *Dictionary of World Literature*, New York, 1953, pp. 174–180.

Saintsbury, George, *A History of Criticism and Literary Taste in Europe* (3 vols.; Edinburgh and London, 1928), II, 239–322.

Spingarn, Joel E., *A History of Literary Criticism in the Renaissance*, 2d ed., New York, 1908.

Adam, Antoine, *Histoire de la littérature française au XVIIᵉ siècle*, Paris, 1952.

Bourgoin, Auguste, *Les Maîtres de la critique au XVIIᵉ siècle*, Paris, 1889.

Bray, René, *La Formation de la doctrine classique en France*, Paris, 1927.

Brunetière, Ferdinand, *L'Evolution des genres dans l'histoire de la littérature*, Paris, 1890.

Gasté, Armand, *La Querelle du Cid*, Paris, 1898.

Gillot, Hubert, *La Querelle des anciens et des modernes en France*, Paris, 1914.

Lemaître, Jules, *Corneille et la poétique d'Aristote*, Paris, 1888.

Mornet, D., *Histoire de la littérature française classique (1660–1700)*, Paris, 1940.

Peyre, Henri, *Le Classicisme français*, New York, 1942.

Rigault, Hippolyte, *Histoire de la querelle des anciens et des modernes*, Paris, 1856.

Introduction (pages ix–xix)

1. Alfred North Whitehead, *Science and the Modern World* (New York, 1954), pp. 57–58.

2. See *Tristam Shandy*, III, 12.

3. George Saintsbury, *A History of Criticism and Literary Taste in Europe* (3 vols.; Edinburgh and London, 1928), II, 309–310.

4. *Pratique du théâtre*, Première Partie, ch. 4.

5. *Entretiens d'Ariste et d'Eugène*, ch. 4.

6. Voltaire paid Boileau the compliment to have written like Horace, as Racine wrote like Virgil; see the *Preface to Œdipe.*

7. *Art poétique,* Chant IV.

Chapelain (pages 3–54)

Jean Chapelain (1595–1674) is perhaps most commonly known as the author of *La Pucelle,* an unreadable epic poem about Joan of Arc, of which Boileau said:

> La Pucelle est encore une oeuvre bien galante,
> Et je ne sais pourquoi je bâille en la lisant.

But Chapelain deserves to be remembered for his contributions to French criticism, chiefly in his letters (ed. Tamizey de Larroque, 2 vols., Paris, 1880–1883), in *Les Sentiments de l'Académie sur le Cid* (1638), and in the two essays here translated.

Though the essay on Marino's *Adone* (1623) is an early and perhaps not typical work, it is interesting on two counts: (1) it shows both Chapelain's derivation from Italian critical method in its rationalistic analysis of the question of genre, and his disposition to consider the possibility of new forms not provided for in classical criticism; (2) it seems to have been influential in the criticism of Davenant (see Preface to *Gondibert*) and Dryden. W. P. Ker, in his Introduction to the *Essays of John Dryden* (Oxford, 1900, I, xxviii), said: "The ancestors of Dryden's prose are to be traced in Chapelain's Preface to the *Adone* of Marino, in Mesnardière's *Poétique,* in the Dialogues and Essays of Sarasin, in the Prefaces of Scudéry, in the *Discours* and *Examens* of Corneille."

Thomas Rymer, in the Preface to his translation of Rapin's *Reflections on Aristotle's Treatise of Poesie* (1674), was influential in making the name of Giovan Battista Marino (1569–1625) a symbol in English criticism for stylistic excess. His reputation in France is summarized in the *Petit Larousse:* "[Marino's] style précieux et contourné (marinisme) eut la plus fâcheuse influence sur le développement du goût français." His poem *Adone,* published in Paris in 1623, similarly became an easy point of reference. For example, in the Dedication of the *Aeneis* (1697), Dryden said: "Whereas poems which are produced by the vigor of imagination only have a gloss upon them at the first which time wears off, the works of judgment are like the diamond. . . . Such is the difference betwixt Virgil's *Aeneis* and Marini's *Adone.*"

The essay on the reading of old romances was written about 1646; it was first published in *Continuations des mémoires de littérature et histoire* (Paris, 1728), VI, i, 281–342, and was later edited by Alphonse Feillet (Paris, 1870). In "A Seventeenth-Century French Source for Hurd's *Letters on Chivalry and Romance*" (*PMLA,* LII [1937], 820–828) Victor Hamm shows that Chapelain anticipated Hurd's opinion about the likenesses between the romances and the classical epics.

The present translations were made from Alfred C. Hunter's edition of Chapelain's *Opuscules Critiques* (Paris, 1936).

1. Giovanni Francesco Straparola (d. 1557?), author among other works of *Piacevole Notte* (Venice, 1550–1557).

2. One of the Seven against Thebes. He defied Jupiter and was struck by lightning while scaling the walls.

3. There is no extant Greek tragedy by this name, but at Rome Varius and Seneca treated the subject under the title *Thyestes.*

4. A novel in Greek by Heliodorus (fl. A.D. 225).

5. Musaeus was a Greek poet (fl. end of the fourth or beginning of the fifth century A.D.); author of *History of Hero and Leander.* He was later than and belonged to the school of Nonnus of Panopolis, who lived in the fifth century A.D. and is the author of a *Dionisyaca* in forty-eight books.

Notes

6. *De raptu Proserpinae*, by the Latin poet Claudian (A.D. 365?–408), of which three books survive.

7. See Catullus *Carm*. lxiv. The poem has 408 lines of which 205 (ll. 50–255) are devoted to the episode of Ariadna.

8. Literally "from the egg," i.e., from the ultimate source of the action (cf. Horace *Ars poet*. 147).

9. On the various interpretations of Aristotle's word περιπέτεια see S. H. Butcher, *Aristotle's Theory of Poetry and Fine Art* (4th ed., 1951), note on pp. 329–331.

10. "departure from logical order."

11. Diomedes: one of the principal heroes in the *Iliad*. Mezentius: legendary king of Caere in Etruria; he appears in the *Aeneid*.

12. Armida appears in Tasso's *Gerusalemme liberata*.

13. Gilles Ménage (1613–1692), a lawyer who entered the service of the Cardinal de Retz and took orders (1648). Later he left the Cardinal and lived independently. Molière pilloried him as Vadius in *Les Femmes savantes*. His works include the *Dictionnaire étymologique* (Paris, 1650), referred to in the dialogue, and *Observations sur la langue française*. A man of the *salons*, he refused an invitation from Queen Christina of Sweden in a Latin eclogue, which was the cause of a quarrel between Ménage and Gilles Boileau. Ménage's detestation of Boileau later forced him to break off his friendship with Chapelain.

Jean-François Sarasin (1614–1654), author of much light verse, of a work in Latin, *Bellum Parasiticum* (1644), of an *Histoire du siège de Dunkerque* (1649), and of an *Apologie de la morale d'Epicure* often attributed to Saint-Evremond. He was a courtier and professional wit whose natural habitat was the *salon*. See also headnote to his *Remarks on Scudéry's L'Amour Tyrannique*, below.

14. *Lancelot*, an interminable prose romance, written about 1225, whose success assured the popularity of tales of that sort.

15. Perhaps an allusion to Sarasin's *Histoire du siège de Dunkerque*.

16. Valentin Conrart (1603–1675). At his house were held the meetings which led to the establishment of the Académie française, whose first secretary he was. Conrart published no such work as the one here mentioned.

17. Jean de Joinville (1224?–1317) accompanied Saint Louis (Louis IX) to Egypt and chronicled the life of that king (1309); Geoffroi de Villehardouin (1150–1218) is the chronicler of an adventure in which he participated: *La Conquête de Constantinople*, the first printed edition of which appeared at Venice in 1573.

18. Julius Caesar Scaliger (1484–1558), in his commentary on Aristotle's *Poetics*, *Poetices libri septem* (1561), was one of the first to praise Virgil above Homer.

19. Olaüs Magnus (1490–1558), Swedish author of the famous *Historia de gentibus septentrionalibus* (Rome, 1555); Saxo Grammaticus (1150–1206?), Danish historian and poet, author of *Gesta danorum* (Paris, 1514); Polydore Virgil (1470?–1555), English historian also known as P. V. Castellensis, author of the *Historia anglica* (1534); George Buchanan (1506–1582), author of numerous tragedies in Latin and of *Rerum scoticarum historia* (1582); the *Life* of Saint Louis is by Joinville (see above, note 17); Bertrand du Guesclin, Constable of France (1320?–1380), eclipsed the fame of all the military leaders of his time; Jean le Meingre Bouciquaut II, Marshal of France (1366?–1421), was taken prisoner in the battle of Agincourt and died in England; Pierre Terrail, seigneur de Bayard (1473?–1524), called the *chevalier sans peur et sans reproche*, was considered the perfect incarnation of French chivalry; Jean Froissart (1333?–1400), best-known chronicler of events in the fourteenth century, whose writings are the mirror of the aristocratic society of his time; Enguerrand de Monstrelet (1390?–1453), whose *Chronique* details events in the period 1400–1444.

20. André Duchesne (1584–1640), author of, among other works, *Les Antiquités et recherches de la grandeur et de la majesté des rois de France* (1609) and of *Series auctorum omnium qui de Francorum historia et de rebus Francicis, cum ecclesiasticis tum secularibus, ab exordio regni ad nostra usque tempora* etc. (1633).

21. Marc de Vulson de Colombière (d. 1658) created the science of heraldry. In 1648 appeared his *Vrai théâtre d'honneur et de la chevalerie, ou Mémoires historiques de la noblesse, contenant les combats, les triomphes, les tournois, les joutes, les carrousels, les courses de bague, les cartels, les duels, les dégradations de noblesse.*

22. Ménage was the author of a *Mamurrae, parasito-sophistae metamorphosis,* and of a *Vita Gargilii Mamurrae parasito-pedagogi,* satires aimed at the pedantry of Pierre de Montmaur (1654–1648), professor of Greek in the Collège de France. Sarasin's sentence, with its exuberant Latinity, also parodies the pedantic style. "Apedestic" means ignorant.

23. William II, Bishop of Tyre (d. 1190), a historian of the crusades, is the author of *Historia rerum in partibus transmarinis gestarum* in twenty-three books, two of which have the value of personal memoirs.

24. *Silvestres homines sacer interpresque deorum caedibus et victu foedo deterruit Orpheus.* Horace *Ars poet.* 391: "While men still roamed the woods, Orpheus, the holy prophet of the gods, made them shrink from bloodshed and brutal living."—Trans. H. R. Fairclough, Loeb Classical Library.

25. *Ars poet.* 122: "He denies that laws were framed against him; he arrogates everything to himself by force of arms."—Fairclough.

26. Gothia is the Crimea; Scandia is Scandinavia; Sarmatia designates central and southern Russia; Scythia is the name for regions north and northeast of the Black Sea.

27. Eurystheus, King of Tiryns, who imposed the famous labors upon Hercules. See *Iliad* xix. 76 ff.

28. *Morata* rather than *urbana:* that is to say suited to their primitive way of life rather than refined and genteel.

29. Numa Pompilius is the second legendary king of Rome (715–672 B.C.). His name is here synonymous with primitive conditions as opposed to the refinement of the Republic and the Empire.

30. *Toxaris* is one of Lucian's dialogues. It describes remarkable instances of friendship among the Scythians and the Greeks.

31. Logres is variously identified in the Arthurian romances as Gascony, Saxon England, and as a town in England.

32. Tannegui Lefèvre (1615–1672) produced numerous editions of classical authors. No work by him on the Arthurian legends is known.

Sarasin (pages 55–79)

Jean-François Sarasin (1614–1654) published his *Discours sur la tragédie* in 1639 to support Scudéry in the quarrel over Corneille's *Cid.* Scudéry probably hoped to show by his play *L'Amour tyrannique,* the plot of which Sarasin summarizes in his essay, that he could write as good a play as *Le Cid* and still not violate any of the classical rules. One of the interesting things about Sarasin's treatment is his use of Heinsius's *De constitutione tragoediae* (1610), which was beginning to influence the common interpretation of Aristotle's *Poetics.* See Albert Mennung (i.e., Georg Heinrich Albert), *Jean-François Sarasin's Leben und Werke,* etc. (Halle, 1902–1904), I, 76. The present translation was made from the text of Sarasin's *Oeuvres,* edited by Paul Festugière (Paris, 1926), II, 3–36. See also Chapelain, *On the Reading of Old Romances,* note 13.

1. Horace *Epist.* II. i. 175: "That done, he cares not whether his play fall or stand square on its feet."—Trans. H. R. Fairclough, Loeb Classical Library.

Notes

2. Jean Mairet (1604–1686). His *La Silvanire ou la morte-vive,* a pastoral tragicomedy, was presented in 1625. *Sophonisbe,* a tragedy, was presented in 1629.

3. Daniel Heinsius (1580–1655), to whose commentary on Aristotle, *De constitutione tragoediae* (Leyden, 1611), Sarasin is much indebted.

4. Seneca *Hercules Oetaeus* 797: "Then with dreadful cries he filled the air."—Trans. Frank Justus Miller, Loeb Classical Library.

5. *Ibid.,* 739: "And whatever that poison touched begins to shrink."—Miller.

6. *Aeneid* ii, 26: "So all the Teucrian land frees herself from her long sorrow." —Fairclough.

7. *Ibid.,* 554: "Such was the close of Priam's fortunes."—Fairclough.

8. Aristotle *Poetics, xxvi.* 5: "Moreover the art attains its end within narrower limits; for the concentrated effect is more pleasurable than one which is spread over a long time and so diluted."—Trans. S. H. Butcher (London, 1917).

9. *Ars poet.* 147: "Nor does he begin . . . the war of Troy from the twin eggs" (i.e., from the birth of Helen).—Fairclough.

10. Joachim du Bellay (1522–1560), author of the famous *Défense et illustration de la langue française* (1549).

11. Alexandre Hardy (1560–1632). The full title of the play mentioned is *Elmire ou l'heureuse bigamie.*

12. "Complex." *Poetics* x.

13. Seneca *Agamemnon* 918: "I am Strophius—I have just left Phocis my kingdom, and am now returning, honored and distinguished through having gained a prize in the chariot race at the Olympic Games."—Trans. Watson Bradshaw (London, 1902).

14. *Ibid.,* 919: "And the cause for my coming on hither was simply to congratulate an old friend."—Bradshaw.

15. *Ibid.,* 942: "And Greece! be now my witness that you, my swift coursers, fly with your headlong speed from these treacherous regions."—Bradshaw.

16. *Poetics* xi.

17. *Ars poet.* 450: "He will prove an Aristarchus. He will not say, 'Why should I give offense to a friend about trifles?' "—Fairclough. The name of Aristarchus had become proverbial as that of a keen critic.

18. *Poetics* xvi: "But, of all recognitions, the best is that which arises from the incidents themselves."—Butcher.

19. *Ars poet.* 186: "Medea is not to butcher her boys before the people, nor impious Atreus cook human flesh upon the stage, nor Procne be turned into a bird, Cadmus into a snake."—Fairclough.

20. Suetonius *Nero* xii.

21. *Poetics* xiv.

22. *Ars poet.* 12: "But not so far that savage should mate with tame or serpents couple with birds, lambs with tigers."—Fairclough.

23. Apparently a reference to the last part of *Poetics* xiv, where Aristotle says that of the events that move pity and fear the best is one in which the agents are related to one another, and in which one in ignorance is about to kill the other but discovers the truth in time. This seems inconsistent with his earlier (xiii) statement that in the best tragedies the fortune of the hero goes from good to bad.

24. Horace *Epist.* II. i. 174: "[See] with what a loose sock [Plautus] scours the scene."—Fairclough.

25. Hippolyte-Jules Pilet de la Mesnardière (1610–1663) published the first volume of his *Poétique* in 1639. The remainder of the work was never published.

26. Virgil *Eclog.* vii. 5: "Ready in a match to sing, as well as to make reply."—Fairclough.

Hédelin (pages 80–100)

François Hédelin, abbé d'Aubignac (1604–1676), was perhaps the most mechanical and dogmatic of all the neoclassical critics of the drama. His criticism of Corneille, in which he was encouraged by Richelieu, was only part of his campaign to establish correctness. In 1647 he published a prose tragedy called *Zénobie,* of which Saint-Evremond said: "I remember that the Abbé d'Aubignac wrote one according to the laws he had imperiously prescribed for the stage. This piece had no success, notwithstanding which he boasted in all companies that he was the only French writer who had exactly followed the precepts of Aristotle; whereupon the Prince of Condé said wittily: 'I am obliged to Monsieur d'Aubignac for having so exactly followed Aristotle's rules, but I will never forgive the rules of Aristotle for having put Monsieur d'Aubignac upon writing so bad a tragedy.' "

La Pratique du théâtre (1657) is a long treatise (385 pages in a modern edition), consisting of four books. The three unities are discussed in Book II. It is hard to say definitely how strong was d'Aubignac's influence. Much of the evidence is collected in A. F. B. Clark, *Boileau and the French Classical Critics in England (1660–1830)* (Paris, 1925), pp. 239–241. Certainly Dennis, Dryden, Addison, and Joseph Warton knew his work. The anonymous English translation does not always stay very close to the original, and a few obscure passages in the text have been retranslated. Most of the following notes are from the excellent modern edition of *La Pratique* by Pierre Martino (Paris, 1927).

1. Josias de Soulas (1608–1672), a famous actor who under the stage name of Floridor played in Corneille's tragedy *Horace* (1639).
2. *La Dorinde* (1631), by le Sieur Auvray.
3. *Trucul.,* the opening lines.
4. Samuel Petit (1594–1643), author of several scholarly works, notably *Miscellaneorum libri novem* (1630) and *Observationum libri tres* (1641).
5. Aelius Donatus, fourth-century commentator on Terence.
6. Scudéry's *L'Amour tyrannique,* I, i.
7. Alessandro Piccolomini (1508–1578) and Bernardo Segni (d. 1558), Italian commentators on the *Poetics.*
8. *Discorsi di Nic. Rossi vicentino, intorno alla tragedia.* Vicenza, 1590.
9. *La Mariamne* (1637), by Tristan.

Corneille (pages 101–115)

The dramatic criticism of Pierre Corneille (1606–1684) consists of three discourses on drama and a series of short criticisms, called *Examens,* of his own plays. They were published in 1660 in a three-volume edition of his works. Each play was followed by its *examen,* and each volume of the edition was prefaced by one of the *Discours.* None of these was translated into English until the twentieth century, nor is there much reference to them in English criticism. But, if for no other reason than that they greatly influenced Dryden in the *Essay of Dramatic Poesy,* we can say that they had a significant influence on eighteenth-century England.

The three discourses should be read together. The first, translated (and slightly abridged) in Barrett H. Clark (*European Theories of the Drama* [New York, 1947], pp. 139–147), deals with the moral "uses" of tragedy and with its "parts." The morality of a play can be expressed by (1) speeches put in the mouths of characters, (2) simple descriptions of virtues and vices, (3) poetic justice, (4) the total effect of the tragedy—the purgation of pity and fear. After a brief notice of the "quantitative parts"—prologue, episode, exodus, and chorus—Corneille devotes the last half of the discourse to an interpretation of Aristotle's "parts"—subject, manner, sentiment, and diction, neglecting music and stage setting. The second discourse, translated in Adams and Hathaway (*Dramatic Essays of the Neoclassic Age* [New York, 1950], pp. 1–34), is on the subject of Aristotelian purgation and the means of effecting it. The third is different from the first two in its more technical concern for dramaturgical problems. It shows as well as the other two what is meant by "the vacillating compromises of [Corneille's] long duel with Aristotle," a phrase of Jules Lemaître, in *Corneille et la poétique d'Aristotle* (Paris, 1888).

1. Corneille's note: *Poetics* x. 3.
2. Corneille's note: *Ibid.*
3. Corneille's note: *Ibid.* xviii. 1.
4. Seneca *Medea* 975: "But thee, .poor senseless corse, within mine arms I'll bear."—Trans. Frank Justus Miller, Loeb Classical Library. Corneille, *Médée*, IV, 5.
5. Corneille's note: *Ars poet.* 189: *Neve minor, neu sit quinto productior actu/fabula.* ["A play should consist of five acts—no more, no less."]
6. Corneille's note: See *Poetics* xxvi.
7. Corneille's note: *Rodogune*, V, 3.
8. Corneille's note: *Poetics* v. 4.
9. Corneille's note: *Suppliants* 598–634. Besides, Aethra says nothing and merely listens to the chorus, which is divided into two parts.
10. Corneille's note: See Aeschylus *Agamemnon* 650 ff.
11. In the *Examen de Mélite,* which precedes the present *Discourse* in the editions published by Corneille.

Saint-Evremond (pages 116–139)

Charles de Marguetel de Saint-Denis, seigneur de Saint-Evremond (1610–1703), lived the last forty years of his life in England, where he wrote almost all of the essays for which he is now remembered, and where most of his work was first published. Some of the essays were privately circulated in manuscript; some were pirated and printed without Saint-Evremond's knowledge. The first authorized edition of his complete works was published posthumously by his friends Dr. P. Silvestre and Pierre Desmaizeaux, *Les Véritables oeuvres de M. de Saint-Evremond, publiées sur les manuscrits de l'auteur* (3 vols.; London, 1705). Later editions appeared in 1706 (Amsterdam), 1708, 1709, etc. But the English translations of various essays had been published in London as early as 1684. In 1692 Dryden wrote an introductory essay on Saint-Evremond for a volume of *Miscellaneous Essays by Monsieur St. Evremond,* which contained anonymous translations previously published. To this volume a second was added in 1694, containing translations by "Dr. Drake, Mr. Brown, Mr. Savage, Mr. Manning," and others. In 1700 a two-volume *Works* appeared, claiming to be a "translation . . . done from a copy of the last French Edition and corrected in many Places by the Pen of the Author." This was, however, only a reprint of the 1692–1694 edition with minor changes. When in 1714 Desmaizeaux published his scholarly edition of the works in translation, based on his 1705 edition of *Les Véritables oeuvres,* he followed the earlier translations, but these he carefully corrected and revised. Our text follows Desmaizeaux's second edition (1728); we have made a very few changes for the sake of clarity.

The dates accompanying the titles are those of composition, not publication.

Saint-Evremond's influence on Dryden, Temple, and Dennis can be discovered in their essays and in modern editions of those essays. The evidence has been summarized by A. F. B. Clark (*op cit.,* pp. 288–293). See also W. Melville Daniels, *Saint-Evremond en Angleterre* (Versailles, 1907). Ernst Mollenhauer, *Saint-Evremond als Kritiker* (Greifswald, 1914); Quentin M. Hope, *Saint-Evremond:*

Notes

The Honnête Homme *as Critic* (Bloomington, 1962); H. T. Barnwell, *Les Idées morales et critiques de Saint-Evremond* (Paris, 1957).

1. Racine's play was first performed in 1665.
2. Velleius Paterculus *Hist. Rom.* 11. 41: "He greatly resembled Alexander the Great, but only when Alexander was free from the influence of wine and master of his passions."—Trans. Frederick W. Shipley, Loeb Classical Library.
3. Quintus Curtius *De rebus gestis Alexandri Magni.*
4. Corneille, *La Mort de Pompée.*
5. Corneille, *Cinna,* I, i.
6. Corneille, *La Mort de Pompée.*
7. Corneille, *Oedipe.*
8. Corneille, *Sophonisbe.*
9. *De bell, civ.* i. 128: "If the victor had the gods on his side, the vanquished had Cato."—Trans. J. D. Duff, Loeb Classical Library.
10. *De rerum nat.* i. 101: "So potent was religion in persuading to evil deeds." Trans. W. H. D. Rouse, Loeb Classical Library.
11. *Ars poet.* 343: "He has won every vote who has blended profit and pleasure."—Trans. H. R. Fairclough, Loeb Classical Library.
12. *De rerum nat.* v. 107: "Which may pilot fortune steer from us."—Rouse.
13. *Ars poet.* 61.
14. Des Maizeaux's note: "Diogenes Laertius has transmitted to us that saying of Epicurus. M. de Saint-Evremond quotes it according to the translation of my Lord Bacon, *Serm. Fidel.* XVI, but this is more literal: *Impius est, non is qui multitudinis deos tollit, sed qui multitudinis opiniones diis adhibet.* Diog. Laert. x. 123." The text of Epicurus has: "Not the man who denies the gods worshipped by the multitude but he who affirms of the gods what the multitude believes about them is truly impious."—Trans. R. D. Hicks, Loeb Classical Library.
15. Virgil *Eclog.* iii. 60: "From Jove the Muses sprang."—Trans. T. C. Williams, *The Georgics and Eclogues of Virgil* (Cambridge, Mass., 1915), p. 135.
16. *De bell. civ.* ix. 1035 ff. and ix. 550.

Huet (pages 140–159)

Pierre Daniel Huet (1630–1721), Bishop of Avranches, was one of the most devoted scholars of his day. A few of his works bear such titles as: *Origenes commentaria in sacram Scripturam* (1668), *Demonstratio evangelica* (1679), *Censura philosophiae Cartiseanae* (1689), *De la situation du Paradis terrestre* (1691), and *Histoire du commerce et de la navigation des anciens* (1716). The following essay, *De l'Origine des romans,* appeared first as an introduction to the 1670 edition of Mme. de La Fayette's novel *Zayde,* which was published under the name of Jean-Regnauld de Segrais (1624–1701), to whom the letter is addressed. An English translation of the essay was published anonymously in London in 1672. A translation in Stephen Lewis, *The History of Romances,* was published in 1715. The present text is that of a third translation, which was prefixed to Volume I of *A Select Collection of Novels,* edited by S. Croxall, in 1720.

It cannot be proved that Huet's essay had much influence on English scholarship. Thomas Warton refers to it once in his *History of English Poetry,* and to William Warburton's criticism of it in a Supplement to the Translator's Preface of Charles Jarvis's *Don Quixote* (1742). Clara Reeve devoted several pages (90–96) to ridiculing it in her *Progress of Romance* (1785). Nevertheless, the number of times it was reprinted in English suggests that it was one of the classics in what became an important subject of study in the eighteenth century. And its intrinsic interest is not inconsiderable.

1. Lilio Gregorio Giraldi (1479–1552), author of numerous learned works.

Notes

Giambattista Nicolucci Pigna (1530–1575) is the author of, among other works, *I Romanzi* (Venice, 1554) which treats of Ariosto.

2. *Satyricon* v.

3. On Hanno see Diodorus Siculus xiii. 80. Philostratus intended to rehabilitate his hero and to defend him against the charge of being a magician in his *Life of Apollonius of Tyana* (about A.D. 220).

4. Annius Viterbensis (Giovanni Nanni, 1432–1502) attributed hitherto unknown works to ancient authors in his *Antiquitatum variarum volumina* XVIII (1498).

5. Tarik (born second half of the seventh century) was the leader of the Arab forces in the invasion of Spain, although subordinate to the Emir Musa Ben Nasser (660?–718).

6. *Geography* XV. ii. 18 and XI. vi. 2.

7. *Instit.* V. xi. 1 ff.

8. *On Sacrifices* xiv; *The Goddesse of Surrye.*

9. The work of Clearchus of Soli (born about 355) is described in the *Histoire de la littérature grecque* of A. and M. Croiset (Paris, 1901, V, 32) as "clever badinage, elegant in form, serious in intention, and passably original."

10. The reference is to Parthenius of Nicaea, who came to Rome in A.D. 73. He is the author of *The Pangs of Love* (περὶ ἐρωτικῶν παθημάτων), a collection of legends dealing with love which usually end in catastrophes or metamorphoses.

11. Longus composed a well-known work in four books entitled *Daphnis and Chloë.*

12. Eustathius of Epiphanius (end of fifth century A.D.) is known only from fragments. Theodorus Prodromus, Byzantine writer of the first half of the twelfth century, is the author of a verse novel, *The Loves of Rhodonte and Dosicles.*

13. Apparently a reference to Xenophon, the author of the *Anabasis;* to Xenophon, a historian of the third century A.D. about whom nothing is known; and Xenophon of Ephesus (third century A.D.), the author of a novel entitled *The Ephesian Tales* concerning the loves and trials of Habrocomes of Ephesus and Antheia.

14. Hesychius of Miletus, Greek biographer, lived during the sixth century. He composed a work on the same plan as the *Lives of the Philosophers* of Diogenes Laertius entitled *Concerning Those Distinguished for Their Learning.*

15. Suidas, Greek lexicographer of the eleventh century. The work bearing his name is a dictionary, an encyclopedia, and a collection of biographies.

16. Probably "The Old Commentary," the famous Alexandrian variorum edition of Aristophanes.

17. Claudius Aelian *Various History* XIV. xx.

18. See *The Ignorant Book-Collector,* 23.

19. Taliessin, a late sixth-century British bard to whom is attributed the collection of poems known as the *Book of Taliessin.*

20. Balaeus (John Bale, 1495–1563) is the author of a work called *Illustrium majoris Britanniae scriptorum summarium in quasdam centurias divisum* (Basle, 1559).

21. Hunibaldus, author of a chronicle history from the fall of Troy to the time of Clovis.

22. The so-called *Chronicle of Turpin,* composed at some unknown date before 1122 by a monk, purports to be the work of Charlemagne's friend Turpin, Archbishop of Rheims.

23. *Geography* IV. i. 1.

24. Salmasius (Claude de Saumaise, 1588–1653) published many editions of Latin and Greek authors.

25. Aristotle *Rhetoric* ii. 20.

Notes

26. Claude Fauchet (1529–1601), author of *Antiquités gauloises* (1579) and of *Recueil de l'origine de la langue et poésie françaises* (1581). Thibaut de Champagne, King of Navarre, and the Châtelain de Couci were poets who took part in the fourth crusade (1204). "Gace's Brussez" should read "Gace Brulé," a poet of about 1180.

27. *Symposium* 203.

28. François de Malherbe (1555–1628), official poet to Henry IV and a favored poet under Louis XIII and Richelieu.

29. *Eunuchus* iii. 584.

30. The famous novel by Honoré d'Urfé (1568–1625) appeared at intervals between 1610 and 1627.

31. *Epist.* I. ii. 3.

32. Photius, Patriarch of Constantinople, lived during the ninth century; the reference is to remarks made in his *Bibliotheca,* a valuable work consisting of abstracts of 280 Greek works, together with criticisms. Lucius Apuleius, a Roman neo-Platonist of the second century, wrote *The Golden Ass,* a prose romance. "Athenagoras" is the pseudonym of Martin Fumée de Genille. His *Du vray et parfaict amour . . . contenant les amours honnestes de Théogènes et de Chariclée* (Paris, 1599) purports to be a translation; but it was in fact written by him. L. Cornelius Sisenna (c. 120–67 B.C.) was a Roman historian known for his translation of the *Milesian Fables* of Aristides. The *Satyricon* of Petronius is a work of prose fiction. Clodius Albinus, a Roman general of the second century, may have been the same Clodius Albinus who was a senator and who wrote the *Milesian Fables* in verse. Heliodorus, a fourth-century Greek sophist and Christian bishop, wrote the romance *Aethiopica*. Achilles Tatius, a fourth-century Greek of Alexandria who became a Christian and later a bishop, wrote the *Amours de Clitophon et de Leucippe*. To Saint John Damascenus was ascribed (without convincing evidence) the *Histoire du saint ermite Barlaam et de Josaphat, fils d'un roi des Indes,* a "roman de spiritualité."

Bouhours (pages 160–192)

In addition to religious works and biographies of St. Ignatius Loyola and St. Francis Xavier, Dominique Bouhours (1628–1702), a Jesuit teacher of classical studies at Paris and Tours, published two influential works of literary criticism. *Les Entretiens d'Ariste et d'Eugène* (1671), consisting of six dialogues on "La Mer," "La Langue française," "Le Secret," "Le Bel esprit," "Le Je ne sais quoi," and "Les Devises," went through at least three editions, and has been edited in modern times by René Radouant (Paris, 1920). It was never translated into English, but it was almost as well known in eighteenth-century England as Bouhours's other, more ambitious work of criticism, *La Manière de bien penser dans les ouvrages d'esprit,* which was published in 1687. At least five editions of the latter work had appeared by the middle of the eighteenth century, as well as two translations into English: *The Art of Criticism . . . Translated . . . by a person of quality* (London, 1705), and *The Arts of Logick and Rhetorick,* by John Oldmixon (London, 1728), which is an English adaptation "to which are added parallel quotations out of the most eminent English authors in verse and prose." The present text is an abridgment of the first two of the four dialogues which make up the book. The third dialogue consists mainly of a collection and discussion of examples of false wit, and the fourth, of examples of "obscurities." Bouhours's critical doctrine is fully outlined in the first two dialogues. One of the disadvantages of the present abridgment is that many of the examples have been omitted, and it is the loving and leisurely concern with the hundreds of examples that gives the work its characteristic style.

A. F. B. Clark (*op. cit.,* pp. 262–274) has summarized the evidence of Bou-

Notes

hours's influence in England. The list of English critics who admired, or quoted, or referred to Bouhours is long: Rymer, Dennis, Addison, Spence, Joseph Warton, Arthur Murphy, and George Campbell. Lord Chesterfield several times in letters to his son recommended Bouhours. In his poem "An Essay Upon Unnatural Flights in Poetry" (1701), George Granville, Lord Lansdowne (1667–1735), "borrowed freely from Bouhours's *La Manière de bien penser,*" and several of his "Explanatory Annotations" are paraphrases from Bouhours. (See J. E. Spingarn, *Critical Essays of the Seventeenth Century* [New York, 1908], III, 292–298, 337.) For a full study of the background of the *Je ne sais quoi,* see Samuel H. Monk, "Grave Beyond the Reach of Art" (*Journal of the History of Ideas,* V [1944], 131–150).

In *La Manière de bien penser* we have enclosed in brackets the places where we have corrected or improved the translation of the "person of quality."

1. ["Its splendor is proportionate to its solidity."]

2. [Pierre Fortin de la Hoguette, French military man, composed a *Testament, ou Conseils d'un père à ses infants* which appeared in 1655 and in which the author examines the duties of man toward God, toward himself, and toward his fellow men.]

3. Suet. in *Caesar.*

4. August. in Psalms 58.

5. [Charles, Duke of Schomberg (1601–1656), had a brilliant military career under Louis XIII.]

6. ["first in that coarseness than second in delicacy."]

7. ["It always bears ripe fruit along with blossoms."]

8. Ludov. Vives *de Budaeo.*

9. [Daniel Bartoli (1608–1685) was an Italian Jesuit. His *Man of Letters* was translated into French by Father Livoy.]

10. [Vincent Voiture (1597–1648) was a master of light poetry and a much-admired wit of the *salons.*]

11. *The History of the French Academy.*

12. [Giovanni Baptista Mancini was a Bolognese writer of the first half of the seventeenth century, several of whose works were translated into French by Scudéry; Virgilio, marquis de Malvezzi (1599–1644), wrote many works dealing with history and diplomacy, among them an historical novel entitled *Il Romulo* (1629), translated into French in 1645; Giovanni Francesco Loredano (1606–1651) wrote *Dianea* (1636), a collection of libertine tales, and published various collections of *concetti* which were very successful not only in Italy but abroad.]

13. Tacitus *Annals* xiii. 45: ["She paraded modesty and practiced wantonness. In public she rarely appeared, and then with her face half-veiled, so as not quite to satiate the beholder—or, possibly, because it so became her."—Trans. John Jackson, Loeb Classical Library.]

14. ["She neither hid her beauties nor did she display them."]

15. I Cor. 13:12.

16. [Claude de Mesmes, comte d'Avaux (1595–1650), French diplomat. For Cardinal Duperron, see below, note 18.]

17. ["Talent and intelligence are the two axes of splendor and success: one without the other leads only to half of the desired goal; intelligence is not enough, for talent too is needed.] Baltasar Gracián, *Oraculo manual y arte de prudencia.*

18. [Bouhours cites for this anecdote the collection (*Perroniana*) made by Christophe Dupuy of the witticisms and criticisms attributed to Jacques Davy, Cardinal Duperron (1556–1618).]

19. [In the first edition of the *Conversations* (1671) Bouhours credited this reform to Ronsard but apparently repented of this rashness. All later editions mention Malherbe. For Voiture see note 10 above. Jean-Louis Guez de Balzac (1594–1654) was much admired for the style of his *Letters* (1624; in reality

383

carefully turned essays) which had many editions (and several English translations) during the century. He is said to have imposed on French prose style a kind of classical discipline. Bouhours's reference is to a letter written to M. de Bois Robert in 1623.]

20. [Paris, comte de Saint-Pol, second son of the Duc de Longueville, whose tutor Bouhours had been. The young prince died in 1672, the year following the first appearance of the *Conversations.*]

21. [Tasso, *Jerusalem Delivered*, Canto I, stanza 58:

> Hope and his years he far outstrips; scarce blown
> Appear his blossoms, than the fruit's reveal'd;
> So sweetly fierce, that when his face is shown
> You deem him Love, but Mars when helm'd and steel'd.
> —J. H. Wiffen (New York, 1881).]

22. [*L'Art de connaître les hommes* . . . (Paris, 1659, 1664, 1666), by Marin Cuneau de la Chambre. De la Chambre had convinced Louis XIV of his ability to judge character and even talent from physiognomy. In the work mentioned he shows himself an opponent of the whole female sex.]

23. [Sappho.]

24. [Athenaïs is better known as Eudoxia, wife of Theodosius II.]

25. [Vittoria Colonna (1490–1547) was a friend of Michelangelo.]

26. [Isotta Nogarola (1420–1466) composed a Latin dialogue in defense of Eve.]

27. [Serafina Contarini is known as a letter-writer.]

28. [Margareta Sarrochi was the center of an enthusiastic literary group at the beginning of the seventeenth century.]

29. [Margaret More (1505–1544) was the eldest daughter of Sir Thomas More. Her devotion to him was exemplary.]

30. [Elizabeth Tanfield (1585–1639) married Sir Henry Cary, first Viscount Falkland. She mastered French, Spanish, Italian, Latin, Hebrew, and Transylvanian.]

31. [Isabel de Roseres preached in Barcelona Cathedral (sixteenth century).]

32. [Catherine, wife of John II of Portugal, defended her country against Philip II in 1580. She was as learned as she was energetic.]

33. [Queen Margaret of Navarre, first wife of Henry IV of France, left some very interesting *Mémoires* (1522–1615).]

34. [Louise Marguerite de Lorraine, later Princess de Conti (1577–1631), wrote a description of life at the court of Henry IV under the title *Les Amours du grand Alcandre* (1652).]

35. [Saint Pulcheria, Empress of the Eastern Roman Empire (399–453), served as regent for Theodosius II, her younger brother.]

36. [Blanche of Castile (1188–1252) became regent of France after the death of Louis VIII, during which time she broke up a league of the barons and repelled an attack by the king of England.]

37. [Isabella (1451–1504), la Católica, queen of Castile and León, married Ferdinand of Aragon. She supported Columbus in his project.]

Bouhours (pages 193–205)

1. [*Doutes sur la langue françoise proposez à messieurs de l'Académie françoise par un gentilhomme de province,* 1674. This work is by Bouhours himself.]

2. *Ars poet.* [309.]

3. [Lucan *De bell. civ.* i. 128.]

4. Sallust *Bell. Catil.*

5. Velleius Paterculus *Hist. Rom.* ii.

6. [Guillaume de Brébeuf (1618–1661), whose epic poem *Pharsale* was ridiculed by Boileau in *L'Art poétique.*]

Notes

7. *De orat.* ii.
8. Vavasseur *De epigramm. lib.*
9. [Honoré de Bueil, marquis de Racan (1589–1670), composed a pastoral *Arthenice ou les Bergeries,* elegiac verse, and translations of the Psalms.]
10. [See Montaigne, *Essays,* I, 31.]
11. *Cavillationes,* Macrob.; *Vafrae et ludicrae conclusiones,* Senec.; *Cannochiale Aristotelico* [by Manolo Tesauro (1591–1677). The *Cannochiale* appeared at Venice in 1669.]
12. *Rhetoric* iii. 4.
13. [Vincent Voiture (1597–1648) during the last half of his life enjoyed a great reputation as one of the leading wits among the brilliant writers who gathered at the Hôtel de Rambouillet (Malherbe, Chapelain, Saint-Evremond, La Rochefoucauld, the Scudérys, and others). His letters and poems were widely read. The reference here is to the opening sentence of a letter to Mlle. de Rambouillet written over the name of the King of Sweden. The poems quoted in the following paragraph are called *Placets.*]
14. [Marc-Antoine Gerard, sieur de Saint-Amant (1594–1660).]
15. [The pun turns on *palais* meaning "palate," and *palais* meaning "palace."]
16. [The pun turns on *plomb* meaning "lead," and *plomb* meaning "plumb," with overtones of "aplomb."]
17. *In amphit. Caesar.*
18. Quint. viii. 6.
19. *Iliad* ii. [This appears to be a mistake; Homer says "Nireus the comeliest man that came beneath Ilios." (ii. 673).]
20. Lib. ii [epigram 92].
21. *De ben.* vii. 23.
22. *Aeneid* viii.
23. *Hist. Rom.* [i. 17.]
24. Senec. Rhet. *Suasor.* ii.

Boileau (pages 207–269)

Nicolas Boileau-Despréaux (1636–1711), called "the law-giver of Parnassus," is the first true literary critic in France. Antoine Adam, in a notably unfriendly chapter of his important *Histoire de la littérature française au XVIIᵉ siècle* (Paris, 1952; Vol. III, *L'Apogée du siècle: Boileau et Molière,* pp. 135–137), argues that Boileau succeeded only in blunting and muddling the literary theories worked out by the *cercle Lamoignon,* especially by Father Rapin and Claude Fleury. Yet Adam is forced to admit (p. 132) that for two centuries Frenchmen saw in the *Art poétique* the image of eternal Reason. No doubt Boileau reflected the ideas of the *cercle Lamoignon,* and no doubt also he accommodated his critical maxims as much as he could to the practice of his friends La Fontaine, Molière, and especially Racine. In the famous Quarrel he was an Ancient; and if he mocks the Italian influence, and Ariosto and Tasso in particular, it is in the name of true art, which for him, as for many of his contemporaries, was synonymous with the Greek and Roman example. Boileau did not invent classicism; he only codified its practices, which, by 1674, were widely accepted. His notions of literary history were extremely hazy, and his ideas are either the commonplaces of his age or tags recollected, as he himself says, from the *Ars poetica* of Horace. Even admitting all this, to Boileau must be granted the merit of understanding the critic's task: he classified and he judged in the name of Reason and Common Sense, couching his statements of principle and his verdicts in often lapidary verse whose felicity is such that it has in many instances become almost proverbial.

The effect of Boileau's *L'Art poétique* on English poetry and literary theory is described by A. F. B. Clark in *Boileau and the French Classical Critics in England (1660–1830)* (Paris, 1925). But the equally significant effect of Boileau's transla-

Notes

tion of Longinus was first noticed by Samuel H. Monk, who said that by publishing these two works in the same year (1674) Boileau simultaneously published doctrines that "eventually became mutually hostile" (*The Sublime: A Study of Critical Theories in XVIII*th *Century England* [New York, 1935]). Dryden read Boileau's Longinus in French, but his countrymen were soon able to read it in English. J. Pulteney's English translation of Boileau's French translation was published in London in 1680, and it was followed by an anonymous translation in 1698. A third translation appeared in *The Complete Works of Boileau-Despréaux, made English by several hands* (3 vols.; London, 1711–1713; reissued in 1714; 2d ed., 1736). Our text of the translation of Boileau's Preface to his translation is taken from Vol. II of *The Complete Works,* as is our text of the translation of "Reflection VII" from Boileau's *Critical Reflections on Some Passages out of Longinus, Wherein answer is occasionally made to some objections of Monsieur Perrault against Homer and Pindar,* originally published in 1711.

The first English translation of *L'Art poétique* was published anonymously in 1683. According to Jacob Tonson, "This translation . . . was made in the year 1680 by Sir William Soame of Suffolk, Baronet; who being very intimately acquainted with Mr. Dryden, desired his revisal of it. [Tonson] saw the manuscript lie in Mr. Dryden's hands for above six months, who made very considerable alterations in it, particularly the beginning of the Fourth Canto; and it being his opinion that it would be better to apply the poem to English writers than keep to the French names, as it was first translated, Sir William desired he would take the pains to make that alteration; and accordingly that was entirely done by Mr. Dryden" (Clark, *op. cit.,* pp. 127–128). The poem was reprinted (with two minor revisions, probably not by Dryden or Soame) in the *Annual Miscellany* of 1708. It was reprinted separately in 1710 and 1715, and reissued in 1717. The translation in *The Complete Works* (1712) is a revised version of the Soame-Dryden translation. Our text follows the first edition, of 1683, which differs from later reprints or editions in only two places: in Canto I, lines 203–204, all texts after 1683 read,

> Reprove of words the too-affected sound,—
> Here the sense flags, and your expression's round;

and line 16 in Canto II reads, "And frighted nymphs dive down into the floods," which seems to be an ignorant effort to correct the misprint of the first edition, where nayads is spelled "Nageds."

Our text of the original *L'Art poétique* is that of the Classiques Garnier (Boileau, *Oeuvres,* Paris, 1961), used by permission of Garnier frères, with the exception that paragraph indentations have been made to correspond to those in the English translation, which in turn are those used by A. S. Cook in his edition of the poem (with the Soame-Dryden translation) in his *The Art of Poetry* (Boston, 1892).

In the following notes the editors are indebted to Cook, as well as to other previous editors, from Claude Brossette, Boileau's first editor, to Ernest Dilworth, whose excellent prose translation of *L'Art poétique* appears in his *Boileau: Selected Criticism,* in the Library of Liberal Arts (Indianapolis, 1965).

Boileau's debt to Horace's *Ars poetica* was so pervasive that it seemed better not to cite the parallels in separate footnotes. In the following list, the lines from Boileau are cited from the French text.

B.I.150–H.40-41, 309ff.; B.I.172–H.292-94; B.I.178-80–H.152, 153;
B.I.186–H.419-52; B.III.33-35–H.319-22; B.III.47–H.338; B.III.51ff.–H.182ff.;
B.III.66–H.220; B.III.67ff.–H.275ff.; B.III.105–H.120-22; B.III.124ff.–H.125-27;
B.III.133-34–H.105ff.; B.III.142–H.102-103; B.III.143-44–H.95ff.;
B.III.269–H.136ff.; B.III.335ff.–H.281ff.; B.III.375ff.–H.161ff.;

B.IV.29ff.–H.368ff.; B.IV.41ff.–H.426ff.; B.IV.55ff.–H.474; B.IV.71ff.–H387, 438ff.; B.IV.88ff.–H.343-44; B.IV.133ff.–H.391ff.

The Art of Poetry

I

1. This commentary on the idea that poets are born, not made, serves also to distinguish verse from poetry, since verse is all that the "bold author" can achieve if unaided by native gift.

2. Brunetière in his edition of the *Art poétique* (Paris, 1912), p. 190, points out that these lines assume that the various poetic genres derive from differences in individual talent.

3. Edmund Waller (1606–1687) wrote poems in praise of Charles I, Cromwell, and Charles II.

4. François de Malherbe (1555–1628) reacted in his verse against what he took to be the extravagances of Ronsard and the Pléiade and so became one of the forerunners of the classicism of 1660.

5. Rosalind appears in several of the pastorals that make up *The Shepherd's Calendar.*

6. Honorat de Bueil, marquis de Racan (1589–1670), author of the *Bergeries,* a pastoral play. Philis (Phyllis) is a traditional name for shepherdesses in pastoral poems.

7. *La Semaine ou Création du monde,* a poem by Guillaume du Bartas (1544–1590), was well known in England in the translation by Joshua Sylvester, *Divine Weeks and Works* (1598).

8. M. A. Girard de Saint-Amant (1594–1661), author of the epic poem *Moïse sauvé,* is one of Boileau's favorite whipping boys.

9. Nicolas Faret (1596–1646), a friend of Saint-Amant, was one of the original forty members of the Academy. As Brunetière points out (*loc. cit.,* his name was predestined to rhyme with *cabaret.*

10. Jules Brody (*Boileau and Longinus* [Geneva, 1958], p. 63) says of this passage: "This language of subservience and submission is rooted in the ancient distinction between prose and verse. When Cicero asserted that the plain style (*sermo humilis*) should avoid the *vincula numerorum,* he was criticizing the metaphor latent in the Latin expression for rhythmical or poetic language: *oratio vincta* as opposed to the *oratio soluta.* Thus the Roman mind conceived of versification as the "imprisonment" or "fettering" of words within metrical configurations (*numeri*). But when in the modern literatures rhyming became the distinctive feature of versification, the role of *vinculum* fell to rhyme. . . ."

11. This famous couplet, which has become practically proverbial in French, needs to be read carefully. Lanson (*Boileau* [Paris, 1919], p. 94) points out that the meaning of words has changed between Boileau's time and our own. "Reason" here is not a positivistic, calculating attitude of mind, nor yet the analytical and critical, generalizing and abstracting reason of philosophers. It is, rather, the Cartesian reason which directs the human soul and distinguishes the true from the false.

12. Boileau is in full reaction against the earlier popularity of the Italian manner in literature, which he considered false, affected, and trashy. For contrast, consider Chapelain's discussion of Marino's *Adone* elsewhere in this book.

13. This line is misquoted from Scudéry's *Alaric,* Book III: "Ce ne sont que festons, ce ne sont que couronnes" (La Haye, 1685, p. 83).

14. Barbin was a bookseller of the time.

15. There was a vogue for burlesque in the first half of the seventeenth century. A better than average example would be Scarron's *Virgile travesti.*

16. Antoine Girard (1584–1626), known as Tabarin, was famous as a charlatan

Notes

(one who sold quack remedies) and as an actor (a buffoon) in popular farces. "Tabarin's facetiae . . . were published as early as 1619. Two of his farces have been reprinted as lately as 1945."—Dilworth.

17. The footnote to the first edition (1683) reads: "a play, written by Mr. Duffet." In his edition of Dryden (1808), Sir Walter Scott identified Duffet as "a low author employed by the players of the King's-house to compose parodies on the operas, by which the Duke's Company at one time attracted large audiences." The first of these operas was D'Avenant and Dryden's ballad opera, or operatic play, *The Tempest* (1667), an adaptation of Shakespeare's play.

18. Charles Coypeau d'Assoucy (1605–1677) wrote a burlesque of the *Metamorphoses* called *Ovide en belle humeur.*

19. Dryden's *Mac Flecknoe* was published in 1682, a year before this translation of Boileau's poem.

20. *Typhon,* also known as *Gigantomachie,* by Scarron, was published in 1644.

21. Samuel Butler's *Hudibras* appeared in three parts, in 1663, 1664, and 1678.

22. Clément Marot (1496–1544), a skillful court poet, continued to write in outmoded medieval forms though he was contemporary with Ronsard. His verse is charming and superficial.

23. " 'Quacks and marionette showmen,' says Boileau, 'have long been in the habit of stationing themselves on the Pont Neuf [in Paris].' "—Dilworth.

24. This line is from Book VII of a translation of Lucan's *Pharsalia,* by Georges de Brébeuf (1617–1661). Boileau's words "Même en une Pharsale" suggest that he was aware that some of the exaggeration to which he objects is attributable to Lucan himself.

25. From the "Second Week," First Day, Fourth Part.—Cook.

26. The capsule history of French poetry which follows bears little relation to that history as it is understood today. Like most men of his time, Boileau knew nothing about the Middle Ages, and he is completely unjust to Ronsard.

27. Edward Fairfax (d. 1635) published in 1600 his translation of Tasso's *Jerusalem Delivered,* which he called *Godfrey of Bulloigne.* Dryden, in *Preface to the Fables* (1700), said, "Many besides myself have heard Waller own that he derived the harmony of his numbers from Godfrey of Bulloigne."

28. François de Montcorbier, called after his uncle François de Villon (1431–1465?), is the greatest French lyric poet of the Middle Ages. Many of the poems included in his *Grand Testament* and *Petit Testament* are still widely read. As an artist he was rediscovered by the Romantics.

29. On the romances, see in this book Chapelain's *On the Reading of the Old Romances.*

30. See note 22. The verse forms mentioned here—*ballades, triolets, rondeaux*—were those Marot continued to use even after the innovations of the Pléiade. Cook notes that "strictly speaking Marot did not rime mascarades as Ronsard did" and says that the mascarade "corresponded nearly to our Elizabethan masque" (p. 271).

31. William Davenant (1605–1668) published his heroic poem *Gondibert* in 1651.

32. Pierre de Ronsard (1524–1585) was indeed sometimes pedantic especially in his early *Odes,* but he is a great lyric poet in, for example, the sonnets addressed to his innamoratas, Cassandre Salviati and Hélène de Surgères.

33. Apparently a reference to "The Incomparable Poem of Gondibert vindicated from the Wit-Combats of Four Esquires: Clinias, Dametas, Sancho and Jack Pudding." "[This tract] is a continuation of [an earlier] satire; a mock defence whose sarcasm and pretended remonstrance are sometimes keener than the open attack" (Isaac Disraeli, *The Calamities and Quarrels of Authors* [New York, 1868], II, 241–242).

34. Philippe Desportes (1546–1606) was more of a wit than a lyric poet. Jean Bertaut (1552–1611) is a minor, primarily elegiac poet.

35. Dryden's praise of Waller's verse (e.g., "nothing so even, sweet, and flowing"—*An Essay of Dramatic Poesy*) was echoed by later English critics.

36. See note 4. Regarding these four famous lines one may mention the poem of Théodore de Banville, "Enfin Malherbe vint," in which the following lines occur:

> pour mettre le holà
> Malherbe vint, et que la Poésie
> En le voyant arriver, s'en alla.

37. These four lines are a paraphrase of Horace *Ars poet.* 309 ff. For other parallels between Boileau and Horace, see headnote.

38. This is the Latin proverb *Festina lente*.

39. Lines 172 to 186 are primarily a paraphrase of various passages of Horace; see headnote.

II

1. The question of what, in subject matter and diction, is appropriate to pastorals was discussed by Rapin in his *De Carmina pastorali* (1659), and again in his *Réflexions sur la poétique* (1674), and by Fontenelle in his essay on the pastoral (1688). See below, pp. 295, 304, and 339 ff., and the Notes. The translators' *Randal* (for Boileau's *Ronsard*, whose shepherds Rapin thought were "too gross") might be an error for Thomas *Randolph* (1605–1635), who wrote some satirical eclogues, but this conjecture of Scott's, in his edition of Dryden, is not very satisfactory.

Pierrot and Toinon, like Tom and Bess, are names more appropriate to clownish villagers than to classical shepherds.

2. Theocritus and Virgil are the great exemplars of pastoral poetry in Greek and Latin, but at Virgil's hands the form took on that artificiality which was to distinguish it in later European literature. Lanson reminds us that for Boileau "reason" and "nature" are equivalent to a third term which is "antiquity" (*op. cit.,* p. 104).

3. This is a reference to Virgil *Eclog.* iv. 3: "Si canimus silvas, silvae sint Consule dignae."

4. Albius Tibullus (c. 60–19 B.C.), Roman elegiac poet. Publius Ovidius Naso (43 B.C.–A.D. 18); the reference is to his poems entitled *Amores* and perhaps to the *Ars amatoria*.

5. The city in Greece where the Olympic Games were held.

6. The Simois was one of the three rivers of ancient Troy; see *Iliad* xxi.

7. The translators here make a British adaptation of Boileau's allusion to contemporary French history. The British East India Company established a trading station in Calcutta in 1690.

8. The Escaut is a river flowing through France, Belgium, and Holland. The reference is to the wars of Louis XIV.

9. Horace *Odes* II. xii. 20–24, but the girl's name there is Licymnia.

10. In the campaign to regain Alsace, the French took Courtrai in July, 1667, Lille in August, 1667, and Dôle in 1668. François Eudes de Mézeray (1610–1683) is a historian of the period.

11. Boileau is describing the Italian or Petrarchan sonnet.

12. Of the poets named here only François de Maynard (1582–1646) is still remembered. Charles de Sercy was a bookseller.

13. "Points" are the same as conceits.

14. In Italy, France, and England, the madrigal, which was originally a short, simple idyl, very early tended to become epigrammatic. Cook (*op. cit.* pp. 276–278) supplies a long note on the madrigal in Italy, France, and England.

15. The commentators agree that Boileau was here thinking of the *Sylvie* of Mairet.

16. The preacher referred to is André Boulanger, Augustinian.

Notes

17. The name of this actor (born Henri Legrand) has become a synonym for punsters and specialists in verbal humor. (*Petit Larousse*)

18. In the first edition a footnote to the word "Madrigal" (l. 107) seems intended for the word "round." It reads: "An old way of writing, which began and ended with the same measure"—a rough definition of what is meant in English by *rondeau,* a rare form in English poetry. "Round" as defined by the translators is not in the *O.E.D.* See Irène Simon, "Critical Terms in Restoration Translations from the French, II" (*Revue Belge de Philologie et d'Histoire,* XLIII [1965], 916).

19. Gaius Lucilius (180–102 B.C.) wrote thirty books of *Sermones* "which included outspoken criticism of authors and men in public life and protests against luxury and gluttony. These Sermones, except for fragments, have perished" (*Oxford Companion to Classical Literature*).

20. Aulus Persius Flaccus (A.D. 34–62) wrote six satires of which only the first is in the style of Lucilius. (*Oxford Companion to Classical Literature*).

21. Decimus Junius Juvenalis (A.D. 65?–128?), the bitterest of the great Roman satirists whose work was imitated by later European poets, was Dryden's favorite (as is evident in his *Discourse Concerning the Original and Progress of Satire*). The four subjects Boileau lists are treated in the following: *Satires* x. 61–89; iv. 72–149; iv. 74–75; vi. 115–32.

22. Mathurin Régnier (1573–1613) left some remarkable pictures of life in the France of Henri IV in his *Satires.*

23. The *vaudeville* was a brief poem more often Bacchic than satirical.

24. Elkanah Settle (1648–1724), the playwright ridiculed by Dryden in *Absalom and Achitophel* and by Pope in *The Dunciad.*

25. The Place de Grève, now the Place de l'Hôtel de Ville, was the site of the execution of criminals. Claude Le Petit (1639–1662), a lawyer, was burned alive there after having been denounced as a libertine author. His very mild writings include *Le B*** des Muses* and *Paris Ridicule* (*Grand Larousse*).

26. Linière (François Payot de Lignières, 1628–1704) was a satirist (J. M. Quérard, *La France littéraire* [Paris, 1833]).

27. David Loggan was the engraver of the plate of the portrait of Settle prefixed to the *Empress of Morocco* (1671).

28. Robert Nanteuil (1623–1678) was an engraver noted for his lifelike portraits (*Larousse*).

III

1. An allusion to Aristotle's notion (*Poetics* vi. 2) that the aim of tragedy is to arouse pity and fear in the audience.

2. Many French writers of the century insisted on the importance of pleasing the audience. Thus Molière, in the *Critique de l'Ecole des Femmes:* "I wonder whether the great rule of all rules is not to please." Thus also Racine, in the Preface to *Bérénice:* "The principal rule is to please and to move; all the others have been invented only to conduce to that first one."

3. Brunetière's note to this line (*ed. cit.*) points out that Boileau erects Racine's technique into a rule and often versifies the *Pratique du théâtre* of the Abbé d'Aubignac.

4. The Spanish poets referred to are Calderón and Lope de Vega, specifically to the latter's *Valentine and Orson.*

5. This pithy résumé of the three unities describes the almost universal practice of the French drama after Corneille's *Cid* (1636). See elsewhere in this book the text of Corneille's *Of the Three Unities of Action, Time, and Place.*

6. Cf. Aristotle *Poetics* ix. 1: "The poet should prefer impossibilities which appear probable to such things as, though possible, appear improbable."—Trans. Thomas Twining (Everyman's Library).

7. Aristotle, *Poetics* x, defines the *peripeteia* or change of fortune as follows:

390

Notes

"a change . . . into the reverse of what is expected from the circumstances of the action."—Twining.

8. As Dilworth notes, *"Cothurne* (buskin) would have fitted into the line, but the error remains."

9. This discussion of the medieval theater is no more reliable than the earlier one on medieval poetry.

10. The first example of tragedy in French is the *Cléopâtre captive* of Jodelle (1552). Among seventeenth-century French tragedies, only Racine's *Esther* and *Athalie* have a chorus.

11. Thyrsis, the shepherd in love, appears in Theocritus *Idyl* i, and Virgil *Eclog.* vii. Dilworth says of Philène: "For this apparently un-Carthaginian Philaenus, see Molière's *Pastorale Comique."* Artamène is the name for Cyrus the Great in Mlle. de Scudéry's *Artamène ou le grand Cyrus* (10 vols.; 1650–1658), an example of the endless novels of the time, to which love was thought to be better suited than to tragedy—despite the success and prestige of Racine.

12. Boileau is the author of a dialogue of the dead in the manner of Lucian entitled *The Heroes of Romance,* which satirizes the style and pretensions of novels like those of Mlle. de Scudéry.

13. *Clélie,* another novel by Mlle. de Scudéry, contains the famous Map of the Land of Love—the *Carte du Tendre.*

14. George Chapman's tragedy *Bussy D'Ambois* was published in 1607.

15. Juba is the hero of La Calprenède's novel *Cléopâtre* (12 vols., 1647).

16. As in Seneca's *Troades.*

17. This is a summary of the beginning of the *Aeneid.*

18. The reference is to Desmarets de Saint-Sorlin (1596–1676), who made use of Christian marvels in his epics *Clovis ou la France chrétienne* and *Esther.* He defended this practice in "Discours pour prouver que les sujets chrétiens sont les seuls propres à la poésie héroique" (1673) and in "Défense du poème héroique" (1674). Cf. Brunetière (*op. cit.,* p. 213). Adam (*op. cit.,* III, 142) says that as early as 1672 Boileau had objected to the use of Christian machinery in the epic. Desmarets merely answered him in the preface to *Clovis* (1673) and so made himself the target for these remarks. Dryden cited this passage from Boileau with approval in his discussion of this subject in his *Discourse on Satire.* The propriety of Christian machinery was much discussed by eighteenth-century critics. Cook quotes an interesting Romantic rebuttal to Boileau by Brunetière: "The restoration of the Christian ideal to its rights over sentiment and imagination we owe to Chateaubriand and the *Genius of Christianity.* . . . By the *Genius of Christianity* the precept of Boileau, who nevertheless knew the *Jerusalem Delivered,* if neither the *Divine Comedy* nor *Paradise Lost,* stands henceforth convicted of error; its purely heathen ideal is convicted of narrowness, of inadequacy, and especially of coldness. . . . Classical art, we have seen, is at bottom heathen. Its object and its ideal were fixed by the heathens of the Renaissance, and its models have remained for more than two centuries exclusively heathen. So that it was not merely Boileau who was here on trial, but, as it were, the Renaissance itself" (*L'Evolution des genres dans l'histoire de la littérature* [Paris, 1890], 181–182).

19. The allusion is to Tasso's *Jerusalem Delivered,* which is always invoked by those defending the use of Christian machinery in the epic (for example, in Georges de Scudéry's preface to his epic *Alaric* of 1654). Boileau never misses a chance to attack Italian taste and example.

20. The allusion is to Ariosto.

21. As did Carel de Sainte-Garde in his *Childebrand* (1666).

22. The war between Eteocles and Polynices, the sons of Oedipus and Jocasta, is the subject of the *Thebaid* of Statius.

23. The word was not pejorative in the seventeenth century; it merely meant splendid.

Notes

24. The culprit is Saint-Amant in his *Moïse sauvé* (1653), in which the following line occurs: "Les poissons ébahis le regardent passer." On Saint-Amant see Alain Seznec, "Saint-Amant, le poète sauvé des eaux," in Jean-Jacques Demorest, ed., *Studies in Seventeenth-Century French Literature* (Ithaca, 1962), pp. 35–64. On the line Boileau attacks, see esp. p. 63, n. 17.

25. The first line of Scudéry's *Alaric*.

26. The first lines of the *Aeneid*.

27. Ariosto, *Orlando furioso*.

28. *Iliad* xiv. 187–223.

29. Cook says, "Boileau specifically refers to Desmarets de Saint-Sorlin." See note 18, above.

30. Aristophanes *The Clouds*.

31. Of Menander's approximately one hundred comedies only fragments survive, but it can be deduced from these that Menander "presents the life of contemporary Athens in its serious and pathetic as well as in its more amusing aspects . . ." (*Oxford Companion to Classical Literature*).

32. As the context here makes clear, "nature" for Boileau is to be taken in the narrow sense as human nature.

33. A character in Ben Jonson's *The Silent Woman*.

34. In other words, only the best society can serve as a model for the student of human nature.

35. Of the two principal Roman writers of comedy, Plautus and Terence, the latter follows Menander more closely and is the more refined. For Tabarin, see note 16 to Canto I, above.

36. It is always pointed out that it is not Scapin but Géronte who gets into the sack in Molière's *Les Fourberies de Scapin. Le Misanthrope* is probably Molière's greatest comedy; certainly it is his most cerebral one.

37. In Ben Jonson's *The Fox,* Sir Politic Wouldbe disguises himself as a tortoise.

38. It should be remembered that all "base," technical, dialectical, and colloquial usages were banished from French tragedy. Boileau is arguing for the parallel refinement of dialogue in the comedy which, especially in the farce, was often gross and indecent.

39. An example of the principle mentioned above (note 2 to Canto II), that for Boileau "nature" and "antiquity" are synonymous. The characters of Terence referred to are Simo in *Andria,* Demea in the *Adelphi,* and Chremes in the *Heautontimorumenos ("The Self-Torturer")*.

40. See note 23 to Canto I, above.

41. Smithfield was a place in London, north of St. Paul's, where fairs were held. Jack-Puddings are buffoons, clowns.

IV

1. Claude Perrault (1613–1688), the celebrated designer of the east façade of the Louvre.

2. Dilworth notes that senna is used as a purge. The translators missed the antithesis: empty of blood—full of senna.

3. Jules Hardouin-Mansart (Mansard) (1646–1708) was Louis XIV's favorite architect. He designed Versailles.

4. Sir Christopher Wren (1632–1723) was at the height of his career when Soame and Dryden were translating this poem. Baptist May (1629–1698) was a member of the committee that with Wren planned the reconstruction after the great fire in 1666, and he served as clerk of the works, under Wren, in the renovation of Windsor Castle in 1671.

5. Galen the physician lived at Rome in the time of Marcus Aurelius.

6. Henry Herringman was one of Dryden's publishers.

Notes

7. All of these writers are, as Boileau says, completely forgotten, and there appears to be no point in resuscitating them here.

8. The *Counter-scuffle* is "a burlesque poem on a quarrel and a scuffle in the Counter-prison, which occurs in Dryden's *Miscellanies,* Vol. III" (Scott's note). Notice that Boileau named nine "cold writers," and that Soame and Dryden cite only Davenant.

9. Savinien Cyrano de Bergerac (1619–1655) wrote comedies and an imaginary journey to the moon. He was later used as the subject of a neo-Romantic drama by Edmond Rostand. Pierre Motin (d. 1614) was a satirist.

10. Thomas Shadwell (1642–1692), who attacked Dryden in *The Medal of John Bayes* (1682), was in turn satirized by Dryden in *Mac Flecknoe* and *Absalom and Achitophel.*

11. The reference is to Chapelain, who had a great reputation as a poet until he published part of his *Pucelle* in 1656.

12. Jean Oger de Gombauld (1588–1666) was a favorite to the *salons* and a member of the Academy.

13. "Referring to an actual experience of Boileau with Charles du Perrier, who one day talked incessantly in church about his own poetry, scarcely pausing at the elevation of the host" (Cook's note). As Cook pointed out, Pope imitated Boileau in these well-known lines from the *Essay on Criticism* (ll. 622–625):

> No place so sacred from such fops is barred,
> Nor is Paul's church more safe than Paul's churchyard;
> Nay, fly to altars; there they'll talk you dead;
> For fools rush in where angels fear to tread.

14. Cf. Pope's *Essay on Criticism,* 631–642 and 141–160.—Cook.

15. Dilworth quotes Huet's *Huetiana* (1722): "Malherbe gave the preference to Statius over all the Latin poets. And with my own ears I have been astonished to hear P. Corneille give it to Lucan over Virgil."

16. Rodrigue and Chimène are the lovers in Corneille's tragicomedy *Le Cid.* According to Dilworth, "The great Jansenist Nicole, in *Les Visionnaires, ou seconde partie des Lettres sur l'hérésie imaginaire* [the *Visionnaires* was a comedy by Desmarets de Saint-Sorlin], had said, in January 1666: 'A maker of novels, and a poet of the theatre, is a public poisoner, not of bodies but of the souls of the faithful.' " The translators' "make a murderer of Roderigue" misses the point of Boileau's allusion.

17. In the *Aeneid* iv.

18. This insistence on social polish indicates the extent to which seventeenth-century French literature was the product of *salon* life rather than of life in the raw.

19. "According to [Claude] Brossette [editor of Boileau], Boileau congratulated Corneille on the success of his tragedies and the glory they had brought him: 'Yes,' said Corneille, 'I've had a bellyfull of glory, and I'm famished for money.' "—Dilworth.

Boileau was himself independently wealthy. Much of this feeling that literature should be above money-making continued into the next century. Voltaire frequently gave away money earned by his writings (John Lough, *An Introduction to Eighteenth Century France* [London, 1960] p. 242).

20. The reference is to the Delphic oracle.

21. In his *Works and Days* Hesiod deals with practical matters instead of re-counting the myths.

22. The Permessus was a river in Boeotia sacred to Apollo and the Muses which rose on Mount Helicon.

23. Juvenal *Satires* vii. 59–62.

24. Horace *Odes* II. xix.

Notes

25. François Colletet (1628–1680?) was not so good a poet as his father, Guillaume. He barely made his living as a tutor and a literary hack.

26. Here begins the praise of Louis XIV which ends the poem. For the English translators the "sharp-sighted prince" was Charles II, who with Louis XIV had been at war against Holland.

27. Dryden published a slightly revised edition of *An Essay of Dramatic Poesy* in 1684, a year after this translation appeared.

28. Isaac de Benserade (1613–1691) composed librettos for the court ballets. A "ruelle" is the space around the huge court bed where in the seventeenth century great ladies often held their receptions.

29. Jean de Segrais (1624–1701) composed some pastoral poems published under the title *Eglogues.*

30. Another name for Hercules.

31. The dikes were opened as a defensive move against the fleet of Louis XIV.

32. Mastricht fell to Louis XIV on July 1, 1673, after bloody fighting.

33. At this point the translators, writing nine years after Boileau, depart entirely from the original. Boileau's panegyric focuses on the recent military successes of Louis XIV, but Soame and Dryden praise their king for his powers as a peacemaker. Charles II, who for four years had been Louis' ally in the Dutch Wars, was forced to make a separate peace in 1674. In the years following he was busy with domestic threats to his power. Dryden was Poet Laureate and Historiographer Royal.

34. Dôle, Salins, and Besançon surrendered in May and June, 1674.

35. Throughout the passage the reference is to the third of the Dutch Wars, 1672–1678. Spain, Brandenburg, Denmark, and other powers were allied with the Dutch. One of the Allied generals, Montecuculli, boasted that he had evaded a battle with the French.

36. *Boutefeus,* "a Gallicism for *incendiary;* in Dryden's time it was a word of good reputation, but is now obsolete" (Scott's note).

37. This acknowledgment is no more than just, since the precepts of Horace are everywhere to be found in Boileau's poem. See headnote for list of parallels between the two poems.

38. Boileau is the first critic in the modern sense. Not a mere annotator, he provided judgments on literary works for the court and for the reading public whose basic values were his own.

Boileau (pages 270–278)

1. The *Lexique de Suidas,* though compiled about the tenth century, from late and unreliable sources, contains much information about Greek literature.

2. A Roman rhetorician whose work Longinus refers to at the beginning of his treatise.

3. Isaac Casaubon (1559–1614), a great classical scholar.

4. Pierre-Daniel Huet (1630–1721) defended his opinion on this point in a letter to the Duc de Montausier, who did not make the letter public. Leclerc included it in volume X of his *Bibliothèque choisie* with a commentary of his own ("Huet," in Michaud, *Biographie universelle* [Paris, 1858]).

5. Dilworth quotes Brossette's note: "The gentlemen of Port-Royal, and especially M. Lemaistre de Saci" (1613–1684), a Jansenist theologian, one of the translators of the Bible.

6. Gnæus Nævius, epic poet and playwright of the third century B.C.; Titus Livius (59 B.C.–A.D. 17), the historian; and Quintus Ennius (239?–169 B.C.), poet and playwright, one of the "founders" of Roman literature.

7. "Quintilian's time" was A.D. c. 35–c. 95; Aulus Gellius, author of *Noctes Atticae,* a collection of essays on various subjects, lived during the second century.

Notes

8. Jean Bertaut (1552–1611), a follower of Ronsard; for Malherbe, see note 7 to La Bruyère, below; for Racan, see note 6 to Canto I, above; "Distingendes" is a misprint for De Lingendes (Jean, d. 1616) who was best known for an elegy on the death of Ovid freely imitated from the Latin of Politian. See Boileau, *Oeuvres complètes* (Paris, 1866), III, 201n.

9. Etienne Pasquier (1529–1615), in *Recherches de la France*.

10. For Marot see note 22 to Canto I, above. Mellin de Saint-Gelais (1491–1558), poet, musician, and favorite wit of Francis I.

11. Charles Perrault (1628–1703), author of *Les Parallèles des anciens et des modernes*, Boileau's frequent opponent in the *Réflection;* see headnote to Fontenelle, below.

12. Jean-Louis Guez de Balzac (1594–1654) was much admired by his contemporaries for his prose style, first revealed in his collection of *Lettres* (1624), carefully turned essays, which went through many editions (and several English translations) during the century. He is said to have done for French prose what Malherbe did for French poetry, freeing it from excesses of ornament and imposing upon it a kind of classical discipline.

13. François Maynard (1582–1646), a poet of sonnets, odes, and epigrams.

14. Lycophron, an Alexandrian poet of the third century B.C.; Nonnius (i.e., Nonnus), a Greek epic poet of the early fifth century B.C.; Silius Italicus, a Latin epic poet of the first century A.D.

Rapin (pages 279–306)

Among the seventeenth-century French critics, René Rapin (1621–1687) shared with Boileau and Saint-Evremond the distinction of having all his critical works translated into English. The *Whole Critical Works* appeared in London in two volumes in 1706 (second and third editions in 1716 and 1731), but the *Réflexions sur la poétique* had been translated and published by Thomas Rymer in 1674, the same year in which the essay first appeared in France, and had been reprinted in 1694. Rymer's important Preface is in Spingarn's *Critical Essays of the Seventeenth Century* (Oxford, 1908–1909). Rapin was thus not only "the first of the formalist critics to be translated into English" (Curt A. Zimansky, *The Critical Works of Thomas Rymer* [New Haven, 1956], p. 179), he was also one of the most widely read. Some of his other works translated and published separately were *A Comparison Between Demosthenes and Cicero* (1672); *A Comparison of Plato and Aristotle* (1673); *Reflections Upon the Eloquence of These Times* (1672 and 1673); *A Discourse of Pastorals* (1684); and *Of Gardens* (1673).

Rapin's influence in the criticism of the Augustan period was pervasive. In 1677, in *The Author's Apology for Heroic Poetry* Dryden called Boileau and Rapin "the greatest of this age" in France, and said that "were all the other critics lost," Rapin alone was "sufficient to teach anew the rules of writing." And from then on through the first half of the eighteenth century English critics referred frequently to him. A. F. B. Clark (*op. cit.,* pp. 275–285) has sketched his career.

Our text, over half the whole essay, follows that of the 1694 edition.

1. A paraphrase of *Epist.* ii. 1.

2. Honorat de Bueil, marquis de Racan (1589–1670), follower of Malherbe and author of the pastoral drama *Les Bergeries.*

3. *Ars poet.* 5–15.

4. Giovan-Giorgio Trissino (1478–1550) worked twenty years on *L'Italia liberata da' Goti.*

5. *Inst. Orat.* II. xix.

6. *On the Sublime* XXXIII.

7. Apelles and Protogenes were Greek painters of the fourth century B.C.

8. Jean Bonnefons (1554–1614), a French poet who wrote erotic verse in Latin.

Phaleusiacs are lines in an ancient meter consisting of a spondee, a dactyl, and three trochees.

9. Aristotle *Poetics* xxv; Horace *Epist.* I. ii. 3.

10. *Poetics* xv.

11. *Rhetoric* III. ii.

12. *Inst. Orat.* VIII. iii.

13. The reference is to the treatise *On Style* (first century A.D.), commonly, but probably wrongly, attributed to Demetrius Phalerius.

14. In the dialogue *Gorgias*.

15. Vincent Voiture (1597–1648) was a master of light verse and a much-admired wit of the *salons*. For Sarasin, see headnote to his *Discourse on Tragedy,* above. Phillippe Habert (c. 1605–1637) wrote an elegy called "Le Temple de la Mort" (1637). Pierre de Lalane (d. 1661?) wrote love poems, in a highly artificial style.

16. *Ars poet.* 99.

17. *Inst. Orat.* vi.

18. [Athenaeus *Deipnosophists* XIV. 620. b.]

19. *Ars poet.* 178 sqq.

20. [In *Of the Writing of History.*]

21. Marco Girolamo Vida (1490–1560), author of a Latin poem, *The Art of Poetry,* and of the *Christiad*.

22. Giacomo Sannazaro (1458–1530), Italian poet, author of the pastoral romance *Arcadia* and called by his contemporaries "the Christian Virgil." Luís de Camoëns (1524–1580), Portuguese poet, author of the *Lusiads*.

23. Armand, prince de Conti (1629–1668), opposed the theater in a *Traité de la comédie et des spectacles* (1666) although he had previously been a friend of Molière.

Le Bossu (pages 307–323)

No work of French criticism was better known in eighteenth-century England than the *Traité du poème épique,* by René Le Bossu (1631–1680). First published in Paris in 1675, and reissued several times during the following years, it was well known in England before it was translated by "W. J." in 1695. During the next thirty years the translation was reprinted in England in various forms at least fourteen times (A. F. B. Clark, *op. cit.,* p. 243). Our text consists of selections from the abridgment of W. J.'s translation published by Pope in the first edition of his *Odyssey* (1725–1726).

As early as 1727 Voltaire said, in his English essay *On Epic Poetry,* that "to believe Homer and Virgil submitted beforehand to the rules laid down by Le Bossu, who bids an epic poet invent and dispose the constitution of his fable before he thinks of the name of his heroes, is indeed not natural." And Johnson in his *Life of Milton* indirectly criticized Le Bossu's thesis by saying that Milton was the only poet to compose an epic by Bossu's method. Nevertheless, critics from Dryden and Dennis and Shaftesbury to Blair and Twining took the *Treatise* very seriously either by following it as a guide in criticism or by condemning it. Clark (*op. cit.,* pp. 243–261) has a long and interesting account of Le Bossu's fame in England. The *Treatise* is divided into six Books: I, "The Nature of the Epic Poem and of the Fable"; II, "The Matter, or the Action"; III, "The Form, or the Narration"; IV, "The Manners"; V, "The Machines"; VI, "The Sentiments and the Expression." Pope's abridgment represents about one tenth of the original.

1. *Ars poet.* 23: "In short, be the work what you will, let it at least be simple and uniform."—Trans. H. R. Fairclough, Loeb Classical Library.

Notes

La Bruyère (pages 324–338)

The fame of Jean de La Bruyère (1644–1696) rests on one book, *Les Caractères de Théophraste, traduits du grec, avec les caractères ou les moeurs de ce siècle,* published in Paris in 1687. With various alterations, it went through several editions before La Bruyère's death. It was translated "by several hands" and published in London in 1699; later editions appeared in 1700, 1702, 1708, 1709, 1713. The translation by Henri Van Laun (London, 1885), from whom we have borrowed a few notes, was reprinted in 1929. The text used here, except for a few corrections (enclosed in brackets), is that of the anonymous translation of 1699.

The popularity of La Bruyère in England, attested by the numerous editions of his work, is about all there is to suggest that his "Des Ouvrages de l'esprit" ("Of Polite Learning") was familiar to English critics. A. F. B. Clark found no references to him among the English critics. But Addison, Dennis, Swift, Pope, and others all referred at least once to him. Though Murphy (*Johnson Miscellany,* I, 416) said Dr. Johnson was a "profound admirer of Boileau and La Bruyère," Johnson scolded Mrs. Piozzi for preferring La Bruyère to La Rochefoucauld. Perhaps no argument need be made for the intrinsic interest of the essay.

We have omitted from our notes most of the identifications of the characters supplied by the "key" which accompanied later editions.

1. "Qui sentent la pension ou l'abbaye." Presumably, "which suggest the style of one who hopes to gain a pension or the office of abbot."

2. Here the translator omitted the following paragraph:

"If certain men of quick and resolute mind are to be believed, words would even be superfluous to express feelings; signs would be sufficient to address them, or we could make ourselves be understood without speaking. However careful you may be to write closely and concisely, and whatever reputation you may have for so doing, they will think you diffuse. You must give only the merest suggestion of what you mean, and write for them alone. They understand a whole phrase by reading the first word, and an entire chapter by a single phrase. It is sufficient for them to have heard only a bit of your work, they know it all and understand the whole. A collection of riddles would be amusing reading to them; they regret that the wretched style which delights them becomes rare, and that so few authors employ it. Comparisons of a river flowing rapidly, though calmly and uniformly, or of a conflagration which, fanned by the winds spreads afar in a forest, where it devours oaks and pine-trees, give to them not the smallest idea of eloquence. Show them some fireworks to astonish them, or a flash of lightning to dazzle them, and they will dispense with anything fine or beautiful."—Van Laun.

3. Here the translator omitted the following paragraph:

"When, after having read a work, loftier thoughts arise in your mind and noble and heartfelt feelings animate you, do not look for any other rule to judge it by; it is fine and written in a masterly manner."—Van Laun.

4. "Capys" is Edmé Boursault (1638–1701), whom Boileau ("Damis") attacked in his Satire IX. Roger de Rabutin, comte de Bussy (1618–1693), was "banished from the court for more than twenty years for writing the 'licentious and satirical' *Histoire amoureuse des Gaules.*"—Van Laun.

5. The original reads simply, "Le nouvelliste se couche . . ."

6. See discussion of prose style of Voiture and Balzac in Bouhours's *The Art of Criticism,* and notes to it (10 and 19).

7. François de Malherbe (1555–1628), official poet under Henri IV and later under Louis XIII and Richelieu, was famous for his vigorous opposition to the excesses of style of earlier poets, the followers of Ronsard, the Pléiade. Théophile de Viau (1590–1626) disagreed in theory and practice with Malherbe.

Notes

8. La Bruyère is here disagreeing with the then current estimate of Ronsard, who was no longer considered a great poet.

9. Clément Marot (1495–1544), a court poet in the reign of Francis I.

10. Rémy Belleau (1528–1577), Etienne Jodelle (1532–1573), poets of the Pléiade, and Mellin de Saint-Gelais (1491–1558), a court poet. In later editions La Bruyère replaced Saint-Gelais with Guillaume du Bartas (1544–1590), the author of a long poem on the Creation. Honorat de Bueil, marquis de Racan (1589–1670), follower of Malherbe, wrote the pastoral *Les Bergeries.*

11. Jacques Amyot (1513–1593) and Nicolas Coëffetau (1574–1623), Bishop of Marseilles, were translators of classical writing.

12. A periodical.

13. Here the translator omitted the following paragraph:

"Busybodies have created the theatre and its machinery, composed ballets, verses, and music; theirs is the whole spectacle, even to the room where the performance was held, from the roof to the very foundation of the four walls. Who has any doubt that the hunt on the water, the delights of "La Table," the marvels of the Labyrinth were also invented by them? I think so, at least, by the agitation they are in and by the self-satisfied air with which they applaud their success. Unless I am deceived, they have not contributed anything to a festival so splendid, so magnificent, and so long kept up, and which one person planned and paid for; so that I admire two things: the ease and quietness of him who directed everything, and the fuss and gesticulations of those who did nothing."—Van Laun. "La Table" was an ingenious meal served in the Labyrinth, which was itself in the forest of Chantilly.

14. Mithridates, King of Pontus (132–63 B.C.), is the hero of Racine's *Mithridate;* Porus and Burrhus are characters in his *Alexandre* and *Britannicus,* respectively.

Fontenelle (pages 339–370)

The Quarrel between the Ancients and the Moderns has been said to have begun on January 27, 1687, at a special meeting of the Academy held to celebrate the convalescence of the king. There, as Charles Perrault read his poem *Le Siècle de Louis le Grand,* Boileau became so indignant that he interrupted Perrault by shouting that the poem was a shame to the Academy. What so moved Boileau was Perrault's suggestion that the age of Louis the Great was the equal of the age of Augustus:

> Que l'on peut comparer, sans crainte d'être injuste,
> Le siècle de Louis au beau siècle d'Auguste.

Shortly thereafter Boileau wrote two violent epigrams about Perrault and within a year Boileau and Perrault had lined up their teams. Most of the leading writers supported Boileau in his thesis that the works of the ancient poets had not been, and were not likely to be, equaled by the work of modern poets. La Fontaine, Racine, and La Bruyère, as well as the critics Ménage, Huet, and Dacier, defended Boileau. Perrault's chief allies were Saint-Evremond and Bernard Le Bovier de Fontenelle (1657–1757), a nephew of Corneille, who published in 1688, as appendices to a collection of pastoral poems, "A Discourse on the Nature of the Pastoral" and "A Digression on the Ancients and the Moderns."

Actually, Fontenelle had, like others before 1687, concerned himself with some of the ideas involved in the Quarrel, in particular with the idea of progress, which he treated in his *Dialogues of the Dead* (1683) in a colloquy between Socrates and Montaigne. Fontenelle was not a good poet or dramatist, but his essays must have been effective against the intense seriousness of men like Boileau and Dacier. The

398

definitive treatment of the Quarrel is Hubert Gillot's *La Querelle des anciens et des modernes* (Paris, 1914).

As J. E. Congleton has made clear in his *Theories of Pastoral Poetry in England, 1684–1798* (Gainesville, 1952), Fontenelle's "Discourse" in its rationalistic and "impertinent" disregard for the Ancients was not, as Pope implied, similar to René Rapin's *De Cormina pastorali* (1659), which was translated into English in 1684. Rapin's work was, as its author claimed, modeled on Aristotle's *Poetics* in that the rules were derived from a study of the practice of the great classical pastoral poets—chiefly Virgil. Fontenelle's work was, therefore, completely different from Rapin's both in assumptions and in method.

Motteux's translation of the "Discourse" was published with "Monsieur Bossu's Treatise of the Epick Poem" in London in 1695. Motteux omitted two introductory paragraphs, which reveal Fontenelle's bias:

"While I was composing the preceding eclogues, several ideas on the nature of this kind of poetry came to me, and to investigate the matter a little further I undertook to review the majority of those authors who have any reputation as pastoral poets. These ideas, and the criticism of these authors, make up the following essay. I place it after the eclogues, for that represents the order in which the essay and the poems were written. The eclogues came before the reflections; I wrote the poems first; then I thought of the theories; and, to the shame of reason, that is what usually happens. So I shall not be surprised if it is discovered that I have not followed my own rules—I did not yet know them very well when I wrote. Besides, it is much easier to make rules than to follow them, and it has been established by custom that the one never requires the other.

"I hope that the criticism I have rather liberally made of a large number of authors, will not render me suspect of having wished to insinuate that my eclogues are better than all others. I would much rather suppress this essay than excite such a belief in the minds of others. But I maintain that because I have sometimes recognized where others have gone astray, I do not consider myself less likely to be wrong even in the matters where I have seen their mistakes. Criticism exercised on the works of others does not require the writer to do better, unless it is bitter, peevish, and arrogant, like that of professed satirists. But criticism which is an examination, not a satire, which is unrestrained but without hatred and without spite, and above all which is accompanied by a sincere recognition of one's own limitations allows one the liberty of doing even worse, if one wishes, than all those one has undertaken to correct. It is this latter kind of criticism that I have chosen together with its privileges, which, I flatter myself, no one will deny me."

The "Digression" was translated by John Hughes and appeared as an addition to the fourth edition (1719) of John Glanvill's translation of Fontenelle's *Conversations with a Lady on the Plurality of Worlds.*

There is a good text of the original, edited, together with *Entretiens sur la pluralité des mondes,* by Robert Shackleton (Oxford, 1955), from which we have taken our notes on the "Digression."

1. Dryden's translation has been here substituted for Motteux's, which makes nonsense of the passage.

2. Titus Calpurnius Siculus (fl. A.D. 50–60) wrote seven pastorals that are extant. Fontenelle refers specially to number VII.

3. Eclog. iii. 8.

4. The *Bucolica* of Johannes Baptista Spagnuolus Mantuanus (1448–1516) were published in Paris in 1513; they were widely read, translated, and imitated during the following one hundred and fifty years.

5. Fontenelle says, "have added to it in the way of what is foreign and evil."

6. Fontenelle says, "c'est cette idée qui fait tout," meaning "that notion [of simple pleasures] produces the happiest effect."

Notes

7. The five piscatory eclogues of Jacopo Sannazaro (1458–1530) were first published in Naples in 1526.

8. The famous romance *Amadis de Gaule* was written in the fifteenth century; the pastoral romance *L'Astrée,* by Honoré d'Urfé (1568–1626), is set in the seventh century.

9. Marcus Aurelius Olympius Nemesianus (fl. A.D. 290) wrote four pastorals that were long supposed to have been by Calpurnius.

10. Adrien Turnèbe (1512–1565), Guilaume Budé (1467–1540), and François Vatable (d. 1547).

11. Honoré de Racan (1589–1670) wrote a pastoral play called *Les Bergeries.*

12. Giovan Battista Guarini (1537–1612) wrote *Il Pastor Fido* (1590) at about the same time Tasso wrote the other famous, similar, Italian pastoral drama, *L'Aminta.* Guidobaldi Bonarelli della Rovere (1563–1608) wrote *Filli di Sciro* (1607), a poor pastoral drama (his only work), which was several times translated into French during the century. For Marino, see headnote to notes on Chapelain, above.

13. Here Motteux omitted a one-sentence criticism of a "ridiculous" passage from an eclogue of Marot.

14. Jean de Segrais (1624–1701), a contemporary of Fontenelle's and secretary of Mme. de La Fayette, was famous for his eclogues.

15. France exchanged ambassadors with Siam for the first time in 1680.

16. Motteux omitted Fontenelle's last paragraph, which is as follows:

"I beg then permission to add here a short digression which will serve both as my apology and as a plain expression of my feelings on the question of the ancients and moderns. I hope this permission will the more easily be forthcoming since M. Perrault's poem has made the question one of current interest. Since he is preparing to treat it more fully and more deeply, I shall touch on it only lightly: I esteem the ancients highly enough to leave them the honor of being opposed by an adversary both illustrious and worthy of them."

17. (This and the following notes are from Shackleton's edition, as explained in the headnote.) The comparison of men to trees was first made by Montaigne (in the *Apologie de Raymond Sebond*), in a discussion of the effects of external physical influences on men.

18. Fontenelle here speaks in the terms of Cartesian physiology.

19. The theory of climatic influence was very popular in the sixteenth and seventeenth centuries, its principal exponent being Jean Bodin in his *République* and *Methodus.* Montaigne and Charron caused the theory to become well known. In *De l'origine des fables* Fontenelle rejects the climatic explanation of fables, as inspired by the vivid imagination of the inhabitants of the torrid zone. In the *Digression,* on the other hand, he accepts climatic influence. Shortly before the *Digression* . . . there appeared a work which argued vigorously in favor of climatic influence. This was *De l'utilité des voyages,* by Baudelot de Dairval (Paris, 1686). Baudelot, in the Quarrel, was a supporter of the ancients, and it seems likely that Fontenelle in the *Digression* is turning against the ancients one of their own arguments.

20. The effects of climate on the brain had been discussed by Juan Huarte, whose *Examen de Ingenios* (1577) had been translated into French and had been widely read.

21. The notion that the temperate zone was the best region in the world for intellectual achievement was common. See Girolamo Cardano, *De animorum immortalitae* (*Opera omnia* [1663], II, 533–534), and Huarte, *Examen de Ingenios* (ed. R. Sanz, Madrid, 1930, p. 182).

22. Theagenes and Chariclea are characters in the Greek prose narrative *Aethiopica,* by Heliodorus (fl. A.D. 225); Clitophon and Leucippe are characters in a romance by Achilles Tatius, an Alexandrian Christian of the fourth century. Both

these romances were popular in French translations. The French romances are *Cyrus,* by Mlle. de Scudéry, *L'Astrée,* by Honoré d'Urfé, and *Zayde* and *Princesse de Clèves,* by Mme. de La Fayette.

23. The "excellent authors" of these three types were, presumably: Quinault, of operas; La Fontaine, of tales; and Fontenelle, himself, whose *Lettres galantes de M. de chevalier d'Her**** appeared anonymously in 1683.

Index

Index

Balzac, Jean-Louis Guez de (*cont.*)
  Boileau criticizes, 277; praised for wit and style, 330; mentioned, 331, 332, 337
Bartoli, Daniel, 165
Bel esprit, Bouhours on, 160-181
Belleau, Rémy, 331, 355, 356
Benserade, Isaac de, 266
Bertaut, Jean, 214, 276
Bible, 144
Bion, 347
Boccaccio, Giovanni, 35, 152, 279, 296
Boiardo, Matteo Maria: model for romances, 140; his romantic poetry produced by genius, not rules, 283
Boileau-Despréaux, Nicolas: *The Art of Poetry,* 207-269; Preface to his translation of Longinus, 269-274; Reflection VII on Longinus, 275-278; mentioned, 338
Bonarelli, Guidobaldi, 351
Bonaventure, Saint, 152
Bonnefons, Jean, 287
Bouhours, Dominique: on the *bel esprit,* 160-181; on the *je ne sais quoi,* 182-192; selections from *The Art of Criticism,* 193-205; mentioned, 329, 351
Boulanger, André, 226
Brébeuf, Guillaume de, 196, 212
Brulé, Gace, 152
Buchanan, George, 40, 103
Budé, Guillaume, 349
Burlesque, 213
Butler, Samuel, 213, 251

Caesar, Julius, 149
Calderon de la Barca, Pedro, 235
Callimachus, 286
Calpurnius, 342-343, 348
Camoëns, Luis de, 291, 300
Capella, Martianus, 151
Casaubon, Isaac, 270
Castelvetro, Lodovico, 88, 92
Catharsis: impossible without credibility, 12; Sarasin's interpretation of, 56; Saint-Evremond says ancient tragedy made people fearful, 126; Saint-Evremond on Aristotle's theory of, 127; Rapin's interpretation of, 300
Catullus, 10, 287
Cecilius, 270, 272
Cervantes, Miguel de, 51, 151
Chapelain, Jean: on Marino's *Adone,* 3-30; *On the Reading of the Old Romances,* 31-54; Boileau on, 258
Chapman, George, 239
Characterization: consistency in, 24; should be true to life and type, 239, 253
Charles, duc d'Anjou, 152
Châtelain de Couci, 152
Chaucer, Goeffrey, 231

Cicero: his eloquence compared with Caesar's, 178; discussion of urbanity, 190; superior to Homer, Virgil, and Demosthenes, 364; can be compared with French writers, 365; mentioned, 193, 196, 275, 276, 325, 365
Claudian, 10, 23, 28
Clearchus of Soli, 145
Climate: effect on intellect, 176, 359; effect on humors, 238
Coëffeteau, Nicolas, 332
Colletet, François, 264
Comedy: mixture with tragedy a fault, 77; burlesque of moral maxims permissible in, 100; Boileau on, 251-255; an image of common conversation, 283; image of common life, 303; produced by genius, not art, 303; Spaniards and Italians superior to French in, 303-304
Comic elements, appropriate in nonheroic epic, 9
Comparisons, *see* Metaphors and Similes
Complication, aspect of plot, 21
Conceits: Marino achieves diversity and the marvelous by means of, 25; where inappropriate, 227
Conrart, Valentin, 33
Consistency: aspect of structure, 15; aspect of good fictional characters, 24
Conti, Armand, prince de, 303
Corneille, Pierre: *On the Unities of Action, Time, and Place,* 101-115; *Horace* observes unity of place, 89; praised for using small compass of time, 94; in *Horace* and *Cinna* begins action immediately before catastrophe, 95; successful use of didactic expressions, 100; *Sophonisbe* mentioned, 118; praised for decorum of heroes' speeches, 122; praised for greatness of soul of women characters, 122; discovered beauties of stage that Aristotle did not know, 123; *Le Cid* referred to, 261; example of sublime in his *Horace,* 273-274; Boileau on, 277; *Le Cid* praised by La Bruyère, 329; compared with Racine, 334-335; *Cinna* and *Horace* superior to works of Greek dramatists, 368; mentioned, 266
Corneille, Thomas, 368
Cowley, Abraham, 267
Credibility: of subject of *Adone,* 11; necessary to hold attention, 11-12; without it no catharsis, 11-12; how achieved, 11-12; defined, 12; magic in *Lancelot* as plausible as Homer's divinities, 37; only the natural or well-known is believable, 39; unity of place essential to, 82; characters should not appear on stage

Index

Index

Fable: three kinds of, defined, 18-19; consists of events and descriptions, 20; see also Plot

Fairfax, Edward, 214

False wit, see Wit, true and false

Fancy, confused with wit, 280

Faret, Nicolas, 208

Fauchet, Claude, 152, 156

Fiction distinguished from falsehood, 197-198

Figures give force to passions, 292; see also Tropes

Flecknoe, Richard, 213

Floridor (Josias de Soulas), 83

Florus, 205

Fontenelle, Bernard Le Bovier de: Of Pastorals, 339-357; A Digression on the Ancients and Moderns, 358-370

Froissart, Jean, 40

Galen, 257

Garin le Loheran, 156

"Gay science," 149, 150, 152

Gellius, Aulus, 275

Genesis, the book of, 272-273

Genius: inadequate alone for writing well, 194; poetic g. innate, 209; defined, 280; rewards of irregularity in men of g., 337

Genre: novelty of, 4-10; the nonheroic epic, a new g., 8; Adone a mixture of heroic, tragic, comic, and epic, 11; different genres suit different talents, 209

Giraldi, Lilio, 140, 141, 142, 150

Girard, Antoine (i.e. "Tabarin"), 212

Gombauld, Jean Ogier de, 226, 258

Gothic: characters and events in Lancelot, 33; courage and ignorance of Goths, 45; should be banished, 325

Grace, see Delicacy

Gracián, Baltasar, 166, 174, 187

Grotius, Hugo, 103

Guarini, Giovanni Battista, his Pastor fido: too long for spectators, 90; censured for didacticism, 97; shepherds too polite in, 295; example of affection, 351

Hardy, Alexandre, 66

Hédelin, François, abbé d'Aubignac: The Whole Art of the Stage, 80-100; Saint-Evremond on, 123

Heinsius, Daniel, 61, 103

Heliodorus, 10, 147, 159, 368

Hemitheon the Sybarite, 148

Heraclitus, 168

Hermogenes, 204, 270, 271

Herodotus, 142, 143, 147

Herringman, Henry, 257

Hesiod, 265

Hesychius of Miletus, 147

History: compared with poetry, 13, 17-18; Lancelot as good history of mores as Livy, 38; writing of h. reached height in Augustan Age, 364

Hoguette, Pierre Fortin de la, 162

Homer: inventor of epic, 5; descriptions in, 27; compared with Lancelot, 36; not guided by rules, 37; seeds of modern arts and sciences in, 38; unity of action in, 64; gods essential to his poems, 130; his faults those of his time, 131, 132; false character of gods in, 138; his poems masterpieces but not models, 153; metaphorical license in, 198, 200; his use of hyperbole, 204, 205; best model, 249; to love him a kind of praise, 249; his greatness incontestable, 276; delightful descriptions in, 281; never uttered impiety or obscenity, 282; source of Aristotle's rules, 283; no false wit in, 285; hymns of, 286; treatment of gods, 289; simplicity of expression, 291; loftiness of expression, 292; harmony of his verses, 295; not self-indulgent, 298; long speeches in, unnatural, 299; moral of Iliad and Odyssey compared, 309-313; praised for uniting four morals in one fable in Iliad, 315-316; structures of Iliad and Odyssey compared, 318-322; excels in making vivid images, 325; modern can equal him, 358; inferior to Demosthenes, Cicero, Virgil, 364; irrelevancies in, 365; poetic license in, 367; mentioned, 10, 163, 288, 290

Horace: Ars poet., 64, 69, 106, 129, 134, 283, 284, 286, 290, 294, 295, 298, 299, 314, 338; Epist., 158, 280, 288; imitated by Voiture, 165; Serm., Boileau on, 229; chief interpreter of Aristotle, 281; his odes praised, 265, 286, 287; superior to Pindar, 364; mentioned, 193

Huet, Pierre-Daniel, The Original of Romances, 140-159

Humors, mixture required for a bel esprit, 168

Hunibaldus Francus, 149, 150

Hyperbole, in Tasso and Ariosto, 199

Imagination, distinct from understanding, judgment, wit, 279

Imitation in descriptions, 27; see also Plagiarism

Irony, as didactic device, 99

Isocrates, 176

Jamblicus of Chalcis, 147

Je ne sais quoi, Bouhours on, 182-192

Jodelle, Etienne, 331

John Damascenus, Saint, 147, 159

Index

Index

Index

Index

412